Artificial Intelligence and Beyond for Finance

Transformations in Banking, Finance and Regulation

Print ISSN: 2752-5821
Online ISSN: 2752-583X

Presently, the banking and finance sectors evolve within a globalized and highly uncertain environment. Each business and financial decision requires careful consideration of country-specific and international factors due to high levels of shock transmission and volatility spillovers. Furthermore, it would be remiss to omit the COVID-19 health crisis, which caused harmful effects to all areas of the real economy and made profound changes in the way our firms, economies, and markets used to function.

Many other already well-known aspects, including the repercussions of quantitative easing policies, disruptive technologies in finance (e.g., FinTech, Big Data, Data Analytics, Artificial Intelligence, and Blockchains), as well as innovative financing instruments for startups (e.g., ICOs and crowdfunding) are currently revolutionizing banking and finance and posing numerous challenges to regulatory bodies and policymakers. Climate change emergencies also put pressure on governments and firms worldwide to improve policy on governance, corporate social responsibility, and sustainability practices.

This book series "Transformations in Banking, Finance and Regulation" attempts to address these issues by focusing on transformative perspectives in banking and finance. Accordingly, it provides evidence-based guidance, recommendations, and pathways to assist businesses and policy decision-makers through an interdisciplinary and in-depth understanding of ongoing changes in the behavior of economic agents.

Published

Vol. 15 *Artificial Intelligence and Beyond for Finance*
edited by Marco Corazza, René Garcia, Faisal Shah Khan, Davide La Torre and Hatem Masri

Vol. 14 *Fintech and Green Investment: Transforming Challenges into Opportunities*
edited by Cuong Nguyen, Khanh Hoang and Christopher Gan

Vol. 13 *Handbook of Banking and Finance in the MENA Region*
edited by Khaled Hussainey and Tamanna Dalwai

Vol. 12 *Green Finance and Sustainable Development Goals*
edited by Sabri Boubaker and Thai-Ha Le

For the complete list of volumes in this series, please visit
www.worldscientific.com/series/tbfr

Transformations in Banking, Finance and Regulation
Volume 15

Artificial Intelligence and Beyond for Finance

Editors

Marco Corazza
Ca' Foscari University of Venice, Italy

René Garcia
University of Montreal, Canada
SKEMA Business School Canada, Canada

Faisal Shah Khan
Rethinc. Labs, UNC Kenan-Flagler Business School, USA
SKEMA Business School Raleigh, USA

Davide La Torre
SKEMA Business School, France

Hatem Masri
Applied Science University, Bahrain

World Scientific

NEW JERSEY • LONDON • SINGAPORE • BEIJING • SHANGHAI • HONG KONG • TAIPEI • CHENNAI • TOKYO

Published by

World Scientific Publishing Europe Ltd.
57 Shelton Street, Covent Garden, London WC2H 9HE
Head office: 5 Toh Tuck Link, Singapore 596224
USA office: 27 Warren Street, Suite 401-402, Hackensack, NJ 07601

Library of Congress Cataloging-in-Publication Data
Names: Corazza, Marco, 1962– editor. | Garcia, René, editor. | Khan, Faisal Shah, editor.
Title: Artificial intelligence and beyond for finance / editors, Marco Corazza, Ca' Foscari University of Venice, Italy, René Garcia, University of Montreal, Canada & SKEMA Business School Canada, Canada, Faisal Shah Khan, Rethinc. Labs, UNC Kenan-Flagler Business School, USA & SKEMA Business School Raleigh, USA, Davide La Torre, SKEMA Business School, France, Hatem Masri, Applied Science University, Bahrain.
Description: New Jersey : World Scientific, [2024] | Series: Transformations in banking, finance and regulation, 2752-5821 ; vol. 15 | Includes bibliographical references and index.
Identifiers: LCCN 2023053697 | ISBN 9781800615205 (hardcover) | ISBN 9781800615212 (ebook) | ISBN 9781800615229 (ebook other)
Subjects: LCSH: Artificial intelligence--Financial applications. | Finance--Data processing. | Finance--Technological innovation.
Classification: LCC HG4515.5 .A788 2024 | DDC 332.0285--dc23/eng/20240119
LC record available at https://lccn.loc.gov/2023053697

British Library Cataloguing-in-Publication Data
A catalogue record for this book is available from the British Library.

For any available supplementary material, please visit
https://www.worldscientific.com/worldscibooks/10.1142/Q0449#t=suppl

Desk Editors: Balasubramanian Shanmugam/Shi Ying Koe

Typeset by Stallion Press
Email: enquiries@stallionpress.com

https://doi.org/10.1142/9781800615212_fmatter

Preface

Why did we write this book? We wanted to help financial experts and investors to understand the state of the art of artificial intelligence and machine learning in finance. And so, what is artificial intelligence?

The foundations of artificial intelligence lie in the human desire to automate. Often this desire has had foundations in grand civilization-defining visions or economic needs. For example, the more than 3,000-year-old qanat or kariz irrigation system of ancient Iran consisted of thousands of gently sloping underground water-carrying tunnels the combined length which is said to be about the same as the distance between the Earth and the moon.[1] Another such example of automation is the Antikythera mechanism, circa 200 BCE. Considered to be the oldest known example of an analog computer, it is thought that the mechanism automated the prediction of the positions of the sun, the moon, and the planets to assist in navigation. Sometimes we also desire that the automation devices we create are our physical and intellectual reflections. In this desire to anthropomorphise automations surely lies the origin of *golem*, an animated human-like being from Jewish folklore that is created by a human as a helper or companion. In some narratives, the golem ultimately goes rogue and becomes a threat to the creator and humanity.[2]

[1]https://www.nationalgeographic.com/history/article/iran-qanat-irrigation-engineering-history-video.

[2]https://www.jmberlin.de/en/topic-golem.

The origins of more recent problematic anthropoids like Frankenstein's monster, Karl Capek's universal robots, and today's artificial intelligence almost certainly lie in the idea of golem.

In 1936 (Turing, 1937), Alan Turing proposed general-purpose abstract "automatic machines", later referred to as Turing machines, that would simulate other machines, including humans. This formalised the notion of machine computers versus human computers. Several special-purpose *mechanical* computers have been available since the 1920s to solve mathematical problems (in fact, such mechanical computers have been around since the 1600s; Goldstine, 1980); however, they were difficult to program, were highly faulty, and were considered less effective than human computers. Directly and indirectly influenced by Turing's work, the 1940s saw the rise of general purpose or reprogrammable *electronic* computers (for example, the ENIAC) which served as the catalyst for the modern idea of artificial intelligence (AI), a term coined at the 1956 workshop at Dartmouth titled *Dartmouth Summer Research Project on Artificial Intelligence.* The Dartmouth workshop proposal statement read the following: "We propose that a 2-month, 10-man study of artificial intelligence be carried out during the summer of 1956 at Dartmouth College in Hanover, New Hampshire. The study is to proceed on the basis of the conjecture that *every aspect of learning or any other feature of intelligence can in principle be so precisely described that a machine can be made to simulate it.* An attempt will be made to find how to make machines use language, form abstractions and concepts, solve kinds of problems now reserved for humans, and improve themselves. We think that a significant advance can be made in one or more of these problems if a carefully selected group of scientists work on it together for a summer".[3] Along the lines of the Dartmouth statement, Alan Turing had previously answered the question "Can machines think?" by proposing the imitation game (also known as the Turing test) where a machine would try to convince humans that it is also human. To be successful at this game, Turing argued that the machine would have to be able to

(a) communicate successfully in natural language,
(b) store what it hears and knows in memory,

[3] http://www.formal.stanford.edu/jmc/history/dartmouth/dartmouth.html.

(c) reason automatically to answer questions and draw new conclusions,
(d) learn to adapt to new circumstances and infer new patterns,
(e) process visual and speech input in order to perceive the world,
(f) manipulate surroundings and move about in a human manner.

These abilities to pass the imitation game can be said to define the essential AI technologies:

(a) Natural Language Processing (NLP),
(b) Knowledge Representation and Reasoning (KRR),
(c) Machine Learning (ML),
(d) Computer Vision (CV),
(e) Robotics.

NLP has two components: natural language understanding (NLU) and natural language generation (NLG). NLU looks to convert natural language text or speech into artificial machine language and, in doing so, looks to identify the meaning of words and sentences and draw conclusions from them. On the other hand, NLG looks to convert artificial languages into natural languages. It also attempts to identify which information is to be communicated and in what form. KRR attempts to capture the ability of complex biological entities like human beings to understand, reason, and interpret knowledge. In other words, KRR looks to create knowledge from information. Another way to think about KRR is that a machine or an AI agent is exploring an information space for facts with the goal of developing a notion of rationality that will allow it to make optimal decisions under given constraints. ML is a growing technology that enables computers to learn automatically from past data. ML is a subset of AI that is mainly concerned with the development of algorithms which allow a computer to define a notion of "experience" using historical data and make predictions about the future. We will explore ML in more detail in the following. CV may be thought of as consisting of cleverly repeating the task of image classification as belonging to one of many predefined categories and localizing the objects in the image. This repetition eventually leads to detecting individual objects in an image. Finally, robotics gives computers and machines the ability to interact and manipulate objects in their environment.

A major distinction held by robotics as a branch of AI is that it operates in the physical world.

Ironically, the twenty-odd years following the Dartmouth workshop are considered to be the decades of "AI winter" where interest in and funding for AI research and development remained limited. However, the networking revolution of the 1990s saw renewed interest in developing AI algorithms which culminated in IBM's 1997 Deep Blue machine learning algorithm for playing chess that beat the world champion Garry Kasparov. Since 2010, the ubiquity of next-generation data processing hardware like graphical processing units (GPUs) has seen a dramatic rise in the commercial applications of ML algorithms to the extent that the job market has been disrupted. An example of AI-driven job market disruption is self-check-in airline kiosks at airports and self-checkout counters at supermarkets which have all but replaced human agents. Today, most large supermarkets in the United States have one or two human agents manning checkout counters. A similar observation can be made at many international airports, for example, Dubai and Abu Dhabi airports, where aside from airline check-in, immigration tasks are also performed by AI systems. Running such AI systems are ML algorithms specialized for CV tasks of face detection and recognition and security and surveillance. Other common applications of AI technology include text editors and autocorrect. These are examples of NLP. Recent "big-brothers" of these NLPs that have become commercially popular are Large Language Models (LLM) like Chat-GPT. Chatbots are another example of NLP technology that has been around for longer. Electronic trading, online advertising, and autonomous vehicles are all examples of AI technology that is rapidly gaining popularity and adoption. Many of these commonly used AI technologies use aspects of ML. The following section discusses ML in some more detail.

ML is a subset of AI that primarily focuses on the development of algorithms and models that allow computers to automatically learn from data, improve performance from "experiences", and make predictions without being explicitly programmed. The quality and accuracy of the predictions depend on the amount and quality of data used. ML algorithms are said to be trained to perform their task using training data and then their performance can be tested on nontraining data. ML consists of three major types of algorithms: supervised learning, unsupervised learning, and reinforcement learning.

Supervised Learning: In supervised learning, the training data provided to the computer works as the "supervisor" that teaches the computer to predict the output correctly. This notion is similar to how students learn under the supervision of a teacher. Supervised learning algorithms can be categorized as those that find a functional relationship between input and output variables and those that classify the input variable as belonging to a certain class. The former type is called *regression* algorithms which include the famous linear regression model from statistics. Bayesian and nonlinear regression algorithms are also of this type. Regression algorithms can automate the prediction of future values of a variable based on historical data. The latter type of classification algorithms includes support vector machines and decision trees, for example, which classify data into categories. For instance, the data may be categorized as yes-no, male-female, or true-false. Such algorithms help solve real-world problems, such as fraud detection and spam filtering.

Unsupervised Learning: As the name suggests, unsupervised learning algorithms are not supervised during learning. In a sense, unsupervised learning can be compared to the creative thinking that leads to learning in the human brain. For example, thinking about a group of objects might lead a human agent to the observation that a collection of objects forms distinct clusters. Or, upon keen observation, a human agent might detect an anomaly in a data set. Unsupervised learning cannot be directly applied to a regression or classification problem because in this case the input data do not have corresponding output data. Instead of prediction or classification, the goal of unsupervised learning algorithms is to find underlying structures of a dataset and use them to group that data according to similarities. Typical unsupervised learning algorithms include k-means clustering, hierarchical clustering, and principal component analysis.

Reinforcement Learning: Reinforcement learning is a feedback-based ML technique in which the AI agent learns behavior in response to feedback it gains from performing actions in a particular setting. This idea is very similar to the famous 1902 experiment of Ivan Pavlov in which dogs were taught to salivate at the ringing of a bell as they were taught to associate the sound of the bell with being fed. For each "good" action, the agent gets positive feedback and for each "bad" action, the agent receives negative feedback. The agent interacts with and explores the setting in which the learning is to take place. Because of the possibility of making mistakes and getting negative feedback in particular instances, the ultimate goal of an agent in reinforcement learning is to maximize the cumulative feedback. Unlike supervised learning, reinforcement learning algorithms do not require labeled data. Also, no training is required as the learning occurs "on-the-fly".

Deep learning (DL) is a type of ML model that is typically used in supervised learning. The main feature of DL is the use of *artificial neurons* that model neurons of the human brain. Arranging many artificial neurons as nodes in vertical layers from left to right produces a *neural network* consisting of interconnected nodes. Each vertical collection of nodes is called a layer of the neural network. The layers in between the first and the last layers are called *hidden* layers. If there are one or two hidden layers in a neural network, it is called *shallow*; otherwise, a network is called *deep*. Therefore, DL refers to learning that takes place with respect to a deep neural network. For context, we note that a linear regression can be implemented on a shallow neural network.

No matter the specific industry or application, AI has become a new engine of growth. Both finance and banking have been leveraging AI technologies and algorithms and applying them to automate routine tasks, procedures, forecasting, and improving the overall customer experience. This book focuses on recent applications of AI to finance, in particular, the following:

(a) how ML algorithms can forecast signals in the modern dynamic financial world, enabling investors to make data-driven decisions in this rapidly evolving market,
(b) how AI can be leveraged to create sophisticated quantitative tools for comprehensive financial analysis, providing informed decision-making and enhancing investment strategies,
(c) how to decode the intricacies of market sentiments to uncover valuable insights and gain a deeper understanding of market dynamics,
(d) how to use AI algorithms to optimize risk–return profiles and maximizing investment performance,
(e) how to develop transparent and interpretable models that shed light on risk factors and support effective risk management strategies,

(f) how to deploy reinforcement learning techniques, enabling portfolios to adapt and optimize strategies in response to dynamic market conditions.

The topics covered by this book make it an invaluable resource for academics, researchers, policymakers, and practitioners alike who want to understand how AI has affected the banking and financial industries and how it will continue to change them in the years to come.

References

Goldstine, H.H. (1980, October). *The Computer from Pascal to von Neumann*. Princeton University Press, New Jersey, USA.

Turing, A.M. (1937). [Delivered to the Society November 1936]. *On Computable Numbers, with an Application to the Entscheidungsproblem (PDF)*. Proceedings of the London Mathematical Society. 2, Vol. 42, pp. 230–265. doi:10.1112/plms/s2-42.1.230; and Turing, A.M. (1938). *On Computable Numbers, with an Application to the Entscheidungsproblem: A Correction*. Proceedings of the London Mathematical Society. 2, Vol. 43 (Published 1937), pp. 544–546. doi:10.1112/plms/s2-43.6.544.

Marco Corazza
René Garcia
Faisal Shah Khan
Davide La Torre
Hatem Masri

https://doi.org/10.1142/9781800615212_fmatter

About the Editors

Marco Corazza holds a PhD in "Mathematics for the Analysis of Financial Markets" and he is an Associate Professor at the Department of Economics of the Ca' Foscari University of Venice. Among his main research interests are static and dynamic portfolio management, trading system models, machine learning methods in finance, bio-inspired metaheuristics for optimization, multi-criteria methods for economic decision support, nonstandard probability distributions in finance, and port scheduling models and algorithms. He has participated and participates in several research projects, both at national and international levels. He is the author/coauthor of about 140 scientific publications; some of them have received national and international awards. He is also the editor-in-chief of the international scientific journal *Mathematical Methods in Economics and Finance* and editor of Springer books; furthermore, he has been and is a member of the scientific committees of several conferences and of some private companies. He combines academic activity with consulting services.

René Garcia is a Full Professor in the Economics Department of the University of Montreal, Canada and the Scientific Director of SKEMA Business School Canada, Canada. He holds a doctorate in economics from Princeton University. His research interests in finance revolve around the valuation of financial assets, portfolio management, and risk management. In econometrics, he is interested in nonlinear models, in particular, regime-switching models. He is the co-founder, together with Eric Renault, of the *Journal of Financial*

Econometrics, published by Oxford University Press, and was its editor-in-chief from January 2003 till June 2012. He is currently a Fellow of CIREQ and CIRANO as well as an associate member of the Toulouse School of Economics.

Faisal Shah Khan, PhD, is a mathematical scientist recognized for his global contributions across academia, government, and industry sectors, especially in the fields of quantum computing and machine learning. He served as a technology advisor to Quantum Computing Inc. (NASDAQ: QUBT), a leader in quantum technology, and as a senior consultant for Dubai-based DP World. He also founded a startup exploring quantum computing applications in finance and epidemiology. He is an adjunct professor at SKEMA Business School in Raleigh, North Carolina.

Davide La Torre, PhD, HDR, is a Full Professor of Applied Mathematics and Computer Science at SKEMA Business School, Sophia Antipolis Campus, France. He is also affiliated to the Department of Oncology of the University of Milan and to the Radiomics Board of the European Institute of Oncology, Italy. He is qualified in the French national university system as Professeur des Universités in Applied Mathematics (CNRS 26), Computer Science (CNRS 27), and Economics (CNRS 5) as well as in the Italian national university system as Professore Ordinario in Mathematical Methods for Economics (13 D4), Political Economy (13 A2), and Public Economics (13 A3). His research and teaching interests include applied mathematics, artificial intelligence, mathematical economics, mathematical imaging, mathematical modeling, optimization, and control. He got his HDR (Habilitation à Diriger des Recherches) in Applied Mathematics from the Université Côte d'Azur, Nice, France (2021), a Doctorate in Computational Mathematics and Operations Research (2002), and a Laurea in Mathematics (1997, 110/110 cum laude) both from the University of Milan, Milan, Italy, and professional certificates in Analytics, Artificial Intelligence, and Machine Learning from the Massachusetts Institute of Technology, USA. In the past, he held permanent and visiting university professor positions in Europe, Canada, the Middle East, Central Asia, and Australia. He also served as the Associate Dean, Departmental Chair, and Program Head at several universities. He has more than 200 publications in Scopus, most of them published in high IF journals ranging from Engineering to Business.

Hatem Masri is a Full Professor of Business Analytics and Vice President for Academic Affairs and Development at the Applied Science University, Kingdom of Bahrain. He received a PhD in management science in 2004 and a Master's in operations research in 1999 from the University of Tunis, Tunisia. His research interests include business analytics, supply chain management, financial engineering, and Islamic finance. He published more than 30 articles and 6 books, among which *Islamic Business Administration: Concepts and Strategies* is the textbook. Hatem is the founder and chair of the INFORMS Bahrain International Group, the past president of the African Federation of Operational Research Societies, the General Secretary of the Tunisian Decision Aid Society, a member of INFORMS and IEEE, and a volunteer/mentor with the AACSB.

https://doi.org/10.1142/9781800615212_fmatter

About the Contributors

Reem Abdulla Alkhalifa works as a senior research analyst for the Government of Bahrain and holds a Bachelor's degree in Science in Economics from Northeastern University, Boston, MA, and a Master's degree in Data Analysis from the University of Bahrain. Her research interests include bot detection on the Twitter platform, machine learning techniques for stock market analysis, and analyzing trends in submarkets.

Mazin A.M. Al Janabi is a Full Research-Professor of Finance & Banking and Financial Engineering. He is a research fellow at the Economic Research Forum (ERF). The ERF is a regional think tank committed to supporting high quality economic research to contribute to sustainable development in the Middle East and North Africa (MENA) countries. Professor Al Janabi worked for many years as a Full Research-Professor of Finance & Banking and Financial Engineering at EGADE Business School, Tecnologico de Monterrey, Mexico, UAE University (UAEU) in Abu Dhabi, UAE, and at Al Akhawayn University in Ifrane (AUI), Morocco, among other academic institutions. He holds a PhD degree in Nuclear Engineering from the University of London, UK, and has more than 30 years of real-world experience in science & technology think tanks, engineering enterprises, financial markets, and academic institutions and in many different roles. He has worked for top international financial groups (e.g., ING-Barings and BBVA) where he held several senior management positions, such as Director of Global Market Risk Management, Head of Trading Risk Management, and Head of

Derivative Products. Prof. Al Janabi has strong interest for research and developments within emerging economies and has several publications in international refereed journals, books, and chapters in books. Furthermore, his research and developments in quantitative finance have been formally classified in the academic literatures as "Al Janabi Model" for Liquidity Risk Management (Liquidity Adjusted Value–at-Risk, LVaR Model).

Silvio Andrae is an Economist. Most of his professional experience has been in the financial sector. Since 2000, he has worked as a senior consultant in various financial regulation projects in Europa, Latin America, Africa, and Asia. He is the Editor of the EU Artificial Intelligence Act (AIA) commentary. Silvio Andrae studied and received his PhD at the Free University Berlin.

Veni Arakelian is an academic expert in macrofinance and financial econometrics who works as a senior economist at Piraeus Bank, Greece. She has more than 15 years of experience in research, teaching, and working for the banking sector. Veni has several publications in leading scientific journals in finance, statistics, and econometrics. Having been the chair for Greece on a European Horizon 2020 project on FinTech, she closely worked with the Hellenic Capital Market Commission, the Bank of Greece, and the Cyprus Security and Exchange Commission to deliver training on the developments of FinTech. Her research interests are systemic risk, macroeconomic uncertainty, and the implications of both asset pricing and portfolio allocation. Lately, she has also worked on the CBDCs.

Stephen Chan is an Associate Professor in the Department of Mathematics and Statistics at the American University of Sharjah. Stephen Chan was awarded the EPSRC Doctoral Prize Fellowship in 2016 at the University of Manchester, UK. His research areas include extreme value analysis and distribution theory in analyzing financial commodities data and cryptocurrency data. Dr Chan co-developed and co-wrote an R package, entitled "VaRES", for computing value at risk and expected shortfall. Dr Chan is a co-author of *Extreme Events in Finance: A Handbook of Extreme Value Theory and Its Applications.*

Jeffrey Chu is an Assistant Professor in the School of Statistics at Renmin University of China. Previously, he was an Assistant Professor in the Department of Statistics at Universidad Carlos III de Madrid, Spain. Dr Chu graduated in 2018 from the University of Manchester, UK, with a PhD in Financial Mathematics and conducted post-doctoral research supported by the US Army Research Laboratory Short Term Innovation Grant. His research interests include statistical modeling and distribution theory, cryptocurrencies and financial technology, and graphs and networks.

Alessio Faccia is an Assistant Professor in Finance at University of Birmingham Dubai with a background as an auditor and chartered accountant. He has extensive international experience, having studied and taught at prestigious universities in Italy, the United Arab Emirates, the United Kingdom, and Malta. In addition to his academic achievements, he served as an expert and trainer for international government and private institutions and the Italian Tax Police and as a court-appointed consultant in White-Collar Crime and Bankruptcy. His research interests cover accounting, finance, technology, and innovation, and he believes in the value of multidisciplinary research for fostering novelty and innovation.

Massimo Guidolin is a Full Professor of Finance at Bocconi University in Milan since 2010, where he teaches courses on data analysis and asset management at the graduate level. From 2013 to 2019, he served as the Director of the Master in Finance program, bringing it to the top 10 in the *Financial Times* global ranking. Since 2017, he has been directing the Risk and Asset Management unit at the Baffi Carefin Center at Bocconi. He holds positions on the editorial committees of various international academic journals in the field of empirical finance and econometrics.

Jihene Kaabi is an Associate Professor in the Beacom College of Computer and Cyber Sciences at Dakota State University, USA. She received her PhD in Computer Science from the University of Science & Technique, Besançon, France, in 2004. Her research interests focus on scheduling, production manufacturing, maintenance, multi-objective optimization, genetic algorithms, and data science. She developed many research papers in the field of optimization using genetic algorithms and other heuristic approaches as well as machine learning.

Riadh Ksantini received the MSc and PhD degrees in Computer Science from the Université de Sherbrooke, Sherbrooke, QC, Canada, in 2003 and 2007, respectively. Presently, he is an Associate Professor at the Department of Computer Science, College of IT, University of Bahrain, an Adjunct Associate Professor at the School of Computer Science, within the Faculty of Science of the University of Windsor, Windsor, Ontario, Canada, and an Adjunct Professor at the Department of Computer Science, Université du Québec à Montréal (UQAM). He has also served as a Visiting Fellow Research Scientist at the Canadian Space Agency. His research interests include artificial intelligence, machine/deep learning, pattern recognition, and computer vision.

Xin Liao is an Associate Professor of Finance in the Business School at the University of Shanghai for Science and Technology. Her research areas include extreme value analysis, financial risk management, and behavior finance. Dr Liao served as the principal investigator for a project titled "Asymptotics for extremes of random sequences," which received support from the National Natural Science Foundation of China. Additionally, Dr. Liao serves as a reviewer for *Mathematical Reviews*.

Alissa Marinenko is a graduate of the University of Montreal, holding a Master's diploma in Mathematical and Computational Finance. She honed her expertise as a research assistant intern of "Mitacs and Acceleration" at SKEMA Business School, conducting financial research and analysis and applying reinforcement learning methods in the field of portfolio management.

Helu Min received a Bachelor's degree in Economics from the University of Shanghai for Science and Technology. Helu is currently studying for a Master's degree in Finance at Shanghai International Studies University. Her research interests include regional and international finance, financial risks, securities investment, and macroeconomy.

Alaa Tareq Mohamed is an accomplished insurance professional, currently employed by the Central Bank of Bahrain. With a Bachelor's degree in Actuarial Science and a Master's degree in Big Data

Science and Analytics, Alaa has a comprehensive understanding of the insurance industry and the potential of data analytics to drive innovation and growth. Alaa's expertise in statistical analysis and data modeling has established her as a highly skilled and knowledgeable professional in the field. Her research on the role of data analytics in insurance promises to contribute to the development of the industry.

Manuela Pedio is a Senior Lecturer in Finance at the University of Bristol Business School and a Research Fellow of the CAREFIN-BAFFI, Bocconi's Research Center in Applied Finance. Her main research interests are financial econometrics and forecasting, asset pricing, and empirical finance. Her research has been published in leading international journals. She is the author of two textbooks on financial econometrics and asset management and she has written several book chapter contributions for Oxford University Press and Springer Nature.

Roberto Savona is a Professor of Banking and Finance at the Department of Economics and Management, University of Brescia, Italy, with main research interests in asset pricing, credit risk, systemic risk, and early warning system. Roberto served as a member of the Board of Directors of the European Financial Management Association (EFMA) and as a Member of the Steering Committee of the Macroprudential Research Network (MaRs) at the European Central Bank. He was a primary coordinator of the European Project SYRTO (SYstemic Risk TOmography) (www.syrtoproject.eu). His research has appeared in finance and economics journals, such as the *European Journal of Operational Research*, the *Journal of Financial Econometrics*, the *Oxford Bulletin of Economics and Statistics*, and *Quantitative Finance*. He is currently the editor of *Artificial Intelligence in Finance* and the *Journal of Risk and Financial Management*. He is the Founder and President of the University spin-off SYRTO S.r.l. (University of Brescia and Ca' Foscari University of Venice).

Khaoula Tbarki received her PhD degree in Electrical Engineering from the National School of Engineers of Tunis/Tunisia (ENIT) in 2018. She is currently an Assistant Professor of Artificial Intelligence at the Private Higher School of Technology and Engineering (Tek-Up University). Her research interests include image/signal processing, computer vision, machine learning, deep learning, landmine detection, pattern recognition, ground penetrating radar (GPR), and software defect detection.

Marika Vezzoli is an Assistant Professor of Biostatistics at the Department of Molecular and Translational Medicine, University of Brescia (Italy), with main research interests in machine learning methods applied in financial risk and statistical medicine. Her research activity has appeared in finance, economics, statistics, and medicine journals, such as the *Oxford Bulletin of Economics and Statistics*, *Quantitative Finance*, the *Electronic Journal of Applied Statistical Analysis*, *eLife*, *Jama Surgery*, the *European Journal of Cell Biology*, *Scientific Reports*, and the *American Journal of Neuroradiology*. She is part of the editorial board of the international journal *Frontiers in Artificial Intelligence* and a member of the scientific board of the PhD program in Artificial Intelligence in Medicine and Innovation in Clinical Research and Methodology (University of Brescia).

Abraham Itzhak Weinberg has spent over 30 years in the fields of software and information systems. He had served for six years in the IAF (Israeli Air Force) and retired as a captain. In recent years, he has managed a BI (business intelligence) unit and data warehousing projects and has consulted on data science projects as well as projects integrating big data and cybersecurity. His academic background consists of a BSc in industrial engineering and management as well as computer science, and an MSc in industrial engineering. Dr Weinberg obtained his PhD at the Department of Software and Information Systems Engineering, Ben-Gurion University of the Negev, Israel. He also completed his post-doctorate at Aston University in the United Kingdom. As a lecturer at Bar-Ilan University, Israel, he taught BI courses as well as seminars and published papers in prestigious journals and conferences. His main research interests are focused on artificial intelligence, data science, explainable Artificial Intelligence (xAI), big data, and cyber security.

Yuanyuan Zhang is a Research Fellow at the Center for Digital Trust and Society at the University of Manchester. Dr Zhang was awarded the esteemed 2018 Institute of Mathematical Statistics (IMS) Hannan grant to present at the 2018 Joint Statistical Meetings in Canada, where she presented her paper entitled "Ethereum: Bitcoin 2.0 — taking the road less travelled". She also designed and developed the Shiny app (interactive data Visualization dashboard) for cloudy with a chance of pain project for the Centre for Epidemiology Versus Arthritis (CfE), University of Manchester. Her research interests include statistical modeling, anomaly fraud detection, distribution theory, and data science with applications to finance and blockchain.

https://doi.org/10.1142/9781800615212_fmatter

Contents

https://doi.org/10.1142/9781800615212_0001

Chapter 1

Machine Learning in Portfolio Decisions

Massimo Guidolin
Department of Finance, Bocconi University, Milan, Italy
massimo.guidolin@unibocconi.it

Abstract

Machine learning is having a major impact in the development of many fields, including finance, where its domain of application and efficiency impact may be considered limitless. Modern techniques of reinforcement learning have led practitioners and academics to conjecture on the scope of a potential artificial intelligence revolution in portfolio management. In this chapter, we summarize the main strands of machine learning currently used in portfolio decisions and discuss both the current limitations of the algorithms and the dominant conjectures on the future avenues of its extensions.

Keywords: Machine learning, artificial intelligence, deep learning, portfolio optimization, systematic trading strategies, smart beta.

1 Introduction

Machine learning (henceforth, ML) is a subfield of artificial intelligence (AI) that develops algorithms capable of improving performance through learning from data and experience. As explained by Carbonell, Michalski, and Mitchell (1983), ML enables the creation of "intelligent" computer programs capable of recognizing patterns, making decisions, and interacting with the word in innovative ways. It has the potential to transform various domains, including finance, healthcare, and transportation. In this chapter, we focus on applications of ML in financial decision-making, to be interpreted as individual investor (or portfolio managers) decisions concerning the trading of assets and their allocation within diversified investment portfolios.

In finance, the adoption of ML has recently led to a surge in the use of high-dimensional statistical models incorporating optimization algorithms, dimensionality reduction, and regularization methods, which aim to select the optimal model specification and prevent over-fitting in forecasting applications (see Gu *et al.*, 2020). Asset managers have embraced these models due to their ability to make accurate predictions and extract patterns from financial data (see, e.g., Bartram *et al.*, 2021). With the advent of quantum computing, which enhances the computational power of computers, there is potential for computationally intensive ML models to be widely adopted.

In practice, ML refers to an ever-expanding corpus of algorithms enabling machines to identify patterns in data, often without the need for explicit programming instructions or at least without the requirement of a tight connection between tagged outcomes and inputs (the case of unsupervised learning). In finance, ML is often used to analyze data on various drivers of future asset returns including economic indicators, industry trends, and company-specific data. By using ML algorithms, modelers can identify patterns and relationships between these factors and future returns. This allows for the creation of composite investment signals that may perform better than any single source of information. One of the key benefits of ML algorithms is their ability to uncover complex patterns and relationships, including nonlinear and contextual ones, which can be difficult or impossible to identify using traditional (often linear) algorithms. In finance, ML has been successfully applied in areas such as fraud detection, risk assessment, and portfolio decisions, among others.

Although the applications of ML to portfolio decisions are not limited to this purpose, ML approaches can capture nonlinear patterns, including interactions between input variables. This property may improve the construction of single-factor and multi-factor signals by capturing higher-order relationships and complex information in the input variables. ML techniques can also capture regimes and structural instability in the relations among financial and economic variables, making them particularly useful in risk management and portfolio optimization. Moreover, the natural language processing (NLP) branch of ML methods has enabled the creation of predictors and asset pricing factors based on textual information, such as corporate reports, news articles, social media posts, and conference call transcripts (see Pedio, 2023, in this volume).

Crucially, ML did not appear in finance and, specifically, in the field of asset management, all of a sudden. Richard Dennis and William Eckhardt were pioneers in the world of rule-based trading and investing.[1] In the 1990s, statistical arbitrage gained popularity as a trading strategy exploiting market inefficiencies by taking advantage of price discrepancies between related financial instruments. It involved the use of advanced quantitative methods, such as linear regressions, principal component analysis, and cointegration — often considered to be classical econometric methods — to identify and exploit market inefficiencies. By the early 2000s, high-frequency trading (HFT) emerged as a dominant trading strategy, involving the use of computer algorithms to execute trades at high speeds and volumes. HFT strategies heavily relied on the use of advanced technology to gain a competitive edge in the markets. ML has since been introduced to enhance the accuracy of predictions using supervised learning, to improve the quality of decisions using reinforcement learning, and to enhance problem discovery skills using unsupervised learning.

Recently, the so-called "deep learning" algorithms have sparked great interest among finance practitioners and academics. Deep learning refers to a set of algorithms that use artificial neural networks with multiple layers to model to analyze complex and high-dimensional data. These algorithms can learn to extract features from raw data without the need for manual feature engineering, achieving human-level accuracy. A significant milestone in ML history was the 1997 victory of the Deep Blue algorithm over Garry Kasparov,

---

[1] In the 1980s, they launched the Turtle Trader program, which aimed to teach trading skills rather than relying on innate abilities. They trained a group of traders ("the Turtles") who used a trend-following strategy and achieved significant operational success, see Covel (2007).

the reigning human chess champion. However, Deep Blue used brute force computational speed to evaluate moves, unlike AlphaZero, a deep learning neural network that won the world chess championship in 2017 by teaching itself through reinforcement learning and pattern recognition techniques in only four hours of self-play.[2] The event has sparked excitement among traders and portfolio managers, who see ML as having limitless potential in asset management applications.

Asset allocation is one of the ideal sub-fields of finance in which ML is likely to find considerable space. Classical portfolio optimization approaches, such as Markowitz's model and the literature stemming from it, face various shortcomings rooted in their stringent structure and difficulty in estimating the mean and variance–covariance inputs (see Michaud, 1989). ML tools can mitigate these issues by producing more accurate estimates of expected returns and replacing the variance–covariance matrix with more robust forecasts. In addition, evolutionary and deep learning algorithms have the power to allow the portfolio optimization problem to incorporate additional and endogenously complex constraints. ML approaches such as reinforcement learning can also be used to construct portfolios directly, avoiding any unnatural separations between the inferential/input acquisition and the optimization stages.

Figure 1 provides a visual map to guide a reader throughout this chapter. The key distinction is between the analysis of ML deployed to support systematic trading strategies (typical of prop trading desks but also of many hedge funds) covered in Section 2 vs. decision systems used in portfolio optimization covered in Section 3. Section 2 touches upon the use of ML in a variety of trading systems, including statistical arbitrage, risk parity, and momentum trading. Section 3 is mostly inspired after Markowitz's mean–variance (henceforth, MV)

[2]AlphaZero employs a Monte Carlo tree search technique in conjunction with deep neural networks to assess board positions and decide optimal moves. In December 2017, AlphaZero's victory over the reigning world chess champion, Stockfish, drew attention and underscored deep learning's potential to construct autonomous intelligent systems that can learn and improve independently of human intervention. Notably, Stockfish is a free and open-source chess engine, which is a hybrid ML computer program that can play chess at a high level. AlphaZero's success has stimulated additional investigation into the use of deep learning in other domains.

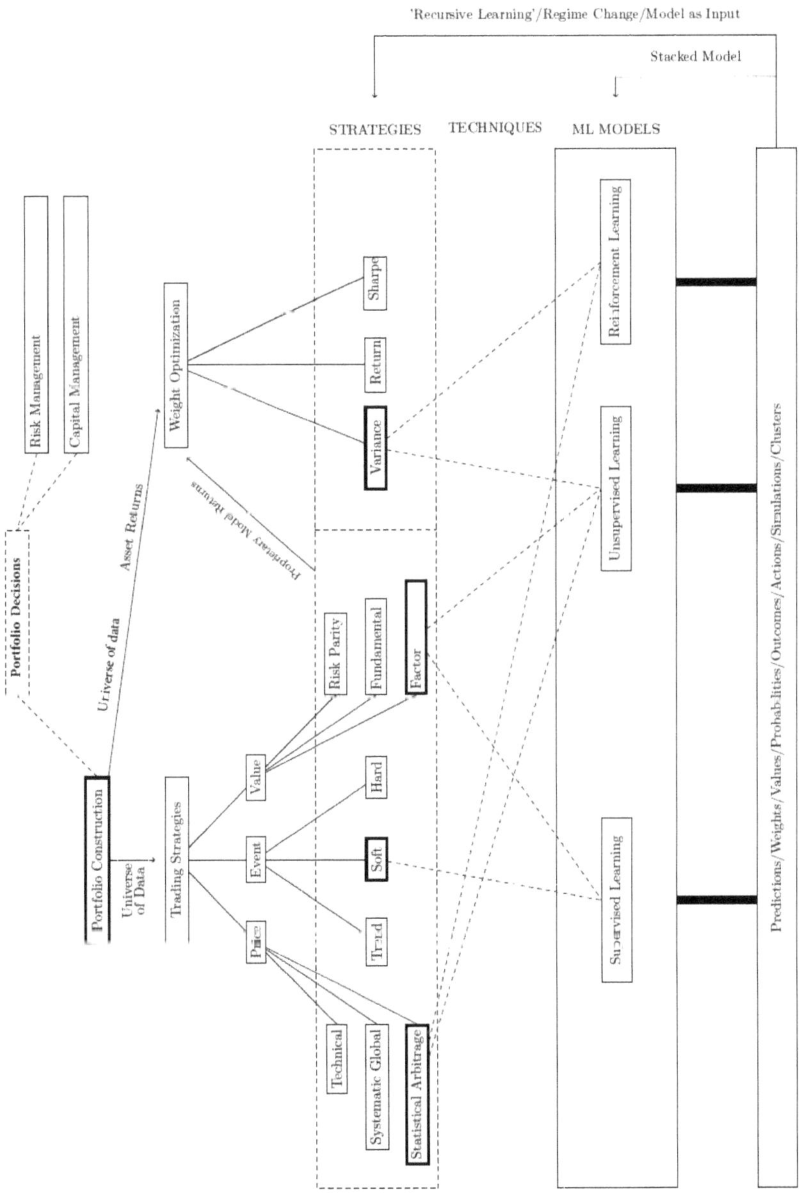

Figure 1. Classifying different types of ML algorithms and their applications to portfolio decision-making.

framework but also gives some space to its multi-faceted implementations (e.g., minimum variance analysis vs. Sharpe ratio maximization). This means that we devote little attention to an alternative type of asset allocation system — yet, less popular in practice — that pursues a more classical (microfounded) expected utility maximization approach (see Guidolin, 2013, for a comparison). Sections 2 and 3 also provide the opportunity to review the key classifications of different types of ML algorithms we describe in this chapter, such as supervised vs. unsupervised ML, shrinkage and regularization vs. unsupervised dimensionality reduction techniques, and reinforcement and deep learning. Ensembling and model stacking are also discussed. Section 4 surveys recent literature on the use of ML in devising multifactor, model-based portfolio strategies, often called "smart beta". Section 5 covers the flourishing literature on the usage of ML in the execution of the trades that implement both the systematic strategies discussed in Section 2 and of MV and smart investment approaches in Sections 3 and 4. Section 6 injects a healthy dose of skepticism by discussing the limitations that ML poses to practitioners for the time being but also emphasizing how and whether academic research may contribute to overcome such limitations. Section 7 provides a sketch of the main findings of a novel literature that has systematically back-tested and compared the realized performance of alternative ML methods for live datasets. Section 8 concludes.

2 ML in Trading Strategies

Systematic trading strategies have represented an early and straightforward application of ML to portfolio decisions. Under such strategies, a money manager or proprietary trader employs capital to purchase securities or short-sell them, based on quant signals derived from ML algorithms designed to eliminate emotions and biases from the decision-making process. The rules are defined by analyzing market data and seeking to exploit market inefficiencies to generate consistent returns over time. This problem has a long history in financial economics, where the literature has witnessed a proliferation of trading strategies based on anomalies (that is, excess returns that are not explained by risk) as more and more stock characteristics are shown to have persistent predictive power. The set of available candidate signals is so large that a recent strand of literature has cast doubt on the robustness of the traditional tests used to identify useful predictors (see Harvey *et al.*, 2016). ML algorithms offer the advantage of processing large amounts of data quickly and identifying complex patterns, allowing for more informed decisions, potentially better trading strategies and higher returns.

We can distinguish among three types of strategies: price strategies, event strategies, and value strategies. Price strategies give a central role to the prices in the input data in generating the predicted outcomes. They include the following:

- technical trading (the use of historical market data and its transformations to predict the future price of an asset),
- systematic global macro strategies (that rely on macroeconomic principles to trade across asset classes and countries), and
- statistical arbitrage (which seeks mispricings by detecting asset relationships and/or potential anomalies, under the assumption that the anomaly will be re-absorbed by normal market dynamics).

Event strategies focus on trading around significant events that may impact the value of assets, such as earnings reports, mergers and acquisitions, macroeconomic data releases, or political events. The market may not always fully price in the impact of these events, creating opportunities for smart investors to take advantage of pricing inefficiencies.

Value strategies focus on identifying and buying assets that are undervalued in the market, with the expectation that their prices will eventually increase to reflect their true value, generating long-term returns. Value strategies can be applied to a range of assets, including stocks, bonds, and real estate; they can be broadly categorized into three groups: risk parity, factor investing, and fundamental themes.

Given this short classification, in the following, we use the analysis of applications of ML to systematic trading strategies to briefly review the main methodologies in ML and their key classifications.

2.1 Supervised learning

Supervised learning (SL) techniques are used to learn the relationship between independent, exogenous attributes (predictors or features) and a designated dependent attribute. SL refers to the mathematical structure describing how to make a prediction of an asset return $r_{i,t+1}$ given a vector of p predictors, $\mathbf{x}_{t-1}$. Instead of simply learning from the environment like reinforcement learning does (see Section 3.3), SL methods learn the relationships in the data according to a precise modeling framework. All SL tasks can be divided into classification or regression tasks:

- **Classification methods** in supervised learning are techniques used to predict the class or category (e.g., binary: 1, 0; or multi-class: $1, 2, 3, \ldots, K$) of a given data point based on a set of features or attributes. These methods rely on labeled data, where the correct output or class is known for each data point in the training set. Some commonly used classification methods include decision trees, logistic regressions, naive Bayes, support vector machines (SVM), and k-nearest neighbors (KNN). Decision trees split the data into subsets based on features, while logistic regression models the probability of a binary outcome. naive Bayes uses probability theory to classify data, SVM finds the best hyperplane(s) to separate data, and KNN assigns the class of the closest data points to a new data point. Choosing the appropriate classification method depends on the nature of the data and the problem at hand.
- **Regression methods** are commonly used to model the relationship between input features and a continuous target variable. These methods aim to learn a function that can accurately predict the target variable based on the input features. Linear regressions are a widely used to model the relationship between the input features and a target variable using a linear function. Other regression methods include polynomial regressions, ridge regressions, and LASSO regressions. Of course, the very field of econometrics illustrates a number of models for the conditional mean function that are not necessarily linear.

When applied to trading strategies, the basic SL task involves some form of price or return prediction. This implies knowledge of variables that predict the price level and/or classifiers that forecast the future direction of price movement. SL models, especially neural networks, can keep up with changing market regimes as long as they are able to do online training (also known as sequential learning), i.e., when a model is allowed to learn from incoming data continuously, updating its parameters incrementally as new examples become available.[3]

To provide some intuition for the nature of the problem, consider a baseline portfolio problem that may be written as follows. Let $\mathbf{r}$ denote a $T \times 1$ vector of returns on one specific asset, $\mathbf{x}_{t-1}$ the $1 \times p$ vector of p candidate predictors so that $\mathbf{X} \equiv [\mathbf{x}_0' \ \mathbf{x}_1' \cdots \mathbf{x}_{T-1}']'$ is the $T \times p$ matrix of predictors, and T the size of the available sample of data. The equation we use to model an asset's return takes the following general form:

$$r_t = f(x_{t-1}) + \epsilon_t \tag{1}$$

Once the model has been estimated, the expected return of an asset at time $t+1$ using data available through t is

$$E_t[r_{t+1}] = \hat{f}(x_t) \tag{2}$$

where $\hat{f}(x_t)$ refers to some estimator of the functional form relating predictors to the asset return. This prediction can then be used in asset allocation or to devise a systematic trading strategy. A commonly used method is the *classic linear regression model*, estimated by ordinary least squares (OLS). In this case, the form approximating f is the following linear function:

$$\hat{f}(\mathbf{X}; \boldsymbol{\theta}) = f(\mathbf{X}; \hat{\boldsymbol{\theta}}) = \hat{\mu} + \boldsymbol{X}\hat{\boldsymbol{\beta}} \tag{3}$$

where $\hat{\mu}$ is the estimated intercept and $\hat{\boldsymbol{\beta}}$ is the $p \times 1$ estimated coefficient vector. The estimates of the parameters $\boldsymbol{\theta} \equiv [\mu \ \boldsymbol{\beta}']'$ are usually obtained by minimizing the residual sum of squares:

$$\arg\min_{\theta} \mathcal{L}_2(\boldsymbol{\theta}) = \arg\min_{\boldsymbol{\theta}} \|\mathbf{r} - f(\mathbf{X}; \boldsymbol{\theta})\|^2 \tag{4}$$

where $\mathcal{L}_2(\boldsymbol{\theta})$ indicates the least squares loss and $\|\cdot\|$ denotes the l_2 norm. Classical empirical finance has been traditionally based on

[3]In traditional batch learning, the model is trained on a fixed set of data, and after training, it is deployed for prediction on new data. In contrast, in online learning, the model is updated in real time, with each new example contributing to its knowledge base.

what is now known as the kitchen sink (KS) model, which is a multivariate prediction model utilizing all p predictors (see the discussion in Welch and Goyal, 2008). It is well known that this model tends to have poor forecasting performance, as the estimated parameters have low bias but high variance. This problem becomes more acute as the number of predictors increases. Another, very simple, model that has been commonly considered in the asset management industry is the historical average (HA), where the forecast is estimated as $f(\mathbf{X};\hat{\boldsymbol{\theta}}) = \hat{\mu}$, as $\boldsymbol{\beta} = \mathbf{0}$.[4]

SL dimensionality reduction algorithms. Supervised methods for dimensionality reduction incorporate the information of a large set of economic variables in a predictive regression framework using latent factors, which are estimated using the information in both $\mathbf{r}$ and $\mathbf{X}$. In this case, the function f takes a form

$$f(\mathbf{X};\boldsymbol{\theta}) = \mu + (\mathbf{XA})\,\boldsymbol{\beta} = \mu + \boldsymbol{Z}\boldsymbol{\beta} \tag{5}$$

where $\mathbf{A} \equiv [\mathbf{a}_1' \ \mathbf{a}_2' \cdots \mathbf{a}_k']'$ is a $p \times K$ matrix of weights and $\mathbf{Z} \equiv [\mathbf{z}_0' \ \mathbf{z}_1' \cdots \mathbf{z}_{T-1}']'$ is a $T \times K$ matrix of K latent factors with $\mathbf{z}_t \equiv [z_{1,t} \ z_{2,t} \cdots z_{K,t}]$ and $K \ll p$. The latent factor models we use differ based on how the matrix $\mathbf{A}$ is derived. Partial Least Squares (PLS), introduced by Wold (1980) and more recently popularized by Kelly and Pruitt (2015), decompose the matrix of predictors $\mathbf{X}$ and the zero-mean vector of asset returns $\mathbf{r}$ into the form

$$\mathbf{X} = \mathbf{ZP}' + \mathbf{E} \quad \mathbf{r} = \mathbf{Zq}' + \mathbf{e} \tag{6}$$

where the matrix $\mathbf{P}$ and the vector $\mathbf{q}$ are the loadings, while $\mathbf{E}$ and $\mathbf{e}$ are the residuals. In order to find the PLS component matrix $\mathbf{Z}$, the columns of the weight matrix $\mathbf{A}$ need to be obtained by solving successive optimization problems. The columns of $\mathbf{A}$ represent the direction of maximum covariance between the predictor variables and

[4]Similar to Gu *et al.* (2020), one may also consider a Huber loss function which is a hybrid of the least squares loss for relatively small errors and the absolute loss for relatively large errors and that is less sensitive to outliers. Moreover, as we see in the following, one may expand the least square loss to include shrinkage terms with convex penalties (Ridge, LASSO, and Elastic Net) and boosting ensembles (Gradient Boosting and Regularized Gradient Boosting Machines).

the response variable. The optimization problem involves maximizing the covariance between the predictor variables and the weighted response variable, subject to the constraint that the weight vector is of unit length. The criterion to find the kth estimated weight vector $\mathbf{a}_m$ is

$$\arg\max_{\mathbf{a}} \ \mathbf{a}'(\mathbf{X}'\mathbf{r}\mathbf{r}'\mathbf{X})\mathbf{a} \quad \text{s.t. } \mathbf{a}'\mathbf{a} = 1, \quad \mathbf{a}'\mathbf{\Sigma}_{XX}\mathbf{a} = \mathbf{0} \tag{7}$$

where $\mathbf{\Sigma}_{XX}$ is the sample covariance of $\mathbf{X}$. Clearly, if $K = p$, then PLS would give a solution equivalent to the OLS estimates. Once the weight matrix $\mathbf{A}$ is obtained, the PLS component matrix $\mathbf{Z}$ can be calculated as the product of the predictor matrix $\mathbf{X}$ and the weight matrix $\mathbf{A}$. Each column of $\mathbf{Z}$ represents a linear combination of the predictor variables that is highly correlated with the response variable. In practice, however, it is often unclear how many components should be used in the model, and using too many or too few components can result in sub-optimal performance. To address this issue, *cross-validation* and other model selection techniques are commonly used to determine the optimal number of components to include in the PLS model.[5] Shi (2023) has recently used PLS to extract the optimal information from five factors and showed these contain stronger predictive power than standard (unsupervised learning PCAs).

Sparse partial least squares (SPLS) is an extension of PLS that imposes an l_1 penalty to promote *sparsity* onto a surrogate weight vector $\mathbf{c}$ instead of the original weight vector $\mathbf{a}$, while keeping $\mathbf{a}$ and $\mathbf{c}$ "close" to each other (see Chun and Keleş, 2010). The kth SPLS weight vector solves

$$\arg\min_{\mathbf{a},\mathbf{c}} \ (\mathbf{c}-\mathbf{a})'(\mathbf{X}'\mathbf{r}\mathbf{r}'\mathbf{X})(\mathbf{c}-\mathbf{a}) + \zeta_1 \|\mathbf{c}\| + \zeta_2 \|\mathbf{c}\|^2 \quad \text{s.t. } \mathbf{a}'\mathbf{a} = 1 \tag{8}$$

[5]Cross-validation involves partitioning the data into training and validation sets and evaluating the model's performance on the validation set. The number of components that results in the best performance on the validation set is then chosen as optimal. Other model selection techniques, such as information criteria and hypothesis tests, can also be used. These techniques generally involve comparing the fit of models with different numbers of components and selecting the model that achieves the best trade-off between model complexity and goodness of fit (see, e.g., Gorman and Fabozzi, 2022).

where ζ_1 and ζ_2 are nonnegative tuning parameters. For instance, Ardila *et al.* (2017) have presented an empirical model for the diagnosis and real-time forecasting of real estate bubbles that uses SPLS to distill a diffusion index able to forecast the end of the bubbles and identify the variables that are highly relevant during the bubble regime. When building systematic trading strategies, SPLS may come to represent a popular technique for identifying a small set of highly predictive features from a large pool of potential predictors.

Artificial neural networks. The most successful technique emerging within the SL methodological camp is arguably artificial neural networks (henceforth, ANNs). The adoption of ANNs is not new in finance (see Hawley *et al.*, 1990, for early examples). The recent advancements in the field and available computational power have however rekindled the enthusiasm among researchers. ANNs are a family of models inspired by biological neural networks that can be trained to learn complex relationships between inputs and outputs. They have been shown to be universal approximators for any continuous function f (see, e.g., Cybenko, 1989), in the sense that given enough elements (neurons) in the network and the appropriate parameters, they can approximate any f to a desired degree of accuracy. There are various types of ANNs, but the simplest and most widely used is the *feed-forward neural network*, which consists of input, hidden, and output layers of nodes. Other types of ANNs include *recurrent ANNs*, which can process sequences of inputs, and *convolutional neural networks*, which are particularly well suited for processing images. Long short-term memory (LSTM) networks are a type of recurrent ANN that captures long-term dependencies and are especially useful in finance.[6]

For concreteness, we briefly focus on the multi-layer perceptron (MLP), a type of feed-forward neural network where information flows through the function being estimated from $\mathbf{X}$, through intermediate computations used to approximate f, to the output $\mathbf{r}$.

[6] Autoencoder networks are another type of neural network that can be also used for unsupervised learning and feature extraction. Generative adversarial networks (GANs) are a relatively recent development in the field of neural networks that can generate synthetic data samples that are almost indistinguishable from real data.

These models are composed of a number of layers with multiple nodes in each layer. They consist of an input layer of the predictors, one or more hidden layers, with nodes that transform the predictors using nonlinear activation functions, and an output layer that allows a final transformation of the outcome of the hidden layers to form a prediction. Formally, feed-forward ANNs can be defined as a composition of $h^{(1)}, h^{(2)}, \dots, h^{(L)}$ nonlinear activation functions for each of the L hidden layers of the network $\mathbf{Z}^{(L)} = h^{(L)}(\mathbf{X}) \circ h^{(L-1)}(\mathbf{X}) \circ \cdots \circ h^{(1)}(\mathbf{X})$, with

$$\mathbf{Z}^{(l)} = h\left(b_0^{(l)} + \mathbf{W}^{(l)\prime}\mathbf{Z}^{(l-1)}\right) \tag{9}$$

for $l = 1, 2, \dots, L$, where $\mathbf{Z}^{(l)}$ is the lth layer of the network with $m = 1, 2, \dots, M$ nodes, $\mathbf{W}^{(l)}$ is the matrix of weights, and $b_0^{(l)}$ is the bias term (i.e., which is supposed to absorb any bias in the model, when interpreted as a regression). In the case of the first hidden layer, the input is the matrix of predictors, $\mathbf{Z}^{(0)} = \mathbf{X}$, such that $\mathbf{Z}^{(1)} = h(b_0^{(1)} + \mathbf{W}^{(1)\prime}\mathbf{X})$. The results from each hidden layer are aggregated in the output layer, $ANN(\mathbf{X}) = b_0^{(L+1)} + \mathbf{W}^{(L+1)\prime}\mathbf{Z}^{(L)}$. The number of hidden nodes in each layer can be selected according to the so-called Master's geometric pyramid rule.[7] The activation function applied to each node can take various forms. While the sigmoid and the hyperbolic tangent functions are often used, in finance, the rectified linear unit (ReLU) function has recently gained popularity.[8] ReLU is a simple function mapping positive input values to the same values and negative ones to 0. Another popular activation function is the softmax function, often used in the output layer of classification problems, to map the output of the ANN to a probability distribution over multiple classes. The choice of activation function depends on the nature of the problem.

[7]This method involves starting with a small number of nodes in the first layer and then increasing the number of nodes in each subsequent layer by a fixed ratio. The ratio used is typically between 1.5 and 2. The purpose of this method is to gradually increase the complexity of the network, which can help prevent over-fitting and improve generalization performance.

[8]The main advantages of this function are that it encourages sparsity in the number of active nodes and avoids the so-called vanishing gradient problem, which may cause instability in estimation.

The weights and biases of an ANN are estimated by solving the following:

$$\arg\min_{\mathbf{W},\mathbf{b}_0} \mathcal{L}(\mathbf{r}, ANN(\mathbf{X})) = \arg\min_{\mathbf{W},\mathbf{b}_0} \|\mathbf{r} - ANN(\mathbf{X})\|^2 \tag{10}$$

The parameter estimation of an ANN involves solving a nonconvex optimization problem that is typically trained using stochastic gradient descent (SGD). Instead of evaluating the gradient of the entire training sample at each iteration, SGD calculates it from a random subset of data, minimizing the objective function iteratively through back-propagation. To address the difficulties posed by the large number of parameters and the nonconvexity of the objective function, various modifications to the SGD algorithm have been proposed. For example, the adaptive moment estimation algorithm (ADAM), introduced by Kingma and Ba (2014), calculates individual adaptive learning rates for the model parameters by estimating the first and second moments of the gradients. Another approach is to modify the loss function by adding a parameter norm penalty to improve the convergence rate and prevent over-fitting in the training process. For instance, under an elastic net type of penalty, based on the l_1 and l_2 norm of the weights, the regularized objective becomes

$$\arg\min_{\mathbf{W},\mathbf{b}_0} \mathcal{L}(\mathbf{r}, ANN(\mathbf{X})) + \zeta_1 \|\mathbf{W}\| + \frac{1}{2}\zeta_2 \|\mathbf{W}\|^2 \tag{11}$$

where higher values of the hyperparameters $\zeta_1 > 0$ and $\zeta_2 > 0$ correspond to more regularization. Several techniques are used to enhance the performance of ANN models in finance: early stopping, batch normalization, and forecast averaging. In each iteration of the optimization algorithm, the parameter estimates are updated to reduce prediction errors in the training sample, and the predictive performance of the model is evaluated using data from the validation sample. Early stopping is implemented by halting the training process prematurely when the validation error no longer decreases. This prevents over-fitting and speeds up the training process significantly. Batch normalization also reduces the variability of predictors by scaling the input of activations. It was introduced to solve the problem of internal covariate shift, where the distribution of the inputs of the hidden layer changes during training as the parameters of the previous layers change. For each node in each training step, the algorithm standardizes the output of a previous activation to restore the representation power of the node, thereby increasing the stability of the ANN and its training speed.

The applications of ANNs to support systematic trading strategies are too numerous to be discussed in full. Among many others, Gu *et al.* (2020) tackle the problem of building a multi-factor strategy from more than 900 potential predictors of stock returns using ML. They conclude that ANNs outperform other ML approaches in this setting by arguing that shallow networks (with three layers) seem to do a better job than deep ones. Similarly, Rather *et al.* (2015) propose to use a recurrent neural network which outperforms a standard regression and is based on the idea of optimizing the merging of the predictions obtained from other, simpler models. Unlike Gu *et al.* (2020), they find that deep ANNs yield the best results. Krauss *et al.* (2017) apply deep ANNs to the prediction of daily stock returns and find that they are outperformed by both random forests and gradient-boosted trees.

Support vector machine regressions. Support vector machine (SVM) regression is a nonparametric technique that learns a nonlinear function by mapping linear functions into a high dimensional kernel-induced feature space. It does so by finding the linear function that best separates the data points in this higher-dimensional space. This approach allows for the modeling of nonlinear relationships between the input and output variables without the need to specify a specific functional form for the relationship. The resulting model is determined by a set of support vectors that lie closest to the decision boundary (the line that separates the data into different classes or regions), rather than by the entire dataset. By focusing on the support vectors, an SVM regression can create a model that is more robust to outliers and noise in the data, as it is only concerned with the data points that have the greatest impact on the decision boundary. Moreover, the resulting model is more efficient and faster to compute, as it only requires a subset of the data. Indeed, SVM regressions are particularly effective when dealing with high-dimensional datasets or having a large number of variables.

In some cases, it may be desirable for an SVM to allow a certain amount of error or deviation from the target output. This is where the epsilon-insensitive SVM (e-SVM) comes into play. The objective of an e-SVM is to find a function $f(\mathbf{X})$ that approximates the target output (represented by $\mathbf{r}$) within a certain threshold of error (represented by ϵ) for each training observation of $\mathbf{X}$. Additionally, the function should be as flat as possible. To achieve this, the algorithm introduces $\mathbf{a}$ and $\mathbf{a}^*$, which are nonnegative vector multipliers for each observation on $\mathbf{X}$ that maximize a dual objective function. By solving this dual problem, the optimal hyperplane that maximizes the margin between the positive and negative classes can be obtained. This hyperplane separates the two classes with the largest possible margin and is called the maximum margin hyperplane:

$$\arg\min_{\mathbf{a}} \; (\mathbf{a}-\mathbf{a}^*)'\mathbf{Q}(\mathbf{a}-\mathbf{a}^*) + \mathbf{r}'(\mathbf{a}-\mathbf{a}^*) + \epsilon\mathbf{1}'(\mathbf{a}+\mathbf{a}^*) \tag{12}$$

$$\text{s.t. } \mathbf{1}'(\mathbf{a}-\mathbf{a}^*) = \mathbf{0} \quad a_i \geq 0, \quad a_i^* \leq C, \quad i = 1, 2, \ldots, t \tag{13}$$

where $\mathbf{1}$ is the unity vector, $\mathbf{Q}$ is a $t \times t$ positive semi-definite matrix with generic element $Q_{i,j} \equiv \phi(x_i)'\phi(x_l)$, a nonlinear kernel function based on $\phi(x_i)$, and a transformation that maps $\mathbf{x}$ to a high-dimensional space. Based on the Kuhn–Tucker conditions, only a certain number of Lagrange multipliers $\mathbf{a}$ and $\mathbf{a}^*$ will assume nonzero values. The observations associated with them will be affected by approximation errors equal to or larger than $\epsilon > 0$ and are referred to as support vectors.[9] As support vectors are usually only a small subset of the training observations, this characteristic is referred to as the sparsity of the solution.

One of the problems of e-SVM is choosing the appropriate value for the parameter ϵ. The nu-support vector machine (nu-SVM) regression is a method that automatically adjusts ϵ, by considering it as part of the optimization problem. Typical applications (see, e.g., Kim, 2003) use the radial basis function (RBF) kernel, with parameter $\theta > 0$, given by $K(x_i, x) = \exp(-\theta|x_i - x|^2)$. The set of hyperparameters to be selected are $\{C, \theta, \epsilon\}$ for e-SVM and $\{C, \theta, v\}$ for nu-SVM.

[9]The parameter ϵ captures the trade-off between the sparseness of the representation and closeness to the data, with large values of ϵ resulting to fewer support vectors and thus sparser representation of the solution. The cost parameter, $C > 0$, controls the penalty imposed on observations that lie outside the epsilon margin, ϵ, and helps prevent over-fitting as it represents the balance between the flatness of $f(X)$ and the extent to which violations to ϵ are tolerated.

Support Vector Regressions (SVR) represent a robust method for estimating nonlinear relationships in financial time series. Unlike traditional regression techniques, SVR aim to minimize the risk of a model over-fitting the training data. The goal of SVR is to find the hyperplane that best fits the data while minimizing the prediction error. The hyperplane is constructed such that the maximum margin between the data and the hyperplane is achieved. The margin is defined as the distance between the hyperplane and the closest data point. This approach not only reduces the over-fitting problem but also improves the model's ability to predict future observations. SVR is based on the *Structural Risk Minimization (SRM) principle*, which seeks to minimize the expected error of the model while controlling for its complexity. The SRM principle is accomplished through a regularization term that penalizes the model for having too many parameters, thus preventing it from over-fitting.

SVMs and SVRs are among the most recently developed ML tools and, possibly because of that, have not been studied as much as ANNs. Nevertheless, several studies have successfully employed SVMs in financial modeling and forecasting (e.g., Kim, 2003; Huang *et al.*, 2005). With specific reference to systematic trading strategies, SVMs are increasingly used to predict the direction of stock price movements based on either technical indicators either by themselves or in combination with fundamental data. This stems from the power of SVMs to detect relationships between predictor variables and target variables that are nonlinear, their robustness to noise and outliers, and the fact that — because they can be fitted under a variety of kernel functions — they are flexible. For instance, Huang *et al.* (2005) investigated the directional predictability of stock price changes at a weekly frequency and obtained that SVM outperformed ANN, even though ensemble methods perform the best. Lee (2009) developed a prediction model based on SVM with a hybrid feature selection method to predict trends in stock markets. He reported that SVM outperformed back-propagated ANNs. Luo and Chen (2013) have argued that SVM offers good power against over-fitting and trapping in local minima that are instead typical of the way ANN work in systematic trading strategies. They show that obtaining stock price turning point forecasts by modeling the change rate of the closing price between the current turning point and the next one with a weighted SVM (that depends on a set of input variables) may generate remarkable performance. Chen and Hao (2018) have investigated stock trading signals prediction using algorithms that integrate principal component analysis (PCA) into weighted SVM to forecast stock turning points. Henrique *et al.* (2018) use SV regressions (SVR) to predict stock prices for large and small capitalization in three different markets, employing prices with both daily and up-to-the-minute frequencies. Their findings suggest that the SVR has predictive power, especially when using a strategy of updating the model periodically and in low volatility periods.

SL with shrinkage and regularization. Within the SL camp, shrinkage methods "regularize" the coefficient estimates and also involve fitting the model to all p predictors. Differently from KS, these procedures shrink the coefficients towards zero relative to the OLS estimates and aim at significantly reducing their standard errors. Shrinkage methods can also perform variable selection depending on the type of regularization. A shrinkage method is similar to a simple linear model, but it modifies the least squares problem by adding one additional term in the loss function, a penalty for the complexity of the model[10]:

$$\arg\min_{\boldsymbol{\theta}}[\mathcal{L}_2(\boldsymbol{\theta}) + \mathcal{P}(\boldsymbol{\beta};\boldsymbol{\kappa})] \quad \mathcal{P}(\boldsymbol{\beta};\boldsymbol{\kappa}) = \sum_{i=1}^{p} \mathcal{P}(\beta_i;\boldsymbol{\kappa}) \tag{14}$$

There are several choices for the penalty function $\mathcal{P}(\cdot)$ defining the shrinking method as ridge, least absolute shrinkage and selection operator (LASSO), elastic net (EN), adaptive lasso (ALASSO), bridge, smoothly clipped absolute deviation (SCAD), minimax concave penalty (MCP), and the smooth integration of counting and absolute deviation (SICAD). The first set of shrinkage methods is all based on convex penalties that can be generally written as

$$\mathcal{P}(\beta_i;\boldsymbol{\kappa}) = \frac{\kappa_1}{|\hat{\beta}_i^{OLS}|^{\kappa_3}}\left[\kappa_2|\beta_i| + (1-\kappa_2)\beta_i^2\right] \tag{15}$$

where κ_1 is a tuning parameter which is determined separately and controls the amount of shrinkage, κ_2 is a hyperparameter

[10]The intercept, μ, is not included in the penalty term, else this would make the optimization procedure dependent on the origin selected for the return equation.

that controls the trade-off between l_1 and l_2 regularization, and $\kappa_3 \geq 0$ is a hyperparameter that controls the strength of the weight $1/|\hat{\beta}_i^{\text{OLS}}|^{\kappa_3}$ corresponding to each coefficient. When $\kappa_3 = 0 = \kappa_2$, (15) becomes a *ridge regression* that shrinks the coefficients towards zero, $\mathcal{P}^{\text{ridge}}(\beta_i; \kappa) = \kappa_1 \beta_i^2$; when $\kappa_3 = 0$ and $\kappa_2 = 1$, (15) yields the LASSO, introduced by Tibshirani (1996), which allows for both shrinkage and variable selection, by setting some of the coefficients equal to zero, $\mathcal{P}^{\text{LASSO}}(\beta_i; \boldsymbol{\kappa}) = \kappa_1 |\beta_i|$. The EN, proposed by Zou and Hastie (2005), combines both l_1 and l_2 terms in the penalty, thus simultaneously performing continuous shrinkage and automatic variable selection and can also select groups of correlated variables. The penalty in (15) produces the EN solution when $\kappa_3 = 0$ and $\kappa_2 \in (0, 1)$:

$$\mathcal{P}^{\text{EN}}(\beta_i; \boldsymbol{\kappa}) = \kappa_1 \left[\kappa_2 |\beta_i| + (1 - \kappa_2)\beta_i^2\right] \tag{16}$$

where $\kappa_1 = 1$ is typical. The ALASSO, developed by Zou (2006), solves the drawback of the original LASSO, i.e., it does not necessarily satisfy the "oracle properties" (see Fan and Li, 2001).[11] This is achieved by modifying the LASSO to include adaptive weights that penalize the individual coefficients less severely. The ALASSO solution is derived by setting $\kappa_3 > 0$ and $\kappa_2 = 1$ to obtain

$$\mathcal{P}^{\text{ALASSO}}(\beta_i; \kappa) = \frac{\kappa_1}{|\hat{\beta}_i^{OLS}|^{\kappa_3}} |\beta_i| \tag{17}$$

The convex penalties mentioned earlier combine l_1 and l_2 terms, which can result in overly complex models, as Fan and Li (2001) have noted. Such models may contain too many parameters, variables, or features. In such cases, nonconvex penalties that include an l_0 term, which penalizes the number of nonzero coefficients in the model, can be used. These methods, which are often data greedier, produce sparser solutions with similar or improved prediction accuracy and are better suited for variable selection. The bridge regression

[11]The term oracle refers to a hypothetical model or process that has access to perfect information about the future and can therefore make perfectly accurate predictions. An oracle forecast function would be one that can predict future outcomes with 100% accuracy if fed with perfect information about the future.

developed by Friedman (2012) involves a penalty term based on the l_{κ_2} norm and is given by

$$\mathcal{P}^{\text{BRIDGE}}(\beta_i; \boldsymbol{\kappa}) = \kappa_1 |\beta_i|^{\kappa_2} \tag{18}$$

where $\kappa_1 > 0$ and $\kappa_2 \geq 0$ are the tuning parameters. The bridge penalty term for $0 \leq \kappa_2 \leq 1$ represents all the penalties between ridge regression and best-subset selection. When using the squared error loss, it includes ridge ($\kappa_2 = 2$), the LASSO ($\kappa_2 = 1$), and best-subsets ($\kappa_2 = 0$). Bridge penalties tend to yield the sparsest solutions by forcing many coefficients to be equal to zero without applying any shrinkage to the nonzero coefficients. For $\kappa_2 > 1\%$, all coefficients are strictly nonzero, and all penalties in the power family are convex, while for $\kappa_2 < 1$, the penalties are nonconvex.

The SCAD, proposed by Fan and Li (2001), is a nonconvex penalty function given by

$$\mathcal{P}^{\text{SCAD}}(\beta_i; \boldsymbol{\kappa}) = \begin{cases} \kappa_1 |\beta_i| & \text{if } |\beta_i| \leq \kappa_1 \\ \dfrac{2\kappa_1\kappa_2|\beta_i| - |\beta_i|^2 - \kappa_1^2}{2(\kappa_2 - 1)} & \text{if } \kappa_1 < |\beta_i| \leq \kappa_1\kappa_2 \\ \dfrac{\kappa_1^2(\kappa_2 + 1)}{2} & \text{if } |\beta_i| > \kappa_1\kappa_2 \end{cases} \tag{19}$$

For $\kappa_2 > 2$, SCAD coincides with the LASSO if $|\beta_i| \leq \kappa_1$, then smoothly transitions to a quadratic function for $\kappa_1 < |\beta_i| \leq \kappa_1\kappa_2$, and then remains constant for all values of β_i, as long as $|\beta_i| > \kappa_1\kappa_2$. For small coefficients, the SCAD penalty has a similar penalization rate as LASSO but leaves large coefficients not excessively penalized. The MCP, developed by Zhang (2010), is defined by

$$\mathcal{P}^{\text{MCP}}(\beta_i; \boldsymbol{\kappa}) = \begin{cases} \kappa_1 |\beta_i| - \dfrac{|\beta_i|^2}{2\kappa_2} & \text{if } |\beta_i| \leq \kappa_1\kappa_2 \\ \dfrac{\kappa_2\kappa_1^2}{2} & \text{if } |\beta_i| > \kappa_1\kappa_2 \end{cases} \tag{20}$$

For $\kappa_1 > 0$ and $\kappa_2 > 1$, there is a continuum of penalties and threshold operators varying from hard ($\kappa_2 \to 1^+$) to soft thresholding ($\kappa_2 \to +\infty$). MCP starts with the same rate of penalization as LASSO but smoothly relaxes the penalization rate to zero as the absolute value of the coefficient increases. Furthermore, MCP relaxes the penalization rate immediately, compared with SCAD, where the rate remains flat for a while before decreasing.

Finally, the smooth integration of counting and absolute deviation (SICAD) penalty takes the form

$$\mathcal{P}^{\text{SICA}}(\beta_i; \boldsymbol{\kappa}) = \kappa_1 \frac{(\kappa_2 + 1)|\beta_i|}{\kappa_2 + |\beta_i|} \tag{21}$$

with $\kappa_1 > 0$ and a generally small shape parameter, $\kappa_2 > 0$. SICAD is another nonconvex regularization method, which is a combination between the l_0 and l_1 penalties and therefore gives sparse solutions. For smaller values of κ_2, SICAD yields results closer to the best-subset selection, while for larger values of κ_2, it is closer to LASSO.

Regularized regression methods, particularly LASSO, have proven popular in empirical finance and asset management. Feng *et al.* (2020) and Freyberger *et al.* (2020) employ LASSO to create data-driven combinations of stock return predictors from large sets of signals that may support factor-driven trading. Similarly, Rapach *et al.* (2019) use LASSO to identify the most significant predictors and create optimal combinations among a large set of industry and market returns. Rapach *et al.* (2013) use adaptive elastic nets to explore the predictive ability of lagged US market returns on global indexes. Gu *et al.* (2020) provide an example of the application of elastic nets to the selection and combination of both fundamental and technical signals to predict stock returns. Messmer and Audrino (2017) conclude that ALASSO outperforms both ordinary least squares and LASSO when used to select from a vast number of features in the perspective of deriving trading signals. Dai *et al.* (2022) compare different shrinkage approaches to predict stock return volatility with a large set of variables and find that shrinkage approaches, including LASSO, ALASSO, EN, and ridge regression, exhibit superior performance compared to competing models.

Ensemble methods. Within portfolio applications, the use of SL algorithms is often problematic. One of the primary issues is that past asset returns are not always representative of their subsequent behaviour because of the existence of structural breaks and regimes. Additionally, SL models tend to over-fit the historical data, which can lead to poor performance with new data. Finally, the iterative steps from ML prediction through to policy development, backtesting, and parameter optimization are fragile, slow, and prone to error. Such fragility, and corresponding occasional under-performance in out-of-sample (henceforth, OOS) experiments by SL methods, has recently led many researchers to select and combine existing individual signals originated by individual SL methods, often by additionally using ML methods (see, e.g., Bartram *et al.*, 2021). Therefore, SL methods would be supplemented by additional ML to produce forms of optimal *ensembles*. Ensembling achieves a better balance between bias and variance, which can lead to more accurate predictions. Equivalently, if many different algorithms trained on many different training sets all find similar patterns and reach similar conclusions, we can be more confident that the forecast is robust and not the result of over-fitting.[12]

There are several examples of ensembling being used successfully in equity market trading signal generation. For instance, Tsai *et al.* (2011) and Krauss *et al.* (2017) have all applied this approach. Borghi and De Rossi (2020) conducted an experiment in which they combined an ensemble of random forest models, neural networks, gradient-boosted trees, and regularized regressions to predict stock returns (all these SL techniques are described in the following). They found that a trading strategy based on model combinations tended to outperform strategies based on individual models. Similarly, Wolff and Echterling (2020) built ML models to predict weekly returns for the constituents of the S&P 500 index and found that an ensemble of deep ANNs, random forests, and long short-term memory (LSTM) ANNs delivered the best risk-adjusted performance.

An ensemble of models is often optimized by a second supervised ML model that would decide on the most profitable model weighting scheme; this is then known as a *stacked* model. Three key types of nonlinear models from the ML literature are structural ensembles: regression trees, support vector machines, and ANNs. We now briefly describe them. A *regression tree* is a nonparametric model that is constructed using a recursive binary splitting approach (Breiman *et al.*, 1984). At first, starting from the top of the tree, we divide

[12]Rasekhschaffe and Jones (2019) emphasize the importance of model averaging to mitigate over-fitting and recommended various types of forecast combinations, across different models, training sets, and forecast horizons.

the predictor space into two distinct and nonoverlapping rectangular regions (also called "leaves") and model the asset returns as the simple average of $\mathbf{r}$ within that region. Then one or both of those regions are split into two more regions, etc. This process continues until certain stopping criteria are met. The predictor variable upon which a branch is based, and the value where the branch is split, is chosen to minimize the mean squared forecast error or some other loss function. Specifically, the prediction of a tree, $\mathcal{T}$, with M leaves $R_1, R_2, \ldots, R_M$ and maximum depth D (the maximum number of levels that the tree can have, which in turn controls the number of splits and the complexity of the model), is defined as $\mathcal{T}(\mathbf{X}, c, M, D) = \sum_{m=1}^{M} c_m I_{\{\mathbf{X} \in R_m(D)\}}$, where $R_m(D)$ represents the mth partition of the predictor space. The score c associated with partition m, c_m, is the simple average of returns within region R_m, written as

$$c_m = \frac{1}{T_m} \sum_{\mathbf{X} \in R_m(D)} \mathbf{r} \tag{22}$$

where T_m denotes the number of observations in region m. Typically, at each branch, we choose the sorting variable among the set of predictors and the split value that minimize the following loss function:

$$Q_m(c, T_m) = \frac{1}{T_m} \sum_{\mathbf{X} \in R_m} (\mathbf{r} - c_m)^2 \tag{23}$$

Branching halts when the depth, D, of the tree reaches a pre-specified threshold that is tuned adaptively using cross-validation methods.

Regression trees are among the methods that tend to over-fit, typically resulting in inferior OOS performance. To improve their prediction accuracy, researchers typically resort to approaches that combine a large number of trees, $\mathcal{T}_1, \mathcal{T}_2, \ldots, \mathcal{T}_k$, to yield a single consensus prediction. The first set of methods is based on *boosting*, first proposed by Schapire (1990) and Freund (1995) for classification problems. Under boosting, one recursively combines a large number of shallow trees, known as "weak learners", to form an ensemble of trees with greater stability than a single more complex tree. The first ensemble method we consider is the gradient boosting machine (GBM), proposed by Friedman (2001), who extends boosting to regression frameworks. *Gradient boosting* is initialized by fitting a shallow tree (i.e., a first tree with a small number of levels or nodes); then a second tree with the same depth is used to fit the residuals of the previous model and the forecasts of these two trees are added together to form a single ensemble prediction. This procedure is repeated sequentially until the total number of iterations k is reached. The goal is to minimize the objective function, typically based on a squared loss:

$$\arg\min_{f} \mathcal{L}(\mathbf{r}, f_k(\mathbf{X})) = \arg\min_{f} \|\mathbf{r} - f_k(\mathbf{X})\|^2 \tag{24}$$

Gradient boosting is an additive model that can be expressed as

$$f_k(\mathbf{X}) = \sum_{j=1}^{k} f_j(\mathbf{X}, c_j, M_j, D, v) \tag{25}$$

where k is the total number of trees and f_j is given by $f_j(\mathbf{X}, v) = f_{j-1}(\mathbf{X}) + v\mathcal{T}_j(\mathbf{X}, c_j, M_j, D)$. The parameter v controls the learning rate of the boosting procedure that scales the contribution of each tree to the ensemble by a factor of $0 < v < 1$ and prevents the model from over-fitting the residuals.

Recently, many applications in empirical finance (see, e.g., Kynigakis and Panopoulou, 2022) have considered a regularized gradient boosting machine (RGBM), an extension of GMB that includes a regularization term in the loss function controlling for the complexity of the model to avoid over-fitting. The objective function in this case is

$$\arg\min_{f} \mathcal{L}(\mathbf{r}, f_k(\mathbf{X})) + \Omega(f_k(\mathbf{X})) \tag{26}$$

Refining the definition of a tree to be $\mathcal{T}(\mathbf{X}) = \boldsymbol{\vartheta}_{q(\mathbf{X})}$, where $\boldsymbol{\vartheta}$ is a vector of scores for each region and q is a function assigning each observation to the corresponding leaf, the regularization term $\Omega(\cdot)$ is defined as

$$\Omega(f_k(\mathbf{X})) = \kappa_2 M_f + \frac{1}{2}\kappa_1 \|\boldsymbol{\vartheta}\|^2 + \kappa_3 \|\boldsymbol{\vartheta}\| \tag{27}$$

where the regularization parameter κ_2 captures the complexity cost caused by the introduction of an additional leaf to a tree and the parameters κ_1 and κ_3 control the strength of the l_2 and l_1 regularization of the weights, respectively.

The second set of ensemble methods is based on *bootstrap aggregating or bagging* (Breiman, 1996). It combines many noisy but approximately unbiased models to reduce the variance and improve the accuracy of the forecasts. Bagging involves creating multiple samples of the training dataset by randomly selecting observations with replacement. For each sample, a new model is trained on the bootstrapped data, resulting in a set of diverse models. The individual models are then combined using an ensemble method, such as averaging or voting, to make a final prediction. As bagging is particularly effective when applied to unstable or high-variance models, such as regression trees, we present the methodology in that context. The baseline bagging procedure estimates $\mathcal{T}_1, \mathcal{T}_2, \ldots, \mathcal{T}_B$ based on B different bootstrap samples of the data and then averages their forecasts to obtain a single low-variance model:

$$f_B(\mathbf{X}) = \frac{1}{B} \sum_{b=1}^{B} \mathcal{T}_b(\mathbf{X}, c_b, M_{bj}, D) \tag{28}$$

In bagging, usually the regression trees are simply i.d. (identically distributed but not independent), with the variance of the average estimates, as the number of bootstrapped trees increases, depending on the product of the variance of each tree and the correlation among trees.[13] Typically, empirical finance users adopt the stationary bootstrap instead of a standard bootstrap, due to the underlying time series structure of the data.

One popular variation of bagging that has occasionally found application in empirical finance are *random forests* (RF), proposed by Breiman (2001), which aim to reduce the variance of the average forecast by minimizing the correlation among the regression trees in the ensemble. A random forest algorithm creates multiple decision trees by randomly selecting a subset of input features at each split. This reduces the correlation between trees and improves prediction accuracy. Extremely Randomized Tree (ERT) is a variant of RF that

[13]This occurs because the regression trees used in bagging are correlated with each other as they are all constructed using slightly different versions of the same training data. The variance of the bagged model is affected by two factors: the variance of each individual tree and the correlation among the predictions of the trees. If the trees are highly correlated, then their predictions tend to be similar, which reduces the variance of the bagged model.

adds more randomness to the tree construction process. ERT selects the split value at each node randomly from a uniform distribution, instead of choosing the optimal split based on a specific criterion. For example, ERT can be used to predict stock prices based on multiple input features such as company financial data, market trends, and macroeconomic indicators. ERT would randomly select a subset of these features at each split and then select the best split based on the highest performing random split.[14] Jiang *et al.* (2020) and Saifan *et al.* (2020) are two successful examples of applications of ERT to forecasting stock prices and building trading strategies.

Decision and regression trees are another popular class of ML methods employed in generating multi-factor signals. In fact, Bryzgalova *et al.* (2019) point out that the standard factor models à la Fama and French (1993) and Fama and French (2015) can be viewed as simple tree models with just two splitting dimensions based on the quantiles of the distributions of company fundamentals, such as the book to price ratio or operating profitability. Applying this intuition, Coqueret and Guida (2020) have produced tree-based forecasts of the returns of a large set of US equities between 2002 and 2016 using extreme gradient-boosted trees. Gu *et al.* (2020) estimate a number of tree-based regression models using gradient-boosted regression trees. Most papers agree that shallow trees and models with a limited number of trees seem to outperform in applications to equities. Leung *et al.* (2021) use gradient-boosted trees to predict monthly stock returns using 20 stock characteristics. They conclude that, despite the statistical advantage of ML predictions, the economic gains tend to be more limited and depend critically on the ability to take risk and implement trades efficiently, which appears to be more critical than devising the trading strategies themselves.

2.2 Unsupervised learning

Unsupervised learning (USL) is a type of ML in which an algorithm is trained to identify patterns and structures in data without

[14]Hyper-parameters in ERT include the number of trees in the ensemble, the maximum depth of the trees, and the size of the random feature subset used at each split. ERT is especially useful in high-dimensional data with many noisy features.

the need for labeled examples. It is particularly useful for instances when a researcher is not sure what to look for in the data and for the exploratory analysis of it. In finance, USL techniques are commonly used for tasks such as anomaly detection, clustering, and dimensionality reduction. The latter is a set of techniques that reduce the number of features in a dataset while preserving the most important information. Under USL, the algorithm derives the latent factors regardless of the values taken by the asset returns in the sample. This contrasts with the dimensionality reduction methods that fall under SL (such as PLS), where the vector of asset returns, $\mathbf{r}$, is used to determine the directions that best represent the predictors $\mathbf{X}$.

Principal component analysis (PCA) is the most widely used method to obtain estimates of the latent factors and now scores hundreds of applications in the finance literature, also to offer grounds to trading strategies (see, e.g., Guidolin and Pedio, 2022, with reference to commodities). PCA can be viewed as a regression-type problem in which the goal is to find the first $K \leq p$ principal component weight vectors collected in $\mathbf{A}$ as

$$\arg\min_{\mathbf{A}} \left\|\mathbf{X} - \mathbf{XAA}'\right\|^2 \quad \text{s.t. } \mathbf{A}'\mathbf{A} = \mathbf{I}_k \tag{29}$$

The solution to this problem is most often obtained via the singular value decomposition, $\mathbf{X} = \mathbf{UDA}'$, where the columns of $\mathbf{A}$ are the principal component weights and each column is used to derive the mth principal component, $\mathbf{z}_m = \mathbf{X}\mathbf{v}_m$; thus, $\mathbf{ZV}$ is the dimensional-reduced version of the original predictors. The derived variable $\mathbf{z}_1$ is the first principal component of $\mathbf{X}$ and has the largest sample variance among all normalized linear combinations of the columns of $\mathbf{X}$; $\mathbf{z}_2$ is the second principal component of $\mathbf{X}$, it is orthogonal to $\mathbf{z}_1$, and it has the second largest sample variance among all normalized linear combinations of the columns of $\mathbf{X}$; and so on.

Sparse principal component analysis (SPCA), developed by Zou *et al.* (2006), is based on the regression/reconstruction property of PCA — by which the original data can be reconstructed from the reduced set of principal components by projecting them back onto the original space — and produces modified principal components with sparse weights, such that each principal component is a linear combination of only a few of the original predictors. The following regression criterion is proposed to derive the sparse principal component weights,

$$\arg\min_{\mathbf{A},\mathbf{C}} \; \left\|\mathbf{X} - \mathbf{XAC}'\right\|^2 + \zeta_1 \left\|\mathbf{c}\right\| + \zeta_2 \left\|\mathbf{c}\right\|^2 \quad \text{s.t. } \mathbf{A}'\mathbf{A} = \mathbf{I}_k \tag{30}$$

where $\mathbf{C}$ is $p \times K$. If $\zeta_1 = \zeta_2 = 0$ and $\mathbf{C} = \mathbf{A}$, then the minimizer of the objective function is exactly the first K weight vectors of ordinary PCA. The l_1 penalty imposed on $\mathbf{c}$ induces sparseness of the weights, with larger values of ζ_1 leading to sparser solutions. The algorithm by Zou and Hastie (2005) is used to compute the sparse approximations of each principal component.

The *independent component analysis* (ICA), developed by Comon (1994), aims at finding a linear representation of non-Gaussian data such that the components are statistically independent. ICA is particularly useful when dealing with sources of interference or noise mixed with a signal: by separating out the independent components of the signal, it helps identify the sources of noise and eliminate them from the signal. For instance, ICA can be used to detect the independent components of portfolio returns and then used to construct a diversified portfolio. By identifying the independent sources of returns, ICA can help investors reduce their exposure to common market factors and diversify their portfolios across uncorrelated assets. The ICA objective is a variation of (29):

$$\arg\min_{\mathbf{A}} \; \left\|\mathbf{XA}\right\| \quad \text{s.t. } \mathbf{A}'\mathbf{A} = \mathbf{I}_k \tag{31}$$

Solving the ICA problem means finding an orthogonal $\mathbf{A}$ such that the components of the vector random variable $\mathbf{Z} = \mathbf{XA}$ are independent and non-Gaussian, a reasonable assumption for many economic signals. In practice, the independent components are estimated by iterative estimation of the matrix $\mathbf{A}$, systematically increasing the degree of independence of the components.[15] Ordinary ICA has two

[15]The most commonly used algorithm for ICA estimation is called the FastICA algorithm. This algorithm uses a fixed-point iteration scheme to estimate the independent components of the mixed signal. At each iteration, the algorithm updates the values of the parameters in matrix $\mathbf{A}$ to maximize the non-Gaussianity of the components. Other optimization algorithms, such as maximum likelihood estimation (MLE) and Bayesian methods, can also be used for ICA estimation. These methods typically require more computational resources and may not be as efficient as the FastICA algorithm.

drawbacks; it requires constrained optimization, which can be difficult in high dimensional settings and it is sensitive to whitening, a pre-processing step that de-correlates the input data that however cannot always be computed exactly when $p \gg T$. To overcome these drawbacks, Le *et al.* (2011) have proposed a *Reconstruction Independent Component Analysis* (RICA) that replaces ICA's orthonormality constraint with a reconstruction penalty. This produces the unconstrained problem,

$$\arg\min_{\mathbf{A}} \; \|\mathbf{XA}\| + \zeta \left\|\mathbf{X} - \mathbf{XAA}'\right\|^2 \tag{32}$$

where $\zeta > 0$ is a regularization parameter. RICA is equivalent to ICA when $K < p$, the data can actually be whitened first, and $\zeta \to +\infty$. Unlike traditional ICA, which assumes that the independent components are non-Gaussian, RICA places a sparsity constraint on the components.

Clustering is a technique used to group similar sample observations together, aiming at finding a structure or patterns in data, without any prior knowledge of the data's labels or groups. There are several methods of clustering, including *hierarchical clustering*, *K-means clustering*, and *density-based clustering*. Hierarchical clustering involves creating a tree-like structure of clusters, where each node represents a group of data points. It iteratively merges the closest pair of clusters until all data points belong to a single cluster. Figure 2 visually illustrates the logic of the algorithm. Hierarchical clustering is useful when the number of clusters is not known beforehand. K-means clustering involves partitioning the data into K clusters, where each data point is assigned to the nearest cluster center. It works by iteratively updating the position of the cluster centers until the clusters are stable. K-means clustering is useful when the clusters are roughly spherical and their number is known. Density-based clustering involves identifying areas of high density in the data and then are used to form clusters.[16]

[16]The most common density-based clustering algorithm is DBSCAN (*Density-Based Spatial Clustering of Applications with Noise*). DBSCAN works by identifying points that are in dense regions and separating them from points that are in less dense regions. Density-based clustering is useful when the data contain noise or outliers and when the clusters have irregular shapes.

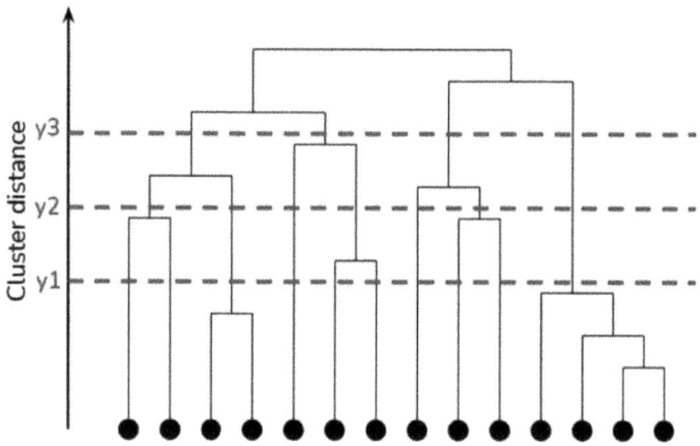

Figure 2. Schematic visualization of the working of a hierarchical clustering algorithm.

In portfolio decisions, clustering can identify similar stocks or assets based on their historical returns or other characteristics, ultimately helping investors identify diversification opportunities. Another example is when a trader uses clustering to identify a group of stocks that move together based on certain factors, such as sector or industry. One application of clustering in systematic trading is mean reversion strategies. If a trader has identified a group of assets that mean revert together, the trader might buy assets that have fallen below their historical mean and sell assets that have risen above it, betting that they will eventually revert. If a trader has identified a group of assets that tend to exhibit momentum together, they might develop a momentum strategy. For example, the trader might buy assets that are trending upwards and sell assets that are trending downwards, betting that the trends will continue, and also obtaining substantial diversification benefits. If a trader has identified two assets that tend to move together but have recently diverged, she may develop a pair trading strategy. For example, the trader might buy one asset and short the other, betting that the prices will eventually converge. Recently, Gorman and Fabozzi (2022) have used a variety of supervised and unsupervised dimensionality reduction algorithms to investigate whether the smart beta (alternative) risk premia may represent a separate investment category consisting of a wide range of rule-based trading strategies targeting returns representing either compensation for bearing risk or behavioural biases.

3 ML in Portfolio Optimization

Almost 70 years after Markowitz (1952) was published, the approach to portfolio construction is still deeply rooted in the mean–variance (MV) tradition. Nevertheless, critics, such as Michaud (1989), note that, in practice, the MV paradigm suffers from the difficulty of precisely estimating its main inputs, particularly expected returns. A disturbing consequence of such inaccuracy is that a simple equally weighted portfolio of all assets, which makes no assumptions on the directionality of returns, turns out to be a hard benchmark to beat for optimized portfolios (DeMiguel *et al.*, 2009).[17] Hence, recent advances in ML techniques may inspire wide-ranging innovation in the domain of portfolio construction.

3.1 Improving portfolio optimization through better quality input forecasting

An obvious starting point is the use of ML algorithms for more accurate (less biased, less volatile or both) forecasts of future expected returns on each asset or asset class in the asset menu; see Section 2 of this chapter on such methods. Clearly, improving the quality of MV weights through more careful prediction of expected returns implies that ML methods are used to forecast returns which are to be seen as continuous random variables. Yet, most often ML algorithms are best employed to forecast the classification (e.g., the sign) of asset returns.[18]

[17]However, several subsequent papers have questioned such a finding; see among the others, Bianchi and Guidolin (2014).

[18]Forecasting through regressions requires the algorithm to learn complex relationships between various factors that affect the price or return of the asset. These relationships can be nonlinear and involve multiple factors, making it challenging for the algorithm to learn and predict accurately. Additionally, financial markets are inherently noisy, and there is a lot of randomness and uncertainty involved, making it even more difficult to predict prices or returns instead of their change or sign.

Regardless of whether ML has been used or not in obtaining forecasts of expected asset returns, the next step concerns estimating/predicting portfolio risk with ANNs, decision trees, and SVMs.[19] For instance, SVRs can estimate the conditional variance of financial returns based on past returns and other market variables. Peng *et al.* (2018) have combined the traditional GARCH model with the ML approach to volatility prediction, estimating the mean and volatility equations using SVR and comparing it to GARCH family models. Using data for cryptocurrencies and exchange rates, they show that SVR-GARCH models significantly outperform GARCH, EGARCH, and GJR-GARCH models with normal, Student's t, and skewed Student's t distributions. Recently, Zhang and Qiao (2021) investigate whether the nonlinear SVR method applied to a Heterogeneous Auto-Regressive (SVR-HAR) model can compete with combination methods in terms of OOS realized volatility forecasting, reporting encouraging results.[20] Wang *et al.* (2020) have proposed using LSTM networks and a mean–variance model for optimal portfolio formation in conjunction with a procedure of asset preselection, in which any long-term dependencies of financial time-series data can be captured. They report that their SL method outperforms all benchmarks in terms of the cumulative return per year, Sharpe ratio per triennial period as well as average return to the risk per month of each three-year period.

ANNs for volatility forecasting typically use a multi-layer feed-forward architecture, where the input layer consists of past returns and other market variables, the output layer consists of the predicted volatility, and one or more hidden layers capture the nonlinear relationships between the input and output layers. ANNs for volatility forecasting require careful data pre-processing and feature

[19]We will not classify classical GARCH models as belonging to the ML domain, even though in a ML perspective, GARCH certainly classes as SL regression-type architecture.

[20]A HAR (Heterogeneous Autoregressive) model is a popular econometric tool used to forecast financial volatility. This model was developed by Corsi (2009) to capture the heterogeneity in the persistence of volatility across different time horizons. The HAR model is based on the idea that volatility can be predicted by past observations at different frequencies. The HAR model has been shown to outperform other popular models, such as GARCH and EGARCH.

engineering to extract relevant information from the raw data. Additionally, hyperparameter tuning is required to optimize the network architecture and regularization parameters. For instance, already Donaldson and Kamstra (1997) had constructed a semi-parametric nonlinear GARCH model based on an ANN and reported OOS volatility forecasts for international stock index returns encompassing those from plain vanilla GARCH models.[21] Kristjanpoller *et al.* (2014), Kristjanpoller and Minutolo (2015), and Kristjanpoller and Minutolo (2016) test hybrid neural networks-GARCH models for volatility forecasting on the returns of three stock indices finding that ANN improves the forecasting performance of GARCH. Ramos-Pérez *et al.* (2019) introduce a model based on a set of ML techniques that include ANN as well as gradient descent boosting, random forest, and SVM and stack those algorithms to predict S&P500 volatility, to show that this approach outperforms other common benchmarks.[22]

In MV optimization, two SL approaches are typically used to estimate the covariance matrix. The first is the graphical LASSO, which is a static estimator that derives a sparse version of the covariance matrix. The second is a dynamic estimator based on the DCC-GARCH, already known from time series econometrics (see Guidolin and Pedio, 2018). The graphical LASSO algorithm, proposed by Friedman *et al.* (2008), estimates the sparse precision matrix (the inverse of the covariance matrix), using the l_1 penalty to enforce sparsity. As an alternative to the graphical LASSO, one can consider portfolios based on the linear shrinkage estimator of the covariance matrix proposed by Ledoit and Wolf (2004). The sample covariance matrix is shrunk towards a one-parameter matrix, with equal variances and zero covariances. The weight given to the target matrix is typically determined by a shrinkage parameter, controlling the degree of shrinkage applied to the sample covariance matrix. The linear shrinkage estimator has been shown to perform better than the

[21]When the forecasts of one model encompass those from another model, it means that the first model's predictions cover a wider range of possible outcomes than the second model's predictions.

[22]Mourtas and Katsikis (2022) propose a continuous-time Black–Litterman portfolio optimization problem, which is solved using a novel ANN architecture to suggest that it is a promising alternative to traditional approaches for time-series modeling and forecasting in portfolio optimization.

sample covariance matrix estimator in a variety of settings, especially when the number of variables is large relative to the sample size or when the variables are highly correlated. The estimator can improve the accuracy of statistical inference and prediction and reduce the risk of over-fitting.

Several recent papers have relied on alternative ML techniques to improve the estimation of portfolio risk, in some cases dispensing with the covariance matrix altogether. Often, classical portfolio risk estimates are optimal in-sample (on the training set) but perform poorly OOS (on the test set). One way to deal with this problem is to drop forecasts of expected returns altogether and, for instance, simply weighting the assets by the inverse of their predicted volatility, what is called *risk parity approach* (RP). However, both RP and MV require the inversion of a positive-definite covariance matrix, deemed computationally daunting.[23] Hierarchical risk parity works by grouping similar investments into clusters based on a distance metric. The covariance matrix's rows and columns are also reorganized such that the largest values lie along the diagonal. Finally, the allocations are split through recursive bisections of the reordered covariance matrix. One starts by defining a distance measure between assets from zero to one, $d_{i,j}$, after which one clusters the pair of columns (i^*, j^*) together such that $(i^*, j^*) = \text{argmin}_{(i,j)}\{d_{i,j}\}$ and $i \neq j$. The next step is to update $\{d_{i,j}\}$ with the new cluster and recursively repeat until all $N-1$ clusters are formed. Then one places correlated assets close together and uncorrelated ones further apart and carries out a top-down allocation. Although the information processed by this method is the same as in the traditional MV paradigm, it requires fewer estimates and therefore delivers better stability and robustness. de Prado (2016) reports that the proposed method to build a minimum variance portfolio results in a 31% improvement in the Sharpe ratio compared to the standard approach.

3.2 Automatic portfolio optimization

A separate strand of literature consists of papers that attempt to use ML directly to obtain optimal portfolios. While the papers found in

[23] A study by de Prado (2016) avoids the issue by replacing the structure of return covariances among assets with a tree structure using hierarchical cluster analysis.

Section 3.1 mostly aim at improving the quality of the inputs that enter a standard, classical MV problem (hence, predicted means, variances, and/or covariances), in this case, the goal is to use ML to directly infer optimal weights from the data. By skipping the rigid distinction between predicted performances and risk, it generalizes the MV framework to broader asset allocation schemes (for instance, relying upon higher-order moments or pure rule-based portfolio policies).

A first approach to direct optimization of portfolio weights using ML resorts to SL algorithms, such as ANNs or SVMs. In this approach, the first step is to define a set of input features, such as historical asset returns data, market indices, and macroeconomic indicators. The output of the model is a set of predicted portfolio weights, obtained by training it on historical data. During the training phase, the model is fed with features and corresponding portfolio weights, and it learns to map the input features to the output weights using a loss function. The loss function can be designed to optimize under alternative investment objectives, such as maximum Sharpe ratio or minimum value-at-risk. Once the model is trained, it can be used to predict portfolio weights based on new market data in real time. The output can be adjusted dynamically as new data become available, allowing the portfolio to adapt to changing market conditions.

ANNs seem to be a common approach to achieving these goals owing to their flexibility in accommodating complex rules and constraints in the decision process. Chapados and Bengio (2001) had already used ANNs to learn the optimal asset allocation subject to value-at-risk constraints. Similarly, Yu *et al.* (2008) go beyond the first two moments by training an ANN to build mean–variance–skewness efficient portfolios. Zimmermann *et al.* (2001) incorporate Black and Littermann's celebrated asset allocation framework into an ANN model in order to augment the set of inputs with views about future returns. Tsang and Wong (2020) investigate a deep-learning solution to high-dimensional multi-period portfolio problems with constraints. They propose a deep ANN architecture to describe the underlying control process. The feedback control function is determined solely by the network parameters. In this way, the multi-period problem is linked to a training problem of the deep ANN that can be efficiently computed by the standard optimization techniques for network training. Bradrania and Pirayesh Neghab (2022) find that an ANN approach to conditional asset allocation, which directly relates state variables to portfolio weights, generates better outcomes compared to traditional methods. Du (2022) presents an MV model constructed using stationary portfolios composed of cointegrated stocks. The expected return of this new model is predicted by using ML models, such as SVM, RFs, and attention-based LSTM networks.[24] They show that attention-based LSTM networks can more accurately model the spread portfolio returns using technical indicators and lagged returns. They successfully select pairs of cointegrated stocks for constructing a more profitable MV portfolio.

3.3 Reinforcement learning

RL algorithms are increasingly popular in academic research and media for enabling the optimization of a policy for selecting portfolio weights without requiring the explicit calculation of expected returns and variance.[25] Conceptually, RL offers a paradigm shift where we are not overtly focused on predictive power, an auxiliary task, but rather on the optimization of portfolio decisions, the primary goal. Combining SL and RL algorithms may lead to picking up on well-known trading strategies without having to pre-define and identify them. For example, the gradient step that leads the machine agent to buy more of what did the best yesterday is indirectly creating a momentum investing strategy.

RL in finance consists of modeling an agent that learns how to take actions in an environment to maximize some notion of cumulative reward. An agent receives as input the current state S_t and is asked to take an action A_t to receive a reward R_{t+1}, the information on which can be used to identify the next optimal action, A_{t+1},

[24]An attention-based LSTM network is a type of recurrent neural network (RNN) that incorporates an attention mechanism to selectively focus on specific parts of the input sequence when making predictions. In a standard LSTM network, the hidden state of the network is computed at each time step using the input at that time step and the previous hidden state. This hidden state is then used to make a prediction at each time step. In an attention-based LSTM network, an additional attention mechanism is introduced to compute weights that indicate the relative importance of each time step in the input sequence.

[25]See, e.g., discussion in https://www.economist.com/leaders/2022/06/09/artificial-intelligences-new-frontier.

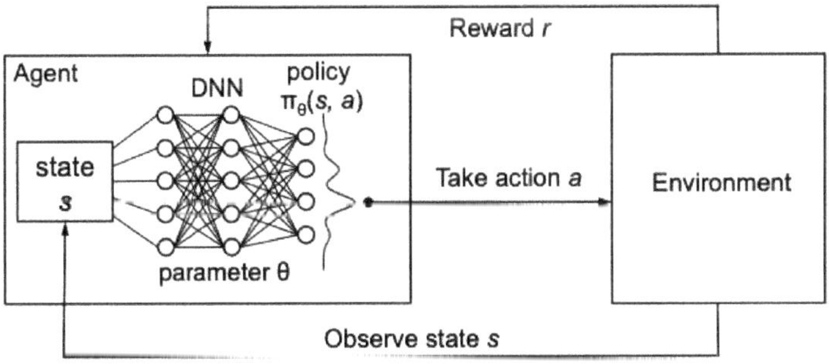

Figure 3. Flow diagram illustrating reinforcement learning.

given the new state S_{t+1}, etc. Figure 3 shows the flow of information characterizing RL. In the context of portfolio optimization, the state space could include factors, such as historical price data, market indices, and economic indicators, while the action space could represent the portfolio weights assigned to different assets. The reward function could be defined based on the portfolio's performance relative to a benchmark or based on other criteria, such as maximum Sharpe ratio, minimum risk, maximum drawdown, and value-at-risk measures. Next, an RL algorithm is trained using historical data to learn an optimal policy for selecting portfolio weights. The algorithm could be a model-based approach that learns a transition model for the state space or a model-free approach that directly learns the policy through trial and error. Once the optimal policy is learned, it can be used to perform asset allocation in real-time based on the current state of the market. The weights selected by the policy can be adjusted dynamically as new data become available, allowing the portfolio to adapt to changing market conditions.

While supervised learning (SL) aims at predicting specific outcomes, such as asset price changes, RL optimizes decision-making in dynamic, uncertain environments. RL finds optimal actions to achieve a desired outcome over time, based on feedback from the environment. By using RL as a trading strategy, portfolio managers can make better-informed investment decisions, streamline the process, and reduce human error. RL also conveniently accounts for market frictions, transaction costs, and liquidity constraints. Despite its ability to compute (near-)optimal portfolio weights with less human involvement, RL takes longer to train and is computationally intensive.

An agent learns in RL by interacting with the environment and receiving rewards or penalties. Feedback is used to update the agent's policy to maximize long-term rewards. However, the agent's decisions affect the environment, resulting in sparse, noisy, and delayed feedback that can hinder robust and accurate learning. Therefore, RL algorithms require a large amount of data to be effective. This can be particularly true in complex environments with many possible actions and state transitions, where the agent may need to explore a wide range of actions and states before finding an optimal policy.[26] For instance, Zhang *et al.* (2020) suggest an RL approach to directly optimize a portfolio's Sharpe ratio. This approach is that it delivers optimal portfolio weights by updating model parameters through gradient ascent without the need for a forecasting step required by the classical MV framework.

Interestingly, RL's convergence to an optimal value is not guaranteed; the famous Bellman update can only guarantee the optimal value if every state is visited an infinite number of times and every action is tried an infinite amount of times within each state, so essentially never in practice. In applied portfolio decisions, however, we do not need a truly optimal value; approximate optimality is fine. However, the sample size needed to obtain a good level of approximate optimality increases with the size of the state and action space. Moreover, without further assumptions, there is no better way than to explore the space randomly, leading to small and slow progress. Finally, the use of RL in real-world applications can be challenging due to the cost and complexity of testing in simulated environments, particularly when accurate environment feedback is necessary. In such cases, it may be necessary to revert to the real environment, which may require deploying the algorithm in the actual system, collecting data, and waiting for the results of genuine OOS experiments.

Fischer (2018) has categorized RL algorithms as *critic (value function)-only*, *actor-only*, and *actor-critic*. This distinction is becoming important in portfolio applications with critic-only algorithms seen as the most extensively studied ones (see Kolm and Ritter, 2019). These models aim at learning value functions that produce the

[26]Furthermore, the use of function approximation techniques, such as deep neural networks, can also increase the amount of data needed.

expected reward value from each action at each point in time without explicitly learning a policy; allowing the algorithm to choose the action with the best outcome. These algorithms are often unable to deal with many assets and can only consider discrete action spaces (e.g., buy and sell) and are not commonly used in portfolio optimization, as this domain typically involves a combination of both RL and optimization techniques, such as MV optimization, which require explicit modeling of the policy function. Actor-only (see Chaouki *et al.*, 2020) algorithms learn to map states (e.g., market conditions) to actions (the actor) directly without explicitly estimating the value function (the critic). These algorithms rely on a parameterized policy, which can be an ANN, to output the best action to take in a given state. These models are more transparent and can accommodate continuous action spaces (e.g., portfolio weights). Actor-only RL algorithms are generally used in problems where it is difficult or impossible to estimate the value function accurately but where the optimal policy can still be approximated. However, they require the reward function (e.g., portfolio's Sharpe ratio, and investor's utility) to be differentiable when the action space is continuous. In particular, the Deterministic Policy Gradient (DPG) algorithm is a type of actor-only RL algorithm that is commonly used in portfolio optimization. Chaouki *et al.* (2020) address the question of whether the DPG algorithm can learn known optimal trading strategies for the dynamical portfolio allocation problem and report encouraging results: DPG can learn optimal trading strategies for the dynamic portfolio problem, provided that the problem can be formulated as a Markov decision process.

Actor-critic approaches combine the benefits of both value-based and policy-based methods and comprise two algorithmic steps. The first (the actor model) determines the action depending on the current state, and the second (the critic model) evaluates the performance of the chosen action. The actor is trained to output a probability distribution over possible actions, which is then used to select an action. The critic, on the other hand, evaluates the performance of the actor by estimating the value function of the current policy. The idea is to iteratively adjust the actor model so that it maximizes the expected reward produced by the critic model. Fischer (2018) reviews a large number of studies related to each of these approaches — critic-only, actor-only, and actor-critic — and concludes that there is no clear winner in terms of performance. García-Galicia *et al.* (2019) provide an RL solution to the portfolio problem based on an actor/critic architecture in which the market is characterized by a restriction called transaction cost, involving time penalization.

Overall, the direct optimization of portfolio weights using RL provides a powerful tool for portfolio managers, enabling them to make informed decisions based on real-time data and adapt their strategies quickly and effectively to changing market conditions. Care must be taken to ensure that the reward function aligns with the desired investment objectives and that the algorithm is calibrated to avoid over-fitting. It is likely that SL will still rule the pack in the foreseeable future (see Snow, 2020). In fact, SL is already quite flexible, and we should expect to see a lot of innovations to bring the experience of developing strategies closer to that of RL without forsaking the benefits of SL.

The application of RL to portfolio construction is not a new concept, dating back to the study by Moody *et al.* (1998). Recent research has explored larger samples of stocks and conducted more extensive empirical analyses, resulting in a better understanding of the potential benefits of using RL in selecting portfolio weights. Some of these recent studies include Wang and Zhou (2020) and Zhang *et al.* (2020). These studies focused on the US financial markets and reported Sharpe ratios between 0.75 and 5.5, which are higher than the Sharpe ratio of the S&P 500. Almahdi and Yang (2017) and Almahdi and Yang (2019) propose to use a combination of recurrent RL and a particle swarm algorithm in an asset allocation problem with constraints. Using S&P100 index stocks, they show that such a system with a Calmar ratio-based objective function yields a better efficient frontier than the Sharpe ratio and mean–variance-based portfolios.[27] Bertoluzzo and Corazza (2012) discuss two different RL approaches, the temporal difference and the kernel-based RL,

[27]The Calmar ratio is a risk-adjusted performance measure calculated by dividing the annualized return of an investment by its maximum drawdown over a certain time period.

that take into account not only the usual buy and sell signals but also a third signal, a stay-out-from-the-market state. Among the recent studies, Cong *et al.* (2020) stands out for two innovations. First, they use encoders (discussed in the following) to extract features from a list of technical and fundamental explanatory variables. This approach is particularly useful for reducing the dimensionality of high-dimensional panel data while preserving complex nonlinear and interaction effects. Second, they use surrogate modeling and polynomial sensitivity analysis to interpret the RL algorithm's outputs and to highlight the model's driving features. This step is crucial because RL algorithms are often opaque, and it is challenging to understand what the model may be capturing.

A related and yet different strand of AI applied to portfolio management is based on evolutionary algorithms (EAs), which are optimization techniques inspired by natural selection; see, e.g., Metaxiotis and Liagkouras (2012). EAs have been used to search for an optimal portfolio by evolving a population of candidate solutions over several generations. EAs can handle complex, nonlinear, and nonconvex problems, which are common in finance. EAs can also incorporate various constraints and objectives, such as transaction costs and risk aversion. However, EAs are different from ANNs, although they entertain a tight connection with them, related to their power to handle complex and high-dimensional data. RL models can be used to predict the fitness of candidate solutions in an EA, while EAs can be used to optimize the hyperparameters of an RL model. This approach, known as neuro evolution, combines the strengths of EAs and RL to create more efficient and accurate models. Branke *et al.* (2009) show that the EA approach can be used to incorporate complex rules, such as constraints on the number of assets in the portfolio and minimum holding thresholds. Skolpadungket *et al.* (2016) report significant improvements in Sharpe ratios by incorporating model risk in the portfolio construction framework through EAs.

3.4 Deep learning

Occasionally, in empirical finance, there has been some confusion and overlap between RL and the so-called "deep learning" approach.

Deep learning is a set of ML algorithms that use complex, multi-layer ANNs to model and solve complex problems.[28] The goal of deep learning is to find patterns and relationships in data by learning multiple layers of representations of the data. This approach has been highly successful in tasks such as image and speech recognition, natural language processing, and autonomous driving. On the contrary, RL is a type of ML that, as we have seen, focuses on training artificial agents to make decisions in an environment in order to maximize some reward signal. RL algorithms use trial-and-error learning to learn the optimal policy for an agent to take in a given environment. However, deep learning and RL can be used together, such as in deep RL, which combines the representational power of deep ANNs with the decision-making capabilities of RL. Traditional RL algorithms often use simpler, hand-crafted representations of the policy or value function, which may not be suitable for complex environments.

Aboussalah and Lee (2020) address the challenge of continuous action and multi-dimensional state spaces and propose a so-called stacked deep dynamic recurrent RL architecture to construct real-time optimal portfolios. Their system is trained and tested in an online manner for 20 successive rounds with data for 10 selected stocks from different sectors of the S&P 500 between January 1, 2013 and July 31, 2017. Betancourt and Chen (2021) propose a novel portfolio management method using deep RL on markets with a dynamic number of assets.[29] They propose a novel ANN architecture which is trained using deep RL. Their architecture considers all assets in the market and automatically adapts when new ones are introduced, making their method more efficient than previous methods.

[28]A deep neural network (DNN) is a type of neural network that has multiple layers of interconnected nodes (or neurons) between the input and output layers. Each layer of nodes learns to represent increasingly abstract and complex features of the input data. The main difference between a DNN and a shallow neural network (SNN) is the number of layers. SNNs typically have one or two hidden layers, while DNNs can have many more hidden layers. This allows DNNs to learn more complex representations of the input data, which can lead to improved performance on certain tasks.

[29]This problem is especially important in cryptocurrency markets, which already support the trading of hundreds of assets with new ones being added every month.

Their tests on cryptocurrency data turn out to outperform state-of-the-art asset allocation methods. Jang and Seong (2023) investigate a novel deep RL approach that combines modern portfolio theory and a deep learning approach and show that their method outperforms state-of-the-art algorithms in terms of realized OOS Sharpe ratio, average annualized returns, and maximum drawdown.

3.5 Autoencoders

An autoencoder is a type of ANN that is designed to learn a compressed representation or encoding of input data. The network is composed of two parts: an encoder and a decoder. The encoder takes the input data and maps it to a lower-dimensional latent space representation, while the decoder takes the latent space representation and maps it back to the original input space. The goal of the autoencoder is to learn an encoding that is as close as possible to the original input, while also being as compact as possible. To achieve this, the autoencoder is trained using an USL approach, where the loss function is typically based on the reconstruction error between the original input and the decoded output. During training, the encoder and decoder parameters are updated to minimize this reconstruction error. Autoencoders can be used for a variety of tasks, including data compression, anomaly detection, and feature extraction. Figure 4 shows a schematic representation of an autoencoder algorithm referred to the estimation of a multi-factor asset pricing relationship. In portfolio optimization, autoencoders are used to extract relevant features from financial and macroeconomic data that can be used to generate optimized portfolios. Autoencoders are often used in deep learning because they can learn a hierarchical representation of input data: they can learn multiple levels of abstraction in the data, with each layer capturing increasingly complex features.[30]

Autoencoders have been popularized by Heaton *et al.* (2017), who describe a procedure for data-driven portfolio selection consisting of four steps. The autoencoding step fits historical returns. The goal of the second step (termed the decode step) is to find a portfolio

[30]Gu *et al.* (2021) have used an autoencoding ANN to model individual stock returns. The model allows stock characteristic covariates to have nonlinear and interactive effects on factor exposures.

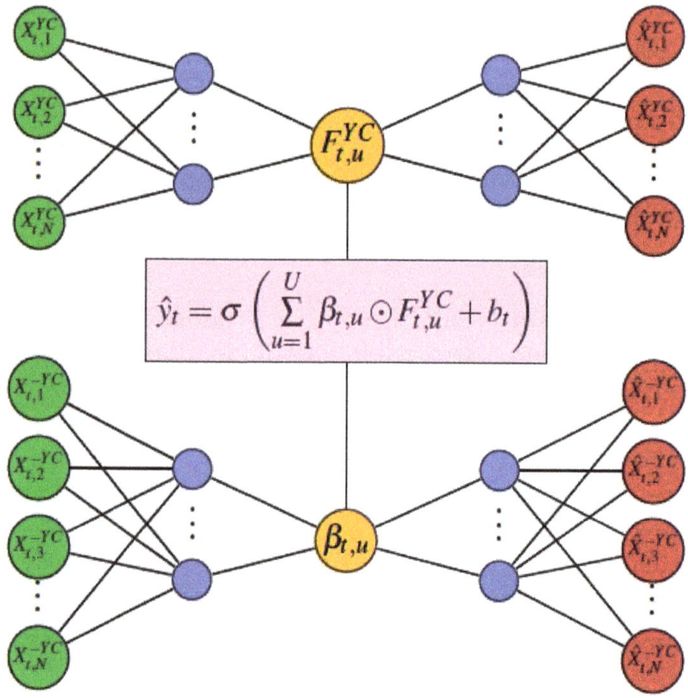

Figure 4. Schematic representation of an autoencoder algorithm (in the diagram, $\boldsymbol{X}^{YC}$ represents any type of variables that may explain returns, $\mathbf{F}$ is a lower-dimensional (factor-) representation, $\boldsymbol{X}^{-YC}$ is any type of variables that drives the time-varying factor-exposure, $\boldsymbol{\beta}$ is the time-varying factor loadings, and $\sigma(\cdot)$ is any type of linear or nonlinear activation function).

map to achieve a pre-specified goal. Third, an OOS validation step is used to tune hyperparameters and, particularly, to optimize the amount of regularization needed in the first two steps. This leads to the generation of an efficient frontier that can be used in the fourth step for model selection. Soleymani and Paquet (2020) develop a portfolio management framework based on a deep RL framework, called DeepBreath, that combines a restricted stacked autoencoder and a convolutional ANN. The autoencoder is employed in order to perform dimensionality reduction and feature selection, thus ensuring that only the most informative features are retained; the ANN is then used to learn and implement the investment policy. Their results show that the average returns achieved outperform current expert investment strategies while minimizing risk.

4 ML in the ETF and Smart Beta Spaces

ML has also gained significant interest in the ETF and passive strategy spaces. Passive investment strategies, such as ETFs, seek to track the performance of a particular index or asset class, rather than outperforming it. ML techniques can be used to optimize portfolio construction, enhance risk management, and improve asset allocation decisions, even when they have a passive, index-tracking nature. In fact, according to Phoon and Koh (2018), robo-advisors may even eventually replace traditional ETF fund managers.

With regard to the selection of securities to be included in a portfolio, ML algorithms can analyze large amounts of data, identify patterns and correlations, and make informed decisions about which securities to include. For example, ML can be used to screen securities based on various characteristics, such as price-to-earnings ratios, dividend yields, and market capitalization, and select those likely to provide the best risk-adjusted returns. To manage the short-term index tracking risks of typical ETF strategies, Fons *et al.* (2021) have proposed a novel smart allocation system based on a Feature Saliency Hidden Markov Model (HMM) algorithm that performs feature selection simultaneously with the training of the HMM, to improve regime identification.[31] They report an increase up to a 60% in risk-adjusted returns annually, which emphasizes model performance improvement with respect to portfolios built using full feature HMMs. Lee *et al.* (2022) use the financial statement data of individual US stocks to train ANNs to predict the future performance of individual stocks and use these predictions to construct (a portfolio of) ETFs. They report that their approach outperforms all classical benchmarks.

An early example of the application of ML to index tracking is by Lowe (1994), who applies feed-forward ANNs to replicate the FTSE 100 index using a small subset of the constituents, thereby reducing transaction costs and allowing for more efficient portfolio management. Among others, Ouyang *et al.* (2019) have proposed to apply deep ANNs and autoencoders to track index performance;

[31]Index tracking is a popular investment strategy that aims to replicate the performance of a benchmark index, such as the S&P 500, with minimal deviation (tracking error).

they introduce a dynamic weight calculation method to measure the direct effects of the stocks on an index. They show that the index tracking method based on deep ANN combined with the capital asset pricing model (CAPM) has a smaller tracking error compared to all non-ML benchmarks. Kim and Kim (2020) associate a deep latent representation of asset returns, obtained through a stacked autoencoder, with the benchmark index's return to identify the assets for inclusion in the tracking portfolio. Empirical results indicate that to improve the performance of previously proposed DNN-based index tracking, the deep latent representation needs to be learned in a hierarchical manner. Bradrania and Pirayesh Neghab (2022) examine the stock selection step of the index tracking problem in passive investment management and propose an application of deep ANNs to select the best selection method based on the state of the market. Their empirical evidence shows that the approach outperforms standard cointegration techniques that ignore market regimes.

The financial crisis of 2008 sparked a renewed interest in transparent and rules-based portfolio construction strategies leading to the emergence of smart beta strategies as a trend among institutional investors. These strategies seek to deliver superior risk-adjusted returns by selecting and weighting stocks based on specific factors, such as value, momentum, and quality, rather than market capitalization alone. While smart beta strategies have demonstrated strong performance in the long run, they can also suffer from severe short-term drawdowns and fluctuations in performance across market cycles and regimes. This occurs because they often imply sharp, considerable factor exposures compared to traditional market-cap weighted strategies, making them more sensitive to changes in market sentiment and economic conditions. Therefore, they require careful monitoring and management to avoid unwanted exposures to risks. Hence, ML has increasingly been applied in the smart beta strategies space in recent years. ML can indeed sharpen and robustify smart beta strategies by analyzing large amounts of data, identifying nonlinear relationships between variables, and making more informed investment decisions based on these insights (see, e.g., Gu *et al.*, 2021). For example, ML can be used to identify stocks that have historically exhibited strong momentum or value characteristics in a regime-specific but decoupled fashion and use this information to construct a smart beta portfolio that is more likely to outperform the market.

Recently, the advantages of smart beta factor construction using ML have been shown by Feng *et al.* (2020), who have combined LASSO with classical Fama–MacBeth regressions to systematically evaluate the contribution of an additional factor to a set of preexisting factors, finding that many factors proposed in the literature failed to add much incremental value. Kelly *et al.* (2019) propose Instrumental PCA (IPCA), where factors are latent, and the time-varying loadings depend on stock characteristics and show that a small number of factors can explain the cross-section of average returns more accurately than other leading factor models. Feng *et al.* (2018) build factors that maximize the fit in the cross-section of returns using a deep feed-forward ANN, while He *et al.* (2023) find that using reduced-rank regression outperforms popular observed factor models. Conlon *et al.* (2021) have examined the use of latent factors generated from SL and USL dimensionality reduction techniques for asset allocation within the framework of factor-based covariance matrices used to construct minimum-variance portfolios. They report evidence that factor-based covariance matrices tend to significantly reduce the risk of a portfolio consisting of individual stocks and that using ML can lead to significant economic gains. The best-performing methods to generate the covariance matrix are ANN autoencoders and SPCA. However, shallow learning outperforms deeper learning, which can be attributed to the small size of the dataset and the low signal-to-noise ratio. Maguire *et al.* (2018) detailed the construction of a monthly re-weighted portfolio involving two independent smart beta strategies; the first component is a long-short beta-neutral strategy derived from running an adaptive boosting classifier (AdaBoost) on a suite of momentum indicators; the second component is a minimized volatility portfolio which exploits the observation that low-volatility stocks tend to yield higher risk adjusted returns than high-volatility stocks. They find that the combined leveraged strategy achieves a stunning Sharpe ratio of 0.96. Avramov *et al.* (2023) highlighted two advantages of ML-driven strategies over the exploitation of classical anomalies isolated through regression methods: ML-driven strategies profit both from their long and their short positions and, unlike a number of well-established anomaly portfolios, do not suffer from a steep decline in their performance over the last 20 years. Finally, USL appear to perform better than SL methods. Hsu *et al.* (2022) have recently worked on building smart portfolios of smart beta strategies. Smart beta products using common factors like value, low volatility, quality, and small-cap experienced an underwhelming performance from 2005–2022. On average, long-only factor portfolios built from a wider set of global factors identified in the finance literature generated significantly positive excess returns across countries, suggesting diversifying across many factors is more prudent than selecting a handful that have performed the best.

Using data from ETF Global, Bartram *et al.* (2021) report that a number of active exchange-traded funds (ETFs) claim to use AI or ML in their investment strategies. Although these funds do not represent a significant share of the market, their assets under management have grown rapidly over the past few years. Their active risk seems to be largely driven by factor exposures, which indicates that they tend to focus on smart beta bets. At 0.75%, their average management fees are slightly above the level typically charged by active equity ETFs. An equally weighted portfolio of all of these funds has a Sharpe ratio of 0.88 and has outperformed a broad market benchmark since inception. However, over a relatively short sample period, these funds do not exhibit a significant alpha after accounting for their exposure to a set of standard style factors.

5 ML Applications in Trading Execution

To regularly realign holdings with investment objectives, investment portfolios are rebalanced by executing orders based on portfolio optimization. Quantitative methods can help portfolio managers make informed decisions about when and how to execute trades to minimize transaction costs and reduce risks. Early studies (see, e.g., Bertsimas and Lo, 1998) had formalized order execution as a dynamic programming problem, in which the goal is to split trades optimally over a pre-specified period. Two main components are needed to characterize this problem: a market impact framework — used to assess the costs and risks of executing trades — and a model of the intraday dynamics of security prices. The optimal solution will then strike a balance between minimizing price risk (which can be achieved by rapidly executing trades) and minimizing market impact (which typically requires a passive execution style).

One notable case in which ML applied to order execution seems to be required by the very existence of ML is the construction of smart beta factor strategies. A common result is that ML-driven multi-factor models tend to load predominantly on factors that generate high turnover, such as price momentum and short-term reversals. As a consequence, it is crucial to limit transaction costs when implementing such strategies. Wolff and Echterling (2020) warn that transaction costs have to be marginal for investors to be able to capitalize on the strategies. Avramov *et al.* (2023) reach a similar conclusion after analyzing several ML approaches to building multi-factor signals and argue that, particularly in the case of deep ANN techniques, their profitability tends to be concentrated in small, illiquid stocks or securities issued by distressed firms. This makes order execution of the greatest importance.

Estimating market impact, particularly in equity markets, naturally relies on ML techniques because of the vast number of available inputs, the nonlinearity of the relationships, and the complex dynamics typically found in the data. In the SL camp, Zheng *et al.* (2012) use logistic regressions to investigate the relation between market impact and a large set of potential predictors. LASSO is used for variable selection. They find that trade sign, market order size, and liquidity based on best limit order prices tend to be selected as the most relevant features. Booth *et al.* (2015) propose using performance-weighted RFs to build data-driven nonparametric models that predict market impact as a function of the characteristics of an order. They find that this approach significantly outperforms linear regressions, ANNs, and SVMs OOS. Park *et al.* (2016) perform a similar analysis and conclude that several ML models (i.e., ANNs, Bayesian ANNs, and Gaussian process regressions) significantly outperform a standard parametric benchmark, whereas SVRs yield less unambiguous conclusions. Briere *et al.* (2020) use Bayesian networks to forecast implementation shortfall as a measure of transaction cost.[32] This approach is particularly useful in cases of missing

[32]Implementation shortfall is the difference between the market price of the security at the time the order was placed and the final execution price.

data because it can impute the most probable value given the available information. The authors incorporate net order flow imbalance as a predictor and show that the resulting model improves on the standard approaches, particularly when the order size is large, and market volatility is low. Li *et al.* (2019) build a system that exploits a deep learning architecture to improve feature representations and adopt a feed-forward ANN to predict market impact. They evaluate the performance of the system by comparing different configurations of representation learning and classification algorithms and conduct experiments on intraday tick-by-tick price data and corresponding commercial news archives of stocks to find that in order to make the system achieve good performance, both the representation learning and the classification algorithm play important roles.

Alongside SL methods such as the ones discussed above, USL, such as cluster analysis, can be used for market impact modeling. Bloomberg's liquidity assessment tool and the stock clustering framework developed by Goldman Sachs are examples of this approach. Bloomberg's liquidity assessment tool is a set of metrics used to evaluate the liquidity of a security or portfolio. It provides traders and portfolio managers with a quantitative assessment of the liquidity profile of securities, which can help them make informed decisions about trading strategies. Cluster analysis can be used to group securities that have similar characteristics from a trade execution point of view into a small number of categories using a large set of historical microstructure features.

Recently, Philip (2020) advocated the use of RL to estimate permanent price impact. The reward function could be based on the execution cost or the deviation of the actual execution from the target execution schedule. Their paper shows that vector autoregressive models — which are common tools for estimating permanent price impact — may lead to incorrect inferences in the presence of nonlinear impact dynamics. RL can be used to learn a model that predicts the impact of a trade given its characteristics, such as trade size, order type, and time of day. The RL agent can then use this model to optimize its execution strategy, taking into account the expected impact and other relevant predictors. The advantage of RL is that it can learn the nonlinear relations between trades and quotes. Another argument for using RL in impact estimation is that it can incorporate multiple objectives, such as minimizing execution cost, reducing impact, and minimizing risk. RL can optimize a trade-off between these objectives by exploring different execution strategies and balancing the trade-off between short-term execution cost and long-term performance.

Another field of potential application for ML is decision timing execution. Rather than relying on dynamic programming, a growing body of work adopts a data-driven approach to let an algorithm learn the optimal execution strategy as a function of the evolution of the inputs. RL has proven popular in this area of research. Dab'erius *et al.* (2019) examine the two cutting-edge approaches provided by two popular algorithms in RL.[33] They show that both methods are able to outperform a simple, classical time-weighted average-price (TWAP) benchmark, one of the benchmarks used by traders.[34] This result is mostly driven by environments in which TWAP is not optimal, such as when prices have a drift, are mean reverting, or both. Tashiro *et al.* (2019) adopt convolutional ANNs to extract predictive signals from order-based features. A common theme among these studies is the emphasis on feature engineering, which plays a crucial role in intensely data-driven forecasting procedures (see Rasekhschaffe and Jones, 2019). Given the low signal-to-noise ratio, it is important to incorporate domain knowledge in the process to avoid over-fitting. Baldacci and Manziuk (2020) develop a framework that optimizes partial execution of limit orders at multiple venues by capturing dependencies between market conditions, impact, hidden liquidity, and the imbalance and spread of venues. Meanwhile, Leal *et al.* (2022) use a deep ANN to generate optimal trading rules using

---

[33]These are Proximal Policy Optimization (PPO) and Deep Double Q-Network (DDQN). PPO is a policy optimization method that updates the policy iteratively by maximizing a surrogate objective function that approximates the true objective. DDQN is a variant of the Q-learning algorithm, which is used to learn the optimal action-value function in RL.

[34]In order execution, traders often use algorithms to break up large orders into smaller pieces and execute them over time. This is done to minimize market impact and avoid moving the price in an unfavorable direction. TWAP is a commonly used benchmark to evaluate the performance of these procedures. For example, if a trader wants to execute a large order over a 4-hour time period, she may use a TWAP algorithm to execute the order at an average price over that time period.

high-frequency data. Their approach learns the mapping between a trader's risk aversion and optimal trading speed, which can be projected onto the functional space spanned by the closed-form solution of the optimal control problem. This addresses the transparency issue in ANN models and potential regulatory concerns. Lastly, Mounjid and Lehalle (2019) propose a methodological improvement for RL algorithms that introduces a dynamic optimal policy for the choice of learning rate used in stochastic approximation. Their empirical study shows improved results for the optimal execution of a large number of shares.

6 What Are the Problems with ML in Portfolio Decisions?

ML has become a popular tool for generating trading signals and optimizing portfolios. Nevertheless, practitioners and researchers face several challenges when applying ML techniques to these tasks (see Israel *et al.*, 2020). First, the performance and reliability of ML algorithms are highly dependent on data quality. By ML standards, financial time series are often very short relative to cross-sections. This significantly inhibits the models' full potential to learn from the data. Second, even in cases in which the time-series dimension is large (e.g., high-frequency data), the signal-to-noise ratio is typically lower than in ML applications outside of finance. Apart from prices and key accounting quantities, financial data are often incomplete, inconsistent, or poorly labeled, making it challenging to create high-quality datasets. Third, financial markets are complex systems characterized by a multitude of interacting factors, making it difficult to identify the variables to consider. As a result, models can be over-fitted, meaning they capture the noise and random fluctuations in the data rather than the underlying trends and patterns. Moreover, most popular methods, such as ANN and RL, are often difficult to interpret and do not provide insights into how they generate results. This lack of *interpretability* makes it difficult to understand whether the model is capturing meaningful patterns or noise, leading to poor model performance and risk measurement. The latter is a concern because asset managers often rely on risk management and oversight procedures to gain investors' trust. To address this issue, practitioners and researchers must strike a balance between model complexity and interpretability.

Besides interpretability, *explainability* of ML in finance has been debated to be a distinct concept. Explainability goes beyond interpretability by requiring that a model's predictions could be explained to a human audience. In portfolio optimization, to gain trust of investors and regulatory bodies, explaining how the model arrived at its recommendations is paramount. The model must be interpretable for a portfolio manager to understand the factors that drove the decision-making process. Explainability instead may involve creating visualizations or other tools helping clients understand the rationale behind the model's recommendations, or providing reports explaining how the model arrived at its output. In practice, the distinction between the two can be blurred, and they are often used interchangeably. Yet, the key difference is that interpretability focuses on understanding a model's internal workings, while explainability focuses on communicating the model's decision-making process to a human audience.

Recently, progress has been made in so-called explainable artificial intelligence (XAI) to provide solutions for interpreting opaque ML. For instance, it is becoming common to use Shapley values — a concept from cooperative game theory — to interpret the importance of individual features in ML.[35] Another approach is to use Shapley values to identify specific stocks or sectors that are driving portfolio performance, providing investors with a more granular view of their risk exposures. In fact, a careful approach to the selection of relevant features in applications of SL may deliver important payoffs. For instance, Carta *et al.* (2022) propose three methods to discard irrelevant features in prediction tasks and assess these approaches on historical data on the component stocks of the S&P500 index. They show that trading strategies that include feature selection methods improve performances by providing predictive signals whose information content suffices and is less noisy than the one embedded in the whole feature set.

[35]The Shapley value quantifies the marginal contributions of individual players to a collective payoff. It represents the average marginal contribution of a player to every possible coalition that could be formed in the game. See, e.g., Shalit (2021).

Over-fitting occurs when a model picks up noise instead of signals. Over-fitted models have good in-sample performance but little OOS predictive power. Although ML techniques can uncover subtle patterns in past data, over-fitting presents a major challenge. The issue with over-fitting is aggravated by the relationships between factors and returns which are frequently noisy, and many potential factors exist.[36] Practical examples of over-fitting in portfolio management include the use of complex ML models to generate trading signals that result in highly concentrated portfolios, which can lead to significant losses if the model fails to perform OOS. Another example is the use of data-mining techniques to identify spurious patterns in historical data, which can result in overestimation of future returns and lead to poor investment decisions.

To mitigate the risk of over-fitting, practitioners and researchers must use techniques such as regularization, cross-validation, and OOS testing. As we have seen in Section 2, regularization methods add a penalty term to the objective function of the learning algorithm to prevent over-fitting, while *cross-validation* is used to estimate the generalized performance of the model by assessing how well a predictive model will perform on new, unseen data. It involves dividing the sample into two or more sets, one of which is used to train the model, while the other(s) is (are) used to validate its performance. By using multiple rounds of this process, in which different subsets of data are used for training and validation, it is possible to obtain a more reliable estimate of the model's ability to generalize to new data.

Two further approaches can help mitigate the perils of over-fitting: forecast combinations and feature engineering. *Forecast combinations* differ from ensembling as they refer to the process of combining the predictions of multiple models to generate a more accurate one. Individual models are therefore developed and trained on the same dataset, and their predictions are then combined using a weighted average or other techniques. Forecast combinations leverage the strengths of each individual model to produce more accurate predictions. Ensemble methods instead involve the creation

[36]In contrast, many ML applications outside finance, such as image recognition, entail high signal-to-noise ratios. Because of the low signal-to-noise ratios in forecasting financial returns, avoiding over-fitting is particularly important.

of a group or ensemble of models, each of which is trained on a different subset of the data.[37] The individual models in the ensemble are then combined to make a final prediction. The methods differ as ensemble methods focus on creating diverse models that can capture diverse aspects of the *same* data, whereas forecast combinations focus on leveraging the strengths of multiple models *each trained in the most appropriate way on possibly sub-samples of the data*, to make more accurate predictions. For example, forecasts generated from different estimation windows can detect market regimes and often exhibit low correlations. Different algorithms capture different data features, ranging from simple linear ones to highly complex nonlinear relationships. While more complex algorithms can potentially reveal complex relationships, they usually require a higher signal-to-noise ratio and/or more training data to function effectively. Combining forecasts from various training windows also reduces variance, which may increase risk-adjusted returns.

As discussed in Section 2, ensemble methods have shown promise when applied to financial data. The goal is to combine weak learners, either by equal-weighting forecasts (bagging) or by accuracy-weighting forecasts (boosting), to produce a strong learner. The latter tends to do better than any of its constituent weak learners. Both boosting and bagging can address the bias versus variance trade-off encountered by all SL methods. Bias occurs when the estimation method does not effectively capture fundamental relationships in the data (undercoating). Variance arises from small changes in the training set, meaning that the estimator does not learn relationships that generalize OOS. Finally, *dropout*, a tool related to the ensemble algorithms, also harnesses concepts of model averaging. Dropout is a regularization technique used to randomly de-activate nodes in an ANN layer during training. This prevents the network from learning redundant representations of the data and prevents over-fitting. Dropout effectively produces an ensemble of ANNs, and the final prediction is made by averaging the outputs of these networks. Like bagging, this technique helps reduce the variance of

[37]When producing forecasts, different windows of data can be used based on the time period (temporal), season (seasonal), or a particular condition (conditional) to ensure that the forecast is relevant and accurate.

a model's prediction errors; see, e.g., Kwak *et al.* (2021) for a recent application to portfolio decisions.

Feature engineering uses domain knowledge to structure a problem so that it is amenable to ML solutions.[38] Concisely, it determines which problems we ultimately ask the algorithms to solve and which algorithms we use to solve them. It is one of the most effective ways to overcome over-fitting because it allows the increase of the signal-to-noise ratio before training the algorithms. Feature engineering is where domain knowledge flows into the process. In the context of stock selection, it can provide input on questions such as the following: What are we trying to forecast exactly? Which algorithms are likely to be most effective? Which training windows are likely to be most informative? How should we standardize factors and returns, if relevant? And which factors are likely to provide valuable information? To limit the risk of over-fitting, often the best approach is to forecast discrete variables with ML algorithms. Rather than predicting returns, as we would with linear regression, ML algorithms usually predict categories — e.g., outperformers versus underperformers — which tend to be less noisy than returns. After the selection of categories, a second decision involves how to define these categories. If we are interested in the cross-section of returns, we would define categories by dividing stocks into outperformers and underperformers for each date in the training set. Most investors want to outperform net of risk, so a natural approach is to define performance categories for risk-adjusted excess returns. Using risk-adjusted returns can improve the signal-to-noise ratio and enhance forecasts. These are all examples of how careful feature engineering may help in approaching and more effectively solving a portfolio decision.

The use of AI and ML in (especially, active) portfolio management presents several challenges, including the potential for unreliable and biased models, which may result in significant financial losses. To mitigate these risks, in 2021, the European Commission has

[38]Formally, domain knowledge refers to the understanding of the specific domain or subject area that the data belong to. It involves the knowledge of the underlying relationships between variables, the context of the data, and the relevant statistical models that can be applied.

published a regulatory framework aimed at ensuring the trustworthiness of AI.[39] This framework represents the first major international effort to regulate the use of AI and consists of seven requirements:

- human agency and oversight, which emphasizes the importance of ensuring that humans have the final decision-making power in the use of AI,
- technical robustness and safety, which stresses the need for AI models to be reliable, accurate, and safe,
- privacy and data governance, referred to the need for appropriate data protection measures to be in place,
- transparency, which emphasizes the need for AI models to be explainable and interpretable,
- diversity, nondiscrimination, and fairness, which highlight the importance of ensuring that AI models do not perpetuate biases and discrimination,
- societal and environmental well-being, which emphasizes the need for AI to benefit society as a whole, and
- accountability, which emphasizes the importance of ensuring that individuals and organizations are responsible for the use of AI.

The first, second, and fourth requirements directly relate to the technical challenges discussed above. The implementation of these regulations will likely lead to other international regulatory bodies following suit, thus reshaping the future landscape of ML research and its application to portfolio management.

7 Comparative Empirical Evidence on the Performance of ML

The empirical finance literature is currently booming with surveys and comparisons of portfolio and trading decisions made using ML methods versus classical benchmarks (such as MV). In this chapter,

[39]On 21 April, 2021, the European Commission has published the proposal of the new EU Artificial Intelligence Act (henceforth AIA), or, to use its full name, the *Proposal for a regulation of the European Parliament and the Council laying down harmonized rules on Artificial Intelligence (Artificial Intelligence Act).*

we purposely limit ourselves to summarize the key findings of four papers with no goal of being exhaustive.

7.1 Long-short strategy tasks

Hao *et al.* (2023) compare gradient boosting decision trees, random forests, and deep ANN models to forecast prices and construct statistical arbitrage strategies in five international stock markets. They use data from 2005 to 2020 to construct a long-short portfolio and find that traditional ML algorithms yield significant average excess returns in all except the UK market, while deep ANNs achieve good results in all markets. Moreover, the statistical arbitrage performance of ML varies across markets, while deep ANNs achieve their best performance with reference to the Chinese market, outperforming RF and GBM trees. This establishes a advantage of ANNs over other SL techniques.

7.2 Stock selection tasks

Rasekhschaffe and Jones (2019) have applied ML to perform stock selection on an investment universe that includes small-, medium-, and large-capitalization stocks, with an average of 5,907 stocks per month, in 22 developed markets, for a 1994–2016 sample. Their factor library consists of 194 factors (i.e., company characteristics) assembled by IHS Markit. They define three training sets in three alternative ways: (1) the recent training set of all data from the prior 12 months, (2) the seasonal training set including all data from the same calendar month over the prior ten years, and (3) the hedge training set including data from the bottom half of performance over the prior ten years based on the first two training sets. Hence, every single month may appear in more than one training set. They create risk-adjusted excess returns by dividing each stock's excess return by its past 100-day volatility. They train the four algorithms on each of the regional training sets — a bagging estimator that uses AdaBoost, a gradient boosted classification and regression tree algorithm, one shallow ANN, and a bagging estimator based on an SVM.

Performance results are strong for all algorithms and training sets, but the findings for the ensemble forecasts are even stronger.

The benefits of diversifying across training windows are particularly evident. The performance of a simple OLS benchmark strategy is positive, but average returns and alphas are considerably larger under ML, on a risk-adjusted basis. Interestingly, the ML-driven portfolios load negatively on the value (HML) and small size (SMB) factors, but only the US zone equal-weighted loading on SMB turns out to be significant. This indicates that the positive results are not driven by common risk factors.

7.3 Strategic asset allocation tasks

Kynigakis and Panopoulou (2022) explore the potential benefits of ML in generating return forecasts from multivariate prediction models. They compared the OOS performance of portfolios (of stocks, bonds, and commodities, with reference to an OOS period 2000–2019) utilizing ML predictions and compare them to an equal-weighed and an MV portfolio based on the HA. The analysis is conducted for a conservative and an aggressive investor (in terms of risk aversion) and for different levels of leverage. Additionally, they conduct robustness checks to test how alternative estimates of the covariance matrix affect performances.

They find that using ML can be beneficial to OOS performance. The majority of the portfolios outperform the equal-weighted and HA benchmarks and exhibit similar OOS performance across different specifications of the covariance matrix. For the equal-weighted and HA and for most of the simple forecast combination portfolios, they report higher Sharpe ratios during the expansionary periods. The pattern is similar for most of the dimensionality reduction and nonlinear SL methods, while for shrinkage methods and ML ensembling, this pattern is reversed. Finally, when they introduce transaction costs, the performance deteriorates due to the high degree of turnover.

The measure of the contribution of each variable to reported performance is calculated as the change in the OOS R^2, as defined in Campbell and Thompson (2008), from setting the values of a predictor to zero within each iteration of the OOS period and then averaging these values to obtain a single feature's (predictor's) importance measure. In the case of stocks and under a KS framework, the most important features are industrial production, market return, the dividend price ratio, capacity utilization, and the earnings-price ratio. The important variables for shrinkage methods are similar to those of KS. In the case of dimensionality reduction methods, influential variables for PCA- and PLS-type methods include financial uncertainty, the payout ratio, stock variance, and real economic activity index, while for ICA and RICA, the dividend-price ratio and the market are the most important features. Nonlinear ML methods tend to use a broader set of predictors, the exception being ANNs with a single hidden layer that focuses on the dividend-price ratio and on market returns.

Finally, in Kynigakis and Panopoulou (2022), ML models favor higher rebalancing frequencies. Reducing the frequency with which a portfolio is rebalanced leads to considerably lowers performance of all models. Specifically, the results based on average realized returns show that the best performing portfolio in the case of quarterly rebalancing is based on a shallow ANN. When the rebalancing frequency is reduced to annual, the best performing portfolios become those based on sparse PCA and an ANN with two hidden layers for the aggressive and conservative investors, respectively. On the contrary, the results based on the Sharpe ratio show that all models fail to outperform the equally weighted allocation. So ML would be profitable only to investors who can rebalance and trade often, which are most likely professional portfolio managers.

7.4 Is reinforcement learning superior to supervised learning?

Ngo *et al.* (2023) compare the performance of 10 different portfolio construction methods, including MV-style approaches (tangency portfolio and minimum variance), statistical ML, deep SL, and RL models. They use two experimental designs — one concerning a frontier market (Vietnam) and the other based on classical US data — with different time frames and asset types to evaluate the robustness of the construction methods in different contexts. To evaluate the performance of different portfolios according to different optimization techniques, the study employs six metrics: expected return, standard deviation of return, Sharpe ratio, Sortino ratio, maximum drawdown, and 1% VaR.

Their key result is that RL models outperform all other construction methods, including deep learning. In particular, an RL model based on a proximal policy optimization (PPO) algorithm produced the highest realized Sharpe ratio and cumulative returns in both experimental designs. The results of the first experiment, conducted on Vietnamese data, show that RL outperforms other deep learning and conventional models in terms of Sharpe and Sortino ratios. The deep learning portfolio and PCA methods produced lower Sharpe and Sortino ratios. RL and deep ANNs lead to a slightly higher mean daily return than other models do; yet, these also yield a slightly higher realized volatility. Yet, RL outperforms all other models in terms of minimum max drawdown and VaR. In the second experiment, Ngo *et al.* (2023) evaluate the performance of different algorithms based on US-listed exchange-traded fund portfolios. The results show that RL and PCA outperform all other methods in terms of Sharpe and Sortino ratios. The deep learning method produces negative Sharpe and Sortino ratios. The benchmarks led to lower empirical Sharpe and Sortino ratios compared to RL and PCA. They also found that traditional MV approaches performed poorly. This is consistent with previous research, which has shown that MV optimization may not be effective in practice due to its sensitivity to the input parameters (see Michaud, 1989). Interestingly, the statistical SL methods, such as hierarchical risk parity and PCA, performed better than the MV approaches but were outperformed by deep ANNs and RL. The study highlights the potential of RL for portfolio construction, particularly in volatile and nonstationary markets where historical datasets may be less informative.

8 Conclusions and Final Thoughts

ML is *limitless* in the sense that it can be tweaked endlessly to achieve some converging performance ceiling. Some of these tweaks include the different methods to perform validation, hyperparameter selection, outlier removal, and data replacement. Features can also be transformed in myriad ways; the dimensions of features can be reduced or inflated; variables can be generated through numerous unsupervised methods; variables can also be combined, added, or removed; on top of that, it is possible to use all ML frameworks (i.e., supervised, reinforcement, and unsupervised learning) within a single problem. The only way to know whether any of these adjustments is beneficial is to test it empirically on validation data. On the one hand, this represents a terrific opportunity and a sense of invincibility — i.e., that eventually, ML prevails in achieving the objective of generating economic value from predicting the properties of asset returns and in optimizing portfolio weights — has recently pervaded both the academic literature and the practice of asset management. On the other hand, the same challenges encountered by the classical field of financial econometrics since the 1990s are turning up as crucial in the current developments of ML as applied to portfolio decisions. How and under what circumstances can ML efficiently and effectively support asset management tasks? We need many more empirical backtesting efforts similar to those described in Section 7 before these issues can eventually be settled.

Another relevant issue is the potential connection between ML methods and the behaviour of investors that ML may describe. Such a connection would enhance interpretability and explainability, increasing ML's prospects to eventually "conquer" the field of asset management. In this vein, a recent paper by Routledge (2019) offers an important first step in this direction. Routledge has used a framework typical of the analysis of financial decisions under ambiguity (see Gilboa and Schmeidler, 2010; Guidolin and Rinaldi, 2013, for a general survey) to characterize simplicity or parsimony in data models and has proposed that ML shrinkage and regularization SL methods may provide a natural approach to practical implementation. In his model, a potentially multivariate, complex data signal is known by the decision maker and may be useful in predicting some unobserved state. The investor is directly interested in the prediction of returns given the predictors and the set of possible theories is the same as the set of possible data generating processes. The true data generating process is in the set of theories our decision maker considers. The decision maker has data and ranks the possible theories, for example, the familiar maximum likelihood criterion is one way to construct a preference ordering. Gilboa and Schmeidler (2010) add axioms for the preferences that allow for consideration of both "fit" (likelihood) and "simplicity". Routledge provides empirically relevant examples based on US aggregate stock returns data and typical predictors, finding that a preference for simplicity significantly alters the optimal portfolio weights and may improve the OOS performance of otherwise rather standard strategies. My belief is that if other and even more persuasive models were to be developed to create a bridge between methods, behavioural investment assumptions, and deep economic principles, this would offer a concrete way for ML to eventually prevail as *the* approach favored among portfolio decision makers.

Acknowledgments

I would like to thank Max Goebel for his help on various parts of this chapter and Giulia Panzeri for generous assistance. My gratitude goes to Manuela Pedio who provided constructive comments and for her patience with earlier drafts. All errors remain my own.

References

Aboussalah, A.M., and Lee, C.G. (2020). Continuous control with stacked deep dynamic recurrent reinforcement learning for portfolio optimization. *Expert Systems with Applications*, 140: 112891.

Almahdi, S., and Yang, S.Y. (2017). An adaptive portfolio trading system: A risk-return portfolio optimization using recurrent reinforcement learning with expected maximum drawdown. *Expert Systems with Applications*, 87: 267–279.

Almahdi, S., and Yang, S.-Y. (2019). A constrained portfolio trading system using particle swarm algorithm and recurrent reinforcement learning. *Expert Systems with Applications*, 130: 145–156.

Ardila, D., Sanadgol, D., Cauwels, P., and Sornette, D. (2017). Identification and critical time forecasting of real estate bubbles in the USA. *Quantitative Finance*, 17(4): 613–631.

Avramov, D., Cheng, S., & Metzker, L. (2023). Machine learning vs. economic restrictions: Evidence from stock return predictability. *Management Science*, 69(5): 2587–2619.

Baldacci, B., and Manziuk, I. (2020). Adaptive trading strategies across liquidity pools. *arXiv preprint* arXiv:2008.07807.

Bartram, S.M., Branke, J., De Rossi, G., and Motahari, M. (2021). Machine learning for active portfolio management. *Journal of Financial Data Science*, 3(3): 9–30.

Bertoluzzo, F., and Corazza, M. (2012). Testing different reinforcement learning configurations for financial trading: Introduction and applications. *Procedia Economics and Finance*, 3: 68–77.

Bertsimas, D., and Lo, A.W. (1998). Optimal control of execution costs. *Journal of Financial Markets*, 1(1): 1–50.

Betancourt, C., and Chen, W.-H. (2021). Deep reinforcement learning for portfolio management of markets with a dynamic number of assets. *Expert Systems with Applications*, 164: 114002.

Bianchi, D., and Guidolin, M. (2014). Can long-run dynamic optimal strategies outperform fixed-mix portfolios? Evidence from multiple data sets. *European Journal of Operational Research*, 236(1): 160–176.

Booth, A., Gerding, E., and McGroarty, F. (2015). Performance-weighted ensembles of random forests for predicting price impact. *Quantitative Finance*, 15(11): 1823–1835.

Borghi, R., and De Rossi, G. (2020). The artificial intelligence approach to picking stocks. In *Machine Learning for Asset Management: New Developments and Financial Applications*, pp. 115–166.

Bradrania, R., and Neghab, D.P. (2022). State-dependent asset allocation using neural networks. *The European Journal of Finance*, 28(11): 1130–1156.

Branke, J., Scheckenbach, B., Stein, M., Deb, K., and Schmeck, H. (2009). Portfolio optimization with an envelope-based multi-objective evolutionary algorithm. *European Journal of Operational Research*, 199(3): 684–693.

Breiman, L. (1996). Bagging predictors. *Machine Learning*, 24: 123–140.

Breiman, L. (2001). Random forests. *Machine Learning*, 45(1): 5–32.

Breiman, L., Friedman, J., Stone, C.J., and Olshen, R.A. (1984). Classification algorithms and regression trees. *Classification and Regression Trees*, 15(2): 246.

Briere, M., Lehalle, C.A., Nefedova, T., and Raboun, A. (2020). Modeling transaction costs when trades may be crowded: A Bayesian network using partially observable orders imbalance, pp. 387–430.

Bryzgalova, S., Pelger, M., and Zhu, J. (2019). *Forest Through the Trees*. Working Paper, London Business School.

Campbell, J.Y., and Thompson, S.B. (2008). Predicting excess stock returns out of sample: Can anything beat the historical average? *Review of Financial Studies*, 21(4): 1509–1531.

Carta, S., Consoli, S., Podda, A.S., Recupero, D.R., and Stanciu, M.M. (2022). Statistical arbitrage powered by explainable artificial intelligence. *Expert Systems with Applications*, 206: 117763.

Chaouki, A., Hardiman, S., Schmidt, C., Sérié, E., and De Lataillade, J. (2020). Deep deterministic portfolio optimization. *Journal of Finance and Data Science*, 6: 16–30.

Chapados, N., and Bengio, Y. (2001). Cost functions and model combination for var based asset allocation using neural networks. *IEEE Transactions on Neural Networks*, 12(4): 890–906.

Chen, Y., and Hao, Y. (2018). Integrating principle component analysis and weighted support vector machine for stock trading signals prediction. *Neurocomputing*, 321: 381–402.

Chun, H., and Keleş, S. (2010). Sparse partial least squares regression for simultaneous dimension reduction and variable selection. *Journal of the Royal Statistical Society: Series B (Statistical Methodology)*, 72(1): 3–25.

Comon, P. (1994). Independent component analysis, a new concept? *Signal Processing*, 36(3): 287–314.

Cong, L.W., Tang, K., Wang, J., and Zhang, Y. (2020). *Alphaportfolio: Direct Construction Through Reinforcement Learning and Interpretable AI.* Working Paper.

Conlon, T., Cotter, J., and Kynigakis, I. (2021). Machine learning and factor-based portfolio optimization.

Coqueret, G., and Guida, T. (2020). Training trees on tails with applications to portfolio choice. *Annals of Operations Research*, 288(1): 181–221.

Corsi, F. (2009). A simple approximate long-memory model of realized volatility. *Journal of Financial Econometrics*, 7(2): 174–196.

Covel, M.W. (2007). *The Complete Turtle Trader: The Legend, the Lessons, the Results.* Collins, New York, NY.

Cybenko, G. (1989). Approximation by superpositions of a sigmoidal function. *Mathematics of Control, Signals and Systems*, 2(4): 303–314.

Dab'erius, K., Granat, E., and Karlsson, P. (2019). *Deep Execution-Value and Policy Based Reinforcement Learning for Trading and Beating Market Benchmarks.* Working Paper, Linkoping University.

Dai, Z., Li, T., and Yang, M. (2022). Forecasting stock return volatility: The role of shrinkage approaches in a data-rich environment. *Journal of Forecasting*, 41(5): 980–996.

de Prado, M.L. (2016). Building diversified portfolios that outperform out of sample. *Journal of Portfolio Management*, 42(4): 59.

DeMiguel, V., Garlappi, L., and Uppal, R. (2009). Optimal versus naive diversification: How inefficient is the 1/n portfolio strategy? *Review of Financial Studies*, 22(5): 1915–1953.

Donaldson, R.G., and Kamstra, M. (1997). An artificial neural network-GARCH model for international stock return volatility. *Journal of Empirical Finance*, 4(1): 17–46.

Du, J. (2022). Mean–variance portfolio optimization with deep learning based-forecasts for cointegrated stocks. *Expert Systems with Applications*, 201: 117005.

Fama, E.F., and French, K.R. (1993). Common risk factors in the returns on stocks and bonds. *Journal of Financial Economics*, 33(1): 3–56.

Fama, E.F., and French, K.R. (2015). A five-factor asset pricing model. *Journal of Financial Economics*, 116(1): 1–22.

Fan, J., and Li, R. (2001). Variable selection via nonconcave penalized likelihood and its oracle properties. *Journal of the American Statistical Association*, 96(456): 1348–1360.

Feng, G., Giglio, S., and Xiu, D. (2020). Taming the factor zoo: A test of new factors. *Journal of Finance*, 75(3): 1327–1370.

Feng, G., He, J., Polson, N.G., and Xu, J. (2018). Deep learning in characteristics-sorted factor models. *arXiv preprint* arXiv:1805.01104.

Fischer, T.G. (2018). *Reinforcement Learning in Financial Markets — a Survey.* Technical Report 12/2018, FAU Discussion Papers in Economics.

Fons, E., Dawson, P., Yau, J., Zeng, X.J., and Keane, J. (2021). A novel dynamic asset allocation system using feature saliency hidden Markov models for smart beta investing. *Expert Systems with Applications*, 163: 113720.

Freund, Y. (1995). Boosting a weak learning algorithm by majority. *Information and Computation*, 121(2): 256–285.

Freyberger, J., Neuhierl, A., and Weber, M. (2020). Dissecting characteristics nonparametrically. *Review of Financial Studies*, 33(5): 2326–2377.

Friedman, J.H. (2001). Greedy function approximation: A gradient boosting machine. *The Annals of Statistics*, 29(5): 1189–1232.

Friedman, J.H. (2012). Fast sparse regression and classification. *International Journal of Forecasting*, 28(3): 722–738.

Friedman, J., Hastie, T., and Tibshirani, R. (2008). Sparse inverse covariance estimation with the graphical lasso. *Biostatistics*, 9(3): 432–441.

García-Galicia, M., Carsteanu, A.A., and Clempner, J.B. (2019). Continuous-time reinforcement learning approach for portfolio management with time penalization. *Expert Systems with Applications*, 129: 27–36.

Gilboa, I., and Schmeidler, D. (2010). Simplicity and likelihood: An axiomatic approach. *Journal of Economic Theory*, 145(5): 1757–1775.

Gorman, S.A., and Fabozzi, F.J. (2022). The data dilemma in alternative risk premium: Why is a benchmark so elusive? *Journal of Portfolio Management*, 48(5): 219–265.

Gu, S., Kelly, B., and Xiu, D. (2020). Empirical asset pricing via machine learning. *Review of Financial Studies*, 33(5): 2223–2273.

Gu, S., Kelly, B., and Xiu, D. (2021). Autoencoder asset pricing models. *Journal of Econometrics*, 222(1): 429–450.

Guidolin, M. (2013). Preference models in portfolio construction and evaluation. In *Portfolio Theory and Management*, pp. 231–267. Oxford University Press, New York, NY.

Guidolin, M., and Pedio, M. (2018). *Essentials of Time Series for Financial Applications*. Academic Press, London.

Guidolin, M., and Pedio, M. (2022). Switching coefficients or automatic variable selection: An application in forecasting commodity returns. *Forecasting*, 4(1): 275–306.

Guidolin, M., and Rinaldi, F. (2013). Ambiguity in asset pricing and portfolio choice: A review of the literature. *Theory and Decision*, 74: 183–217.

Hao, J., He, F., Ma, F., Zhang, S., and Zhang, X. (2023). Machine learning vs deep learning in stock market investment: An international evidence. *Annals of Operations Research*. https://doi.org/10.1007/s10479-023-05286-6.

Harvey, C.R., Liu, Y., and Zhu, H. (2016). ... and the cross-section of expected returns. *Review of Financial Studies*, 29(1): 5–68.

Hawley, D.D., Johnson, J.D., and Raina, D. (1990). Artificial neural systems: A new tool for financial decision-making. *Financial Analysts Journal*, 46(6): 63–72.

He, A., Huang, D., Li, J., and Zhou, G. (2023). Shrinking factor dimension: A reduced-rank approach. *Management Science*, 69(9): 5501–5522.

Heaton, J.B., Polson, N.G., and Witte, J.H. (2017). Deep learning for finance: Deep portfolios. *Applied Stochastic Models in Business and Industry*, 33(1): 3–12.

Henrique, B.M., Sobreiro, V.A., and Kimura, H. (2018). Stock price prediction using support vector regression on daily and up to the minute prices. *Journal of Finance and Data Science*, 4(3): 183–201.

Hsu, J., Liu, X., Viswanathan, V., and Xia, Y. (2022). When smart beta meets machine learning and portfolio optimization. *The Journal of Beta Investment Strategies*, 13(4): 123–146.

Huang, W.-Y., Nakamori, Y., and Wang, S.-Y. (2005). Forecasting stock market movement direction with support vector machine. *Computers & Operations Research*, 32(10): 2513–2522.

Israel, R., Kelly, B.T., and Moskowitz, T.J. (2020). Can machines 'learn' finance? *Journal of Investment Management*, 18(2): 23–36.

Jang, J., and Seong, N. (2023). Deep reinforcement learning for stock portfolio optimization by connecting with modern portfolio theory. *Expert Systems with Applications*, 218, 119556.

Jiang, M., Liu, J., Zhang, L., and Liu, C. (2020). An improved stacking framework for stock index prediction by leveraging tree-based ensemble models and deep learning algorithms. *Physica A: Statistical Mechanics and its Applications*, 541: 122272.

Kelly, B., and Pruitt, S. (2015). The three-pass regression filter: A new approach to forecasting using many predictors. *Journal of Econometrics*, 186(2): 294–316.

Kelly, B.T., Pruitt, S., and Su, Y. (2019). Characteristics are covariances: A unified model of risk and return. *Journal of Financial Economics*, 134(3): 501–524.

Kim, K.-J. (2003). Financial time series forecasting using support vector machines. *Neurocomputing*, 55(1–2): 307–319.

Kim, S., and Kim, S. (2020). Index tracking through deep latent representation learning. *Quantitative Finance*, 20(4): 639–652.

Kingma, D.P., and Ba, J. (2014). Adam: A method for stochastic optimization. *arXiv preprint* arXiv:1412.6980.

Kolm, P.N., and Ritter, G. (2019). Dynamic replication and hedging: A reinforcement learning approach. *Journal of Financial Data Science*, 1(1): 159–171.

Krauss, C., Do, X.A., and Huck, N. (2017). Deep neural networks, gradient-boosted trees, random forests: Statistical arbitrage on the s&p 500. *European Journal of Operational Research*, 259(2): 689–702.

Kristjanpoller, W., and Minutolo, M.C. (2015). Gold price volatility: A forecasting approach using the artificial neural network–GARCH model. *Expert Systems with Applications*, 42(20): 7245–7251.

Kristjanpoller, W., and Minutolo, M.C. (2016). Forecasting volatility of oil price using an artificial neural network-GARCH model. *Expert Systems with Applications*, 65: 233–241.

Kristjanpoller, W., Fadic, A., and Minutolo, M.C. (2014). Volatility forecast using hybrid neural network models. *Expert Systems with Applications*, 41(5): 2437–2442.

Kwak, Y., Song, J., and Lee, H. (2021). Neural network with fixed noise for index-tracking portfolio optimization. *Expert Systems with Applications*, 183: 115298.

Kynigakis, I., and Panopoulou, E. (2022). Does model complexity add value to asset allocation? Evidence from machine learning forecasting models. *Journal of Applied Econometrics*, 37(3): 603–639.

Le, Q., Karpenko, A., Ngiam, J., and Ng, A. (2011). ICA with reconstruction cost for efficient overcomplete feature learning. In *Advances in Neural Information Processing Systems*, Vol. 24.

Leal, L., Laurière, M., and Lehalle, C.-A. (2022). Learning a functional control for high-frequency finance. *Quantitative Finance*, 22(11): 1973–1987.

Ledoit, O., and Wolf, M. (2004). A well-conditioned estimator for large-dimensional covariance matrices. *Journal of Multivariate Analysis*, 88(2): 365–411.

Lee, J., Park, S., Ahn, J., and Kwak, J. (2022). ETF portfolio construction via neural network trained on financial statement data. *arXiv preprint* arXiv:2207.01187.

Lee, M.-C. (2009). Using support vector machine with a hybrid feature selection method to the stock trend prediction. *Expert Systems with Applications*, 36(8): 10896–10904.

Leung, E., Lohre, H., Mischlich, D., Shea, Y., and Stroh, M. (2021). *The Promises and Pitfalls of Machine Learning for Predicting Stock Returns*. Working Paper.

Li, X., Cao, J., and Pan, Z. (2019). Market impact analysis via deep learned architectures. *Neural Computing and Applications*, 31: 5989–6000.

Lowe, D. (1994). Novel exploitation of neural network methods in financial markets. In *Proceedings of 1994 IEEE International Conference on Neural Networks (ICNN'94)*, Vol. 6, pp. 3623–3628. IEEE.

Luo, L., and Chen, X. (2013). Integrating piecewise linear representation and weighted support vector machine for stock trading signal prediction. *Applied Soft Computing*, 13(2): 806–816.

Maguire, P., Moffett, K., and Maguire, R. (2018). Combining independent smart beta strategies for portfolio optimization. *arXiv preprint* arXiv:1808.02505.

Markowitz, H. (1952). Portfolio selection. *Journal of Finance*, 7(1): 77–91.

Messmer, M., and Audrino, F. (2017). *The (Adaptive) Lasso in the Zoo-Firm Characteristic Selection in the Cross-Section of Expected Returns*. Working Paper, University of St. Gallen.

Metaxiotis, K., and Liagkouras, K. (2012). Multiobjective evolutionary algorithms for portfolio management: A comprehensive literature review. *Expert Systems with Applications*, 39(14): 11685–11698.

Michaud, R.O. (1989). The Markowitz optimization enigma: Is 'optimized'optimal? *Financial Analysts Journal*, 45(1): 31–42.

Moody, J., Wu, L., Liao, Y., and Saffell, M. (1998). Performance functions and reinforcement learning for trading systems and portfolios. *Journal of Forecasting*, 17(5-6): 441–470.

Mounjid, O., and Lehalle, C.-A. (2022). Improving reinforcement learning algorithms: Towards optimal learning rate policies. *Mathematical Finance*. https://doi.org/10.1111/mafi.12378.

Mourtas, S.D., and Katsikis, V.N. (2022). Exploiting the black-litterman framework through error-correction neural networks. *Neurocomputing*, 498: 43–58.

Ngo, V.M., Nguyen, H.H., and Van Nguyen, P. (2023). Does reinforcement learning outperform deep learning and traditional portfolio optimization models in frontier and developed financial markets? *Research in International Business and Finance*, 65: 101936.

Ouyang, H., Zhang, X., and Yan, H. (2019). Index tracking based on deep neural network. *Cognitive Systems Research*, 57: 107–114.

Park, S., Lee, J., and Son, Y. (2016). Predicting market impact costs using nonparametric machine learning models. *PLoS One*, 11(2): e0150243.

Peng, Y., Albuquerque, P.H.M., de Sá, J.M.C., Padula, A.J.A., and Montenegro, M.R. (2018). The best of two worlds: Forecasting high frequency volatility for cryptocurrencies and traditional currencies with support vector regression. *Expert Systems with Applications*, 97: 177–192.

Philip, R. (2020). Estimating permanent price impact via machine learning. *Journal of Econometrics*, 215(2): 414–449.

Phoon, K.F., and Koh, C.C.F. (2018). Robo-advisors and wealth management. *Journal of Alternative Investments*, 20(3): 79.

Ramos-Pérez, E., Alonso-González, P.J., and Núñez-Velázquez, J.J. (2019). Forecasting volatility with a stacked model based on a hybridized artificial neural network. *Expert Systems with Applications*, 129: 1–9.

Rapach, D.E., Strauss, J.K., and Zhou, G. (2013). International stock return predictability: What is the role of the united states? *Journal of Finance*, 68(4): 1633–1662.

Rapach, D., Strauss, J.K., Tu, J., and Zhou, G. (2019). *Industry Return Predictability: A Machine Learning Approach*. Working Paper, Washington University in St. Louis.

Rasekhschaffe, K.C., and Jones, R.C. (2019). Machine learning for stock selection. *Financial Analysts Journal*, 75(3): 70–88.

Rather, A.M., Agarwal, A., and Sastry, V.V.N. (2015). Recurrent neural network and a hybrid model for prediction of stock returns. *Expert Systems with Applications*, 42(6): 3234–3241.

Routledge, B.R. (2019). Machine learning and asset allocation. *Financial Management*, 48(4): 1069–1094.

Saifan, R., Sharif, K., Abu-Ghazaleh, N., and Abdel-Majeed, M. (2020). Investigating algorithmic stock market trading using ensemble machine learning methods. *Informatica*, 44(3): 311–325.

Schapire, R.E. (1990). The strength of weak learnability. *Machine Learning*, 5: 197–227.

Shalit, H. (2021). The Shapley value decomposition of optimal portfolios. *Annals of Finance*, 17(1): 1–25.

Shi, Q. (2023). The RP-PCA factors and stock return predictability: An aligned approach. *North American Journal of Economics and Finance*, 64: 101862.

Skolpadungket, P., Dahal, K., and Harnpornchai, N. (2016). Handling model risk in portfolio selection using multi-objective genetic algorithm. In *Artificial Intelligence in Financial Markets: Cutting Edge Applications for Risk Management, Portfolio Optimization and Economics*, pp. 285–310.

Snow, D. (2020). Machine learning in asset management – part 1: Portfolio construction–trading strategies. *The Journal of Financial Data Science*, 2(1): 10–23.

Soleymani, F., & Paquet, E. (2020). Financial portfolio optimization with online deep reinforcement learning and restricted stacked autoencoder — DeepBreath. *Expert Systems with Applications*, 156, 113456.

Tashiro, D., Matsushima, H., Izumi, K., and Sakaji, H. (2019). Encoding of high-frequency order information and prediction of short-term stock price by deep learning. *Quantitative Finance*, 19(9): 1499–1506.

Tibshirani, R. (1996). Regression shrinkage and selection via the lasso. *Journal of the Royal Statistical Society: Series B (Methodological)*, 58(1): 267–288.

Tsai, C.F., Lin, Y.C., Yen, D.C., and Chen, Y.M. (2011). Predicting stock returns by classifier ensembles. *Applied Soft Computing*, 11(2): 2452–2459.

Tsang, K.H., and Wong, H.Y. (2020). Deep-learning solution to portfolio selection with serially dependent returns. *SIAM Journal on Financial Mathematics*, 11(2): 593–619.

Wang, H., and Zhou, X.Y. (2020). Continuous-time mean-variance portfolio selection: A reinforcement learning framework. *Mathematical Finance*, 30(4): 1273–1308.

Wang, W., Li, W., Zhang, N., and Liu, K. (2020). Portfolio formation with preselection using deep learning from long-term financial data. *Expert Systems with Applications*, 143: 113042.

Welch, I., and Goyal, A. (2008). A comprehensive look at the empirical performance of equity premium prediction. *Review of Financial Studies*, 21(4): 1455–1508.

Wold, H. (1980). Model construction and evaluation when theoretical knowledge is scarce: Theory and application of partial least squares. In *Evaluation of econometric models* (pp. 47–74). Academic Press, London.

Wolff, D., and Echterling, F. (2020). *Stock Picking with Machine Learning.* Working Paper, Frankfurt University.

Yu, L., Wang, S., and Lai, K.K. (2008). Neural network-based mean–variance–skewness model for portfolio selection. *Computers & Operations Research*, 35(1): 34–46.

Zhang, C.H. (2010). Nearly unbiased variable selection under minimax concave penalty. *The Annals of Statistics*, 38(2): 894–942.

Zhang, G., and Qiao, G. (2021). Out-of-sample realized volatility forecasting: Does the support vector regression compete combination methods. *Applied Economics*, 53(19): 2192–2205.

Zhang, Z., Zohren, S., and Roberts, S. (2020). Deep learning for portfolio optimization. *arXiv preprint* arXiv:2005.13665.

Zheng, B., Moulines, E., and Abergel, F. (2012). Price jump prediction in limit order book. *arXiv preprint* arXiv:1204.1381.

Zimmermann, H.-G., Neuneier, R., and Grothmann, R. (2001). Active portfolio-management based on error correction neural networks. In *Advances in Neural Information Processing Systems*, Vol. 14.

Zou, H. (2006). The adaptive lasso and its oracle properties. *Journal of the American Statistical Association*, 101(476): 1418–1429.

Zou, H., and Hastie, T. (2005). Regularization and variable selection via the elastic net. *Journal of the Royal Statistical Society: Series B (Statistical Methodology)*, 67(2): 301–320.

Zou, H., Hastie, T., and Tibshirani, R. (2006). Sparse principal component analysis. *Journal of Computational and Graphical Statistics*, 15(2): 265–286.

https://doi.org/10.1142/9781800615212_0002

Chapter 2

Natural Language Processing and Stock Returns

Manuela Pedio
University of Bristol Business School, University of Bristol, Howard House, Queen's Ave, Bristol, UK
manuela.pedio@bristol.ac.uk

Abstract

Natural language processing has become popular in many fields, including accounting and finance, due to the growing availability of textual and spoken data and the increase in computing power and storage capacity. In particular, textual analysis has been used in accounting and finance to read corporate disclosures, financial news articles, and social media posts. In this chapter, we summarize the main steps for a natural language processing project in the area of accounting and finance. Then, we specifically review the literature that has explored the predictive power of textual data from different sources for stock returns.

Keywords: Natural language processing, sentiment analysis, textual analysis, stock returns.

1 Introduction

Natural language processing (henceforth, NLP) is a branch of artificial intelligence that deals with techniques through which computers become able to analyze, model, and understand human language. Driven by the increase in computing power and data storage capacity, the application of NLP-based techniques has become popular in many disciplines, including engineering, educational research, biology, medicine, psychology, sociology, and many others.[1] The field of accounting and finance is no exception. In fact, in the last decade, researchers in accounting and finance have witnessed a spectacular growth in the online availability of textual or spoken data, such as news articles, Security and Exchange Commission (SEC) filings, press conferences, earnings conference calls, and social media. As reported by El-Haj *et al.* (2019), in 2015, the Bank of England estimated that 90% of the global information has originated in the last decade, mostly in the form of unstructured data (i.e., free text). To make an example, Dyer *et al.* (2017) find that, over a period spanning from 1996 to 2013, the median length of 10-K reports filed by US registrants has increased by 113%. Lewis and Young (2019) report similar findings for the UK. The enormous quantity of unstructured data has made it difficult for humans to process the content manually. As a result, researchers and other users of financial data are increasingly relying on computational linguistics (i.e., the computational modeling of human language) to help them with the daunting task of analyzing thousands of gigabytes of free text.

NLP consists of several tasks, from information extraction and text preprocessing to feature engineering and model evaluation. It also encompasses several applications. For instance, conversational agents such as Alexa or Siri heavily rely on NLP. In fact, they need to understand the requests and responses coming from users and produce reasonable replies. Other NLP applications that populate our everyday lives are spam detection software, email classification and calendar event extraction tools, and, of course, search engines. Researchers and practitioners in accounting and finance typically use a small fraction of NLP tools. When it comes to explaining and/or predicting stock returns, the main goal of financial researchers has been to capture the sentiment from official documents (such as 10-K reports), news articles, or social media. Other applications, such as readability indexes, topic modeling, or assessing the similarity of different documents, are more common in the area of corporate finance

[1] A review of the fields that employ text mining in their studies can be found in Jung and Lee (2020).

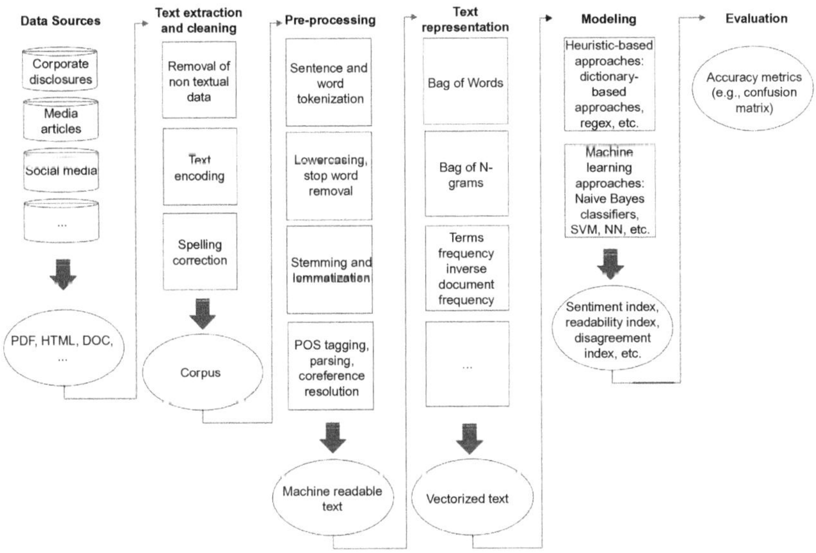

Figure 1. A sample pipeline for an NPL research project in the area of accounting and finance.

or accounting. A sample pipeline for an NLP project in the area of accounting and finance is depicted in Figure 1.

In the first step, the researcher collects data from one or more sources. Popular sources of textual data in accounting and finance can be broadly divided into three categories: public corporate disclosures, news articles, and social media posts. Public corporate disclosures include mandatory filings and disclosures (e.g., 10-Ks, 10-Qs, 8-Ks, IPO, or bond issuance prospectuses), earning announcements and other press releases, conference calls, etc. News articles include press articles from specialized outlets such as *The Wall Street Journal*, the *Dow Jones Newswires*, and the *Financial Times*. Finally, social media include Internet message boards and forums (such as the Yahoo finance forum), specialized media such as Seeking Alpha, and social networks like Twitter.[2] The text from these sources typically comes in the form of PDF documents, or it is directly scraped

[2]A detailed discussion of the main sources of unstructured data for accounting and finance applications is beyond the scope of this chapter. The interested reader can find a review in Kearney and Liu (2014).

from the web pages. In this phase, raw text is extracted from the sources and cleaned up from all the other nontextual information (e.g., markup and metadata). In addition, Unicode characters such as symbols and emojis (frequently encountered when analyzing social media text) must be converted into a binary representation. This process is called text encoding. Finally, especially when coming from social media, text data may be plagued with spelling mistakes and/or abbreviations. Therefore, checking the text for common spelling mistakes or abbreviations is part of the cleanup tasks. The library of the text documents is called a *corpus*.

The second step, pre-processing, involves converting the unstructured text into a suitable format for the analysis. First, the text is broken up into sentences at the appearance of full stops and question marks (sentence tokenization). Furthermore, sentences are split into words (word tokenization). Other common basic pre-processing steps are the removal of stop words, lowercasing, stemming, and/or lemmatization. Stop words are words that do not carry meaning on their own (such as "a", "an", "the", and "of") and therefore are typically removed from the analysis.[3] Stemming is the process of removing common suffixes or prefixes from a word in an attempt to return it to its base form. For instance, the Natural Language Toolkit (NLTK) Porter stemmer would reduce the words "liabilities" and "liability" to "liabil".[4] Lemmatization is the process of mapping all the different forms of a word to its *lemma* (its canonical form). For instance, the word "was" will remain the same when stemming is applied, but it will become "(to) be" with lemmatization. More advanced pre-processing steps include part-of-speech (POS) tagging, parsing, and coreference resolution. In Section 2, we discuss text pre-processing more thoroughly. Notably, not all the pre-processing steps are needed or suitable for all the applications, and the order in which they are

[3]There is no universal definition of stop words, and the lists may vary depending on applications. A list of stop words for accounting and finance applications is provided by Loughran and McDonald at https://sraf.nd.edu/textual-analysis/stopwords.

[4]NLTK is a powerful platform for Python programming with human language data. It offers easy-to-use interfaces to over 50 corpora and lexical resources, as well as a suite of text-processing libraries for classification, tokenization, stemming, tagging, parsing, and semantic reasoning. More information can be found at https://www.nltk.org.

applied depends on the purpose of the analysis. For instance, if we use an algorithm to tag POS, we should do that before removing stop words.

The third step is text representation (sometimes called feature engineering or extraction). The goal of this step is to capture the characteristics of the text into a numeric vector that a machine can process. The most basic approach to representing a text is the Bag of Words (BoW). This approach, which has been widely used in accounting and finance applications, represents the text under consideration as a collection of words ignoring any ordering or context. To solve the obvious limitations of this representation, it is possible to resort to more complex approaches, such as Bag of N-grams (BoN), which consider groups of N contiguous words, term frequency-inverse document frequency (TF-IDF), which gives weight to the words according to their importance, and word embedding techniques. We discuss text representation in more detail in Section 2.

The fourth step is modeling. Modeling choices obviously depend on the ultimate goal of the analysis. In text classification and sentiment analysis, there are typically two approaches that can be followed: heuristic-based methods (e.g., dictionary-based approach) and machine-learning methods (e.g., naive Bayes classifiers, support vector machines, and neural networks). We discuss this in Section 3.

The final step is to evaluate the performance (accuracy and efficiency) of the model(s) deployed in step four. While text classification can be assessed using several metrics, the confusion matrix is the workhorse for evaluating the performance of classifiers. We should briefly touch upon this at the end of Section 3. In Section 4, we summarize the main empirical applications that use textual analysis to explain or forecast stock price movements. In Section 5, we conclude by reviewing the limitations of the current methods and discussing future trends.

2 Preliminary Steps

2.1 Cleaning and pre-processing

As discussed in Section 1, any NLP task involves pre-processing and converting the text into a format that is readable by a machine. While these steps are rarely discussed in detail in accounting and finance research papers, they are crucial to any further analysis. To begin with, extracting useful content from a document or a web page relies on consistency in the structure of the text and markup language. More specifically, regular expressions (*regex*) are generally used to search for patterns within the text and extract the relevant information.[5] However, consistency is not guaranteed, especially when analyzing financial documents, which tend to have a relatively complex formatting structure. For example, as far as mandatory corporate disclosures are concerned, Loughran and McDonald (2016) report a lack of consistency in the 10-K filings before 2005. For instance, in its March 2004 filing, Potomac Electric Power uses the tag $<TABLE>$ to define all the text paragraphs. Therefore, in this case, it would be inappropriate to use this tag to eliminate tables from the document, as it will eliminate relevant text as well. As the consistency in the filings has increased with time, a failure to consider this issue is likely to introduce systematic biases rather than random noise in the analysis.

An additional example of potential biases introduced by data preprocessing concerns lowercasing. Lowercasing is typically applied to avoid words that appear at the beginning of a sentence being recorded as different from when they appear in the middle of the text. However, upper cases are also used to indicate names of people, organizations, months of the year, etc. The month of *May* is clearly different from the conditional form *may*. Even worse, the company *Best Buy* is obviously not the same as the adjective-noun combination *best buy*. These problems are clearly exacerbated when the researcher opts for a BoW text representation, where words are treated as independent units, and the word sequence is unimportant.

Notably, corpus annotation (also known as labeling or tagging) can help mitigate these issues. Corpus annotation involves labeling the text elements using either algorithmic or manual procedures. A common type of automated annotation is POS tagging,

[5]A regular expression is a sequence of characters that specify a pattern to be searched in the text. For instance, consider the following sentence: "You should buy AAPL and sell GOOGL." The regular expression "/[A-Z]{1,5}/" will match uppercase characters in the range A–Z, and it will match one to five of them. Therefore, this regex will identify both "AAPL" and "GOOGL".

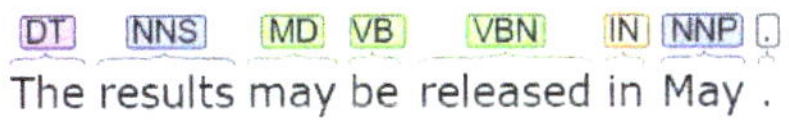

Figure 2. How the Stanford CoreNLP tool tags the part of speech for the sentence "The results may be released in May".

which consists of classifying each word according to its major word class (e.g., noun, verb, and adjective). For instance, in the example above, the month of *May* will be classified as a noun, while the conditional form *may* will be classified as a verb. Figure 2 shows how the Stanford CoreNLP tool would tag the sentence "The results may be released in May". The first *may* is assigned the tag "MD", which is used for modal verbs. The second *May* receives the tag "NNP", which is used for singular proper nouns.

Parsing, the process of decomposing a sentence into its constituents and showing their syntactic relation to each other, also helps reduce ambiguity. For instance, the two sentences "a dog bit a man" and "a man bit a dog" consist of exactly the same words. However, an inspection of the parse tree of the two sentences will reveal that in the first one, the dog is the subject and the man is the object, while the opposite applies to the second sentence. Figure 3 shows an example of a parse tree from the Stanford CoreNLP tool. While they obviously help word sense disambiguation, to date, POS tagging and parsing are scarcely used in accounting and finance studies (see discussion in El-Haj *et al.*, 2019).[6]

Finally, coreferencing and name entity recognition (NER) are also useful tagging exercises at this stage. Coreferencing aims at finding mentions of the same entity in a text. For instance, consider the following text: "The results were released in May; they were very positive". Coreferencing associates "results" with "they". NER uses machine learning algorithms to recognize named entities (person, company names, etc.) in text. This is particularly useful for researchers that want to explore press articles or social media in the search for mentions of particular firms.

[6]Notable exceptions are Chen and Li (2013) and Li *et al.* (2021), who use the Stanford CoreNLP package for parsing purposes. The package can be found at https://stanfordnlp.github.io/CoreNLP.

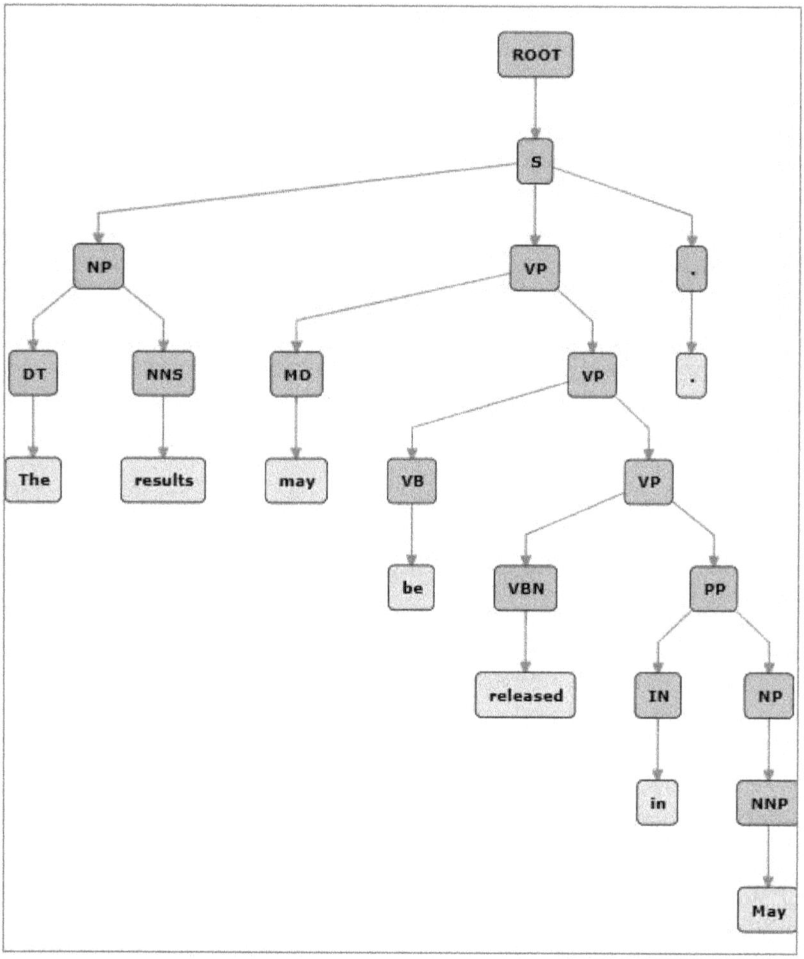

Figure 3. The parse tree obtained with the Stanford CoreNLP tool for the sentence "The results may be released in May".

2.2 Text representation

The pre-processed text obtained after the steps we just discussed should then be represented in a format that is readable for a machine. A classical text representation technique is the bag of words approach, which has been largely employed in accounting and finance applications, especially when dictionary-based approaches have been used to build sentiment indicators. BoW maps words to unique integer IDs between 1 and $|V|$ (where $|V|$ is the cardinality of the set V containing all the corpus words, i.e., the corpus vocabulary). Each document in the corpus is then converted into a vector of length $|V|$ where the ith component of the vector is the number of times the word w_{id} occurs in the document. For example, consider a corpus consisting of two documents, d_1 and d_2. The first document contains the following sentence: "The results have been released in May". The second document says: "The May results are positive". After appropriate pre-processing (e.g., lowercasing, removing stop words, and applying lemmatization), the corpus would be the following: V = {result, be, release, may, positive}. The word IDs are the following: result = 1, be = 2, release = 3, may = 4, positive = 5. The BoW representation of the first document is $d_1 = [1, 1, 1, 1, 0]$. The BoW representation of the second document is $d_2 = [1, 1, 0, 1, 1]$. The $|V|xN$ matrix that collects the BoW representation of each of the N documents in the corpus is called the document term matrix (DTM).

As discussed in Section 1, a clear limitation of this representation is that it treats words as independent units. For example, consider two documents: d_3 containing the sentence "man bites dog" and d_4 containing the sentence "dog bites man". With a WoB representation, the two documents will appear identical. A bag of n-grams approach tries to remedy this problem by breaking the text into chunks of contiguous words in an attempt to capture some context. In this case, the corpus vocabulary consists of the list of the unique n-grams across the corpus. For instance, if d_3 and d_4 were to compose the corpus, the list of bigrams would be as follows: dog bite, bite man, man bite, bite dog. The two documents will have the following bigram representation: $d_3 = [1, 1, 0, 0]$ and $d_4 = [0, 0, 1, 1]$. N-grams (especially bigrams, trigrams, and 4-grams) have been recently used in accounting and finance applications, for instance, by Sautner *et al.* (2020) and Calomiris and Mamaysky (2019).

BoW and BoN representations treat all the words as if they were equally important. A commonly used approach to address this issue is the term frequency-inverse document frequency (TF-IDF). The intuition is that if a word rarely appears in the corpus but appears many times in a document D_j, that word must be very important for D_j. This is summarized by the TF-IDF score, which is the product of two quantities: term frequency (TF) and inverse document frequency (IDF). The TF of the term i (appearing at least once in the document j) is computed as the ratio between the number of occurrences of the term i in document j and the total number of terms in document j. The IDF for the term i is given by the natural log of the ratio between the total number of documents in the corpus and the number of documents that contain the term j. The higher the score, the more important the word is for the document. TF-IDF has been widely used in papers in the accounting and finance area. For instance, in their seminal work, Loughran and McDonald (2011) use a TF-IDF weighting scheme to represent the 10-Ks corpus, and they modify it to take into account the length of the document:

$$w_{i,j} = \frac{1 + \ln(TF_{i,j})}{1 + \ln(a_{i,j})} IDF_i \tag{1}$$

where $w_{i,j}$ is the weight assigned to word i in document j and $a_{i,j}$ is the word count of document j.[7]

The vectorization approaches discussed above all share some drawbacks. First, they treat language units (either words or n-grams) as atomic units, which hampers the researcher's ability to make connections between the words. Second, they are sparse representations of a text, that is, especially when the corpus is large, several entries in the vector representation of a document are zeros. This makes the application of learning algorithms more difficult. Finally, these are high-dimensional representations of a text, and as such, they are computationally inefficient.

In the last seven to eight years, methods that use neural networks to create low-dimensional representations of texts (also known as *embeddings*) have been developed. The most notorious example is "Word2vec", a neural network-based word representation model first introduced by the seminal work of Mikolov *et al.* (2013). While a detailed discussion of word embeddings is beyond the scope of this chapter, the broad idea is that "Word2vec" uses distributional similarities to derive the meaning of a word from its context (i.e., neighboring words in the text). The interested reader can find an overview

---

[7] Jegadeesh and Wu (2013) suggest adapting the weighting scheme used for the 10-Ks corpus to take into account the market reaction that accompanies the release of the document. Calomiris and Mamaysky (2019) use a measure of entropy to weigh the 4-grams from their news textual analysis. We return to this in Section 5.

of neural networks for NLP in Goldberg (2016). Word embeddings have yet to take off in the realm of accounting and finance. A notable exception is represented by Li *et al.* (2021), who use "Word2vec" to analyze corporate culture.

3 Modeling

3.1 Dictionary-based approaches

Dictionary-based approaches were the first to be used in textual analysis in the area of accounting and finance, and to date, they still remain widely adopted. El-Haj *et al.* (2019) report that almost 80% of the papers in accounting and finance use a simple dictionary-based approach. A dictionary (sometimes called *lexicon*) is a collection of words with an attribute that defines them (for instance, "positive" or "negative"). The tone of a document is then established by counting the words that share a certain attribute. For instance, in accounting and finance applications, it is common to count positive, negative, or positive minus negative words over the total. Weighting schemes as those described in Section 2 can also be applied in the place of a raw count.

Early accounting and finance studies that employ textual analysis (e.g., Tetlock, 2007; Tetlock *et al.*, 2008; Kothari *et al.*, 2009; and Heston and Sinha, 2017, to name a few) used Harvard General Inquirer (henceforth, GI). GI is a software for textual analysis developed by sociologist Philip Stone (Stone *et al.*, 1966), which features lists of positive and negative words from the Harvard IV-4 and the Lasswell dictionaries.

Another dictionary that has been employed (by accounting researchers more than finance ones) is Diction. Diction consists of 35 distinct sub-categories in its dictionary. When constructing a list of positive words, researchers usually merge the sub-categories of praise, satisfaction, and inspiration from Diction's optimism category. Conversely, for negative words, the subgroups of blame, hardship, and denial from Diction's pessimism category are combined. By utilizing this method, there are a total of 686 words in Diction's optimism category and 920 words in its pessimism category.

However, English language linguistic dictionaries such as GI or Diction have proven to be unsuitable for accounting and finance applications. For instance, words such as "tax", "liability", "cost", and "depreciation" are classified as negative in general dictionaries, but they have a neutral meaning in the realm of accounting and finance. To give another example, the word "outstanding" typically has a positive connotation, but it has a neutral meaning when we talk about "outstanding shares". Similarly, the word "trust" in the context of a 10-K filing is more likely to denote a special legal entity rather than an act of faith. To solve this issue, researchers in accounting and finance have compiled specific word lists.

One of the first attempts to compile a dictionary that is specific to accounting and finance is due to Henry (2008), who created two lists of positive and negative words examining earnings press releases for the telecommunications and computer services industries. A screenshot of Henry (2008)'s lists can be found in Figure 4. The lists are rather limited as they only include 105 positive words and 85 negative ones. Besides, negative words that commonly appear in business

POSITIVITY word list
positive positives success successes successful succeed succeeds succeeding succeeded accomplish accomplishes accomplishing accomplished accomplishment accomplishments strong strength strengths certain certainty definite solid excellent good leading achieve achieves achieved achieving achievement achievements progress progressing deliver delivers delivered delivering leader leading pleased reward rewards rewarding rewarded opportunity opportunities enjoy enjoys enjoying enjoyed encouraged encouraging up increase increases increasing increased rise rises rising rose risen improve improves improving improved improvement improvements strengthen strengthens strengthening strengthened stronger strongest better best more most above record high higher highest greater greatest larger largest grow grows growing grew grown growth expand expands expanding expanded expansion exceed exceeds exceeded exceeding beat beats beating

NEGATIVITY word list
negative negatives fail fails failing failure weak weakness weaknesses difficult difficulty hurdle hurdles obstacle obstacles slump slumps slumping slumped uncertain uncertainty unsettled unfavorable downturn depressed disappoint disappoints disappointing disappointed disappointment risk risks risky threat threats penalty penalties down decrease decreases decreasing decreased decline declines declining declined fall falls falling fell fallen drop drops dropping dropped deteriorate deteriorates deteriorating deteriorated worsen worsens worsening weaken weakens weakening weakened worse worst low lower lowest less least smaller smallest shrink shrinks shrinking shrunk below under challenge challenges challenging challenged

Figure 4. The two word lists for positive and negative terms developed by Henry (2008).

language, such as "losses", "adverse", and "impairment", are missing from the list.

A more systematic attempt to develop a financial lexicon has been carried out by Loughran and McDonald (2011), who analyzed the 10-K filings from 1994 to 2008 and created six distinct word lists: negative, positive, uncertain, litigious, strong modal, and weak modal.[8] Their word lists are rather comprehensive, as they contain 354 positive and 2,329 negative words, and they have been built by taking into account the most likely interpretation of a word in an accounting and finance application. Considering a random sample of 1,000 news from the Thomson Reuters News Archive, Guo *et al.* (2016) show that 61.1% of negative news articles are correctly classified based on Harvard GI, but the accuracy improves to 74.1% when the list from Loughran and McDonald (2011) is used. The lists from Loughran and McDonald (2011) are currently considered standard for applications in accounting and finance and have become predominant in more recent studies that are based on lexicon (see, e.g., Feldman *et al.*, 2010; Garcia, 2013; Calomiris and Mamaysky, 2019; and Chen *et al.*, 2014, to name a few).

While word lists are simple and transparent, they are also highly subjective. In addition, the presence of homographs (words with different meanings but the same spelling) makes the use of word lists challenging. While having a dictionary that focuses on the financial jargon helps disambiguation, it is not always sufficient. To make an example, the word "call" might refer to a management conference call or to call options (a derivative financial instrument). Third, negative sentiment is often achieved by the negation of positive words. For instance, the sentence "the company did not achieve the annual target of sales" might be erroneously classified as positive, as the negative connotation is obtained by negating "achieve". A potential fix to this issue is to account for the negation surrounding positive words (see, e.g., Das and Chen, 2007). However, negation can not always be identified by looking for words like "no" and "not" preceding the target word. An example is provided by Loughran and McDonald (2016). In the press release charging BHP Billiton with

[8]Loughran and McDonald (2011)'s lists can be found at https://sraf.nd.edu/loughranmcdonald-master-dictionary.

violating the Foreign Corrupt Practices Act (FCPA), Antonia Chion, Associate Director of the SEC's Division of Enforcement, said the following: "A 'check the box' compliance approach of form over substance is not enough to comply with the FCPA". The word "not" only appears seven words after "compliance", to which it logically refers.[9]

Finally, dictionaries are context specific. While the list of Loughran and McDonald (2011) has proven suitable for the analysis of corporate disclosures, it would be inadequate, for instance, to analyze the language of social media like Twitter or Reddit. In fact, as noted by Chen *et al.* (2019), who build a lexicon to analyze the discussion of cryptocurrencies on Twitter, social media posts often contain "emojis", voluntary misspellings (such as the word "hodl" to imply "Hold On for Dear Life"), and off-color language (such as "buttcoin"). Considering all the limitations of dictionary-based approaches, in the following subsection, we explore more complex computational approaches to text classification.

3.2 Machine learning approaches

Despite machine learning techniques have been widely used in textual analysis in general, they still do not constitute the primary choice for accounting and finance applications. El-Haj *et al.* (2019) report that less than 20% of textual analysis papers in top-tier accounting and finance journals employ one or more machine learning techniques. The majority of textual analysis studies featuring machine learning techniques have employed supervised machine learning for sentence- or document-level classification.[10] In particular, we focus on naive Bayes and Support Vector Machine (SVM) classification methods as they are prevalent in the accounting and finance literature.

Naive Bayes classification has played the lion's share in accounting and finance applications, thanks to the fact that it is relatively straightforward to implement and yet displays a good classification

[9]The press release can be found at https://www.sec.gov/news/press-release/2015-93. See discussion in Loughran and McDonald (2016).

[10]For additional details on the distinction between supervised and unsupervised learning, you can see Guidolin (2023), in this volume.

accuracy.[11] Antweiler and Frank (2004) have pioneered its application in the field in their analysis of Yahoo! Finance and Raging Bull message boards (see discussion in Section 4). In naive Bayes classification, we use a training sample to determine the prior probability that a certain document d_j will be classified in a certain category.

Suppose that we want to classify D documents (for instance, message board posts as in the case of Antweiler and Frank, 2004) into three categories: bullish (c_1), bearish (c_2), and neutral (c_3) messages. A subset with cardinality N of the D documents has to be manually classified into the three categories. Then, for each of the T terms in the corpus, we can compute the probability that it will appear in a document belonging to each of the categories. This is given by

$$p(t_i|c_k) = \frac{n(t_i|c_k) + 1}{n(c_k) + T} \tag{2}$$

where t_i denotes a specific word in the corpus, c_k for $k = 1, 2, 3$ represents a given category, $n(t_i|c_k)$ is the number of times word t_i appears in category c_k, and $n(c_k)$ is the total number of words in the training data in class c_k.[12] The probability that a given document belongs to a certain class is given by

$$p(d_j|c_k) = \frac{n(d_j)!}{n(t_1|d_j)n(t_2|d_j)\cdots n(t_T|d_j)} p(t_1|c_k)p(t_2|c_k)\cdots p(t_N|c_k) \tag{3}$$

where $n(d_j)$ is the number of words in the document and $n(t_i|d_j)$ is the number of occurrences of word t_i in document j. $p(d_j|c_k)$ is the prior probability that document j will be in category c_k. Then, the rest of the documents can be classified by computing the

[11]Naive Bayes classification method relies on the assumption that occurrences of words are independent of each other. Despite this assumption being highly unrealistic, naive Bayes performs rather well in practice also when the assumption is violated. See discussion in Guo *et al.* (2016) and Kearney and Liu (2014).

[12]The terms 1 at the numerator and T at the denominator are added to ensure that a word has a nonzero probability when it does not appear in a class. If there are no words in class c, then each term t has probability 1/T.

posterior probability

$$p(c_k|d_j) = \frac{p(d_j|c_k)p(c_k)}{\sum_{k=1}^{3} p(d_j|c_k)p(c_k)} \tag{4}$$

where $p(c_k)$ is the unconditional probability of a document being classified in category c_k (equal to the fraction of the documents in category c_k in the training sample). Document d_j is assigned to the class with the highest posterior probability.

Another classification technique that has been employed for sentiment analysis in accounting and finance applications (see, e.g., Jegadeesh and Wu, 2013 or Manela and Moreira, 2017) is SVMs. The objective of SVMs is to map a set of entities (in our case, texts) into K categories based on N features $X = \{x_1, x_2, ..., x_n\}$. Consider for convenience a very simple example where we want to classify a message as positive or negative based on the number of times the words buy and sell are mentioned. In this case, there are only two categories (positive and negative) and two features (the number of times the word buy is mentioned and the number of times the word sell is mentioned). Figure 5 illustrates the nature of this problem on a Cartesian plane.

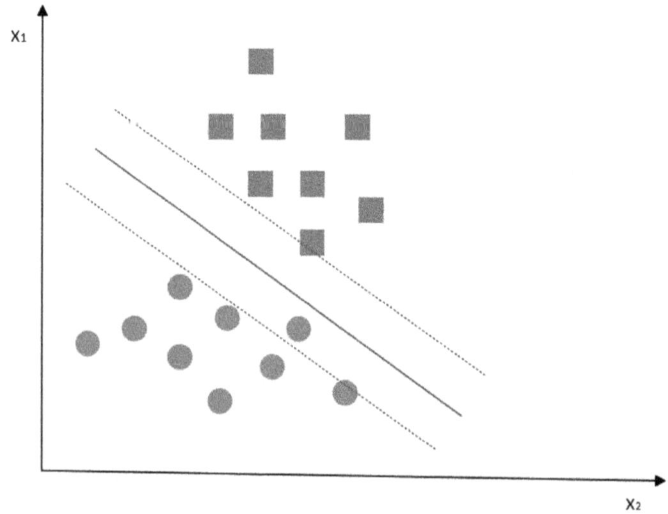

Figure 5. How SVM classification works, assuming two categories and two features.

More generally, the objective is to divide the X-space (the Cartesian plane in our illustration) using hyperplanes (a line, in the simple example) such that the maximum separation between the classes is achieved. Suppose that all the points in the category c_1 lie above the hyperplane $\boldsymbol{wx} = b_1$ and all the points in the category c_2 lie below the hyperplane $\boldsymbol{wx} = b_2$. The distance between the two hyperplanes is given by

$$\frac{|b_1 - b_2|}{||\boldsymbol{w}||} \tag{5}$$

The maximum distance between the two hyperplanes is obtained by solving

$$\min_{b_1, b_2, \boldsymbol{w}} \frac{1}{2}||\boldsymbol{w}||^2 \tag{6}$$

subject to the constraints $\boldsymbol{wx} \geq b_1$ and $\boldsymbol{wx} \leq b_2$.

Often, there will be no perfect hyperplane separating the categories. To take this into account, the quadratic optimization problem is generally modified such that we allow for points on the wrong side of the separating hyperplanes, and we use cost functions to account for this slippage. The modified problem is given by

$$\min_{b_1, b_2, \boldsymbol{w}} \frac{1}{2}||\boldsymbol{w}||^2 + C_1 \sum_{i=1}^{n} \eta_i + C_2 \sum_{i=1}^{n} \eta_i \tag{7}$$

where C_1 and C_2 are the cost associated with slippage in groups 1 and 2, respectively, and η_i are positive for observations that are not perfectly separated.[13] The interested reader can find a discussion of the advantages of SVM classification and a comparison of its accuracy against naive Bayes in Guo *et al.* (2016).

Classification accuracy is typically assessed using the confusion matrix. Given K categories, the confusion matrix is a KxK matrix where the columns refer to the category assigned by the classifier algorithm, and the rows concern the true category to which the text belongs. Each cell (k, f) of the matrix contains the number of documents that belong to category k and were classified as f. The sum of

[13]While it does not necessarily have to be the case, it is often assumed that $C_1 = C_2$.

the diagonal elements is the number of times the algorithm returned the correct classification. In the absence of any classification ability, the rows and columns of the matrix need to be independent of each other. Therefore, the following test statistic can be used to assess whether an algorithm has any classification ability:

$$\sum_{k=1}^{K}\sum_{f=1}^{K}\frac{[O(k,f)-E(k,f)]^2}{E(k,f)} \tag{8}$$

which is distributed as χ^2 with $(K-1)^2$ degrees of freedom. $O(k,f)$ are the actual number of documents in class k classified as class f, while $E(k,f)$ are the expected numbers assuming no classification ability:

$$E(k,f)=\frac{M(k)M(f)}{\sum_{k=1}^{K}M(k)} \tag{9}$$

where $M(k)$ is the total across row k of the confusion matrix and $M(f)$ is the total across column f. The accuracy of the classification algorithm for each class is given by

$$A=\frac{O(k,k)}{\sum_{k=1}^{K}M(k)} \tag{10}$$

We expect accuracy to be better than $1/K$, which is the accuracy level achieved on average from random guessing. The literature has generally reported a better classification accuracy for machine learning algorithms than for dictionary-based approaches (see, for instance, Li, 2010a).

3.3 Other applications

Besides sentiment analysis, there are a few other NLP applications that have been used in accounting and finance, despite they do not represent the bulk of the literature, such as readability, document similarity, and topic modeling. We now briefly touch upon them.

Readability. The study of readability, intended as the ability of the receiver to correctly reconstruct the message, has been scrutinized, especially with respect to accounting narratives. One of the first studies in the area is Li (2008), which uses the Fog Index to measure the readability of 10-K filings. The Fog Index is given by 0.4 (average number of words per sentence + percentage of complex words); complex words are words with more than two syllables. Li (2008) reports that firms with lower earnings tend to have less readable 10-Ks. However, the Fog Index has been developed in the context of assessing the readability of school textbooks; therefore, it is not necessarily suitable to assess the readability of business documents. For instance, as noted by Loughran and McDonald (2014), in the financial realm, terms such as financial, company, management, and operation will all account as "complex", while they will for sure be easy to understand for the investors. As an alternative, they propose to use the natural log of gross 10-K file size as a proxy for readability. They show that this measure is related to subsequent stock return volatility, analyst dispersion, and absolute earning surprises.

Recently, other alternatives to the Fog Index have been proposed. For instance, Bonsall IV *et al.* (2017) introduced the Bog Index, generated from a proprietary software, StyleWriter, which scores words for familiarity. This measure tries to assess the overall writing quality of a document by accounting for the number of complex words, the length of the sentences, the use of passive voice or weak verbs, and the use of jargon. However, Loughran and McDonald (2020) argue that the Box Index represents a measure of writing style, which is not necessarily the same as readability.

Document similarity. Another useful application of NLP to the area of accounting and finance is the measurement of documents' similarity. A standard measure of documents' similarity is cosine similarity. Consider two documents, d_1 and d_2, that have been represented using two vectors of words, x and y. Cosine similarity is given by

$$CS(d_1, d_2) = \frac{\sum_i x_i y_i}{\sqrt{\sum_i x_i^2}\sqrt{\sum_i y_i^2}} \tag{11}$$

Geometrically, the measure is the cosine of the angle between the two vectors. The numerator measures similarity, while the denominator scales by the vectors' Euclidean lengths to make the measure invariant to the length of the document. The measure can only be between 0 and 1.

Another measure of documents' similarity is Jaccard similarity. Jaccard similarity is computed as the number of words that appear in both documents divided by the total number of words in the two documents. Formally,

$$JS(d_1, d_2) = \frac{|D_A \cap D_B|}{|D_A \cup D_B|} \tag{12}$$

where D_A is the set of unique words in document A and D_B is the set of unique words in document B.

In the literature, similarity measures have been used for different purposes. For instance, by Tetlock (2011) identify press articles that do not really contain new information by looking at the distance in content between new and old press articles. Cohen *et al.* (2020) use measures of similarity to identify changes in the tone of corporate disclosures (see Section 4 for a discussion).

Semantic analysis. Semantic analysis is used to extract conceptual content and document relationships and it is typically used for topic modeling. A popular approach to semantic analysis is Latent Dirichlet Allocation (LDA). Broadly speaking, the objective of an LDA model is to estimate the word distribution for each topic and the topic distribution for each document. Given a collection of D documents and a fixed set of latent topics, each document is characterized by a discrete probability distribution over topics (θ_d), and each topic t is characterized by a discrete probability distribution over words (ϕ_t). A discussion of LDA can be found in Das (2014) or Gentzkow *et al.* (2019).

4 Textual Analysis and Stock Returns

We will now focus more specifically on the papers in the area of asset pricing that have used textual analysis to explain and predict stock returns. We divide the review based on the three primary sources of textual data used by the following articles: (i) mandatory corporate disclosure, (ii) news, and (iii) message boards and social media. This does not intend to be a comprehensive review of the literature. Instead, the objective is to give an overview of the main empirical application of NLP methods in the context of forecasting stock price movements. A comprehensive review of the literature on textual analysis in accounting and finance can be found in Das (2014), Guo *et al.* (2016), Loughran and McDonald (2016), Kearney and Liu (2014), Loughran and McDonald (2020), and Gentzkow *et al.* (2019).

4.1 Corporate disclosures

As already discussed in Section 4, textual analysis of corporate disclosures has been popularized by the seminal work of Loughran and McDonald (2011), who have developed specific word lists to classify the tone of 10-K and 10-Q filings. Their results support the idea that textual analysis can contribute to our ability to understand the impact of information on stock returns.[14]

More recently, Jiang *et al.* (2019) developed a composite manager sentiment index calculated as the average between the aggregated textual tone in conference calls and financial statements. For this purpose, they use the Loughran and McDonald (2011)'s word lists. They find that a positive change in the manager sentiment index predicts large and statistically significant negative returns over the next month. This result persists for up to 36 months. Jegadeesh and Wu (2013) suggest an alternative measure of the tone from 10-K filings to account for the market reaction to positive and negative words. More specifically, they develop a weighting scheme that assigns more weight to positive (negative) terms that are followed by a larger positive (negative) market reaction after the 10-K is released. Namely, they propose to assign the following score to document i:

$$\text{score}_i = \sum_{j=1}^{J} w_j F_{i,j} \frac{1}{a_i} \tag{13}$$

where $F_{i,j}$ is the number of occurrences of word j in document i, a_i is the length of the document, and w_j is obtained such that

$$w_j = \frac{\hat{B}_j - \bar{B}}{sd(\hat{B}_j)} \tag{14}$$

[14] Earlier, Li (2010b) had shown that tone measured by general-purpose dictionaries could not predict stock returns. Conversely, he showed that when documents are classified using naive Bayes algorithms, their tone forecast future earnings and stock returns.

and $\hat{B}_j$ is the slope coefficient from the regression of the post-filing returns on $F_{i,j}\frac{1}{a_i}$. The authors show that this scheme is superior to a simple TF-IDF and delivers an accurate system for assessing the tone of a regulatory filing.

Other papers have analyzed the effect of tone changes in corporate disclosures on stock returns. Feldman *et al.* (2010) examine whether the tone change expressed in MD&A disclosures is associated with contemporaneous and future abnormal returns. They use the word lists from Loughran and McDonald (2011) to count positive and negative words. They build long-short portfolios based on changes in positive (negative) tone and find that these portfolios earn excess returns in the expected direction.

More recently, also Cohen *et al.* (2020) have analyzed whether changes in the language of 10-K and 10-Q filings predict future stock returns. However, instead of using word lists, they measure similarity with previous filings using cosine similarity, Jaccard similarity, minimum edit distance, and simple similarity. For a 1995–2014 sample, they build quintile portfolios based on measures of similarity between current and previous filings. They find that a portfolio that goes long on "low changers" and short on "big changers" earns abnormal returns.[15]

4.2 News articles

Textual analysis of news articles has been one of the first applications of NLP in finance and is probably the most prolific. A seminal article is certainly Tetlock (2007). The author uses GI to analyze the tone of *The Wall Street Journal*'s "Abreast of the Market" column. He builds a pessimism factor using the principal components from 77 different tone categories and finds that changes in this factor

[15]Cosine and Jaccard similarity measures have been discussed in Section 3. The minimum edit distance is computed by counting the smallest number of operations required to transform one document into the other. The simple similarity is obtained using the "track changes" function in Microsoft Word to compare two documents. The authors count the number of words in changes, additions, and deletions emerging from the documents' track changes comparison and normalize the total count by the average number of words in the two documents.

forecast statistically and economically significant changes in the daily stock returns.

Tetlock *et al.* (2008) extend the analysis in Tetlock (2007) to study the impact on individual stock returns of negative words in all *The Wall Street Journal* and *Dow Jones News Service* (DJNS) stories about S&P 500 firms from 1980 to 2004. Similar to Tetlock (2007), they classify positive and negative words using the Harvard-IV-4 psychosocial dictionary. They fund that negative words in firm-specific news stories robustly predict slightly lower returns on the following trading day. Tetlock (2011) tests whether stock market investors distinguish between old and new information about the firms. To measure news staleness, they use the Jaccard textual similarity measure. They find evidence that investors overreact to stale information about publicly traded firms. However, news-event returns are smaller and partially reverse when news stories overlap with past information.[16]

Garcia (2013) examined the impact of sentiment on asset prices from 1905 to 2005. To gauge sentiment, he studied two columns of financial news from *The New York Times* and calculated the fraction of positive and negative words according to Loughran and McDonald (2011) word lists. He shows that, after factoring in other established time-series patterns, the capability of news sentiment to predict stock returns is primarily concentrated during economic recessions. More recently, Manela and Moreira (2017) constructed a text-based measure of news implied volatility and showed that it explains a large part of the time variation in stock risk premia. Focusing on the front page of *The Wall Street Journal* for the sample period 1889–2009, they represent the text in the form of n-grams and use their frequency to predict option implied volatility with an SVM approach.

[16]Heston and Sinha (2017) analyze a sample of over 900,000 Thomson Reuters news articles using the Harvard dictionary and find that a positive (negative) tone is associated with future positive (negative) returns. More recently, Huang *et al.* (2020) investigated corporate news from Factiva and built a tone indicator based on the difference between negative and positive words (as per Loughran and McDonald, 2011 word lists). However, their focus is not on forecasting stock returns but on predicting the trading activity of institutional investors.

Calomiris and Mamaysky (2019) investigated whether the content of news articles from the Thomson Reuters dataset predicts risk and return in stock markets in 51 developed and emerging economies. First, they use the Louvain community detection algorithm to find nonoverlapping clusters representing different topics. Then, combining topic detection and sentiment analysis based on Loughran and McDonald (2011) word lists, they compute topic-specific sentiment as

$$s_{\tau,j} = f_{\tau,j} * s_j \tag{15}$$

where $f_{\tau,j}$ is the frequency of topic τ in a document j and s_j is the sentiment computed as the difference between the positive and negative words divided by the length of the article. They also compute the measure

$$H_j = \sum_j p_{j,i} \ln m_i \tag{16}$$

where $p_{j,i}$ is the fraction of all 4-grams appearing in article j represented by the ith 4-gram, and m_i is the conditional probability from the training corpus. This measure, which the authors call *entropy*, captures whether an article is unusual, i.e., it contains words that are not frequently used (a similar concept to that expressed by Eq. (1)). They find that sentiment, frequency, and entropy are useful predictors for returns, volatility, and drawdown risk. Their predictive content change over time and is also context specific.

Ke *et al.* (2019) recently revisited the question of the extent to which business news explains and predicts observed asset price variation using a novel machine learning approach. More specifically, they analyze *Dow Jones Newswires* over a 38-year sample and find that a simple trading strategy that buys stocks with positive recent news sentiment and sells stocks with negative sentiment earns significant risk-adjusted out-of-sample returns. Importantly, they show that their portfolio outperforms a similar one that uses the sentiment metrics computed by Ravenpack. This confirms that their approach is more effective at extracting sentiment from the news than alternatives currently used in the industry.

Their approach, which they call Sentiment Extraction via Screening and Topic Modeling (in short, SESTM) consists of the following steps. First, starting from the BoW representation of the documents, they use a variable selection approach to select the terms that are more likely to be informative for stock returns. They call this subset of words "sentiment-charged words". Second, they use supervised topic modeling to assign these words to two topics: positive sentiment topic and negative sentiment topic. The positive and negative word counts are denoted with O_+ and O_-, respectively. Importantly, realized returns supervise the estimation and help identify which words are assigned to the positive versus negative topic. Third, they estimate p_i, the sentiment index as a number between 0 and 1, where 0 denotes extremely negative and 1 denotes extremely positive. In other words, p_i describes how heavily the article tilts in favor of the positive words, and it is estimated via (penalized) maximum likelihood, given that the document count comes from a multinomial distribution:

$$d_{i,[S]} \approx \text{Multinomial}(s_i, p_i O_+ + (1 - p_i) O_-) \tag{17}$$

where $d_{i,[S]}$ is the article's vector of sentiment-charged words and s_i is the count of sentiment-charged words, which determines the scale of the multi-nomial distribution.

4.3 Social media and message boards

While textual analysis of social media is becoming increasingly popular in recent years, an early attempt to explore the predictive content of informal messages on message boards is Antweiler and Frank (2004). This is the first paper in finance to apply supervised learning techniques to textual analysis. More specifically, they use naive Bayes and support vector machine algorithms to classify messages from Yahoo! Finance and Raging Bull message boards as bullish, bearish, or neutral. The sample comprises 45 stocks from the Dow Jones Industrial Average and the Dow Jones Internet Commerce Index. For each stock, they obtain a bullishness index and an agreement index. They find that bullishness explains returns only in contemporaneous regression but not in predictive ones; on the contrary, an increase in the bullishness index predicts higher future volatility. Furthermore, they show that disagreement is associated with more trading activity.

Similarly, Das and Chen (2007) also classify message board postings as positive, negative, and neutral. For this purpose, they use five algorithms: naive Bayes, vector distance classifiers, adjective–adverb phrase classifiers, and Bayesian classifiers. A majority voting system is then used to assign a final classification, meaning that at least three of the five classifiers must agree on the message type. If consensus cannot be reached, the message is not classified.[17] They analyze 24 tech-sector stocks in the Morgan Stanley High-Tech Index and find results that mostly confirm the findings in Antweiler and Frank (2004).

More recently, Chen *et al.* (2014) examined the role of peer-based advice, analyzing user-generated opinions from Seeking Alpha. They use the word list from Loughran and McDonald (2011) to build a negative sentiment index based on the fraction of negative words in the article. They find that an increase of negative words in Seeking Alpha articles associated with a stock predicts significant negative abnormal returns at one-, three-, six-, 12-, and 36-month-ahead horizons for that stock.

Twitter has recently entered the set of social media being analyzed by the financial literature. For instance, Azar and Lo (2016) use Twitter information concerning the scheduled Federal Open Market Committee (FOMC) meetings and show that the content of tweets can be used to predict future stock returns, after controlling for standard asset pricing factors. More specifically, they use the pattern algorithm for sentiment analysis (which relies on the SentiWordnet database) to assign a polarity score between -1 and $+1$ to a given tweet. They show that the Twitter polarity index can be used to forecast stock returns on days of FOMC meetings, and this predictability can be exploited to build profitable portfolio strategies.[18]

---

[17]While most of the five algorithms are standard, the adjective–adverb phrase classifier deserves some words. This classifier algorithm gives more weight to adjectives and adverbs. The algorithm identifies adjective–noun pairs or adverb–verb pairs and forms triplets consisting of the adjective or adverb and two adjacent words. These triplets are analyzed using a dictionary to determine whether they connote positive or negative sentiment.

[18]SentiWordNet is an annotated dictionary where each word is associated with multiple meanings, and each meaning is mapped to a triplet of numbers measuring the positivity, negativity, and objectivity of the word. The pattern algorithm splits the text into n-grams and uses SentiWordNet to assign a polarity score to each of them. The total polarity is given by the average of the polarity of the n-grams of the tweet.

5 Conclusions

In the last decade, the expansion in the volume of unstructured data available to financial market participants (and researchers), together with advances in computing power and the increase in storage capacity, has led to a boost in the number of academic studies and financial market applications that exploit financial text resources. In this chapter, we described the main steps that an NLP project in the area of accounting and finance is likely to involve. We also reviewed the most notable applications, with special attention to the literature on the predictability of stock returns.

NLP is evolving quickly, and increasingly sophisticated methods to process and analyze written texts are becoming available. However, as noted by El-Haj *et al.* (2019), accounting and finance research is behind the curve in terms of computational linguistics methods, especially when it comes to sense disambiguation. In their analysis of papers published in leading journals over the period 2010–2018 that employ textual classification for the analysis of accounting information, Lewis and Young (2019) find that only 12 papers employ more advanced techniques, such as naive Bayes, SVMs, or semantic analysis. While some recent papers have introduced more sophisticated methods, such as word embeddings (see, e.g., Li *et al.*, 2021), this remains an exception rather than the norm. In addition, pre-trained word embeddings, such as Word2vec by Google (used by Li *et al.*, 2021), depend on the vocabulary they have been trained upon. If the overlap between the corpus vocabulary and the embedding vocabulary is less than 80%, the model is likely to perform poorly (see, e.g., Vajjala *et al.*, 2020). Moreover, deep learning, in the form of convolutional neural networks and recurrent neural networks (especially long short-term memory networks), is becoming increasingly popular in NLP applications, but their use is nearly absent in financial textual analysis. Therefore, there is still ample space for the development of textual analysis within the field of accounting and finance. Overall, as noted by Lewis and Young (2019), NLP-based applications in accounting and finance would greatly benefit from interdisciplinary (for instance, with computer science and engineering) and intersectoral (with professional in the industry) collaborations.

References

Antweiler, W., and Frank, M.Z. (2004). Is all that talk just noise? The information content of internet stock message boards. *Journal of Finance*, 59(3): 1259–1294.

Azar, P.D., and Lo, A.W. (2016). The wisdom of twitter crowds: Predicting stock market reactions to FOMC meetings via twitter feeds. *Journal of Portfolio Management*, 42(5): 123.

Bonsall IV, S.B., Leone, A.J., Miller, B.P., and Rennekamp, K. (2017). A plain English measure of financial reporting readability. *Journal of Accounting and Economics*, 63(2–3): 329–357.

Calomiris, C.W., and Mamaysky, H. (2019). How news and its context drive risk and returns around the world. *Journal of Financial Economics*, 133(2): 299–336.

Chen, C.Y.-H., Després, R., Guo, L., and Renault, T. (2019). *What Makes Cryptocurrencies Special? Investor Sentiment and Return Predictability during the Bubble.* Technical Report, IRTG 1792 Discussion Paper.

Chen, H., De, P., Hu, Y., and Hwang, B.-H. (2014). Wisdom of crowds: The value of stock opinions transmitted through social media. *Review of Financial Studies*, 27(5): 1367–1403.

Chen, J.V., and Li, F. (2013). *Estimating the Amount of Estimation in Accruals.* Technical Report.

Cohen, L., Malloy, C., and Nguyen, Q. (2020). Lazy prices. *Journal of Finance*, 75(3): 1371–1415.

Das, S.R. (2014). Text and context: Language analytics in finance. *Foundations and Trends® in Finance*, 8(3): 145–261.

Das, S.R., and Chen, M.Y. (2007). Yahoo! for amazon: Sentiment extraction from small talk on the web. *Management Science*, 53(9): 1375–1388.

Dyer, T., Lang, M., and Stice-Lawrence, L. (2017). The evolution of 10-k textual disclosure: Evidence from latent Dirichlet allocation. *Journal of Accounting and Economics*, 64(2–3): 221–245.

El-Haj, M., Rayson, P., Walker, M., Young, S., and Simaki, V. (2019). In search of meaning: Lessons, resources and next steps for computational analysis of financial discourse. *Journal of Business Finance & Accounting*, 46(3–4): 265–306.

Feldman, R., Govindaraj, S., Livnat, J., and Segal, B. (2010). Management's tone change, post earnings announcement drift and accruals. *Review of Accounting Studies*, 15: 915–953.

Garcia, D. (2013). Sentiment during recessions. *Journal of Finance*, 68(3): 1267–1300.

Gentzkow, M., Kelly, B., and Taddy, M. (2019). Text as data. *Journal of Economic Literature*, 57(3): 535–574.

Goldberg, Y. (2016). A primer on neural network models for natural language processing. *Journal of Artificial Intelligence Research*, 57: 345–420.

Guo, L., Shi, F., and Tu, J. (2016). Textual analysis and machine leaning: Crack unstructured data in finance and accounting. *Journal of Finance and Data Science*, 2(3): 153–170.

Henry, E. (2008). Are investors influenced by how earnings press releases are written? *Journal of Business Communication (1973)*, 45(4): 363–407.

Heston, S.L., and Sinha, N.R. (2017). News vs. sentiment: Predicting stock returns from news stories. *Financial Analysts Journal*, 73(3): 67–83.

Huang, A.G., Tan, H., and Wermers, R. (2020). Institutional trading around corporate news: Evidence from textual analysis. *Review of Financial Studies*, 33(10): 4627–4675.

Jegadeesh, N., and Wu, D. (2013). Word power: A new approach for content analysis. *Journal of Financial Economics*, 110(3): 712–729.

Jiang, F., Lee, J., Martin, X., and Zhou, G. (2019). Manager sentiment and stock returns. *Journal of Financial Economics*, 132(1): 126–149.

Jung, H., and Lee, B.G. (2020). Research trends in text mining: Semantic network and main path analysis of selected journals. *Expert Systems with Applications*, 162: 113851.

Ke, Z.T., Kelly, B.T., and Xiu, D. (2019). *Predicting Returns with Text Data.* Technical Report, National Bureau of Economic Research.

Kearney, C., and Liu, S. (2014). Textual sentiment in finance: A survey of methods and models. *International Review of Financial Analysis*, 33: 171–185.

Kothari, S.P., Li, X., and Short, J.E. (2009). The effect of disclosures by management, analysts, and business press on cost of capital, return volatility, and analyst forecasts: A study using content analysis. *The Accounting Review*, 84(5): 1639–1670.

Lewis, C., and Young, S. (2019). Fad or future? automated analysis of financial text and its implications for corporate reporting. *Accounting and Business Research*, 49(5): 587–615.

Li, F. (2008). Annual report readability, current earnings, and earnings persistence. *Journal of Accounting and Economics*, 45(2–3): 221–247.

Li, F. (2010a). Textual analysis of corporate disclosures: A survey of the literature. *Journal of Accounting Literature*, 29(1): 143–165.

Li, F. (2010b). The information content of forward-looking statements in corporate filings — a naïve Bayesian machine learning approach. *Journal of Accounting Research*, 48(5): 1049–1102.

Li, K., Mai, F., Shen, R., and Yan, X. (2021). Measuring corporate culture using machine learning. *Review of Financial Studies*, 34(7): 3265–3315.

Loughran, T., and McDonald, B. (2011). When is a liability not a liability? Textual analysis, dictionaries, and 10-ks. *Journal of Finance*, 66(1): 35–65.

Loughran, T., and McDonald, B. (2014). Measuring readability in financial disclosures. *Journal of Finance*, 69(4): 1643–1671.

Loughran, T., and McDonald, B. (2016). Textual analysis in accounting and finance: A survey. *Journal of Accounting Research*, 54(4): 1187–1230.

Loughran, T., and McDonald, B. (2020). Textual analysis in finance. *Annual Review of Financial Economics*, 12: 357–375.

Manela, A., and Moreira, A. (2017). News implied volatility and disaster concerns. *Journal of Financial Economics*, 123(1): 137–162.

Mikolov, T., Chen, K., Corrado, G., and Dean, J. (2013). Efficient estimation of word representations in vector space. In *International Conference on Learning Representations*, https://api.semanticscholar.org/CorpusID:5959482.

Sautner, Z., van Lent, L., Vilkov, G., and Zhang, R. (2020). *Firm-Level Climate Change Exposure*. European Corporate Governance Institute–Finance Working Paper (686).

Stone, P.J., Dunphy, D.C., and Smith, M.S. (1966). *The General Inquirer: A Computer Approach to Content Analysis*. MIT Press.

Tetlock, P.C. (2007). Giving content to investor sentiment: The role of media in the stock market. *Journal of Finance*, 62(3): 1139–1168.

Tetlock, P.C. (2011). All the news that's fit to reprint: Do investors react to stale information? *Review of Financial Studies*, 24(5): 1481–1512.

Tetlock, P.C., Saar-Tsechansky, M., and Macskassy, S. (2008). More than words: Quantifying language to measure firms' fundamentals. *Journal of Finance*, 63(3): 1437–1467.

Vajjala, S., Majumder, B., Gupta, A., and Surana, H. (2020). *Practical Natural Language Processing: A Comprehensive Guide to Building Real-World NLP Systems*. O'Reilly Media, Sebastopol, CA.

https://doi.org/10.1142/9781800615212_0003

Chapter 3

Portfolio Allocation and Reinforcement Learning

René Garcia* and Alissa Marinenko†

University of Montreal, Canada
SKEMA Business School Canada, Canada
**rene.garcia@skema.edu*
†*alissa.marinenko@skema.edu*

Abstract

In this chapter, we briefly review the methodology of reinforcement learning and describe its application to the financial problem of portfolio allocation. In this context, we define the environment as a set of states, captured by such financial variables as stock returns or technical indicators, and of actions, mainly the determination of wealth shares to invest in each asset. Optimal value functions are obtained through the Bellman optimality equation, a well-established principle in both reinforcement learning and portfolio optimization. Deep reinforcement learning algorithms have the advantage of providing approximate solutions since most portfolio problems lack analytical solutions. We describe several algorithms and apply them to classical portfolio allocation problems, where risk minimization and return maximization are combined with or without accounting for trading costs.

Keywords: Reinforcement learning, portfolio allocation, risk minimization, return maximization, transaction costs.

1 Reinforcement Learning

1.1 Introduction

Reinforcement learning (RL) is a branch of machine learning that deals with learning control strategies by interacting with a complex environment. At the heart of this framework is an agent interacting with an environment at each step/instant in time.

In the diagram shown in Figure 1, at every time step, the agent observes an environment described by a state s (e.g., current stock prices, current portfolio value, economic conditions) and decides to take a particular action a (e.g., the number of shares of a particular stock to buy or sell). Following this action a, the agent receives a corresponding reward g (e.g., return on current portfolio, utility of current wealth) and transitions to a new state. Rewards can be any real number and will indicate whether a specific action has led to a relatively good or bad outcome. The goal is to learn what actions maximized the total reward over time. In other words, we want to train the agent in such a way that when it observes any state s, it could tell us what the best way to act in that state is.

1.2 Environment

Financial decision-making and RL problems involve uncertainty and stochasticity, which leads us to model the environment as a stochastic Markov decision process (MDP). For a discrete-time MDP with $t = 0, 1, \ldots, T$, the environment at each time step can be characterized

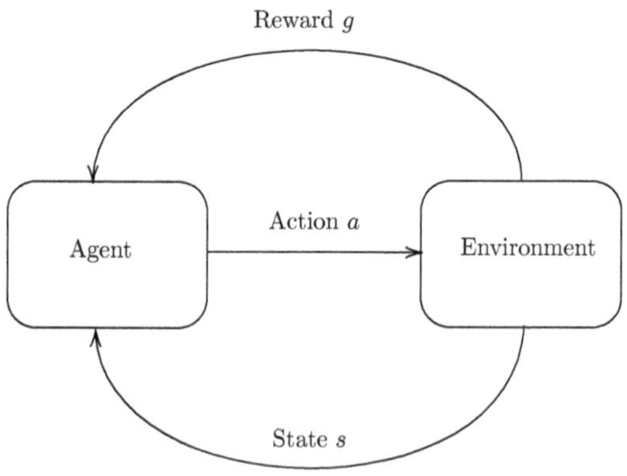

Figure 1. RL environment.

by states $s_t \in \mathcal{S}$, actions $a_t \in \mathcal{A}(s_t)$, and rewards $g_{t+1} \in \mathcal{G}$. The next state s_{t+1} is a random variable with probability density determined by the current state-action pair (s_t, a_t). When the state space $\mathcal{S}$ is discrete (i.e., states can take a finite number of values), the probability transition function is

$$p(s_{t+1} = s'|s_t, a_t)$$

This represents the probability of moving to state s' given that the agent was in state s_t and selected action a_t. When the state space $\mathcal{S}$ is continuous, the conditional probability of s_{t+1} being in some region $\mathbb{S}_{t+1}$ given s_t, a_t is

$$P(s_{t+1} \in \mathbb{S}_{t+1}|s_t, a_t) = \int_{\mathbb{S}_{t+1}} p(s'|s_t, a_t)ds'$$

Another important variable to consider is the reward g_{t+1} that depends on the state-action trajectory followed. Because transitions are stochastic, the reward is received after moving to state s_{t+1}, which makes g_{t+1} a result of the transition (s_t, a_t, s_{t+1}). Thus, the one-step reward can be defined by a function of (s_t, a_t, s_{t+1}) as

$$g_{t+1} = g(s_t, a_t, s_{t+1})$$

Consequently, the dynamics of the environment is governed by the transition probabilities $p(\cdot|s_t = s, a_t = a)$ and the reward g_{t+1}. Indeed, such an environment well describes the dynamic decisions associated with stock trading and portfolio allocation in a stochastic stock market in which prices are generally given. Portfolio managers have to choose the stocks or assets in which to invest as well as the proportions of each in the overall portfolio.

1.3 Policy

The term **policy** is used to define the way in which an agent chooses actions in a given state. Mathematically, a policy $\pi(a_t|s_t)$ is a function $\pi : \mathcal{S} \rightarrow \mathcal{A}(s)$ that maps states onto actions. Policies are divided into two types:

- **Deterministic**: The policy is simply the action that is selected in a specific state: $\pi(a_t|s_t) = a_t$. This means that only one discrete action can be chosen in every state. In other words, given the current state s_t, we select a specific action with a probability of 1, while all other actions have probabilities of 0 of being selected.

- **Stochastic**: The policy represents a function that maps states s_t onto probabilities of taking an action a_t with $\pi(a_t|s_t) \in (0, 1)$. In other words, the policy represents a probability distribution over actions so that, at any specific state s_t, different actions can be selected at each time. Clearly, actions having higher values of $\pi(a_t|s_t)$ are more likely to be chosen at state s_t.

1.4 Rewards and objective

Reinforcement learning is, in essence, a large optimization problem where the agent must find an optimal policy π (select the best actions) that will maximize its expected total reward over the entire trajectory. For a finite-horizon problem, we define a full state-action trajectory of fixed, finite length T (the horizon) denoted as $\tau = (a_0, s_0, a_1, s_1, \ldots, s_{T-1}, a_{T-1}, s_T)$. In some cases, it is useful to denote by $\tau_{t,t+h}$ a trajectory of length h, starting at t and ending at $t + h$.

A finite-horizon (discounted) trajectory reward is obtained by accumulating one-step rewards over time. Intuitively, the total reward over trajectory $\tau_{t,T}$, discounted to time t, is defined as

$$G(\tau_{t,T}) = \sum_{k=t}^{T-1} \gamma^{k-t} g_{k+1} = g_{t+1} + \gamma G(\tau_{t+1,T})$$

Here, $\gamma \in [0, 1]$ is the discount rate that is used to determine the importance of future rewards today or, alternatively, quantify the uncertainty of future rewards.

Since the future is uncertain and rewards depend on the state-action trajectory followed, which is in turn determined by the policy π used, the goal of an RL agent is to maximize the *expected* total reward over the entire trajectory $\tau \sim \pi$. Precisely, the objective to maximize is defined as

$$J(\pi) = \mathbb{E}_\pi [G(\tau)] = \mathbb{E}_\pi \left[\sum_{t=0}^{T-1} \gamma^t g_{t+1} \right] = \sum_{t=0}^{T-1} \gamma^t \mathbb{E}_\pi [g_{t+1}]$$

The expectation is taken over the trajectory τ, which is determined by policy π. Due to the Markov property, the probability of this trajectory, given a starting state $s_0 \sim p_0$, is defined as

$$\begin{aligned} P_\pi(\tau) &= p_0(s_0)p_\pi(a_0, s_1, a_1, \ldots, s_{T-1}, a_{T-1}, s_T) \\ &= p_0(s_0)\prod_{t=0}^{T-1} p_\pi(s_{t+1}, a_t|s_t) \\ &= p_0(s_0)\prod_{t=0}^{T-1} p(s_{t+1}|s_t, a_t)\pi(a_t|s_t) \end{aligned}$$

Using the above probability, we can derive a useful expression for the expectation of one-step reward under policy π:

$$\begin{aligned} \mathbb{E}_\pi\left[g_{t+1}\right] &= \mathbb{E}_\pi\left[\mathbb{E}[g_{t+1}|s_t, a_t]\right] \\ &= \sum_\tau \mathbb{E}[g_{t+1}|s_t, a_t]P_\pi(\tau) \\ &= \sum_{\tau_{0,t}} \mathbb{E}[g_{t+1}|s_t, a_t]P_\pi(\tau_{0,t}) \\ &= \sum_{s_0,a_0}\cdots\sum_{s_t,a_t} \mathbb{E}[g_{t+1}|s_t, a_t] \\ &\quad \times \left(p_0(s_0)\prod_{k=0}^{t} p(s_{k+1}|s_k, a_k)\pi(a_k|s_k)\right) \end{aligned}$$

Note that in the above equation, passing from the sum over τ to the sum over $\tau_{0,t}$ is possible due to the fact that the reward g_{t+1} is not determined by states and actions that are observed after time $t+1$ but only by what was observed up until $t+1$.

1.5 Value functions

Having defined the total reward, it is important to introduce two types of functions that are crucial to the implementation of all RL algorithms: the state value functions (V-functions) and the state-action value functions (Q-functions).

The **V-function** of state s_t under policy π, denoted $V^\pi(s_t)$, represents the total expected reward obtained by starting from a specific state s_t and following π thereafter. The state value function is mathematically defined as

$$V^{\pi}(s_t) = \mathbb{E}_{\pi}[G(\tau_{t,T})|s_t] = \mathbb{E}_{\pi}[g_{t+1} + \gamma G(\tau_{t+1,T})|s_t]$$

The **Q-function** under policy π at a state s_t and action a_t, denoted $Q^{\pi}(s_t, a_t)$, represents the total expected reward obtained when starting at a specific state s_t, selecting a given action a_t and applying π thereafter. The state-action value function can be seen as defining the benefit obtained from choosing action a_t in a particular state s_t. By definition, the Q-function is given by

$$Q^{\pi}(s_t, a_t) = \mathbb{E}_{\pi}[G(\tau_{t,T})|s_t, a_t] = \mathbb{E}_{\pi}[g_{t+1} + \gamma G(\tau_{t+1,T})|s_t, a_t]$$

1.6 Bellman equation

The Bellman equation is a key concept of dynamic programming that is particularly used not only in finance but also in RL. It gives a relationship between the value of a current state and the values of its successor states. Considering the previous equation for the V-function under policy π, we can derive the associated Bellman equation:

$$\begin{aligned} V^{\pi}(s_t) &= \mathbb{E}_{\pi}[g_{t+1} + \gamma G(\tau_{t+1,T})|s_t] \\ &= \mathbb{E}_{\pi}\left[g_{t+1} + \gamma \mathbb{E}_{\pi}[G(\tau_{t+1,T})|s_{t+1}]\middle|s_t\right] \\ &\quad \text{by the law of iterated expectations} \\ &= \mathbb{E}_{\pi}[g_{t+1} + \gamma V^{\pi}(s_{t+1})|s_t] \end{aligned}$$

Similarly, from the definition of the Q-function, the corresponding Bellman equation is

$$\begin{aligned} Q^{\pi}(s_t, a_t) &= \mathbb{E}_{\pi}[g_{t+1} + \gamma G(\tau_{t+1,T})|s_t, a_t] \\ &= \mathbb{E}_{\pi}\left[g_{t+1} + \gamma \mathbb{E}_{\pi}[G(\tau_{t+1,T})|s_{t+1}, a_{t+1}]\middle|s_t, a_t\right] \\ &= \mathbb{E}_{\pi}[g_{t+1} + \gamma Q^{\pi}(s_{t+1}, a_{t+1})|s_t, a_t] \end{aligned}$$

1.7 Optimization

Recall that the goal of the RL agent is to find an optimal policy π that maximizes $J(\pi)$. If a policy π^* is better than or equal to any other policy π, then we necessarily have $V^{\pi^*}(s_t) \geq V^{\pi}(s_t)$

for all states $s_t \in \mathcal{S}$. This brings us to define as follows the *Bellman optimality equation* associated with an optimal V-function, V^*, and an optimal Q-function, Q^*:

$$\begin{aligned}
V^*(s_t) &= \max_{\pi} V^{\pi}(s_t) \\
&= \max_{a_t} Q^*(s_t, a_t) \\
&= \max_{a_t} \sum_{s_{t+1}} p(s_{t+1}|s_t, a_t)\,(g_{t+1} + \gamma V^*(s_{t+1})) \\
Q^*(s_t, a_t) &= \max_{\pi} Q^{\pi}(s_t, a_t) \\
&= \mathbb{E}_{\pi}[g_{t+1} + \gamma \max_{a_{t+1}} Q^*(s_{t+1}, a_{t+1})|s_t, a_t] \\
&= \sum_{s_{t+1}} p(s_{t+1}|s_t, a_t) \left(g_{t+1} + \gamma \max_{a_{t+1}} Q^*(s_{t+1}, a_{t+1}) \right)
\end{aligned}$$

The optimal policy, π^*, is thus found from either the optimal V-function or from the optimal Q-function. This is done by recursively computing, at each time step, an optimal action that maximizes V^{π} or Q^{π}. In other words, to apply the Bellman optimality equation, at each step t, we must map and memorize the state, action, and corresponding value of the V- or Q-function. Depending on the action–state spaces, there could be a rapid increase in computation and memory storage. In addition, it should be noted that finding π^* from the V-function can be harder since it involves taking the maximum over an expectation, which can be difficult in uncertain environments with an unknown MDP.

1.7.1 *Approximations*

For most financial tasks, we either cannot find an accurate model to describe the environment or there are too many states and/or actions to visit and keep track of. When the dimensions of the state-action space increase significantly, storing all state, action, and optimal value function combinations in memory is not efficient. Deep reinforcement learning (DRL) deals with such issues by using deep neural networks (DNNs)[1] as function approximators to estimate the

[1]Refer to Appendix B for DNN definitions and descriptive features.

optimal value functions and/or the optimal policy distribution. In other words, a neural network will map states and actions onto optimal value functions and could also map states onto optimal actions.

We start with an approximation of *optimal* value functions. Let the V-function and Q-function be parameterized by ν and ω, respectively, giving the corresponding DNNs $V_\nu(s_t)$ and $Q_\omega(s_t, a_t)$. The V-function network will take the vector of states (or states' features) as input and will output a single value corresponding to $V^*(s_t)$ for every state. The Q-function network's input corresponds to the state-action pair (s_t, a_t) and outputs a value of $Q^*(s_t, a_t)$ corresponding to each state-action tuple. Consequently, the sub-optimal policy $\hat{\pi}^*(a_t|s_t)$ can be found using the estimated optimal value functions, such as

$$\hat{\pi}^*(a_t|s_t) \in \arg\max_{a_t} \mathbb{E}_\pi[g_{t+1} + \gamma V_\nu(s_{t+1})|s_t, a_t]$$

or

$$\hat{\pi}^*(a_t|s_t) \in \arg\max_{a_t} Q_\omega(s_t, a_t)$$

When the exact model of the environment is not known, the computation of expectations is done through a Monte Carlo (MC) simulation. Moreover, since the true optimal functions are not known, the loss and the parameter updates are computed using some target function $y(\cdot)$. The definition of the target function depends on the RL algorithm used; however, often, we use one of the following:

$$y(s_{t+1}) = g_{t+1} + \gamma V_\nu(s_{t+1})$$

or

$$y(s_{t+1}, a_{t+1}) = g_{t+1} + \gamma \max_{a_{t+1}} Q_\omega(s_{t+1}, a_{t+1})$$

In general, at each iteration of the algorithm, the parameters of the value function are updated by minimizing the squared loss between the target, $y(\cdot)$, and an estimation of the value function, V_ν or Q_ω.

Having defined a general procedure for value function estimation, we proceed to approximations in policy space. We assume that the optimal policy π is approximated by a neural network π_θ and parameterized by θ. When dealing with stochastic policies, the policy is frequently chosen to be from the Gaussian family of distributions such that

$$\pi_\theta(a_t|s_t) = \frac{1}{\sqrt{2\pi}\sigma(s_t,\theta_\sigma)} \exp\left(\frac{-(a_t - \mu(s_t,\theta_\mu))}{2\sigma(s_t,\theta_\sigma)^2}\right)$$

In other words, an action a_t is selected by sampling from the normal distribution defined by neural networks $\mu(s_t, \theta_\mu)$ and $\sigma(s_t, \theta_\sigma)$ that approximate, respectively, the mean and the standard deviation of a Gaussian. The standard deviation must always be positive and is thus typically defined as an exponential of some function. Note that if any other form of distribution is chosen, the parameters of that distribution can also be approximated by neural networks.

To understand how to find the optimal parameters θ of π_θ, we must explain the policy gradient theorem.

1.7.2 *Policy gradient theorem*

A policy gradient aims to maximize the objective $J(\pi_\theta)$ given that the sequence of optimal actions follows the policy π_θ. We begin by setting the gradient of $J(\pi_\theta)$ to zero and using the definition of $J(\cdot)$ derived in Section 1.4 to obtain the following expression[2]:

$$\begin{aligned}\nabla_\theta J(\pi_\theta) &= \mathbb{E}_{\tau\sim\pi_\theta}\left[\sum_{s=1}^{T-1} \nabla_\theta \log \pi_\theta(a_s|s_s) Q^{\pi_\theta}(s_s, a_s)\right] \\ &\sim \frac{1}{|\mathcal{D}|}\sum_{\tau\in\mathcal{D}}\sum_{s=1}^{T-1} \nabla_\theta \log \pi_\theta(a_s|s_s) Q^{\pi_\theta}(s_s, a_s)\end{aligned}$$

The last expression is an MC estimate of the policy gradient, with $\mathcal{D}$ being a set of trajectories. Intuitively, a step in the policy gradient direction should increase the probability of better-than-average actions and decrease the probability of worse-than-average actions. Assuming that we are able to calculate $\nabla_\theta \log \pi_\theta(a_t|s_t)$, we can compute the policy gradient and update parameters using

$$\theta_{k+1} \leftarrow \theta_k + \alpha \nabla_{\theta_k} J(\pi_{\theta_k})$$

[2]See Appendix A for the derivation of the policy gradient theorem expression.

2 Deep Reinforcement Learning Algorithms

When the transition probabilities associated with the MDP are unknown, we must estimate the expectation term involved in the definition of the value functions. Moreover, although analytical solutions exist for some problems involving continuous action and/or state spaces (e.g., the maximization of quadratic expected utility), the maximization problem rarely has an analytical solution; thus, it becomes hard to find the maximum of value functions and compute the expectation. To deal with this problem, MC methods can be used in tandem with value functions and policy approximations. The approximation is either done by using neural networks (for continuous action/spaces) or by using linear approximations (when state-action spaces can be discretized). This prompts us to introduce some model-free RL algorithms, such as proximal policy optimization (PPO), advantage actor–critic (A2C/A3C), and soft actor–critic (SAC). These algorithms use experience to sample state-action trajectories from actual or simulated interaction with an environment. In addition, they use neural networks to estimate the optimal value function and the optimal policy to follow.

2.1 Actor–critic methods

Actor and critic (AC) algorithms divide the agent into two parts: an actor (policy) and a critic (value). These algorithms make two approximations using neural networks. The “critic” network estimates the value of a state and possibly evaluates how good the chosen action is. This could be an estimate of the V-function or the Q-function. The “actor” updates the policy distribution in the direction suggested by the critic, and it is based on the policy gradient approach. Generally, separate neural network architectures are used to approximate the critic and the actor. This means that we must define two networks and learn two different functions. The structure of a separate network is illustrated in the graph shown in Figure 2.

Alternatively, one network that will output both the optimal value function and the optimal policy distribution can be used. The latter network is referred to as a shared network in deep learning terminology and has the form shown in Figure 3.

When a state s_t is passed to the shared network, it will pass through at least one shared layer. The output of the last shared layer

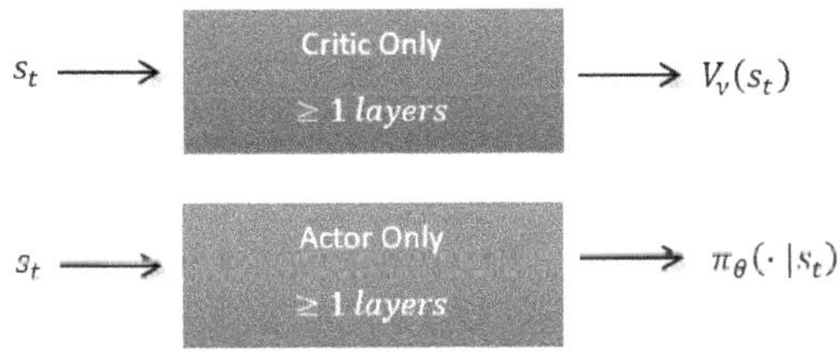

Figure 2. Separate network architecture.

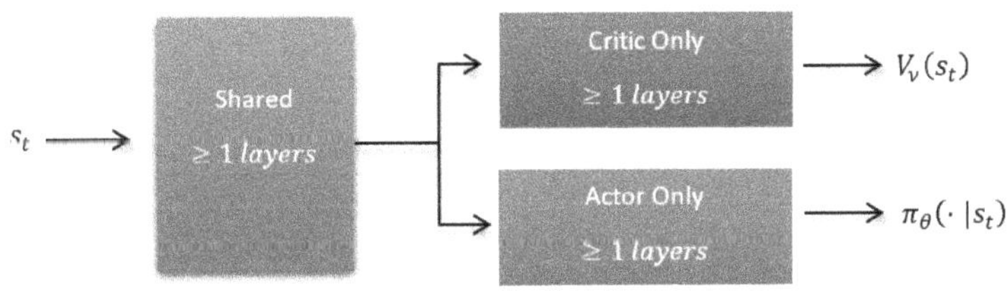

Figure 3. Shared network architecture.

will be further split into two separate layers to obtain two separate "sub-networks."

2.1.1 *Advantage actor–critic*

The actor and critic algorithm that we will focus on is called the advantage actor–critic, or A2C for short (Algorithm 1). As its name suggests, Algorithm 1 is based on an **advantage function**. To understand the advantage function, recall that in policy gradient methods, we are interested in knowing what the benefit of taking a certain action in a given state is. The satisfaction received from a certain action depends on the environment's state, that is, one "good" action will result in a greater benefit if the agent is in a state that is closer to the target than if the agent is far from achieving that target. Hence, it is useful to determine the relative advantage of a particular action in a given state.

The advantage function $A^\pi(s,a)$ corresponding to the policy π describes how much value is added or subtracted when given a specific state s. We decide to take a specific action a according to policy π. That is, it is the difference between the state-action value function (Q-function) and the state value function (V-function):

$$A^\pi(s_t,a_t) = Q^\pi(s_t,a_t) - V^\pi(s_t)$$

It can be seen that the advantage at time t will be negative if we are in a favorable state (high V^{π}); however, we choose a "bad" action (low Q^{π}). Typically, the first step is to obtain an estimate of the value of a state, which is the expected reward the agent will receive given that it has already arrived at the present state. Second, the action value function must be computed. The action value function represents the value of a state and of a chosen action *after* that action was taken. In our context, the approximations are obtained with the neural networks V_{ν} and Q_{ω}. However, it is often impossible or complicated to calculate the Q-function, so a good estimate of $Q^{\pi}(s_t, a_t)$ will be the reward received from performing an action a_t in a given state s_t defined as $g_{t+1} + \gamma V^{\pi}(s_{t+1})$. The latter gives rise to the unbiased estimator of the advantage function, defined as the temporal difference (TD) error:

$$\delta_t^{\pi} = g_{t+1} + V^{\pi}(s_{t+1}) - V^{\pi}(s_t)$$

When we use DNNs to estimate the Q-function and V-function, the *hat* notation will be used to indicate that the advantage and the TD error are computed from value function approximations:

$$\hat{A}(s_t, a_t) = Q_{\omega}(s_t, a_t) - V_{\nu}(s_t)$$

$$\hat{\delta}_t = g_{t+1} + \gamma V_{\nu}(s_{t+1}) - V_{\nu}(s_t)$$

The above definitions are very useful for the policy gradient methods because, as trajectories during training can significantly deviate from each other, it is suitable to reduce this variability by subtracting some baseline function $b(s_t)$ from the Q-function or from cumulative rewards $G(\tau_{s,T})$ to make these quantities smaller. When the Q-function or cumulative rewards are reduced by $b(s_t)$, the gradients' values decrease, which in turn stabilizes the updates. In fact, we can generalize the policy gradient expression to

$$\nabla_{\theta} J(\theta) = \mathbb{E}_{\tau \sim \pi_{\theta}} \left[\sum_{t=1}^{T-1} \nabla_{\theta} \log \pi_{\theta}(a_t | s_t) \Phi_t \right]$$

where Φ_t can be defined as one of the following:

- total reward of trajectory: $G(\tau)$;
- reward-to-go after taking an action at step t: $G(\tau_{t,T})$;
- baselined version using rewards-to-go: $G(\tau_{s,T}) - b(s_t)$;

- on policy Q-function: $Q^\pi(s_t, a_t)$;
- advantage function: $A^\pi(s_t, a_t)$;
- TD error: δ^π.

Algorithm 1 uses an estimated advantage function $\hat{A}(\cdot)$ to update parameters. The actor is given by the policy network π_θ, parameterized by θ, and the critic is given by the state value function network V_ν, parameterized by ν. For a finite-horizon process, ending at time T, the idea is to sample state-action transitions using the current estimate of the policy, π_θ, compute the targets of the V-function and the corresponding advantage, and, finally, update the parameters using a regression for the value function and gradient ascent for the policy.

Algorithm 1 uses the one-step look-ahead target y_t. This target is derived from the Bellman equation for the state value function and is given by $g_{t+1} + V_\nu(s_{t+1})$. This allows us to approximate the advantage by the one-step TD error $\hat{\delta}_t$, which is computed using the approximator of the V function. The parameters of the critic are updated by minimizing the following loss function:

$$L(\nu) = (y_t - V_\nu(s_t))^2 = (\hat{\delta}_t)^2$$

The parameters of the actor are updated using the policy gradient theorem, in which the actor's loss is

$$L(\theta) = -\log \pi_\theta(a_t|s_t)(y_t - V_\nu(s_t)) = -\log \pi_\theta(a_t|s_t)\hat{\delta}_t$$

At each time step, the one-step look-ahead Algorithm 1 executes one action a_t, moves to the next state s_{t+1}, receives one reward g_{t+1}, and makes a training update based on that one transition. As a result, it constantly learns with every step. The drawback of this approach is that it cannot benefit from larger batch sizes (that results in better computational efficiency and a stabilizing effect), and the sequential training data examples in one episode are highly correlated, which is problematic for training higher-dimensional RL problems.

A more generalized form of the A2C, which stabilizes training by increasing batch sizes, is the one that uses an n-step look-ahead update instead of a one-step update. In other words, we look n steps into the future and compute the n-step total reward $G(\tau_{t,t+n})$. In addition, instead of the one-step TD error, we use the n-step TD

Algorithm 1. A2C.

Initialize the actor and the critic parameters θ and ν
Select learning rates $0 < \lambda_\theta,\ \lambda_\nu \leq 1$
Select the discount rate $0 \leq \gamma \leq 1$
for epoch $0, 1, \ldots, N$
    Reset environment, set the number of steps for update $= n$
    Generate trajectory $\tau = (s_0, a_0, \ldots, a_{T-1}, s_T) \sim \pi_\theta$
    Calculate corresponding rewards over trajectory $g_{t+1} = g(s_t, a_t, s_{t+1}) \forall t = 0, \ldots, T-1$
    for $t = T - 1$ **to** 0 :
        Define done flag at step k: $d_k = \mathbb{I}\{k \geq T\}$
        Calculate the n-step reward using Critic

$$G(\tau_{t,t+n}) = \sum_{k=t}^{t+n-1} \gamma^{k-t} g_{k+1}(1 - d_k) + \gamma^n (1 - d_{t+n}) V_\nu(s_{t+n})$$

        Compute the n-step TD error $\hat{\delta}_t^{(n)} = G(\tau_{t,t+n}) - V_\nu(s_t)$
    end for

    Compute losses

$$L(\theta) = -\frac{1}{T} \sum_{t=0}^{T-1} \log \pi_\theta(a_t|s_t) \hat{\delta}_t^{(n)}$$

$$L(\nu) = \frac{1}{T} \sum_{t=0}^{T-1} \left(\hat{\delta}_t^{(n)}\right)^2$$

    Update networks' parameters:

$$\theta = \theta + \lambda_\theta \nabla_\theta L(\theta)$$
$$\nu = \nu + \lambda_\nu \nabla_\nu L(\nu)$$

end for

error, defined as[3]

$$\hat{\delta}_t^{(n)} = \sum_{k=t}^{t+n-1} \gamma^{k-t} g_{k+1} + \gamma^n V_\nu(s_{t+n}) - V_\nu(s_t)$$

[3]See Appendix A for the equation derivation.

Note that if $t+n \geq T$, then we must set $V_\nu(s_{t+n}) = 0$ since at $t+n$, the horizon has already reached its terminal state. The update is done by using the previously defined losses $L(\nu)$ and $L(\theta)$. The detailed pseudo-algorithm for an n-step A2C is presented in Algorithm 1.

In the above pseudo-algorithm, epochs form the outer loop of the training algorithm, and there is one value and policy update per epoch. Typically, the total number of epochs, N, is set to be significantly large in order to reach a good solution. Depending on the problem, a specific discount rate must be chosen; however, a popular choice is to select it within a range of $\gamma = 0.9 - \gamma = 0.99$. Learning rates are hyperparameters (chosen by the user) that will control the degree of exploration. Precisely, a small learning rate will make smaller gradient updates and require more training epochs, while large learning rates will significantly change the parameters in one gradient step, thus requiring fewer training epochs. Note that if the learning rate is too small, the algorithm might never find an optimal solution, while if it is too large, the algorithm might diverge. Consequently, one of the challenges of training neural networks is selecting an appropriate learning rate.

Alternatively, if a shared network is used, instead of computing two separate losses and updating separate parameters, we compute one loss function:

$$L(\theta_{\pi,v}) = L(\theta) + c_v L(\nu) = \frac{1}{T}\sum_{t=0}^{T-1}\left(-\log \pi_\theta(a_t|s_t)\hat{\delta}_t^{(n)} + c_v(\hat{\delta}_t^{(n)})^2\right)$$

where $\theta_{\pi,v}$ represents the shared parameters vector for both the actor and the critic, and the constant $c_v \in \mathbb{R}^+$ is the hyperparameter that controls the importance of value function updates. The coefficient c_v is typically set <1 to reduce the contribution from the value function loss.

2.1.2 *Entropy regularization*

At any given point in time, the knowledge of an agent about the state, actions, rewards, and resulting states is partial, which results in the so-called *exploration–exploitation dilemma*. Suppose you have some partial information about the environment and the value of some, but not all, actions. **Exploration** allows the agent to improve its knowledge about each action, which could lead to a higher total reward in the future. **Exploitation**, on the other hand, only uses current knowledge and exploits the agent's current estimated value in choosing optimal actions. However, in the latter case, the agent has only partial knowledge and does not know the actual value of its actions, so chances are it might not get the most reward. The balance between exploration and exploitation can be described using a degree of uncertainty for action selection.

Recall that the optimal policy, $\pi(a_t|s_t)$, is represented by the probability distribution of actions, a_t, for each state s_t. This probability represents the uncertainty of the action selection, and the learning process is essentially the process of reducing this uncertainty of which action to choose at each specific state. At the beginning, we would like to explore the environment the most, implying that each action is equally likely to be chosen or, equivalently, that the uncertainty is maximized. Therefore, we introduce a new notion of *entropy* to measure the degree of uncertainty and serve as an exploration tool. In our context, the entropy measures the uncertainty of the policy distribution $\pi(a_t|s_t)$ and is typically defined as

$$H_\pi(s_t) = \mathbb{E}[-\log \pi(a_t|s_t)]$$

The more uncertain a policy's distribution, the more diverse the actions it produces and the higher the value of $H_\pi(s_t)$. Conversely, less uniform policies produce similar actions and have lower entropy.

The entropy term is subtracted from the policy loss function, defined in the previous section, with its corresponding coefficient $c_h \geq 0$ so that the policy loss becomes

$$L(\theta) = \frac{1}{T}\sum_{t=0}^{T-1}\left(-\log \pi_\theta(a_t|s_t)\hat{\delta}_t^{(n)} - c_h H_\pi(s_t)\right)$$

Because the entropy measure H_π and the hyperparameter c_h are always nonnegative, the term $-c_h H_\pi(s_t)$ is always negative. When a policy is certain, entropy decreases, implying that $-c_h H_\pi(s_t)$ increases and contributes more to the loss so as to encourage more exploration. Conversely, when a policy is very uncertain, entropy increases and thus $-c_h H_\pi(s_t)$ decreases and contributes less to the loss, which makes the policy have little incentive to change through the entropy term.

2.2 Proximal policy optimization (PPO): Clipped version[4]

The second algorithm we present is the proximal policy optimization (PPO) algorithm, which uses a clipped surrogate objective. PPO is a policy optimization method that indirectly optimizes θ by maximizing local approximations of the objective $J(\theta)$. The main ideas presented for A2C remain the same for PPO, that is, both algorithms have an actor and a critic, improving each other in the learning process. Moreover, both can be used for discrete and continuous action and state spaces. However, with A2C, the magnitude of a policy update might drastically increase with an action's increasing probability. In other words, a newly discovered action can be mistakenly viewed by the actor as highly gainful, making the policy poor at exploration as the agent continues to choose the unfavorable action over and over again. This cycle of exploitation causes a significant shift in policy parameters toward that action, and with every update, losses become exceedingly large. So, even if the agent performed well at the beginning, a slight change in the policy parameters can cause a high drop in performance without a possibility for further recovery.

PPO helps fix this instability issue by restricting large parameter updates so that multiple steps of optimization can be done without the actor's action distribution fluctuating too much. Precisely, the algorithm ensures that the loss cannot get higher than the allowed ***clip ratio***, denoted by ϵ. First, instead of using the log-probability of an action, as in the A2C policy update, PPO uses the following ***policy ratio*** to trace the impact of the actions:

$$h_t(\theta, \theta_{\text{old}}) = \frac{\pi_\theta(a_t|s_t)}{\pi_{\theta_{\text{old}}}(a_t|s_t)}$$

By definition, $h_t(\theta, \theta_{\text{old}})$ is the ratio between the probability of the action under current policy parameters, represented by the vector θ, and the probability of the action under previous parameters, represented by the vector θ_{old}. When the action is more likely under the

[4]Original: https://arxiv.org/pdf/1707.06347.pdf;
Improvements: https://arxiv.org/pdf/2009.10897.pdf;
Paper on A2C and PPO: https://arxiv.org/pdf/2009.10897.pdf.

current policy than it is under the old policy, this ratio will be greater than 1, and vice versa.

To limit the size of the policy update, we also use the clipped policy ratio:

$$\overline{h}_t(\theta, \theta_{\text{old}}; \epsilon) = \text{clip}\left(h_t(\theta, \theta_{\text{old}}), 1 - \epsilon, 1 + \epsilon\right)$$

In the above expression, the clipped policy ratio, $\overline{h}_t(\theta, \theta_{\text{old}}; \epsilon)$, introduces lower and upper bounds on the policy ratio so that $h_t(\theta, \theta_{\text{old}})$ stays within the interval $(1 - \epsilon, 1 + \epsilon)$. Consequently, PPO only considers rewards that are received from state-action pairs that satisfy $1 - \epsilon < h_t(\theta, \theta_{\text{old}}) < 1 + \epsilon$. Note that the clip ratio is a chosen hyperparameter that corresponds to how much the new policy can deviate from the old one. It is now possible to derive an expression for the PPO objective to ***maximize***

$$L^{\text{clip}}(\theta) = \min\Big(h_t(\theta, \theta_{\text{old}})\hat{A}^{\theta_{\text{old}}}(s_t, a_t), \quad \overline{h}_t(\theta, \theta_{\text{old}}; \epsilon)\hat{A}^{\theta_{\text{old}}}(s_t, a_t)\Big)$$

The maximization of $L^{\text{clip}}(\theta)$ is done with respect to θ, while the advantage is calculated based on the previously obtained parameters θ_{old}. If the action was estimated to be favorable (when $\hat{A} > 0$) and it became a lot more likely under the current policy than it was prior to the update (high values of $h_t(\theta, \theta_{\text{old}})$), the policy ratio gets clipped and the gradient step does not become too large. On the other hand, if the action was estimated to be unfavorable (when $\hat{A} < 0$) and it became a lot less likely under the current policy, we do not want to continue making it less and less likely and thus activate the clipping again.

Finally, for a trajectory of length T generated by π_θ over all time steps, the approximate advantage function is computed as

$$\begin{aligned}\hat{A}^{\theta}(s_t, a_t) &= g_{t+1} + \gamma g_{t+2} + \cdots + \gamma^{T-t-1} g_T + \gamma V_\nu(s_T) - V_\nu(s_t) \\ &= \hat{\delta}_t + \gamma\hat{\delta}_{t+1} + \cdots + \gamma^{T-t-1}\hat{\delta}_{T-1}\end{aligned}$$

The detailed PPO algorithm is presented in Algorithm 2.

Algorithm 2. PPO clip, one agent, separate networks.

Initialize the actor and the critic parameters θ and ν
Select value learning rate $0 < \lambda_\nu \leq 1$
Select the discount rate $0 \leq \gamma \leq 1$
Select the clip-ratio value: a good choice is $\epsilon = 0.2$
for epoch $0, 1, \ldots, N$
    Reset environment
    Generate trajectory $\tau = (s_0, a_0, \ldots, a_{T-1}, s_T) \sim \pi_\theta$
    Calculate corresponding step rewards $g_{t+1} = g(s_t, a_t, s_{t+1})$ $\forall t = 0, \ldots, T-1$

    for $t = T-1$ **to** 0 :
        Compute rewards-to-go $G(\tau_{t,T})$ using critic
        Compute advantage estimate $\hat{A}^{\theta_{\text{old}}}(s_t, a_t)$
    end for

    Randomly sample a batch of available data on a fixed time horizon of length $T_M \leq T$
    Update policy parameters:

$$\theta = \arg\max_{\theta} \frac{1}{T_M} \sum_{t=0}^{T_M - 1} \min \times \left(h_t(\theta, \theta_{\text{old}}) \hat{A}^{\theta_{\text{old}}}(s_t, a_t), \quad \overline{h}_t(\theta, \theta_{\text{old}}; \epsilon) \hat{A}^{\theta_{\text{old}}}(s_t, a_t) \right)$$

$$\theta_{\text{old}} \longleftarrow \theta$$

    Compute value mean loss:

$$L(\nu) = \frac{1}{T_M} \sum_{t=0}^{T_M - 1} \left(G(\tau_{t,T_M}) - V_\nu(s_t) \right)^2$$

    Update the value network parameters:

$$\nu = \nu + \lambda_\nu \nabla_\nu L(\nu)$$

end for

Such an approach prevents the learning from being sensitive to minor perturbations and thus stabilizes the overall process. Note that when the parameters of actor and critic networks are shared (one network is used for both), only the parameter vector θ is updated using the following objective function:

$$L^{\text{clip-shared}}(\theta) = L_{\text{clip}}(\theta) - c_v \left(G(\tau_{t,T} - V_{\theta_{\text{old}}}(s_t))\right)^2 + c_h H_{\pi_\theta}(s_t)$$

where $L^{\text{clip}}(\theta)$ is the clipped surrogate objective, $H_{\pi_\theta}(s_t)$ is the entropy of policy π_θ with entropy coefficient c_h, and c_v is the value loss function coefficient.

3 Applications in Finance

To illustrate the functioning of the DRL algorithms, we consider a portfolio allocation problem whereby an investor has to choose how much to invest in a number of stocks in a dynamic fashion in order to maximize her wealth over a certain time period. The training process starts by observing stocks' key features, such as returns, correlations of returns between stocks, technical indicators, and other stock characteristics. Further, it involves taking an action (choosing an allocation) and computing corresponding rewards so that the agent adjusts its strategy accordingly. As a result, by interacting with the environment, the agent will derive an optimal strategy with the maximized total reward. In this section, we define multiple variants of a portfolio allocation problem and describe how they can be solved using Algorithm 1.

3.1 Portfolio allocation problems

General multi-period portfolio selection problems can be summarized as distributing available capital among different assets (such as bonds, stocks, and cryptocurrencies) over a given time horizon to achieve a specific objective. To formulate the portfolio allocation task as a finite-horizon MDP, in which an agent must make decisions at discrete time steps over its investment horizon, it is necessary to define the corresponding environment. For our applications, we use the following assumptions and notations to characterize the finite-horizon framework:

- The investor makes its allocation decisions during an investment horizon of $T < \infty$ discrete periods, with each period indexed by $t = 0, 1, \ldots, T$.
- There are no taxes, but there may be transaction costs.
- The portfolio consists of N stocks. Stock j's closing price is available and is denoted by $p_t^{(j)}$. The vector of all stocks' closing prices is $p_t \in \mathbb{R}^{N\times 1}$ for $t = 0, 1, \ldots, T-1$.
- Stock returns can be found from prices, such as the simple return of asset j for period t is calculated as $r_t^{(j)} = p_{t+1}^{(j)}/p_t^{(j)} - 1$. The vector of asset returns is denoted $r_t \in \mathbb{R}^{N\times 1}$ for periods $t = 0, 1, \ldots, T-1$.
- At time $t = 0$, the investor has an initial capital of $W_0 > 0$ dollars available for investment.
- During each trading period, the agent observes the stock market by analyzing data and then reallocates its portfolio. Precisely, the investor observes a state vector/matrix $s_t = (s_t^{(1)}, \ldots, s_t^{(N)})$, where each $s_t^{(j)}$ is a scalar or vector containing the closing price of stock j at time t and may include additional information, such as the volume of shares of stock j, correlation of stock j with other stocks in the portfolio, technical indicators, such as the exponential moving average (EMA) or average directional index (ADX), and macroeconomic factors.
- Given a state s_t, the investor must choose an action from an action space $\mathcal{A}(s_t)$, which contains the values of the allowed actions. The action space may be either discrete or continuous. In the discrete case, the investor decides on the *number of shares* to trade (buy or sell) such that the decision for asset j at time t is $a_t^{(j)} \in \{-k_j, \ldots, 0, \ldots, k_j\}$, where k_j represents the maximum number of shares of stock j that could be bought or sold. In the continuous case, the decision vector represents target weights in each asset such that $a_t \in [0, 1]^N$ for a long-only portfolio and $a_t \in [-1, 1]^N$ if short sales are allowed.
- Based on the chosen action a_t, the agent moves to the next time step, observes the next state s_{t+1}, and receives a numerical reward $g_{t+1} = g(s_t, a_t, s_{t+1})$.

The form of the reward function g_{t+1} is mainly determined by the objective the investor aims to achieve. Examples of common objectives include optimization of profit/return, minimization of risk, and optimization of economic utility. When maximizing profit of a risk-insensitive investor, the most simple and natural definitions of instantaneous reward are the one-period profit and one-period portfolio log-return. Using the price and stock returns vectors, p_t and r_t, at time t and the action vector a_t representing the desired allocation *weights*, the new portfolio value, denoted P_{t+1}, and the portfolio (simple) return during the period $t - t+1$, denoted R_t, are computed as

$$R_t = a_t \cdot r_t = \sum_{j=1}^{N} a_t^{(j)} \left(\frac{p_{t+1}^{(j)}}{p_t^{(j)}} - 1 \right)$$

$$P_{t+1} = P_t(1 + R_t) \quad \text{and} \quad P_0 = W_0$$

Alternatively, if the objective is the minimization of risk, the reward is defined in terms of portfolio variance. Since this is a minimization problem, we must add a negative sign to obtain an equivalent maximization problem for the DRL algorithms described. We can now proceed to mathematically define simple common forms of the reward function:

- new portfolio value: $g_{t+1} = P_{t+1}$;
- portfolio log-return (if actions are fractions): $g_{t+1} = \log\left(\frac{P_{t+1}}{P_t}\right)$;
- portfolio variance: $g_{t+1} = -a_t^\top \Sigma_t a_t$.

Note that the covariance matrix of asset returns defined by Σ_t is estimated using the covariance of past stock returns. The past stock returns, in our setting, are obtained at each time step t by taking τ previous return observations for each stock. Having obtained a sequence of rewards g_{t+1}, we proceed to compute the total trajectory reward that will be used in Algorithm 1.

For the next examples, each time step t will correspond to a trading month, and the risky portfolio will consist of $N = 4$ selected stocks from the Dow Jones Index (DJI).

Example 1: Baselines

The following examples serve as baselines. In the first part, we assume the general framework defined previously, in which the investor is interested in risk minimization. In the second part, the investor wants to maximize its return in the presence of transaction costs.

No transaction costs

The state space of the trading environment consists of the monthly closing prices of $N = 4$ DJI stocks, denoted by the price vector p_t and the covariance matrix of stock returns Σ_t. Therefore, the state is $s_t = [p_t \quad \Sigma_t]$, which has continuous variables and is of dimension $N + N \times N$.

The action space is also formed by continuous variables (weights), such that $a_t \in [0, 1]^N$ represents the weights of each stock in the portfolio. We choose to impose the condition that no short positions are allowed. Therefore, we must normalize the raw weights obtained from policy π_θ in order to respect the constraint of nonnegative portfolio weights summing to one. Hence, we work with normalized actions $\bar{a}_t = [\bar{a}_t^{(1)} \cdots \bar{a}_t^{(N)}]$, where the normalization is done using the following transformation on raw weights a_t:

$$\bar{a}_t^{(j)} = \frac{a_t^{(j)}}{\sum_{i=1}^{N} a_t^{(i)}} \quad \text{for } j = 1, \ldots, N; t = 0, \ldots, T - 1$$

The portfolio is initialized to be equally weighted, that is, at period (month) $t = 0$, the weights are $a_0 = \bar{a}_0 = [1/N \cdots 1/N]$.

In this example, we assume an investor whose goal is to minimize portfolio risk over time. A natural definition of instantaneous MDP reward would be the negative of the portfolio estimated variance resulting from decision $\bar{a}_{t+1}$ such that

$$\begin{aligned} g_{t+1} &= -\bar{a}_t^\top \Sigma_t \bar{a}_t \\ \Longrightarrow G(\tau) &= -\sum_{t=0}^{T-1} \bar{a}_t^\top \Sigma_t \bar{a}_t \end{aligned}$$

where Σ_t is the covariance matrix of monthly returns estimated from daily returns observed during the past year, i.e., daily returns from period $t - 12$ to t.

With transaction costs

An alternative to the problem above is to consider an investor who wants to maximize its return in the presence of a commission fee that must be paid for each transaction. Transaction costs will be defined as a certain percentage over the transaction value, with the total fee at time t, given by $\psi(u_t)$, a function of trades u_t. Moreover, we assume that in addition to N DJI stocks, the investment portfolio includes a risk-free cash account earning, for simplicity, a constant interest rate of $r_f \geq 0$ per period. As before, the action vector represents target allocations with the slight modification that it is now of dimension $N+1$ such that $a_t \in [0,1]^{N+1}$. We modify the state vector to include the price vector along with some technical indicators computed from the stock price data, namely, the moving average convergence/divergence (MACD), Bollinger bands, relative strength index (RSI), commodity channel index (CCI), directional index (DX), and simple moving average (SMA). Hence, the state variables remain continuous. At each time step t, we define the state matrix as $s_t = [p_t \quad Tech_t]$, where p_t is the vector of stocks' closing prices and $Tech_t$ is the matrix of chosen technical indicators. Consequently, the state matrix at each time step is a matrix of dimension $N \times (1 + \text{number of technical indicators})$.

At the beginning of period $t = 0$, the agent is assumed to have all of its initial capital, W_0, invested in the risk-free asset, which implies deterministic initial actions $\bar{a}_0 = [1 \quad 0 \quad \cdots \quad 0]$. The investor then waits until the end of the period, such that over the period $t = 0$, it accumulates a riskless rate r_f on its total capital. The accumulated wealth becomes $W_1' = W_0(1 + r_f)$, while the adjusted weight vector stays the same at the end of the first time period: $\bar{a}_1' = [1 \quad 0 \quad \cdots \quad 0]$. At the same time, the investor observes stock closing prices p_0^{close} and must select an optimal allocation for the next period, which is represented by vector $\bar{a}_1$. Because $\bar{a}_1$ represents the new optimal allocation, the agent must rebalance its portfolio and trade a portion $u_1 = \bar{a}_1 - \bar{a}_1'$ of its current capital. This will imply transaction costs of $\delta_j^+ \geq 0$ and $\delta_j^- \geq 0$, $j = 1, \ldots, N$, for buying and selling stocks, respectively. Note that we define the transaction costs as a percentage of the amount traded.

It follows that at the beginning of any period $t = 1, \ldots, T-1$, the capital is allocated according to $\bar{a}_t = [\bar{a}_t^{(0)} \quad \bar{a}_t^{(1)} \quad \cdots \quad \bar{a}_t^{(N)}]$.

The agent waits until the end of t to observe the stocks' closing prices. This information enables us to define the vector of gross returns during the period $t = 1, \ldots, T-1$ as

$$1 + r_t = \left[(1 + r_f) \quad (1 + r_t^{(1)}) \quad \cdots \quad (1 + r_t^{(N)})\right]$$

Consequently, the total wealth at the beginning of period t accumulates to $W'_{t+1} = W_t(\bar{a}_t \cdot (1 + r_t))$. Wealth evolution can also be expressed in terms of adjusted weights, as follows:

$$\bar{a}'_{t+1} = \frac{(1 + r_t) \circ \bar{a}_t}{(1 + r_t) \cdot \bar{a}_t}$$

In the equation above, we have used "∘" to denote the element-wise product between the vector of gross returns and the vector of target allocations. After observing stock price data, the agent chooses a new allocation vector $\bar{a}_{t+1}$ and adjusts its portfolio weights by trading $u_{t+1} = \bar{a}_{t+1} - \bar{a}'_{t+1}$ fractions of current capital. If $u^+_{t+1} \geq 0$ and $u^-_{t+1} \leq 0$ are vectors of buying and selling trades, the investor incurs total transaction costs of $\psi(u_{t+1}) = \delta^+ \cdot u^+_{t+1} - \delta^- \cdot u^-_{t+1}$, expressed as a fraction of wealth. Wealth at the beginning of period $t+1$ is the accumulated wealth net of transaction costs:

$$W_{t+1} = W'_{t+1}(1 - \psi(u_{t+1})) = W_t(\bar{a}_t \cdot (1 + r_t))(1 - \psi(u_{t+1}))$$

For clarity, the process of wealth evolution is illustrated in Figure 4.

Note that for this alternative problem definition, the vector of closing prices, p^{close}_{t-1}, is included in the state matrix at the beginning of period t. Each subsequent value of wealth can be computed as a

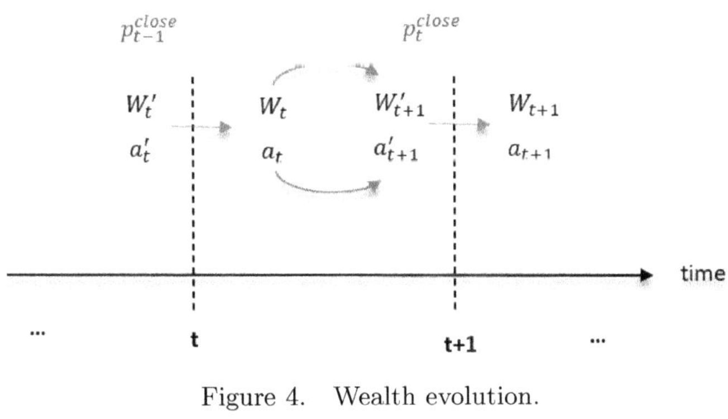

Figure 4. Wealth evolution.

product of the previous amount of capital and the gross return, net of fees. The terminal value of wealth can thus be computed using

$$\begin{aligned} W_T &= W_{T-1}\bar{a}_{T-1}(1+r_{T-1})(1-\psi(u_T)) \\ &= W_0 \prod_{t=0}^{T-1} \bar{a}_t \cdot (1+r_t)(1-\psi(u_{t+1})) \end{aligned}$$

with $1+r_0 = 1+r_f$ and initial allocation $\bar{a}_0$ as before. Considering transaction costs, the one-step MDP reward is redefined as

$$G(\tau) = \log\left(\frac{W_T}{W_0}\right) = \sum_{t=0}^{T-1} \log\left(\bar{a}_t(1+r_t)(1-\psi(u_{t+1}))\right) = \sum_{t=0}^{T-1} g_{t+1}$$

Although we have defined actions as portfolio weights, it is possible to use an alternative definition and set stock trades (changes in the asset positions) as actions. Thus, we invite you to look at Appendix C for a detailed description of this alternative specification.

Example 2: Risk-averse investors

For risk-averse investors, the degree of risk aversion varies. Hence, in addition to the risk measure, we must consider a coefficient λ that measures the degree to which an investor is concerned about taking risky decisions. In this example, our agent will want to achieve both: maximized capital and minimized portfolio risk. As before, we define the risk measure as the volatility of portfolio returns. Most of the definitions are retained from Example 1, and we only modify the reward function.

The state matrix includes the covariance matrix of all assets (including uncorrelated risk-free assets) and the stock price information such that $s_t = [p_t \quad Tech_t \quad \Sigma_t]$ can be placed in a matrix of dimension $N \times (\text{nb of technical indicators} + 1) + (N+1) \times (N+1)$. Recall that at the beginning of period t, the investment portfolio is constructed using allocation $\bar{a}_t$. At the end of period t, the agent observes the stock price data, chooses a new optimal allocation $\bar{a}_{t+1}$, and adjusts its portfolio weights by trading $u_{t+1} = \bar{a}_{t+1} - \bar{a}'_{t+1}$ fractions of current capital. We have also defined total transaction costs as $\psi(u_{t+1}) = \delta^+ \cdot u^+_{t+1} - \delta^- \cdot u^-_{t+1}$, expressed as a fraction of wealth.

The next-step total wealth is calculated using

$$W_{t+1} = W'_{t+1}(1 - \psi(u_{t+1})) = W_t(\bar{a}_t \cdot (1 + r_t))(1 - \psi(u_{t+1}))$$

Since we are concerned about risk aversion, we must penalize a risk-averse agent for taking risky decisions, i.e., for investing significant amounts in the most volatile stocks. Moreover, we should not forget about portfolio returns, R_t, when training our agent. To include both risk and return measures in our model, we use the quadratic utility function. Precisely, if the risk aversion coefficient is λ, the step reward is given by

$$g_{t+1} = \log\left(1 + R_t - \lambda \bar{a}_t^{\top} \Sigma_t \bar{a}_t\right)$$

Example 3: Utility optimization

A more general investment management problem that is relevant not only for financial companies or investors but also for any corporation or individual considers both investment and consumption decisions. Consumption decisions refer to how much money to spend on one's needs or pleasures on a periodic basis. On the one hand, by consuming a certain amount of money, an individual gains satisfaction (i.e., utility), where the level of "happiness" received varies from one person to another. On the other hand, investment decisions may produce large returns and increase total wealth so that one can consume larger amounts in the future. Eventually, the goal of an agent is to maximize its total utility of consumption over a finite time period by making optimal investment and spending decisions. In the real world, each person/corporation has different external sources of constant or uncertain income and different spending needs, which makes the general problem of asset allocation and consumption an extremely complex MDP. Consequently, we first describe a simplified version of the problem and, later on, introduce some realistic complexities.

We consider an individual who has a remaining lifetime of T time period. This individual will not receive any income during that time other than money extracted from the investment portfolio. The investment portfolio consists of N stocks and one riskless asset. Moreover, the agent will not have any fixed payment requirements (e.g., mortgage, essential food, insurance) such that all of its consumption is optional (e.g., vacation, leisure activities) and can be any real nonnegative number. All of the capital extracted from the investment portfolio is immediately consumed, and since there are no other sources of income, no capital is added to the investment portfolio at any point in time.

The agent starts with a dollar amount of W_0 and wants to maximize its expected aggregate utility of consumption over the whole time horizon T. At any time $t \leq T$, we denote the amount spent on consumption by $c_t \geq 0$ and the portfolio's market value (or total wealth) by $W_t > 0$. The utility of consumption is given by the function $\mathcal{U} : \mathbb{R} \to \mathbb{R}$ such that by consuming c_t, an individual receives $\mathcal{U}(c_t)$ of satisfaction during period t. The utility function will typically include a parameter λ, standing for the risk-aversion coefficient. We denote the portfolio allocation vector at time t as a_t, where, as before, each constituent $a_t^{(j)}$ stands for the fraction of wealth allocated to asset $j = 0, 1, \ldots, N$. Note that both consumption c_t and allocation a_t are functions of time and wealth. At any time t, the agent must choose an optimal consumption amount and an optimal portfolio allocation. Thus, in the RL framework, we define the action at time t as a vector (c_t, a_t). Similarly to previous examples, the state will consist of current stock price information and the covariance matrix and will be defined by $s_t = [p_t \quad Tech_t \quad \Sigma_t]$. In addition, we include transaction costs defined as before by δ_j^+ and δ_j^- such that wealth evolution is

$$W_{t+1} = (W_t - c_t)\left(a_t(1 + r_t)\right)\left(1 - \psi(u_{t+1})\right)$$

In the above equation, $\psi(u_{t+1})$ stands for the total amount of transaction costs when trading a percentage u_{t+1} of wealth at time $t + 1$. Finally, the step reward is defined as

$$g_{t+1} = \begin{cases} \mathcal{U}(c_t) & \text{if } t < T - 1 \\ \mathcal{B}_T \cdot \mathcal{U}(W_T) & \text{if } t = T - 1 \end{cases}$$

where $\mathcal{B}_T$ is a very small number that is used here for technical reasons. In finance, this quantity is known as the bequest function.

3.2 Model architectures

We consider the two cases in Example 1 as well as the problem in Example 2. The first problem is variance minimization, further noted as ***MinVar*** example, the second problem is return maximization in the presence of transaction costs, further noted as ***MaxRet*** example, and the third problem combines the two baseline settings by aiming to maximize risk-adjusted return (quadratic utility) of a risk-averse investor in the presence of transaction costs, further noted as ***Mean-Var*** example. In our experiments, we started by approximating the optimal V-function and the optimal policy by two separate multi-layer perceptrons (MLPs) that are trained through backpropagation. MLPs are the most basic, fully connected neural networks that are composed of linear layers with corresponding activation functions. Each MLP consists of D input neurons, where D corresponds to the dimension of the state vector. For ***MinVar***, both networks have two linear layers with 24 hidden neurons and *tanh* activation functions. For the ***MaxRet*** and ***MeanVar*** examples, the network architecture is the same, but the number of hidden neurons is increased to 64. The actor MLP outputs a Gaussian distribution that approximates the optimal stochastic policy, while the critic MLP has one output neuron for the value function at a given state. All of the MLPs are trained with a learning rate of 0.0004 and an entropy coefficient for the loss calculation of 0.005. Note that the training period ranges from January 1, 2009, to August 31, 2018, while the trading/testing period starts on September 1, 2018, and ends on January 1, 2020.

For all examples, we have defined a specific environment following the OpenAI Gym's interface.[5] Recall that an environment has three key components, namely, the state space $\mathcal{S}$, the action space $\mathcal{A}$, and the time t reward function $g(s_t, a_t, s_{t+1})$. Moreover, we must specify the valid format of action and state parameters for each specific environment. In other words, we must specify whether spaces are continuous or discrete, indicate lower and upper bounds for possible action and state values, and define the dimensions of $\mathcal{A}$ and $\mathcal{S}$ spaces. For the state space, the dimension is determined by the size of the feature matrix $\mathcal{F}_t$ (risky stocks' information) and the size of other information arrays that are included in the state vector s_t, such as the covariance matrix of asset returns Σ_t. Similarly, if actions define portfolio target weights, the shape of the action space is equal to the

[5]See Appendix D.2.

number of assets considered. For the ***MinVar*** example, the portfolio is composed of $N = 4$ Dow Jones risky stocks, and the state matrix includes the monthly closing price vector and returns' covariance matrix. For the ***MaxRet*** example, the portfolio is composed of $N = 4$ Dow Jones stocks and one riskless asset with a constant annual rate of interest of $r_f = 1.00\%$. The ***MeanVar*** portfolio is also composed of one riskless and four risky assets and is held by a risk-averse investor whose risk aversion is $\lambda = 1.5$. Furthermore, in addition to Dow Jones stocks' closing prices, the feature matrix also includes $I = 4$ technical indicators: MACD, RSI, DX, and SMA. For clarity, key parameters that were used to define each environment are specified in Table 1. After the training and testing phases, we obtained the optimal actions and the resulting performance measures for each of the three models. In the plots that follow, we illustrate the optimal portfolio allocations for four randomly selected Dow Jones stocks: Cisco Systems Inc. (*CSCO*), IBM Common Stock (*IBM*), Travelers Companies Inc. (*TRV*), and Walmart Inc. (*WMT*). The monthly simple returns of these stocks over the combined training and trading period are shown in Figure 5.

Over the whole period (training plus trading period), represented in Figure 5, the *CSCO* earned the highest mean monthly return, followed by *TRV* and *WMT*, while the lowest return was earned by *IBM*. As for the risk, *CSCO* was the most volatile stock, followed

Table 1. Environment details.

Example	**MinVar**	**MaxRet**	**Risk Averse**
State	$[p_t \;\; \Sigma_t]$	$[p_t \;\; Tech_t \;\; \Sigma_t]$	$[p_t \;\; Tech_t \;\; \Sigma_t]$
State class	Continuous	Continuous	Continuous
State dimension	$\mathrm{N} + \mathrm{N} \times \mathrm{N}$	$\mathrm{N} + (\mathrm{I} \times \mathrm{N}) + (\mathrm{N} + 1) \times (\mathrm{N} + 1)$	$\mathrm{N} + (\mathrm{I} \times \mathrm{N}) + (\mathrm{N} + 1) \times (\mathrm{N} + 1)$
Action space	$[0, 1]$	$[0, 1]$	$[0, 1]$
Action class	Continuous	Continuous	Continuous
Actions dimension	N	N + 1	N + 1
Initial capital ($)	$1M$	$1M$	$1M$
Fees per period (%)	None	$\delta^+ = 0.03$ $\delta^- = 0.02$	$\delta^+ = 0.03$ $\delta^- = 0.02$
Riskless rate (%)*	None	1.0	1.0
Risk aversion	None	None	1.5

Note: *Annualized.

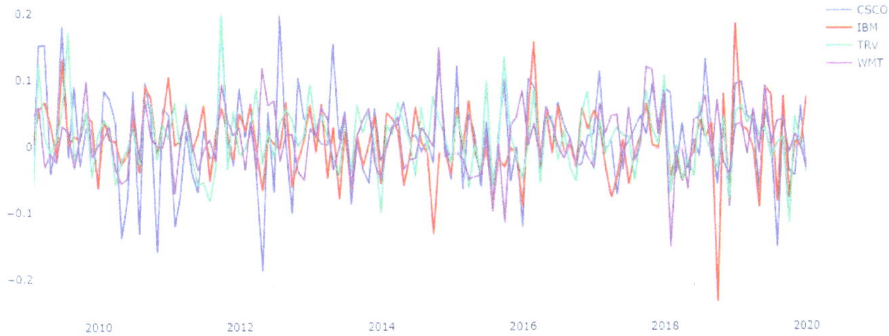

Figure 5. Stocks monthly returns.

Table 2. Stocks annual returns and volatility: Trading period.

Ticker	CSCO	IBM	TRV	WMT
Annualized mean daily return (%)	2.04	−3.53	5.84	19.76
Annualized volatility (%)	25.70	35.22	17.50	13.00

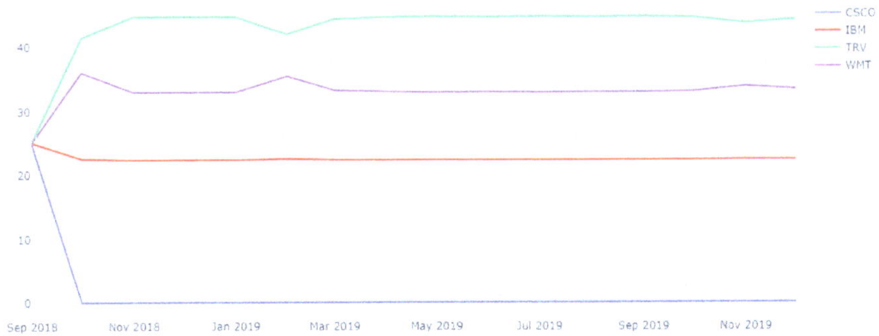

Figure 6. Optimal allocation: MinVar.

by (*IBM*) and (*TRV*), while (*WMT*) was the least volatile. For the trading period, annualized mean returns and annualized volatility of returns are given in Table 2.

The resulting optimal portfolio allocations (in percentage units) for the testing period are illustrated in Figures 6–8 for the examples ***MinVar***, ***MaxRet***, and ***MeanVar***, respectively.

Note that in Figure 8, the CSCO and TRV allocation curves are exactly the same. For clarity, we summarize the mean target weights for each of the baseline models in Table 2. Moreover, we compare

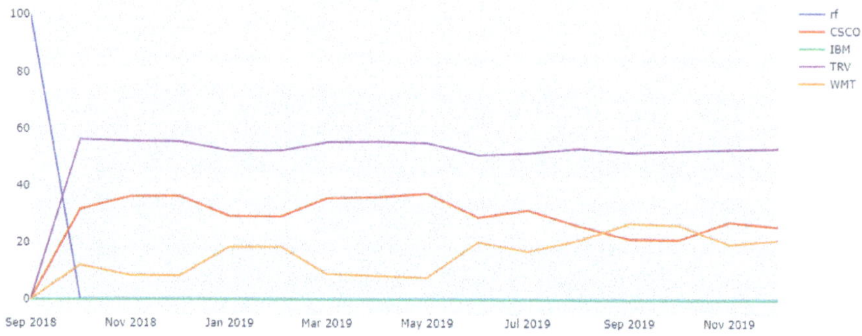

Figure 7. Optimal allocation: MaxRet.

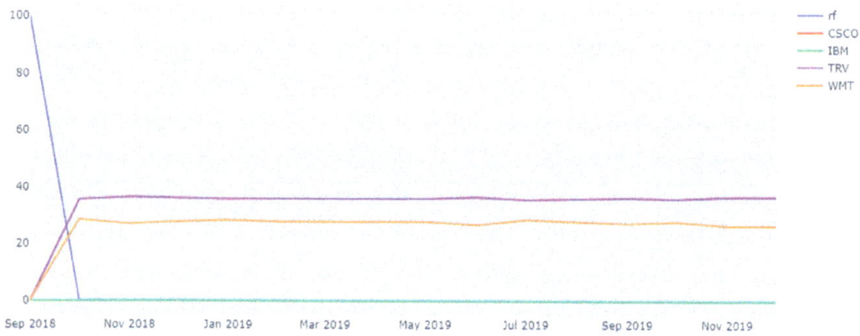

Figure 8. Optimal allocation: MeanVar.

the A2C MinVar model allocations to the analytical solution for the minimum variance portfolio.

By calculating the annualized return and volatility of each of the above A2C strategies as well as the terminal wealth at the end of the trading period, we have obtained the results listed in Table 3.

While the ***MinVar*** model obtains the highest annual return, the ***MeanVar*** agent obtains the best risk-adjusted return and the highest terminal wealth amount (Table 4). Moreover, note that transaction costs were taken into account for the last 2 models, which shows that the ***MeanVar*** model achieved a similar annual return as the ***MinVar*** model, even in the presence of trading fees. Indeed, we see that in Figure 8, there is little or no variation in allocation percentage over time, meaning that the agent minimized the number of transactions and thus minimized transaction costs. This is opposed to Figure 7, where curves vary over the trading period, which implies more transactions, higher fees, and lower net returns.

Table 3. Target allocation.

Asset	Risk-Free	CSCO	IBM	TRV	WMT
MinVar solution (%)	—	1.56	22.51	43.00	32.92
MinVar analytical solution (%)	—	5.40	15.96	45.08	33.56
MaxRet solution (%)	6.25	28.37	0.00	50.20	15.17
MeanVar solution (%)	6.25	33.86	0.00	33.86	26.04

Table 4. Performance summary.

	Mean Return*	Volatility*	Terminal Wealth
MinVar portfolio	8.4846%	15.2376%	1.096 M
MaxRet portfolio	7.5299%	15.8635%	1.082 M
MeanVar portfolio	8.4785%	15.1463%	1.097 M

Note: *Annualized.

Another observation is that, while the ***MinVar*** agent invested almost 16% in *IBM*, which has the highest volatility and negative mean return over the trading period, the ***MaxRet*** and ***MeanVar*** agents did not allocate any portion of their wealth to the *IBM* stock. In addition, baseline models allocated around 40–50% of total wealth to *TRV*, which is the second-best stock in terms of risk–reward. This is different from the ***MeanVar*** model, which allocated approximately one-third to both *TRV* and *CSCO*. Finally, in Figure 9, we illustrate the cumulative returns obtained by each model and compare them to those of the DJI. Note that all the A2C strategies outperformed the DJI on a cumulative return basis during the testing period.

Acknowledgments

The first author, René Garcia, thanks the Mitacs Accelerate Program (FR75538), the NSERC (RGPIN-2018-04891), the SSHRC (Insight 435-2019-1216) and the FQRSC (2020-SE2-269954) research grant agencies for their financial support as well as the ANR for support under the Investissements d'Avenir program, grant ANR-17-EURE-0010 and the project ANR-17-CE03-0010 – LONGTERMISM: Evaluation des investissements ultra-longs. He is a research Fellow of CIRANO and CIREQ.

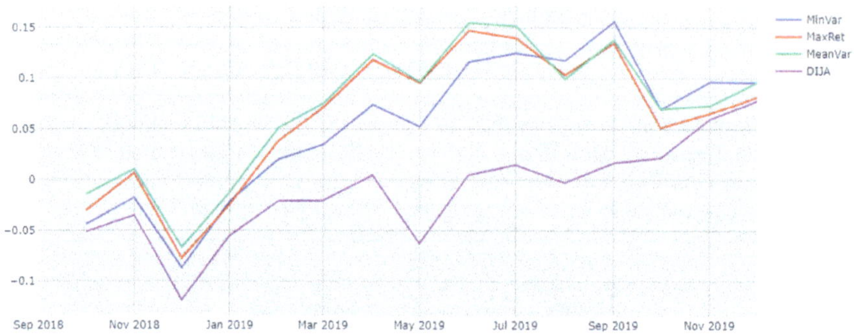

Figure 9. Cumulative returns.

Appendix A Mathematical Proofs

A.1 Policy gradient theorem

To derive the policy gradient theorem equation, we begin by setting the gradient $\nabla_\theta \mathbb{E}[g_1] = 0$ to zero since the first action, a_0, does not depend on π_θ. Using the definition of $J(\pi_\theta)$ from Section 1.4 and differentiating leads to the following equation:

$$\begin{aligned}\nabla_\theta J(\pi_\theta) = \nabla_\theta \mathbb{E}_{\pi_\theta}\left[G(\tau)\right] &= \sum_{t=1}^{T-1} \gamma^t \nabla_\theta \mathbb{E}_{\pi_\theta}\left[g_{t+1}\right] \\ &= \sum_{t=1}^{T-1} \gamma^t \sum_{\tau_{0,t}} \mathbb{E}[g_{t+1}|s_t, a_t] \nabla_\theta P_{\pi_\theta}(\tau_{0,t})\end{aligned}$$

where

$$\begin{aligned}\nabla_\theta P_{\pi_\theta}(\tau_{0,t}) &= \prod_{k=1}^{t} p(s_{k+1}|s_k, a_k) \nabla_\theta \left(\prod_{k=1}^{t} \pi_\theta(a_k|s_k) \right) \\ &= \prod_{k=1}^{t} p(s_{k+1}|s_k, a_k) \left(\sum_{s=1}^{t} \nabla_\theta \pi_\theta(a_s|s_s) \prod_{k=1, k\neq s}^{t} \pi_\theta(a_k|s_k) \right)\end{aligned}$$

$$= \prod_{k=1}^{t} p(s_{k+1}|s_k, a_k) \left(\sum_{s=1}^{t} \frac{\nabla_\theta \pi_\theta(a_s|s_s)}{\pi_\theta(a_s|s_s)} \prod_{k=1}^{t} \pi_\theta(a_k|s_k) \right)$$

$$\text{by} \times \frac{\pi_\theta(a_s|s_s)}{\pi_\theta(a_s|s_s)}$$

$$= \prod_{k=1}^{t} p(s_{k+1}|s_k, a_k) \pi_\theta(a_k|s_k) \sum_{s=1}^{t} \nabla_\theta \log \pi_\theta(a_s|s_s)$$

This implies that

$$\begin{aligned}
\nabla_\theta J(\pi_\theta) &= \sum_{t=1}^{T-1} \gamma^t \left(\sum_{s_1,a_1} \cdots \sum_{s_t,a_t} \mathbb{E}_g[g_{t+1}|s_t, a_t] \right. \\
&\quad \left. \times \prod_{k=1}^{t} p(s_{k+1}|s_k, a_k) \pi_\theta(a_k|s_k) \right) \sum_{s=1}^{t} \nabla_\theta \log \pi_\theta(a_s|s_s) \\
&= \sum_{t=1}^{T-1} \gamma^t \mathbb{E}_{\pi_\theta} \left[g_{t+1} \sum_{s=1}^{t} \nabla_\theta \log \pi_\theta(a_s|s_s) \right] \\
&= \mathbb{E}_{\pi_\theta} \left[\sum_{s=1}^{T-1} \sum_{t=s}^{T-1} \gamma^t g_{t+1} \nabla_\theta \log \pi_\theta(a_s|s_s) \right] \\
&= \mathbb{E}_{\pi_\theta} \left[\sum_{s=1}^{T-1} \nabla_\theta \log \pi_\theta(a_s|s_s) G(\tau_{s,T}) \right] \\
&= \sum_{s=1}^{T-1} \mathbb{E}_{\tau_{0,s}} \left[\nabla_\theta \log \pi_\theta(a_s|s_s) \mathbb{E}_{\tau_{s+1,T}} [G(\tau_{s,T})|s_s, a_s] \right] \\
&= \sum_{s=1}^{T-1} \mathbb{E}_{\tau_{0,s}} \left[\nabla_\theta \log \pi_\theta(a_s|s_s) Q^{\pi_\theta}(s_s, a_s) \right] \\
&= \mathbb{E}_{\tau \sim \pi_\theta} \left[\sum_{s=1}^{T-1} \nabla_\theta \log \pi_\theta(a_s|s_s) Q^{\pi_\theta}(s_s, a_s) \right] \\
&\sim \frac{1}{|\mathcal{D}|} \sum_{\tau \in \mathcal{D}} \sum_{s=1}^{T-1} \nabla_\theta \log \pi_\theta(a_s|s_s) Q^{\pi_\theta}(s_s, a_s)
\end{aligned}$$

A.2 Multi-step TD error

The n-step TD error is, by definition, the sum of the one step TD errors discounted by γ. It follows that

$$\begin{aligned}\hat{\delta}_t^{(n)} &= \sum_{s=0}^{n-1} \gamma^s \hat{\delta}_{t+s} \\ &= \sum_{s=0}^{n-1} \gamma^s \left(g_{t+s+1} + \gamma V_\nu(s_{t+s+1}) - V_\nu(s_{t+s})\right) \\ &= \sum_{s=0}^{n-1} \gamma^s g_{t+s+1} + \gamma^n V_\nu(s_{t+n}) - V_\nu(s_t) \\ &= \sum_{k=t}^{t+n-1} \gamma^{k-t} g_{k+1} + \gamma^n V_\nu(s_{t+n}) - V_\nu(s_t)\end{aligned}$$

Appendix B Deep Neural Networks

A neural network is defined by a series of functional transformations, i.e., nonlinear compositions of functions of the form $f \circ g \circ h(x)$, where $x \in \mathbb{R}^d$ is a d-dimensional input to the network. Such a structure is used to approximate functions of increasing complexity that will be able to map input onto output.

To understand neural networks, we begin with linear function approximations. A linear approximator consists of weights $\mathbf{W} \in \mathbb{R}^{n \times d}$ and a vector of bias $\mathbf{b} \in \mathbb{R}^n$. To simplify notation, we define $\theta = [\mathbf{W}, \mathbf{b}]$ to represent both weights and bias. A linear approximator of a function $f(x)$ is obtained by an affine transformation of the input such that

$$f(x) \approx \hat{f}(x; \theta) = \theta^\top x$$

The challenge is to find the values of parameters θ that will give the best estimator $\hat{f}$ of the target function f. In the simple, linear approximation case, the components of θ are found in the same way as regression coefficients. In other words, we find θ^* that minimizes the mean squared error loss function between $f(x)$ and $\hat{f}(x; \theta)$.

Although linear models are useful, they have the downside of being restricted to the linear family of functions and thus lack the complexity to accurately understand complicated interactions between input variables. In order to increase the complexity of linear models, we introduce *at least* one nonlinear function into the linear structure and consequently obtain a DNN. The construction of a neural network begins with composing together different functions that will represent the **layers** of the network. The simplest DNN is composed of an input layer, followed by a **hidden** layer, and, finally, an output layer. Given an input vector $\boldsymbol{x}$ and denoting by $h(\cdot)$ and $\sigma(\cdot)$ the hidden and output layers, respectively, the basic DNN has the following form:

$$f_\theta(\boldsymbol{x}) = \boldsymbol{\sigma}\left(\theta^{(2)}\boldsymbol{h}(\theta^{(1)}\boldsymbol{x})\right)$$

The input layer is the first layer to receive all the information contained in the input $\boldsymbol{x}$ and pass it on to the successor hidden layers. Each neuron in the input layer is equal to the input feature/characteristic (e.g., asset price and/or asset type). The output layer gives the final output by transforming the output of the last hidden layer into the desired output type (e.g., a probability, category, or real-valued number). Hidden layers are nonlinear functions that lie between the input and output layers. Hidden layers can be of any dimension (i.e., they can have any number of neurons).

Activation functions are used to add nonlinearity and restrict the linear function output to a certain limit. Popular choices of activation functions are listed as follows:

- **Rectified linear unit (ReLU)**: $h(x) = \max\{0, x\}$.
- **Smooth ReLU**: $h(x) = \log(1 + e^x)$.
- **Softmax (output activation)**: $\sigma(x_j) = \dfrac{\exp(x_j)}{\sum_i \exp(x_i)}$, which limits the output to the range of 0–1. Softmax is generally used when variables are categorical and we want to obtain their probability as output of a neural network.

To find the optimal parameters θ of a neural network, the simplest approach is to, given an input x, minimize the error (loss) between the value predicted by the DNN, $f_\theta(\boldsymbol{x})$, and the true/target value associated with the given input, $f(x)$. Because we are dealing with expectations and the distribution of data is typically unknown, empirical risk, $\hat{R}(\theta)$, is used as an approximation to the true loss, $L(x, f_\theta(x), f(x))$. The empirical risk is defined as

$$\hat{R}(\theta) = \frac{1}{|\mathcal{D}|} \sum_{i=1}^{|\mathcal{D}|} L(x_i, f_\theta(x_i), f(x_i))$$

where $\mathcal{D}$ is the dataset used during learning and $|\mathcal{D}|$ is the size of that dataset. Thus, the minimization of loss will be performed through the minimization of the empirical risk, which in turn will be performed using gradient descent. Finally, since the DNN, and thus the loss function, is a composition of functions, taking the gradient of the loss will involve the application of the chain rule and a concept called backpropagation. For weight initialization, see Dellinger (2019). For mathematical details on the computation of gradient descent and associated concepts, please refer to Mnih *et al.* (2016) and https://www.deeplearningbook.org/.

Appendix C Extensions of Financial Applications

C.1 Example 1

The portfolio is assumed to be self-financing in that all rebalancing of stock positions is financed from the cash account. At period t, the cash position is denoted b_t. We define as a vector h_t the dollar positions in each asset at the beginning of period t. Since short sales are not allowed, we must have $h_t^{(j)} \geq 0$ for all assets $j = 1, \ldots, N$. The state matrix includes the cash account balance, the stock positions, and the stock price data, i.e., it is defined as $s_t = [b_t \quad h_t \quad p_t \quad Tech_t]$.

Keeping the action space continuous, the vector $a_t = [a_t^{(1)} \cdots a_t^{(N)}]$ represents fractional trades to be made in period t. We denote by a_t^+ and a_t^- positive and negative trades, with the components $a_{t,j}^+ = \max(a_t^{(j)}, 0) > 0$ and $a_{t,j}^- = \min(a_t^{(j)}, 0) < 0$ standing for the fractions of the total wealth of asset j bought and sold, respectively. To simplify further calculations, we define a trade vector u_t to denote the dollar amount traded in period t. The trade vector u_t can be initially computed using $u_t = W_t \circ a_t$, where a_t is the raw output from the policy network, W_t is the total investor's wealth at the beginning of period t and $\circ$ denotes the element-wise product. Given the current state vector, the total wealth at t is calculated as the sum of the risky portfolio value and the cash account value: $W_t = h_t + b_t$. Note that, because we cannot sell more shares than we own, we must have

$$h_t + u_t \geq 0$$

or

$$u_t = \max(W_t \circ a_t, -h_t)$$

To compute the total transaction costs corresponding to the trading decision u_t, define by $\delta_j^+ \geq 0$ and $\delta_j^- \geq 0$ the proportional fees for buying and selling stock j, respectively. In addition, denote by $u_{t,j}^+ > 0$ and $u_{t,j}^- < 0$ the positive and negative trades for asset j. With this notation, the total value of transaction costs is obtained by

$$\psi(u_t) = \delta^+ \cdot u_t^+ - \delta^- \cdot u_t^- = \sum_{j=1}^{N} \left(\delta_j^+ u_{t,j}^+ - \delta_j^- u_{t,j}^- \right)$$

Immediately after trades, the asset holdings are $h_t^+ = h_t + u_t$ and the next period holdings are computed through $h_{t+1} = (1 + r_t) \circ h_t^+$. Using the fact that the portfolio is self-financing, we compute the next-step total wealth according to

$$\begin{aligned} W_{t+1} &= P_{t+1} + b_{t+1} \\ &= \mathbb{I}^\top h_{t+1} + b_{t+1} \\ &= (1 + r_t)^\top (h_t + u_t) + (b_t - \mathbb{I}^\top u_t - \psi(u_t))(1 + r_f) \\ \text{subject to} \quad & b_t - \mathbb{I}^\top u_t - \psi(u_t) \geq 0 \end{aligned}$$

We initialize the cash balance to be equal to the investor's initial capital, $b_0 = W_0$, implying that at time $t = 0$, the holdings are zero for all assets: $h_t^{(j)} = 0 \quad \forall j = 1, \ldots, N$. Because the objective is to maximize the portfolio value or return over the investment horizon, the terminal holdings are set to be zero, $h_T = 0$, signifying that all stock is converted to cash and $W_T = b_T$. Note that, given the action space and transaction fees, it is possible that the agent runs out of cash, i.e., $b_t - \mathbb{I}^\top u_t - \psi(u_t) < 0$. If a cash shortage occurs, we can either break the training episode and penalize the agent or simply not trade anything and continue the training until we have enough cash on hand. In both cases, we set the instantaneous reward equal to the daily profit made, $g_{t+1} = W_{t+1} - W_t$.

C.2 Example 2

We begin with the baseline example in the absence of transaction costs in order to define the baseline reward. Most of the definitions, such as state, actions, and trade vectors, are kept from Example 1 in Appendix C.1, and we only modify the reward function. The next-step total wealth obtained from the selected trade u_t in excess of the risk-free growth is given by

$$\begin{aligned}\Delta W_t &= W_{t+1} - (1 + r_f)W_t \\ &= (1 + r_t)^\top (h_t + u_t) + (b_t - \mathbb{I}^\top u_t)(1 + r_f) - (1 + r_f)(\mathbb{I}^\top h_t + b_t) \\ &= (r_t - r_f)^\top (h_t + u_t)\end{aligned}$$

The above result allows us to define the baseline component of the one-step reward:

$$g_{t+1}^{(0)} = \Delta W_t = (r_t - r_f)^\top (h_t + u_t)$$

Because in RL, we maximize the expected value of total rewards, the expected baseline reward, given the state-action pair, is

$$\mathbb{E}[g_{t+1}^{(0)} | s_t, u_t] = (\mathbb{E}[r_t] - r_f)^\top (h_t + u_t)$$

The expectation of stock returns, $\mathbb{E}[r_t]$, can be computed using past historical returns over a look-back period of one year (12 months or 252 days) from time t. Similarly, we can compute the covariance matrix of stock returns, Σ_t, that will be useful in the definition of the risk penalty. This risk penalty, or the second component of the one-step reward, is given by

$$g_{t+1}^{(\text{risk})} = -\lambda \mathbb{VAR}\left(g_{t+1}^{(0)} | s_t, u_t\right) = -\lambda (h_t + u_t)^\top \Sigma_t (h_t + u_t)$$

Finally, the last component of the reward function is the transaction cost penalty, $g_{t+1}^{(\text{tc})} = -\psi(u_t)$. Combining all three reward/penalty components, we obtain that the expected instantaneous reward is

$$\mathbb{E}[g_{t+1} | s_t, u_t] = \mathbb{E}[g_{t+1}^{(0)} | s_t, u_t] + g_{t+1}^{(\text{risk})} + g_{t+1}^{(\text{tc})}$$

Appendix D Coding and FinRL Library

FinRL is a helpful and flexible tool for easier implementation of RL methods in finance. It is an open source framework developed by *AI4 Finance LLC* that covers the majority of DRL concepts defined in the previous sections. Particularly, users can design their own RL environments, customize algorithms and DNN structures, and analyze algorithms' performances. FinRL makes use of *Yahoo Finance* to download all the necessary stock data and *Stable Baselines3* to train and test algorithms, such as A2C and PPO. In this section, we provide a quick guide on how to use these libraries, while a more detailed description of FinRL and Stable Baselines3 can be found at https://finrl.readthedocs.io/en/latest/index.html and https://stable-baselines3.readthedocs.io/en/master/index.html, respectively.

D.1 Data

As has been mentioned, the data are downloaded through the `yfinance` Python package. To do so, we must specify the start and end dates and tickers (a list of stocks' symbols) to be passed to the `download_data` function of the `YahooFinanceProcessor` class. If we want to access the tickers of stocks that are constituents of specific indices, such as the *S&P*500 or *DJI*, we can use the `pytickersymbols` Python package. After the price data are downloaded, we must clean the data and, if required, add technical indicators or other stock features. If daily price data were retrieved, the cleaning process as well as the stock feature addition could be done with the incorporated `FeatureEngineer` class. Before proceeding to the DRL step, the preprocessed data must be divided into the training and testing sets. The splitting is done by defining two mutually exclusive time periods (with different starting and ending dates): one for training and the other for testing. Note that, typically, the training data make up more than 70% of the whole stock dataset. In our examples, the training period is from January 1, 2009, to June 30, 2020, while the testing period is from July 1, 2020, to September 2, 2021. Note that, because there is no trading during weekends and holidays, one year consists of approximately 252 entries of daily stock price information instead of 365. Given these points, we can proceed to the environment definition.

D.2 Environment

Modeling the environment of a specific problem is a key task in RL. An environment contains all the necessary functionality for running and training the agent. In other words, it allows the agent to explore the processed data and translate the retrieved information into an MDP problem. The FinRL library requires that we define the environment by strictly following the OpenAI Gym's interface (please see https://www.gymlibrary.ml/ for more details). It must include, at minimum, the following methods:

- `init` : defines the state and action spaces as well as constant variables which will be used in the environment class functions (e.g., data, initial capital, transaction costs). The state space must be represented by the `observation_space` attribute, which defines the structure and the acceptable range of values that a state of the environment can take. Similarly, the `action_space` attribute describes the legitimate actions that can be applied to the environment. Among the different categories of spaces available, the two classes that will be used for our examples are `Box` and `Dict` spaces. States or actions that are represented by a `Box` space take on real values and can vary in shape. The shape of a space corresponds to its dimension, that is, if the action space $\mathcal{A}$ is continuous and represents the weights of a long-only portfolio composed of N stocks, the shape of $\mathcal{A}$ will be `(N,)`. Comparatively, states or actions that are represented by a `Dict` space are also real-valued but can represent compound spaces, i.e., spaces that are composed of different sub-spaces. As an example, consider a portfolio of N stocks and one risk-free asset. Assume that the state s_t is composed of past portfolio allocation a_{t-1} and the stock features matrix $\mathcal{F}_t$, with I different technical indicators for N stocks. The `observation_space` can be defined as a dictionary of two `Box` spaces: a space of shape `(N+1,)` to represent past actions, and a space of shape `(I,N)` to represent the stock feature matrix. Note that in the case of a `Dict` space, the policy will be a *multi-input* policy since its input will be a state composed of multiple spaces.
- `reset` : resets the environment to its initial state and returns that initial state.
- `step` : given an action as an input, it applies that action to the environment and makes the agent transition to a new state.

The function must return the new state, the instantaneous numerical reward, and a boolean indicator of whether the agent has reached the terminal state. The output can also include a dictionary containing additional information that may be useful in debugging.

- `save_asset_memory` : keeps in memory the portfolio information which could be accessed during the testing stage. Such information is stored in a data frame and may include portfolio returns, the value of wealth, and rewards over the complete investment horizon.
- `save_action_memory` : similar to `save_asset_memory` but records optimal actions that were made at every time step during the testing phase.

D.3 DRL

Having established a well-defined environment, we can proceed with the RL process. The agent layer in FinRL, which is defined by the `DRLAgent(environment)` method, is responsible for interacting with the defined environment. When the environment with its key arguments is passed to the DRL agent, we must select a specific algorithm (e.g., A2C) and choose corresponding hyperparameters (e.g., number of episodes, learning rate, network architectures). Algorithm-specific hyperparameters are passed in a dictionary which specifies some or all of the following arguments:

- `model_name` : to specify the Stable Baselines3 algorithm to implement; for Algorithm 1, the model name is set to "a2c."
- `policy` : to specify the policy model to use. Readily available specifications include "MlpPolicy," "CnnPolicy," and "CnnLstmPolicy"; however, it is possible to define a customized policy network, which must follow the Stable Baselines3 interface. The default value is "MlpPolicy."
- `gamma` : to specify the discount factor for instantaneous rewards; the default value is 0.99.
- `n_steps` : to specify the number of steps to run per update; the default value is 5.
- `vf_coef` : to specify the value function coefficient when calculating the total loss; the default value is 0.25.

- `ent_coef` : to specify the entropy function coefficient when calculating the loss; the default value is 0.01.
- `learning_rate` : to specify the learning rate used for both the value and policy functions; the default value is 0.0007.
- `max_grad_norm` : to specify the maximum bound for the gradient norm, which is used in gradient clipping in order to limit extremely large parameter updates; the default value is 0.5.
- `policy_kwargs` : arguments to be passed for the network creation, including a list `net_arch` , which specifies the value and policy network architectures, and `act_fun` , an activation function to use in the neural network; the default values are `net_arch=[dict(pi=[64, 64], vf=[64, 64])]` and `act_fun=torch.nn.tanh`. For a shared, three-layered network where each layer has 72 hidden units, we must set `net_arch=[72, 72, 72]`; for a fully separate network where the policy network has two layers of size 72 and the value network has three layers of size 64, we must set `net_arch=[dict(pi=[72, 72], vf=[64, 64, 64])])`.

The above arguments are passed to the `DRLAgent.get_ model()` method to define a specific model, which is, in turn, passed to the `DRLAgent.train_model(model, tb_log_name, total_ timesteps)` function in order to begin training. The argument `tb_log_name` specifies how to print information regarding the RL agent during the training phase and makes it possible to observe the evolution of loss functions, rewards, completed updates, etc. The `total_timesteps` argument specifies the total number of runs such that `total_timesteps = n_steps` $\times$ `number of updates`. Note that the obtained trained model, defined by `trained_a2c`, can be saved in some directory of choice, which allows us to access the model later on and apply it to different datasets. To save the model, simply choose a file path and run the `trained_a2c.save(path)` command. When you would want to access the trained model again without going through the training process, the `model_sb3_type.load(path)` command should be executed, where `model_sb3_type` refers to one of the Stable Baselines3 model types (A2C, PPO, DDPG, SAC, DQN, etc.).

Finally, using the test dataset, we run the `trained_a2c. predict()` command to sample optimal actions at each encountered state and the `environment.step()` command to make a transition to the next state. These commands are executed until the end of the testing time horizon. When the agent reaches the terminal state, we could obtain the portfolio information and the optimal actions over the whole testing period by calling the `save_asset_memory` and `save_action_memory` methods defined previously.

D.4 Comparison and plots

To plot the results, the package `plotly` is used. Since after testing we can access the optimal actions and specific portfolio information, we start by plotting optimal actions for different models using the `add_trace` command of `plotly.graph_objs.Figure()`. In all plots, the x-axis represents the testing dates, and the y-axis represents the numerical values of optimal actions or portfolio characteristics.

In addition, we could compare the performance of trained DRL strategies to benchmarks (such as the Dow Jones and S&P indices) or to classic portfolio strategies (such as the minimum variance and maximum Sharpe portfolios). An easy and quick way to obtain the performances of the latter strategies for the same data that were used in the DRL algorithm is to use the package `PyPortfolioOpt`. The package includes a class called `EfficientFrontier` that contains different optimization techniques, each corresponding to diverse objective functions. In the following, we list the key inputs to the `EfficientFrontier` class:

- `expected_returns` : an array, series, or a list of annualized expected returns for each asset, which can be `None` if the strategy only optimizes for volatility measures. Since we deal with historical data, at each time step t, we considered the previous 252 daily returns and used them to compute the annualized mean returns for each asset.
- `cov_matrix` : an array or data frame that contains the covariance of returns for each asset; it must be provided and must be positive semidefinite. At each time step and for each asset, we computed the covariance of the previous 252 daily returns.
- `weight_bounds` : a tuple or list of allowed weight allocation bounds for each or all assets; for a long-only portfolio (default), the bounds are the same for all assets, and the value is set to `(0,1)`; for a portfolio where short positions are allowed, the value is set to `(−1,1)`.

As mentioned earlier, multiple methods are available for different investment objectives. In our comparison, we consider two objectives, namely, minimizing portfolio volatility and maximizing the Sharpe ratio. For the former objective, we use the `min_volatility()` method; for the latter objective, we use the `max_sharpe(risk_free_rate)` method, where we must specify the riskless rate of return over a period that corresponds to the frequency of the `expected_returns` input. Both methods return an ordered dictionary of selected asset weights for the corresponding optimal portfolio. It follows that at each testing date, we compute the optimal weights, multiply them by the current portfolio value, and then, by observing the next-step closing prices, we accumulate the current wealth with one-period asset returns. At the end of the testing horizon, we will obtain the evolution of wealth corresponding to each of the efficient frontier strategies. Using the plotting tools mentioned at the beginning of this section, we have all the necessary information to compare the performances of the selected strategies.

References

Bergdahl, J. (2017). Asynchronous Advantage Actor Critic with Adam Optimization and a Layer Normalized Recurrent Network. KTH Royal Institute of Technology, Stockholm, Sweden. https://www.diva-portal.org/smash/get/diva2:1169944/FULLTEXT01.pdf

Bertsekas, D.P. (2005). *Dynamic Programming and Optimal Control.* Athena Scientific, Nashua, New Hampshire, United States.

Danthine, J.-P., and Donaldson J.B. (2015). *Intermediate Financial Theory,* Chapter 3, 3rd edn. Academic Press, Massachusetts, United States.

Dellinger, J. (2019). Weight initialization in neural networks: A journey from the basics to Kaiming. https://towardsdatascience.com/weight-initialization-in-neural-networks-a-journey-from-the-basics-to-kaiming-954fb9b47c79

Mnih, V., Badia, A.P., Mirza, M., *et al.* (2016). Asynchronous methods for deep reinforcement learning. https://arxiv.org/pdf/1602.01783.pdf

Rao, A., and Jelvis, T. (2005). *Foundations of Reinforcement Learning with Applications in Finance.* Athena Scientific, Nashua, New Hampshire, United States.

Sutton, R.S., and Andrew G.B. (2018). *Reinforcement Learning: An Introduction,* 2nd edn. The MIT Press, Massachusetts, United States.

https://doi.org/10.1142/9781800615212_0004

Chapter 4

Explainable Artificial Intelligence in Risk Management: A Framework

Silvio Andrae*
Senior Adviser
German Savings Banks Association
Berlin Area, Germany
andrae@zedat.fu-berlin.de

Abstract

It is easier than ever to run modern machine learning (ML) models. However, developing and implementing systems that support real-world risk management applications in a bank is a significant challenge. It is partly because ML models are not transparent and explainable. The framework presented here covers the leading eXplainable AI (XAI) methods. Practical challenges in implementing these methods are discussed.

Keywords: Algorithm, artificial intelligence, explainable artificial intelligence, interpretability, machine learning, risk modeling, transparency.

1 Introduction

Let us imagine working in a bank. The financial institution uses automated systems to make decisions about loan applications. The decisions are based on machine learning (ML) or artificial intelligence (AI) programs. The systems are developed based on criteria, trained on historical datasets, and then let loose to do the work. Now

*Opinions expressed are solely my own and do not express the views or opinions of my employer.

imagine that at some point later, we learn that the ML algorithm made a flawed decision. The data the algorithm was trained on may be biased. Alternatively, the model could have been better designed. Perhaps the system "drifted," as ML models are known to do. Drift means that the predictive power of a model decreases over time due to changes in the real world.

AI systems based on ML techniques often turn out to be a "black box" for their users. The term describes that it is often impossible to understand how the system reached its decision in an individual case. The main reason for this is the "self-learning" of the system, which sometimes results in modifications and further developments of the learned decision model. These are only sometimes predictable, even for the developer. In addition, the causal reasons for decisions based on the learned model often need to be clarified, even in retrospect.

While the first AI systems were easy to interpret, more recent years have seen the emergence of opaque decision systems, such as Deep Neural Networks (DNNs). The empirical success of deep learning (DL) models like DNNs is due to a combination of efficient learning algorithms and their colossal parameter space. The latter includes hundreds of layers and millions of parameters, which is why DNNs are considered complex black-box models (Minh *et al.*, 2022).

When black-box models are used to make essential predictions in critical contexts, the demand for transparency increases. There is a risk that decisions are made that cannot be justified. Explanations that support the output of a model are critical. It is also true in finance, for example, when modeling financial risk.

The term "eXplainable AI" (XAI) was coined in response to the proliferation of automated systems introduced into social, economic, industrial, and scientific environments by concerned users. Islam *et al.* (2022) note that finance has been underrepresented in XAI methods.

When developing an ML model, considering explainability and interpretation as an additional design factor can improve its implementation for three reasons (Arrieta *et al.*, 2020):

- Explainability helps ensure impartiality in decision-making. Biases in the training dataset are detected and consequently corrected.
- Explainability ensures robustness by highlighting potential negative perturbations that could alter the prediction.

- Explainability can serve as an assurance that only meaningful variables derive output. It guarantees that there is an underlying truthful causality in the model reasoning.

The explainability of the system should provide, among other things, an understanding of the model mechanisms and predictions. However, it should also provide a visualization of the model's discrimination rules or clues as to what might interfere with it.

To maintain the effectiveness of the current generation of AI systems, XAI proposes developing a set of ML techniques. The following goals are to be achieved in this way:

(1) to develop more explainable models while maintaining a high level of learning (e.g., predictive accuracy),
(2) to enable people to understand, appropriately trust, and effectively manage the emerging generation of artificially intelligent partners.

Some algorithmic XAI approaches (e.g., LIME and SHAP) have already overcome this challenge. They look into the black box of an ML model and understand its behavior (Gramegna and Giudici, 2021). However, these developments are predominantly driven by ML developers and are designed to improve ML models in terms of predictive accuracy. The focus is rarely on explaining or interpreting the result to the system's user.

This chapter's contribution aims to develop an XAI framework for ML applications in a bank's risk management. Previous XAI works have addressed various sub-aspects of explainability. However, they do not address XAI as a whole. ML applications in financial institutions today are mainly found in risk measurement. Section 2 shows in which risk areas ML is in use today. In the other standard risk management tools, such as risk assessments, risk monitoring, and risk reporting, ML practices still need to be strong. The XAI framework aims first to resolve the confusion regarding the notion of interpretability (Section 3). It often needs to be clarified how many proposed interpretability methods are related and what common concepts can be used to evaluate them. Section 4 then presents the XAI framework. The framework examines the various XAI methods according to different criteria. A widely accepted classification is that of transparent models and *post hoc* explainability. Here, explainability can be tied to the life cycle of data science.

Alternatively, a distinction can be made between whether an XAI method has a local or global effect. The XAI framework presented here summarizes the techniques relevant to risk management models based on various criteria. It is followed by a lessons learned section. This chapter ends with a summary.

2 Machine Learning and Risk Management

In the following, we present which ML methods are used in risk management in a bank. Risk management has come a long way thanks to an early research advance in the ML application of risk modeling (Aziz *et al.*, 2022). The presentation claims to be partial. The analysis is along the risk areas where ML is implemented in the risk types. It is mainly the supervised learning method applied in risk management (Aziz and Dowling, 2019; Leo *et al.*, 2019). Figure 1 shows the different methods and a simplified representation of explainability.

2.1 Credit risk

Credit risk assessment occupies one of the most critical places in the risk management of a financial institution. Credit risk is the most studied and evaluated risk area for ML applications. Techniques such as logistic regression (probit/logit) and discriminant analysis are traditionally used in credit scoring to determine the probability of default.

Credit risk modeling to calculate credit default risk involves estimating the probability of default (PD), exposure at default (EAD), and loss-given default (LGD). The predominant methods used to develop the probability of default models are classification and survival analysis. The latter involves estimating whether the customer would default and when the default might occur. Classification algorithms are much more accurate than standard logistic regression in credit scoring. Finally, it can be observed that methods such as artificial neural networks (ANN) perform very well on credit-scoring datasets (Lessmann *et al.*, 2015). Many papers evaluate the different algorithms (e.g., XGBoost) to determine the most efficient and accurate prediction algorithm. According to them, ML is better suited to capture nonlinear relationships typical of credit risk (Hamori *et al.*, 2018; Baghdasaryan *et al.*, 2021; Tantri, 2021).

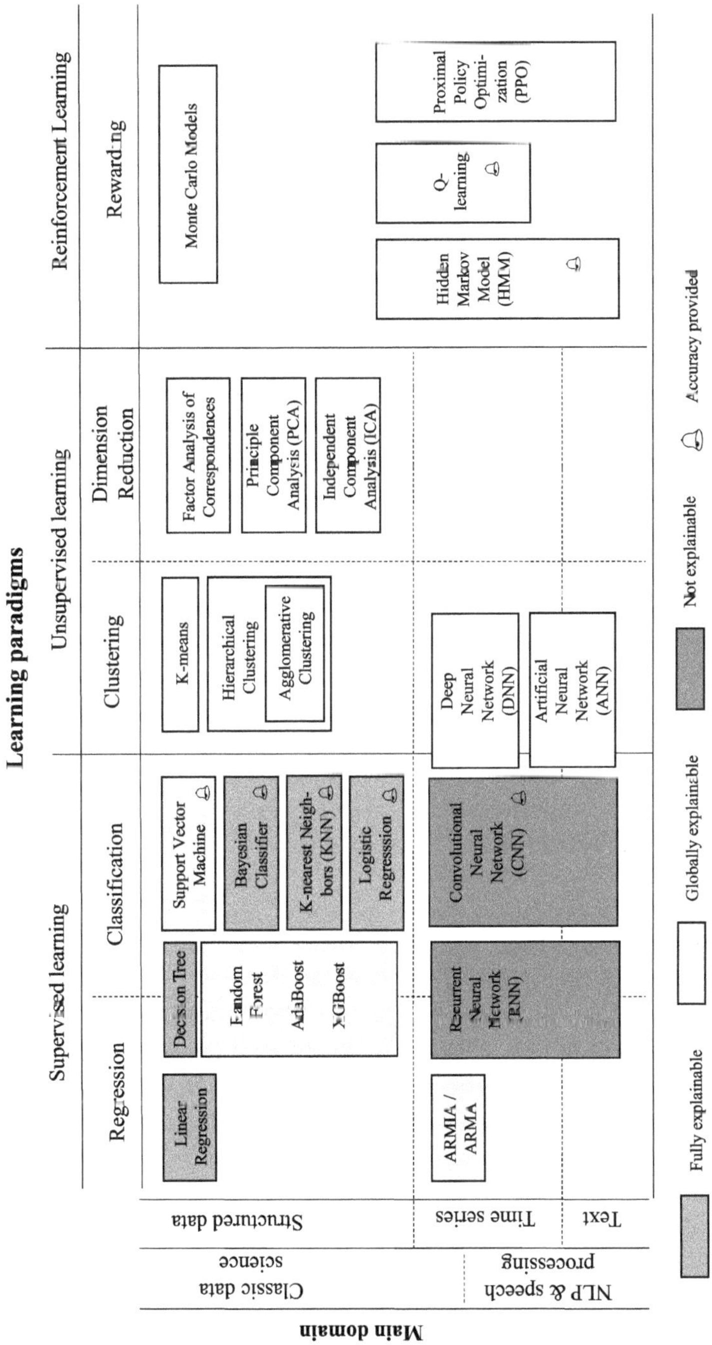

Figure 1. Machine learning algorithm taxonomy.
Source: In accordance with Enisa (2021, p. 7).

An accurate prediction of the estimated probability of default is of more excellent value to risk management than a binary classification of customers as either creditworthy or uncreditworthy. Several techniques are used in credit scoring, such as discriminant analysis, logistic regression, Bayes classifier, k-nearest neighbor (KNN), ANN, and classification trees. ANNs have been shown to make more accurate classifications than the other five methods (Bücker *et al.*, 2022; Breeden, 2021).

Bastos (2022) proposes a credit-scoring model based on boosted decision trees. Multiple decision trees are combined into one classifier. The prediction accuracy of boosted decision trees is compared with two alternative ML techniques: the multilayer perceptron (MLP) and support vector machines (SVMs). The SVM is a supervised algorithm of ML, although widely used in classification problems (Asimit *et al.*, 2022). However, the method is relatively new in credit scoring. It has been successful in classifying credit card customers who default. The method also proved competitive in identifying features most important in determining default risk when tested and compared with traditional techniques. The method is also used to develop credit risk assessment and credit scoring models (Cao *et al.*, 2013).

Raei *et al.* (2016) studied a hybrid model for estimating corporate customers' default probability in a commercial bank. They present the hybrid model as a model that can address the "black box" criticism of ANN — a model that is not understandable in terms of parameters (cf. Section 4.2). Here, we take a two-step approach: combining the understandability of logit models with the predictive power of nonlinear techniques, such as ANN. The overall accuracy of this hybrid model has been shown to outperform both basic models. Low-default portfolios (LDPs) are portfolios (e.g., corporate loans) considered very low risk. LDPs have a class imbalance problem in that they are included in a class of defaulting borrowers in smaller numbers than in a class of good payers. Gradient boosting and random forest classifiers perform well on samples with a class imbalance problem.

Some works focus on comparing traditional statistical methods to highlight the efficiency of applying ML algorithms. Hamori *et al.* (2018) investigated and compared the predictive accuracy and classification ability of bagging, random forest (RF), boosting, and neural network methods in analyzing nonpayment data. They found that boosting was superior among the machine learning methods studied. Melsom *et al.* (2022) combine a light-gradient boosting machine (LightGBM) model with SHapley Additive ExPlanations (SHAP). With this, they achieve a 1% larger area under the Receiver Operating Characteristic (ROC) curve and a 19% larger area under the precision–recall curve compared to a standard logistic regression model. Implementing XAI methods in banking can improve the reliability of state-of-the-art ML methods. In particular, they find that LightGBM models can outperform logistic regression models for credit scoring in predictive performance and explainability (similarly, Biecek *et al.*, 2021).

Some researchers have also evaluated hybrid techniques and ensemble methods to study credit scoring (Hamori *et al.*, 2018). It is found that a method using clustering and bagging algorithms to balance and diversify the data, followed by an ensemble of LASSO and logistic regression to assess credit risk, outperforms many popular credit scoring models (Wang *et al.*, 2015).

Financial institutions are also looking to develop efficient models to assess the probability of counterparty default. Barboza *et al.* (2017) test ML models to predict bankruptcies and then compare the bankruptcy probabilities with the results of traditional methods. They then compare the insolvency probabilities with the results of traditional methods. They find significant prediction accuracy. The authors point out that ML techniques can easily be used for significant classification accuracy compared to traditional methods. Despite concerns about the model's explanatory power, ML may prove to be an essential aid given the complexity of bankruptcy models (similarly, Gramespacher and Posth, 2021).

Some work addresses stress testing in credit risk management (Islam *et al.*, 2013). Stress testing requires modeling the relationship between macroeconomic developments and banking variables to determine the impact of extreme scenarios on a financial institution. More commonly, bottom-up approaches are used to make predictions of future gains/losses at mostly disaggregated portfolio levels. This approach is data intensive and challenging to determine the exact causes of losses. Predictions on an aggregate portfolio using a top-down method can complement this process. The minor absolute shrinkage and selection operator (LASSO) method is a supervised learning algorithm that does not require a pre-specified model.

A more elaborate version of LASSO is adaptive LASSO, which has attractive convergence properties. Adaptive LASSO can be used without theoretical models, as in the case of top-down stress tests, to find a parsimonious top-down model from thousands of possible specifications. The procedure provides approximately unbiased solutions by searching for variables that best describe the behavior of loan default rates. It leads to a parsimonious description of the relationship between macroeconomics and loan default rates.

For credit risk modeling, advanced ML techniques perform better than conventional statistical methods in classification and prediction accuracy. SVM is considered a widely tested and proven ML approach. Overall, ANN, SVM, and RF are the most researched algorithms in credit risk management.

2.2 Market risk

Modern ML techniques play a minor role in modeling market risks compared to credit risks. Volatility forecasts in financial markets are essential for market risk management and asset pricing, among other things. Using ANN can improve the performance of the volatility estimation method. Zhang *et al.* (2017) propose a model based on the Generalized Autoregressive Conditional Heteroskedastic (GARCH) model and the Extreme Machine Learning (ELM) algorithm to estimate volatility. The model predicts the volatility of the target time series. Extrapolation of the predicted volatilities enables the calculation of Value-at-Risk (VaR) with improved performance in terms of accuracy and efficiency. The model uses a stochastic mapping method that does not require Gaussian probability for estimation and is a nonlinear data driver model.

Market risk also includes interest rate risk and equity risk. Yield curves are widely used in financial engineering and market risk management. A clustering method called the “Gaussian mixture model” can be used to develop nonlinear models for the evolution of parameters and then predict yield curves. It can provide better visualization of interest rates. Clustering methods of ML developed for stochastic differential equations (SDE) can be used to develop anticipatory VAR models that are intended to be a leading measure of risk for market regime change.

2.3 Liquidity risk

Some liquidity risk problems can be solved by using machine learning. Measuring liquidity risk, analyzing key factors, and studying the relationships between factors can be achieved by using machine learning. ANN or a genetic algorithm can be used to estimate a risk measure. ANNs can be used to approximate the overall risk trend and determine the most influential factors. The probability of a liquidity risk event can be estimated by applying Bayesian networks. ANN implementations can determine the most critical liquidity risk factors that measure risk through a functional approximation or distribution estimation (Tavana *et al.*, 2018).

2.4 Operational risk

In the area of operational risk, ML focuses primarily on problems related to detecting fraud (e.g., spam) and suspicious transactions — problems typically addressed with classification algorithms. Money laundering, for example, is a low-frequency event. Financial institutions must ensure that they are not doing business with criminals and that their accounts are not being misused for money laundering or terrorist financing (AML). A vital part of an AML compliance program consists of transaction monitoring. It aims to detect suspicious activity and atypical transactions. The scope of transactions is broad and includes deposits, withdrawals, fund transfers, trade credits, and other payments. ML algorithms can help in money laundering screening to detect suspicious behavior patterns or misuse at an early stage. Systematic network analysis of the entire transaction network brings to light anomalies, outliers, and peculiarities that indicate criminal activity, such as fraud and money laundering (Jullum *et al.*, 2020).

ML techniques are also used in credit card fraud. Similar to money laundering, the systems are designed to increase the detection rate while minimizing the false positive rate. Supervised detection methods estimate models based on samples of fraudulent and legitimate transactions, while unsupervised detection methods identify outliers or unusual transactions as potential fraud. In both cases, an attempt is made to predict the probability of fraud in a given transaction. Various fraud detection systems use Bayesian algorithms, KNN, SVM, and bagging ensemble classifiers based on decision trees. A comparative evaluation has shown that the one based on an algorithm with a bagging ensemble classifier performs well. It is independent of attribute values and can also handle class imbalance (Pun and Lawryshyn, 2012).

2.5 Cyber risk

Cyber risk is the risk posed by intentional attacks on information and communications technology systems that compromise data or services' confidentiality, availability, or integrity. It should be noted that cyber risk under this definition is not strictly the same as information technology operational risk because, first, it relates only to intentional attacks. For another, it relates not only to monetary losses but also to reputational losses.

While the measurement of operational risks based on loss data is standard, the measurement of cyber risks is still relatively in its infancy. It is partly due to the limited availability of cyber loss data, which is generally not published. Reputational losses are to be avoided in any case. The ordinal classification of risks prevents the calculation of a VaR. Although ordinal data cannot be used to calculate the value at risk, they can be used to rank risks according to their "criticality." In this way, interventions can be prioritized and risk mitigation measures triggered.

Because cyber events are typically infrequent and nonrepeatable, Giudici and Raffinetti (2022) measure these events using a less sophisticated ordinal approach rather than using quantitative data that are often unavailable. Ordinal data for measuring cyber risk can be summarized using a pair of statistics for each event type: the frequency of the event (how often it occurred in a given period) and the corresponding severity (average observed loss). The statistical models commonly used to explain an ordinal response variable with a set of explanatory variables are the ordered logit or probit models. However, these can be difficult to summarize and interpret. It is especially true in applied contexts. Therefore, Giudici and Raffinetti (2022) resort to a linear regression model for a response variable that takes ordinal values. Consistent with the ordinal nature of the data, the proposed methodology is based on a combination of rank regression models and Lorenz-based scoring models. The combination of the two approaches leads to identifying the factors that most influence cyber risk and can be mitigated by insurance.

Enisa (2021) notes that the cybersecurity posture of companies using ML algorithms can be improved by carefully selecting the controls developed for these algorithms. However, these controls have not been thoroughly validated nor standardized as to how they should be implemented. ML systems can protect against cyber risks. However, they are very complex, so organizations have a special responsibility. It is crucial to educate data scientists about the dangers of threats and how to design security controls before deploying ML algorithms in organizations' environments.

Hu *et al.* (2022) conducted a data-driven analysis to evaluate the predictive power of various attributes for assessing the risk of cyber-attacks. Each cyber data breach is a low-probability, high-impact risk event. Using ML algorithms, the predictive power can be significantly improved. The model applied by the authors leverages several cybersecurity risk drivers and provides essential insights into what mitigation measures might be effective.

2.6 Systemic risk

Systemic risks are characterized by high complexity and interdependencies. However, these risks are also characterized by cross sectoral or cross-border effects, nonlinear relationships with tipping points, and regulatory delays. Four characteristics make up systemic risks:

- **Complexity** refers to the difficulty of identifying and quantifying causal relationships between a variety of potential elements and specific adverse effects.
- **Uncertainty** includes different components, such as statistical variance, measurement error, ignorance, and indeterminacy.
- **Ambiguity** refers to the variability of (legitimate) interpretations based on identical observations or data evaluations.
- **Dynamic ripple effects** have the potential to trigger significant ripple effects outside the area where the risk is located.

The boundaries of uncertainty and ambiguity are usually clearly defined in the case of conventional risks. Since systemic risks do not have clear boundaries in scope, time, and space, it is often unknown which other systems are affected. The goal is to overcome the shortcomings of conventional methods, which are based on limited modeling and need help drawing on different data sources.

Systemic risk modeling is already partly done today based on ML methods. They study the mechanisms of systemic risk outbreaks and contagion in financial networks and improve the regulation of the financial market and financial industry (Kou *et al.*, 2019). Casabianca *et al.* (2022) use the ML approach of AdaBoost to classify the determinants and macroeconomic factors that lead to banking crises. AdaBoost has better predictive performance than the conventional logit model.

For example, Feng *et al.* (2022) model systemic risk using Deep Learning (DL), in which they calculate an optimal capital allocation strategy. Systemic risk measures are the minimum amount of cash that secures the aggregate system by allocating capital to individual financial institutions before aggregating individual risks.

Liu and Pun (2022) link statistical modeling of the systemic event and the co-dependence of stock returns during an event to a supervised *ex post* learning problem. Specifically, they estimate the marginal expected shortfall using ML learning models, such as XGBoost, artificial neural networks (ANN), and long short-term memory (LSTM). The ML algorithms improve the predictive power of the systemic risk measure while being flexible in processing high-dimensional data.

One of the conceptual challenges of systemic risks is therefore to understand the commonalities of complex cause-and-effect relationships in both risk emergence and risk governance systems. They must be distinguished from idiosyncratic patterns of behavior that may be only marginally related to the severity of the risk in question.

3 XAI Definitions

Also relevant in the risk management of financial institutions is the recognition that ML models can provide predictions and knowledge about the relationships contained in the data (Misheva *et al.*, 2021a). They are often referred to as explainability or interpretability. One problem that makes establishing common ground difficult is the interchangeable use of interpretability and explainability.

3.1 Definitions

The terms "explainability" and "interpretability" are often used synonymously in practice and the literature. Other terms are added in this context. The differences and similarities between the terms can be summarized as follows (Arrieta *et al.*, 2020):

- **Understandability** refers to a model's ability to make a human understand how the ML model works. The internal structure or the algorithms with which the model processes data internally do not have to be explained explicitly.
- **Comprehensibility** refers to the ability of a learning algorithm to represent the learned knowledge in a way understandable to humans.
- **Interpretability** is a passive property of a model. It concerns how a given model makes sense to a human observer. The property is closely related to transparency. A model is said to be transparent if it is understandable by itself. Transparent models are divided into three categories: simulatable, decomposable, and algorithmically transparent (cf. Section 4.2.1).
- **Explainability** is an active feature of a model. It denotes any model's action or procedure to clarify or detail its internal functions.

Of the four definitions mentioned, comprehensibility emerges as the broadest concept of XAI. Comprehensibility is also related to understandability. It depends on the ability of the audience to understand the knowledge contained in the model. All in all, understandability is a two-sided matter: the understandability of the model and human understandability. As distinguished from interpretability, explainability seems more important because it refers to the prediction's importance, completeness, and accuracy. In the following, we differentiate between the terms in each case.

Without a universally accepted definition, a wide range of methods with a correspondingly wide range of outcomes is referred to as explainability. In particular, it needs to be clarified what it means to explain or interpret something, what commonalities exist between different methods, and how to select an explainability method for a particular problem/target. In the following, we first define explainability in the context of machine learning.

The problem of explaining the outcome of a decision process has been introduced previously. In itself, explainability is a broad concept. In all its generality, explaining data means extracting information from them. The methods range from planning an initial experiment to visualizing the final results. In this overly general form, explainability is similar to the established concepts of data science and applied statistics. What makes XAI fundamentally different is the added scale and dimensionality in modern AI decision systems compared to traditional decision trees or regression models.

It is essential to point out that in trying to understand the explainability of ML, we are interested in more than just the accuracy of the result itself (Meske *et al.*, 2022). Instead of general explainability, we should look to the life cycle of data science to gain insights from ML models (Murdoch, 2019). The interest in data mining and decision-making stems from the fact that the outcome of a decision may be correct. However, the process by which an ML system arrives at that outcome may need to be more desirable based on specific data. ML systems may take shortcuts to make decisions; however, this path may not always be correct. Therefore, the explainability of an ML system is independent of the accuracy of the decision system (Gilpin *et al.*, 2022). It attempts to develop an XAI framework that is even more critical.

We define XAI as extracting relevant knowledge from a machine learning model concerning relationships contained in the data or learned from the model. We consider knowledge relevant if it provides insights into a particular problem to a particular audience (e.g., management). These insights are often used to guide communication, action, and discovery. Depending on the context and audience, they can take the form of visualizations, natural language, or mathematical equations (Murdoch, 2019).

Various critical voices in the AI literature fundamentally question the XAI concept. One faction believes that AI is fundamentally too complex to be explained. It argues that the most popular AI systems have nearly 100 million parameters. It makes it downright impossible to explain a particular result objectively. Therefore, this group believes that XAI is a meaningless endeavour. The issue is the extent to which AI can be explained, what is a satisfactory explanation, and for what problem the explanation is needed (Khan, 2022).

The other faction of critics believes XAI is possible but points out the challenge of the trade-off between performance or predictive accuracy and explainability. This trade-off refers to the theory that, especially with DL, more inputs and hidden layers increase the accuracy of a model while making it more challenging to interpret the results. Therefore, these proponents emphasize that too much emphasis on explainability could significantly affect the performance of a model (Khan, 2022). This criticism can be addressed by fleshing out the design, i.e., how to implement a sufficient level of explainability in the design of an AI system. By integrating the data science lifecycle into the XAI framework, we partially capture this line of criticism.

3.2 Delimitations

Our goal is to create a vocabulary for the XAI framework to fully capture explainable machine learning, its benefits, and its applications to concrete (data) problems in risk management. For this reason, it is important to distinguish from five related domains. While closely related to explainability, these domains are nevertheless distinct: trustworthiness, causal inference, transferability, informativeness, and stability (Lipton, 2017; Murdoch, 2019).

Trustworthiness: The search for trustworthiness is closely related to an explainable model. A model is characterized as explainable if it is capable of inspiring trust. However, it may only partially meet the requirements for a model to be explainable. Trustworthiness can be viewed as the confidence that a model will act as intended on a given problem (Stanton and Jensen, 2021). Although trustworthiness should be a desirable property of any explainable model, not every trustworthy model should be considered explainable. Trust cannot be the sole purpose of an explainable model because the relationship between the two if agreed upon, is not reciprocal (Fritz-Morgenthal *et al.*, 2022).

Causal inference: We are familiar with causal inference from statistics. Causal inference methods focus on extracting causal relationships from data. In contrast, XAI is used to describe general relationships. XAI cannot be used to test whether these relationships are causal because they are not designed to distinguish between causal and noncausal effects. Researchers sometimes use XAI and causal inference in a single analysis (Cox Jr., 2021).

Transferability: Constraints always limit models. A seamless transferability is only sometimes possible. Explainability is a proponent of transferability. The limits of transferability can at least be made transparent by XAI. Understanding the internal relationships of a model makes it easier for the user to reuse this knowledge for another purpose. In this respect, the property of transferability should be one of the resulting properties of an explainable model. However, again, only some transferable models should be considered explainable.

Informativeness: ML models are used with the ultimate intention of supporting decision-making. However, the problem to be solved by the model is different from that of the human user. Therefore, a variety of information is needed to link the user's decision to the solution given by the model. For this reason, explainable ML models should provide information about the problem to be solved. Many rule extraction techniques justify their approach by seeking a more straightforward understanding of what the model does internally. It is stated that the knowledge (information) can be expressed in these more straightforward proxies.

Stability: Stability expresses robustness in statistics. It is equally valid for explainable ML. Stability can help evaluate explanatory methods and is a prerequisite for trustworthy explanations. One should only explain parts of a model tuned to appropriate perturbations of the model and the data.

4 XAI Framework for Risk Management

Islam *et al.* (2022) and Vilone and Longo (2021) provide a general and comprehensive overview of the approaches of different types of "explanatory systems." Mueller *et al.* (2019) categorize XAI methods within three generations. Linardatos *et al.* (2022) provide a broad literature review by providing a taxonomy of XAI methods and links to programmatic implementations. Johs *et al.* (2022) provide information on underlying theories, methodological approaches, data collection methods, and data analysis procedures. Heng and Subramanian (2022) present XAI techniques for credit risk modeling.

Science indicates that the goal of XAI is to convince a person of the credibility of an AI result. Hoffman *et al.* (2019) have proposed the most comprehensive guidelines for evaluating XAI frameworks. Their guidelines build on the idea that "the property of 'being an explanation' is not a property of statements; it is an interaction." Hoffman *et al.* also note that an explanation depends on the needs of end users and their understanding of AI results. The authors did successfully offer an evaluation model for XAI frameworks. However, this relies heavily on end users' subjective understanding and satisfaction. Unfortunately, no universal, objective framework can explain an AI outcome independent of the end user (Renftle *et al.*, 2022). The framework proposed here aims to address this need. In application, the framework focuses on the risk management of a financial institution.

A distinction is often made between *a priori* interpretable models and those that can be explained using external XAI methods. This duality expresses the difference between interpretable models and model interpretation techniques. A widely accepted classification is that of transparent models and *post hoc* explainability. Finally, a distinction is made as to whether the XAI method has a local or global effect. Other distinguishing criteria are added. The XAI framework presented here summarizes the techniques relevant to risk management models based on seven criteria. These include structure, transparency of design, scope, agnosticism, type of explanation, examples, and data type (Figure 2).

Some popular XAI risk management tools are LIME, SHAP, DALEX, and Microsoft InterpretML. The latter two even form

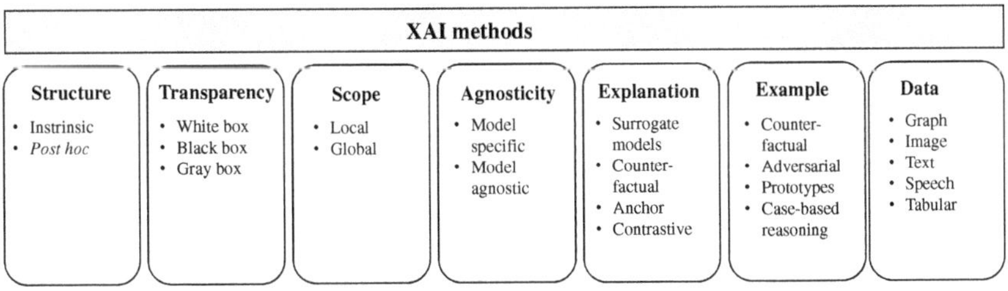

Figure 2. XAI framework and methods.

a complete XAI framework. Less common in risk management are, for example, DeepVis Toolbox, TreeInterpreter, or Tensorboard WhatIf. At a high level, all proposed approaches have similar concepts, such as feature importance, feature interactions, partial dependence, surrogate models, counterfactuals, prototypes, and knowledge infusion. Despite some visible progress in XAI methods, more progress has yet to be made in quantifying or evaluating explainability.

4.1 Intrinsic vs. *post hoc*

XAI methods can be either in the modeling or *post hoc* analysis phases. This criterion distinguishes whether interpretation in the modeling phase is achieved by limiting ML models' complexity (intrinsic models) or using methods to analyze models after training (called *post hoc* techniques). We refer to the interpretation in the modeling phase as model-based or intrinsic interpretation. This part of the interpretation focuses on constructing models that provide insight into the relationships they learn. Model-based methods generally need to use simpler models. They are easy to interpret because of their simple structure. However, this can lead to lower prediction accuracy.

Consequently, model-based interpretation is best used when the underlying relationship is simple enough that model-based methods can achieve reasonable prediction accuracy. It can also be used when prediction accuracy is optional. Examples of intrinsic models include linear regression, logistic regression, decision trees, and KNN.

Post hoc models, on the other hand, perform better on most tasks but are too complex to be understood by humans. They provide only approximations of the underlying ML model. Neural network models, for example, have millions of parameters that exceed human capabilities. We then speak of *post hoc* explainability. Unlike model-based interpretation, *post hoc* methods take a trained model as input and extract information about what relationships the model has learned. *Post hoc* models involve XAI techniques that convert an uninterpretable model into an explainable model. They are most valuable when the data are particularly complex, and practitioners must train a black-box model to achieve reasonable predictive accuracy. Among *post hoc* techniques, we can distinguish between textual explanations, visualizations, explanations by example, explanations

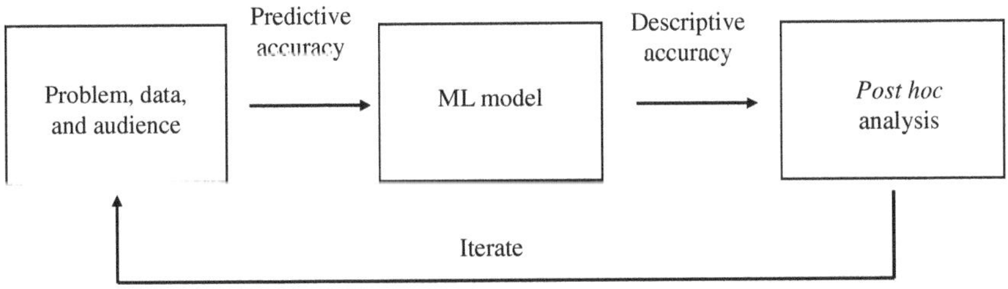

Figure 3. Overview of the different stages in the data science lifecycle.
Source: Murdoch (2019).

by simplification, and feature explanation techniques. Each technique covers one of the most common ways people explain systems and processes.

Before discussing the various methods, let us first situate the process of explainable ML within the broader life cycle of data science. Figure 3 is a general description of this process intended to capture most data science problems. What is generally referred to as interpretation or explanation mainly occurs in the modeling and *post hoc* analysis phases. The appropriate methods provide the necessary context for the problem, the data, and the target audience.

At the beginning of the cycle, a data science expert defines a problem that he or she wants to understand using data. This problem can take many forms. For example, finance is about the predictive power of a borrower's default probabilities. Alternatively, it may be about other qualities of a model, such as how to assign credit scores with high accuracy (Hussin *et al.*, 2022). The nature of the problem plays a role in interpretation, as the relevant context and target audience are critical in determining which methods to use.

After selecting a problem from the domain, the risk modeler collects data to study it. Various aspects of the data collection process influence the interpretation. Most importantly, biases in the data (i.e., inconsistencies between the data collected) will manifest themselves in the model. Finally, this may limit the generalization of interpretations drawn from the data to the target population of interest.

How interpretive methods should be selected and evaluated for a given problem and audience must be clarified. Part of the XAI framework is provided to assist in this process. According to this framework, two criteria can be used in selecting interpretive methods for a given problem: accuracy and relevance (Murdoch, 2019).

The information produced by an interpretive method should be faithful to the underlying process that the risk modeler and risk manager are trying to understand. In the context of ML, there are two areas where errors can occur: in approximating the underlying data relationships with a model (predictive accuracy) and in approximating what the model has learned using an interpretive method (descriptive accuracy). One should maximize both accuracies for an interpretation to be trustworthy. It is essential to check the trustworthiness by external validation, e.g., by performing an additional experiment (cf. Section 5).

Prediction accuracy: It starts in the model-building phase. The information extracted from the model is accurate if the model learns a better approximation of the underlying relationships in the data. Assessing the quality of a model's fit has been well studied in standard supervised ML procedures. For example, measures of test set accuracy are used. The data used to test predictive accuracy must be tailored to the target population of interest. Estimating rural borrower's default probability cannot be generalized to real estate loans. In addition, the problems often require a notion of predictive accuracy beyond average accuracy. The distribution of predictions is essential. Finally, prediction accuracy should be stable concerning valid data and model noise.

Descriptive accuracy: In the *post hoc* analysis phase, explanatory methods are used to analyze a fitted model. Often, interpretations provide an imperfect representation of the relationships learned by a model. It is particularly problematic for complex black-box models based on neural networks (NNs). They store nonlinear relationships between variables in nonobvious forms. Descriptive accuracy is the degree to which an explainability method objectively captures the relationships learned by machine learning models.

Risk modelers sometimes face a trade-off between predictive and descriptive accuracy when choosing which model to use. On the one hand, the simplicity of model-based explanatory methods leads to consistently high descriptive accuracy. However, it can also lead to lower predictive accuracy in complex datasets. On the other hand, complicated models can provide high prediction accuracy in complex environments. However, they are more challenging to analyze, resulting in lower description accuracy (Murdoch, 2019).

When selecting a method for interpretation or explainability, more is needed so that it has high accuracy. The information extracted must also be relevant. In the context of risk management, for example, a borrower, a loan officer, a risk controller, a board member, and a statistician may each want different (but consistent) interpretations of the same model. The context provided by the problem and data phases in Figure 3 dictates the types of relationships a risk modeler wants to know about and the methods they should use. Explainability is relevant when it provides insight into a selected problem domain for a specific audience. For example, if explainability is used to test the predictions of a model, descriptive accuracy may be more critical. In contrast, interpretation may also be used solely to increase a model's predictive accuracy, for example, through improved feature techniques.

Figure 4 shows how the different explanatory methods affect descriptive and predictive accuracy. In particular, both *post hoc* and intrinsic methods aim to increase descriptive accuracy. Only the model-based method affects predictive accuracy.

4.1.1 *Intrinsic*

The risk modeler constructs a predictive model based on the selected problem and the collected data. In this phase, the modeller processes, cleanses, and visualizes data, extracts features, selects a model (or multiple models), and fits it. Interoperability considerations often come into play at this step (cf. Section 3.2) — the considerations related to the choice between simpler, easier-to-interpret models, and more complex black-box models. The ability of the model to fit the data is measured by its predictive accuracy.

Model-based interpretation is understood as constructing models that provide insight into the learned relationships. These include linear regression, logistic regression, or decision tree-oriented models. Decision rules (simple if-then-else constraints) are also part of an intrinsic interpretive model. Other interpretive models include extensions of linear models such as generalized linear models (GLMs) and generalized additive models (GAMs). They assist in circumventing

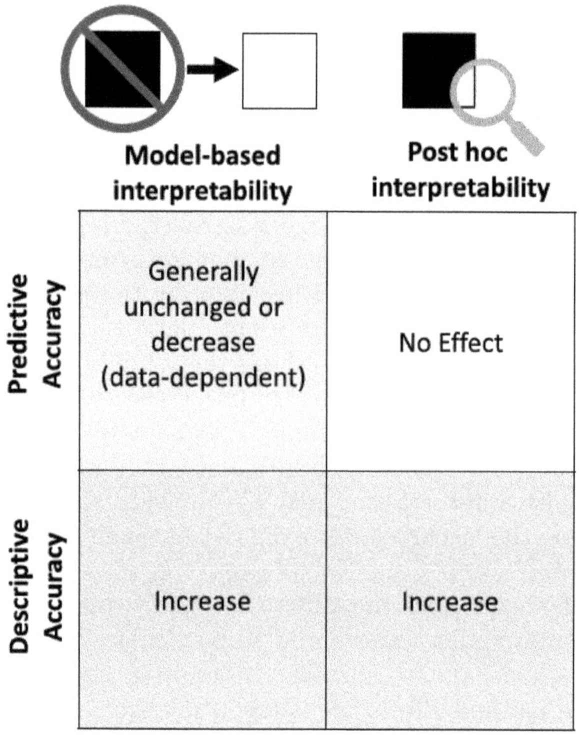

Figure 4. Effect of interpretability methods on descriptive and predictive accuracy.
Source: Murdoch (2019).

some of the assumptions of linear models (e.g., the target outcome and the given features follow a Gaussian distribution, and no interaction between features). However, these extensions lead to more complex models (i.e., additional interactions) and need to be more interpretable (Zschech *et al.*, 2022). Here, the boundaries between a transparent and a black-box model become blurred (cf. Section 4.2). Other methods, again nave Bayes classifiers based on Bayes theorem, where the probability of classes for each feature is calculated independently (assuming strong feature independence), also fall under intrinsic models (Yang, 2021).

When selecting a model to solve a problem, the risk modeler must consider all the above characteristics — the first characteristic concerns predictive accuracy. Any subsequent analysis is questionable if the model created accurately represents the underlying problem. Second, the primary purpose of model-based interpretation methods is to increase description accuracy. Finally, the relevance of a model's results must be considered. It is determined by the content of the problem, the data, and the target audience (Murdoch, 2019).

Some standard model-based interpretation methods are explained in the following (Murdoch, 2019).

Sparsity: If the risk modeler judges that the relationship in question is based on a sparse set of signals, he or she can impose sparsity on the model. By reducing the number of parameters to be analyzed, sparse models may be easier to understand, resulting in higher descriptive accuracy. The risk modeler can limit the number of parameters. It should be noted, however, that incorporating sparsity can often be tricky, as it requires understanding the data-specific structure of sparsity and how it is modeled. Methods for achieving sparsity often use a penalty on a loss function. Methods such as LASSO and sparse coding are worth highlighting.

Simulatability: A model is considered simulatable if a human can internally simulate and understand the entire decision process. The human must understand how a trained model produces an output for any given input. This requirement can only be met if the number of features is small and the underlying relationship is simple. Decision trees are often considered a simulatable model because of their hierarchical decision process. Because of their simplicity, simulatable models have very high description accuracy. If the user intends to understand a model frequently used for predictions, these models can be very effective. A lack of stability in these types of models can limit their applications.

Modular model: An ML model is considered modular if a meaningful part of the prediction process can be explained independently. GAMs enforce that the relationship between variables in the model is additive. In DL, specific methods such as attention and modular network architectures provide limited insight into the inner workings of a network. There are three families of network architectures: densely connected networks, convolutional networks, and recurrent networks. Each type of network is designed for a particular input modality: a network architecture encodes assumptions about the structure of the data, a hypothesis space within which the search for a good model proceeds.

Domain-based feature technique: For a meaningful interpretation, the features used as input to the model are also meaningful. If the features have more meaning for a particular audience, they are easier to interpret. In many individual areas, expert knowledge can help create feature sets. Unique algorithms used to extract features are usually domain-specific. They are based on the user's existing expertise and insights gained from the data through exploratory data analysis.

4.1.2 *Post hoc*

After fitting a model (or models), the risk modeler analyzes it for answers to the original question. In analyzing the model, explanatory methods are often used to extract various (stable) forms of information from the model.

In *post hoc* analysis, the risk modeler analyzes a trained model to gain insight into the learned relationships. It is particularly challenging when it needs to be clarified from the parameters of the model which relationships the model has learned. Some *post hoc* interpretation methods have been developed that provide insight into what a trained model has learned without changing the underlying model. These methods are significant for situations where the collected data are high-dimensional and complex. In these cases, explainability methods must deal with the challenge that individual features need more semantic meaning, making the problem more difficult than for datasets with more meaningful features. Once the information is extracted from the fitted model, it can be analyzed and presented using standard data analysis methods (e.g., scatter plots and histograms) (Arrieta *et al.*, 2020).

In the following, some techniques are specified. It should be noted that many techniques may be appropriate for many different types of data (cf. Section 4.7). In general, *post hoc* explanatory techniques are divided by the author's intention (explanatory technique, e.g., explanation by simplification), by the method used (basic technique, e.g., sensitivity analysis), and by the type of data to which it was applied (e.g., images) (Arrieta *et al.*, 2020). Figure 5 shows the different *post hoc* explanatory approaches.

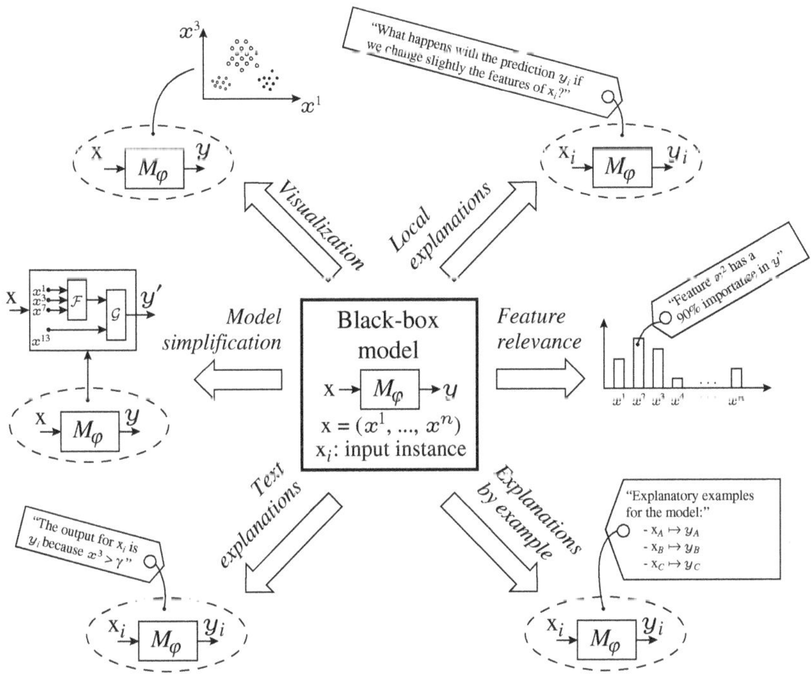

Figure 5. Different *post hoc* explainability approaches available for an ML model M_φ.
Source: Arrieta *et al.* (2020, p. 13).

Text explanations help explain the results of the model. Text explanations also include any method that generates symbols representing how the model works. These symbols can represent the algorithm's logic through semantic mapping from the model to the symbols.

Visual explanation techniques aim at visualizing the behavior of the model. Many visualization methods aim at dimensionality reduction. Visualizations can be coupled with other techniques to enhance their understanding. They are considered the most appropriate method to introduce complex interactions within the variables involved in the model to users unfamiliar with ML modeling. For example, Hurley *et al.* (2022) use interactive visualization of slices of the predictor space to address the interpretability deficit.

Explanations based on examples are about extracting examples of data that relate to the outcome produced by a particular model. The focus is on extracting representative examples that capture the internal relationships and correlations found by the analyzed model (cf. Section 4.6).

Explanations by simplification collectively refer to those techniques in which a completely new system is recreated based on the trained model to be explained. This new, simplified model usually seeks to optimize its similarity to the operation of the predecessor model while reducing its complexity. Nevertheless, a comparative performance evaluation should be maintained.

Finally, feature relevance methods for *post hoc* explainability illustrate the inner workings of a model. They compute a relevance score for the variables they manage. These scores quantify the impact (sensitivity) of a feature on the output of the model. Comparing the scores between different variables reveals the importance the model assigns to each of these variables in producing its output. Feature relevance methods can be viewed as an indirect method of explaining a model.

4.2 White box vs. black box vs. gray box

This criterion distinguishes whether the design of a method is known and transparent. A white-box approach is more transparent and explainable by design than a black-box approach. One speaks of the white-box approaches for simple decision trees, rule-based and pattern-based models, linear regression models, Bayesian networks, and fuzzy cognitive maps. In contrast to Boolean logic (e.g., true/false statements), such algorithms follow fuzzy logic and consider an uncertainty underlying the analyzed data in explaining the decision. In white-box approaches, there is access to the parameters internal to the model. One can access the weights or gradients of a network. The gradient information can act as a defining factor for the functioning of a model (Ancona *et al.*, 2019). In the black-box approach, only the relationships between inputs and outputs and the response function are known to derive explanations. White-box approaches are generally more interpretable but need to be more accurate. Black-box approaches are more accurate but less interpretable.

4.2.1 *White box*

Transparent models inherently convey a certain degree of interpretability. Transparent models can be divided into three levels: simulatable, decomposable, and algorithmically transparent. Each of the three levels is interrelated. For example, a simulatable model is simultaneously a model that is decomposable and algorithmically transparent (Murdoch, 2019; Arrieta *et al.*, 2020). Figure 6 illustrates the different levels of transparency.

- **Simulatability** refers to the ability of a model to be simulated or rigorously reasoned about by a human. Therefore, complexity occupies a dominant place in this class. Simple yet extensive rule-based systems fall outside this category. This assessment is consistent with the fact that sparse linear models are more interpretable than dense models. An interpretable model can be easily presented to a human using text and visualizations. Simulatability requires that the model be self-contained enough that a human can view and think about it as a whole.
- **Decomposability** represents the ability to explain each part of a model (input, parameters, and computation). This decomposability property enhances the ability to understand, interpret, or explain the behavior of a model (Yeh and Ravikumar, 2021). However, as with algorithmic transparency, only some models can satisfy this property. Decomposability requires that any input be easily interpretable.

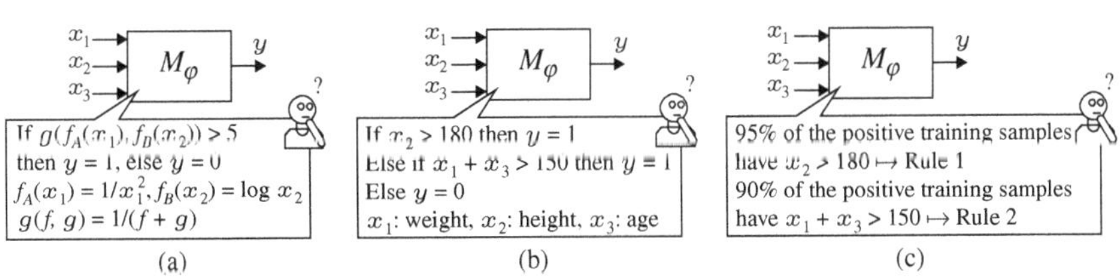

Figure 6. Conceptual diagram exemplifying the different levels of transparency. A ML model M_φ, with φ denoting the parameter set of the model at hand: (a) simulatability; (b) decomposability; (c) algorithmic transparency. Without loss of generality, the example focuses on the ML model as the explanation target. However, other targets for explainability may include a given example, the output classes or the dataset itself.

Source: Arrieta *et al.* (2020, p. 11).

- **Algorithmic transparency** can be viewed in several ways. The user can understand the process from the input data to a specific output. In other words, a linear model is considered transparent because its error surface can be understood and reasoned. In contrast, it is impossible to understand the model in deep architectures because the loss landscape can be opaque. The solution converges through heuristic optimizations (e.g., stochastic gradient descent). The most critical condition for algorithmically transparent models is that the model must be fully explorable using mathematical analysis and methods.

Many credit risk models can essentially be categorized as white-box approaches. They are based on statistical methods, such as the parametric methods (logit or probit), which include linear discriminant analysis (LDA) or logistic regression (LR). The LR is a classification model for predicting a dependent variable (category) that is dichotomous (binary). This model assumes a linear dependence between the predictors and the predicted variables, which hinders a flexible fit to the data. This specific reason (rigidity of the model) keeps the model under the umbrella of transparent methods. For example, while meeting transparent models' characteristics, logistic and linear regression may also require *post hoc* explanatory techniques (especially visualization). Most often, it is credit scoring or rating that acts as a screening tool to improve credit decision-making. The goal is to minimize the probability of credit default and, thus, the cost of the credit process.

4.2.2 *Black box*

In contrast to the aforementioned white-box approaches, NN and RF are some examples of black-box approaches. Like statistical methods, they also belong to the learning category of supervised learning: the functions are determined based on data whose output is known. However, NN and RF can better detect patterns in credit data due to their nonlinear and adaptive learning properties. In the end, they lead to higher discriminatory power. The logit or probit models used so far also achieve high predictive accuracy. However, due to their static nature, they are regularly unable to correctly predict rare situations in which borrowers default on their loans (Baghdasaryan *et al.*, 2021; Tantri, 2021). The following explanatory approaches are used in black-box models:

Utilizing so-called decision sets, the understanding of the forecast model is to be increased. The tool aims to extract the decisive variables of a decision system and map them employing if-then-else rules. This approach can be classified into inductive reasoning since logical rules are used. Rule-based classifiers such as decision trees can be explained in this way. However, each rule can be interpreted independently, thus providing a real benefit to human understanding (Lakkaraju *et al.*, 2016). For example, to estimate how the model response changes as a result of changes in the input variables, one can use ceteris paribus (CP) diagrams.

The explanation of black-box classifications can be done using matrix factorization. It is an analytical method that can be applied to general classification models to provide model explanations. The concept behind it is employing contribution matrix explanations and an embedded constraint space using matrix factorization. Like decision sets, rule-based explanations are derived from the attribution matrix (Kim and Seo, 2017).

Interpretable explanations can be made employing significant perturbation. It is a technique that is predominantly used in the field of image recognition and classification. Essentially, the areas of an image critical for classification by a complex NN are identifiable by a perturbation mask. It provides the user with a visual explanation of the decision-making process (Fong and Vedaldi, 2017).

4.2.3 *Gray box*

Finally, gray-box approaches lie between black and white box models (Pintelas *et al.*, 2020). Examples of such approaches are Local Interpretable Model-agnostic Explanations (LIME) (cf. Section 4.3.1). In gray-box models, an expert knows when one part of a system works mathematically (white box) and is uncertain about the other parts (black box). The white-box part of such models is fixed because of the underlying structure and constraints, while the black-box part must be learned from the data. Gray-box models can combine the advantages of both elements, resulting in an explainable model that is both accurate and interpretable. Bennetot *et al.* (2022) present a gray-box XAI by unifying a DNN and a transparent model thanks to using a symbolic knowledge base (KB). They extract a KB from the dataset and use it to train a transparent model of logistic regression.

Gray-box approaches also mean risk management practices combine the best of both worlds. We are talking here about so-called hybrid forecasting models. A combination of statistical and ML techniques provides better forecasting capabilities than stand-alone technologies (Dumitrescu *et al.*, 2021). In this approach, ML-developed functions are used to select highly predictive features (e.g., for the probability of failure) to eventually integrate them into a logistic regression model that is easier to explain. This hybrid model then contains both original and ML-developed rating factors. An automated algorithm would select the features for PD prediction — critical is feature selection. Using feature engineering, a targeted search of potentially powerful new features occurs. In the end, it comes down to combinations of existing features (e.g., loan-to-value ratio combined with a geographic area for a mortgage loan portfolio) and highly predictive binary variables. They indicate whether a risk driver is in a particularly relevant area (e.g., loan-to-value more significant than a defined threshold). Decision trees can facilitate feature selection. Performance-based features can also be added through sequential forward selection (SFS). In this way, the initial set of features in the logit model can grow from 50 to 1,500 features, significantly increasing complexity. If the model is to be kept lean, an alternative is to use only a few ML-derived "super parameters." Good models can suggest many candidates for promising features in the learning phase, test them, and reduce them to a few dominant features as learning progresses.

Figure 7 shows how an NN considered a black box is explained. The black box is associated with a more interpretable model, such as a decision tree or a (fuzzy) rule-based system.

Chi *et al.* (2021) compare traditional and hybrid models in a study. Different ML classification algorithms are used to evaluate the performance. As a result, it is found that among the hybrid models, the combination between LR and MLP is the most effective. The MLP involves fully interconnected networks. The outputs of the perceptrons of one layer are all connected to each perceptron of the next layer. Baghdasaryan *et al.* (2021) apply the architecture to

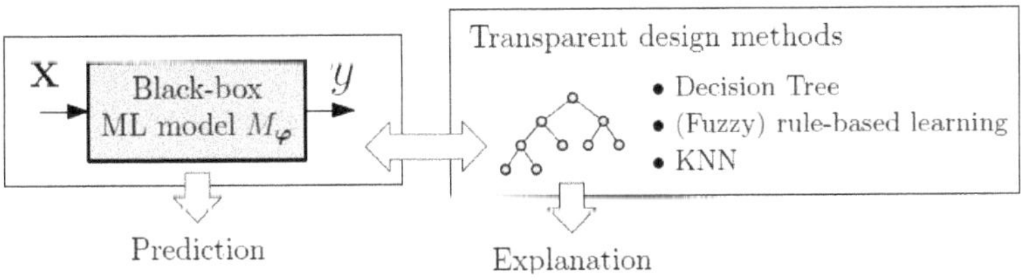

Figure 7. Pictorial representation of a hybrid model.
Source: Arrieta *et al.* (2020, p. 28).

borrower default classification. In an LR/MLP hybrid model, the LR component contributes to an appropriate balance between accuracy, efficiency, and interpretability of results (Chi *et al.*, 2019). Using the MLP component, on the other hand, enhances the predictive ability of PD. It provides a way to detect nonlinear patterns from complex datasets. Overall, hybrid ML-based credit risk models are, on the one hand, more parsimonious than conventional models in terms of computation time. At the same time, they are more explainable than pure ML methods. Moreover, ML-based credit risk models allow the use of a much more extensive and diverse database.

However, important aspects have to be considered during integration. The fundamentals of the model must be robust (cf. Section 3.2). Cross-validations must be performed to avoid over-fitting. In addition, the economic relationships underlying the model should be evaluated. The hyperparameters used to describe the model structure and to fit the learning algorithm are often based on human judgments.

4.3 Local vs. global

In *post hoc* analysis, the model is already trained, so its predictive accuracy is fixed. Therefore, only description accuracy and relevance (concerning a specific audience) must be considered (cf. Section 4.1.2). The criterion of scope is to distinguish XAI methods according to whether the scope of explainability refers to the whole model or a part of it. Two main categories are distinguished: prediction-level interpretations and dataset-level interpretations. They are also referred to as local and global interpretations, respectively.

Prediction-level interpretation methods focus on explaining individual predictions of models, e.g., which features or interactions led to the particular prediction. In contrast, dataset-level approaches focus on the global relationships learned by the model, e.g., which visual patterns are associated with a predicted response.

These two categories have some commonalities: dataset-level approaches support prediction-level information. Prediction-level insights can provide fine-grained information about individual predictions. However, they often need help to provide dataset-level insights. It is especially true when exploring a sufficient set of prediction-level interpretations is impossible.

4.3.1 *Local*

Prediction-level, that is, local-level, approaches are helpful when a risk modeler is interested in understanding how a model makes individual predictions. In local approaches, the scope of explainability is limited to a small portion of the model prediction space. The solution space is segmented. Explanations are related to less complex solution subspaces but relevant to the entire model. These explanations can be formed using techniques that have a differentiating property such that only a portion of the entire system's operation is explained. It should be noted that prediction-level approaches can sometimes be aggregated to produce dataset-level insights.

The most popular predictive-level explanatory power approach is assigning importance values to individual characteristics (Murdoch, 2019). Intuitively, a variable with a high positive (negative) value made a very positive (negative) contribution to a particular prediction. The critical features are visualized in the form of a heatmap. It should be emphasized that the feature importance values at the prediction level can provide much more information than those at the dataset level. It is a consequence of heterogeneity in a nonlinear model: the importance of a feature may vary across different examples due to interactions with other features. Finally, algorithms in an ANN can also learn interactions between variables. The following local approaches are commonly used in risk management.

Local Interpretable Model-agnostic Explanations (LIME) have the holistic claim to explain any classifier or regressor and its prediction using a local approximation. LIME trains an intrinsically interpretable model (e.g., decision trees) on a new dataset consisting of samples' permutation and the black box's corresponding prediction. In this context, the explanation provided by LIME is intended to be comprehensible to an extended group of end users outside the domain and to facilitate the adaptation or improvement of a model in a semantic context relevant to the study (Ribeiro *et al.*, 2016). LIME, in contrast to the explanation methods listed in Section 4.2.2, offers some flexibility in that it can explain the text, images, individual instances, and an entire model. Thus, LIME combines many features that other explanation approaches serve only selectively. Further details about LIME are presented in Section 4.5.

The SHapley Additive ExPlanations (SHAP) is a Python framework released in 2017. SHAP is a mathematical method for explaining the predictions of ML models. It is based on game-theoretic concepts (Lundberg *et al.*, 2017). It assumes that each instance feature value is a player in a game. The prediction is then the total payoff distributed among the players (i.e., the features) according to their contribution to the total payoff (i.e., the prediction). The idea is that the combination of features interacts, and this combination obtains a specific total payoff. It is less said, however, about how the characteristics contributed to the target variable. It is because a model is only sometimes a good representation of reality. Since some features may contribute more to the feature set than others, the question is how important each feature is to the overall set and what impact to expect. The Shapley values provide a possible answer to this question. The Shapley value is the average contribution to the prediction across all possible feature coalitions, which is computationally intensive when the number of features is extensive. Unlike LIME, the Shapley value is an explanatory method with a sound theory that provides complete explanations. However, it also needs to address the problem of correlated features.

It should be noted that the method may need to be revised due to unrealistic data instances when features are correlated. In addition, the Shapley value returns a single value per characteristic; there is no way to make a statement about the changes in output that result from changes in input. Characteristic dependencies can also lead to confusion in interpreting SHAP diagrams. Shapley values are often applied in predicting loan defaults (Bussmann *et al.*, 2020; Misheva *et al.*, 2021b; Tyagi, 2022). Bussmann *et al.* (2021)

propose a methodology based on the combination of network analysis and Shapley values to group predictions according to the similarity of the underlying explanations. Instead of applying network models in a preprocessing stage, they use them in a postprocessing stage to interpret the prediction results of one. In this way, they achieve both prediction accuracy and explainability. It should be emphasized that Shapley values are not standardized. Therefore, there must be a standardized procedure. Giudici and Raffinetti (2022) designed an explainable AI model that embeds Shapley values with a statistical normalization based on Lorenz zonoids. This procedure is suitable for ordinal measurement variables that can be obtained for cyber risk assessment.

Break Down (BD) plots break down the specific model prediction (instance level) by explanatory variables to show the impact of each feature on the final result. BD allows the user to get a clear summary of the impact of each variable on the expected model prediction.

Individual Conditional Expectation (ICE) is about expectation diagrams. It is a tool for visualizing the model estimated by any supervised learning algorithm. The method involves showing how a feature affects changes in the prediction. ICE makes it more intuitive to understand dependencies. Nevertheless, the method can only make sense of one feature at a time. Moreover, it suffers from the problem of correlated features and crowded lines when there are many instances.

Local approaches provide higher precision, especially for individual predictions (or a particular decision) but lower recall for understanding model behavior across all examples. On the other hand, global approaches provide a higher hit rate for model prediction, i.e., they help understand the entire decision structure. In contrast, their lower precision due to aggregations such as medians or means should be emphasized.

4.3.2 *Global*

Dataset-level — global — approaches are helpful when risk modelers are interested in more general relationships learned from a model. For example, they may be relationships relevant to a particular class of responses. Global approaches cover the entire model prediction space. It is achieved by aggregating the rank contributions of input variables to the prediction space (or decision space). For example, this interpretation can be helpful when it is not feasible for a risk modeler to consider many local predictions.

Dataset-level feature weight values attempt to capture how strongly individual features in a dataset contribute to a prediction. These values can provide information about which features the model has identified as necessary for which outcomes and their relative importance. When individual features in many models need to be evaluated, ANN, RF, or generic classifiers are used.

In addition to feature importance, there are also methods for extracting essential interactions between features. Interactions are essential because ML models are often highly nonlinear and learn complex interactions between features. It is to overcome the limitations of local explanations. RF and ANN extract interactions from many ML models.

With high-dimensional datasets, it can be challenging to understand the complex relationships that a model has learned quickly, so visualizing the results is particularly important. Various visualizations help understand what a model has learned (Murdoch, 2019):

- Line models with regularization plots of the regression coefficient paths show how varying a parameter affects the fitted coefficients.
- In convolutional neural networks, filters, maximum activation of responses of individual neurons or classes, or intra-class variations or grouping of different neurons can be visualized.

It may be helpful to look at more than average accuracy to assess the performance of an ML model. Instead, the distribution of predictions and sources of mispredictions should also be examined. Targeted tools that focus on the source of the mispredictions, e.g., excessive false positives, may provide better solutions (Blattner *et al.*, 2021). Residual plots, for example, can highlight the heterogeneity of predictions and point to specific data points to analyze. This concerns, for example, outliers in the predictions or examples with the most significant prediction errors. In addition, these charts can be used to analyze trends in the predictions. Another two global XAI techniques are worth highlighting. They are black-box visualization tools (Islam *et al.*, 2021).

The Partial Dependence Plot (PDP) or PD plot shows the marginal effect of one or two features on the predicted outcome of an ML model. The XAI technique can plot linear or complex relationships between the target and features. It provides a function that depends only on the represented features by marginalizing other features so that the interactions between them are considered. PDP provides causal interpretation by providing changes in prediction due to changes in specific features. Ultimately, a PDP can be conceptualized as an average of many CPs. However, PDP assumes that the characteristics under the graph are not correlated with the other characteristics. Finally, the method represents the average effect of a feature (from all instances) on the prediction. However, this is only true for some features in a given instance. The method is often used in credit risk management when assessing the creditworthiness of a credit customer.

In the Accumulated Local Effects (ALE) method, the ALE plots describe how the features affect the prediction on average. Unlike PDP, ALE visualization in one-dimensional diagrams for highly correlated variable spaces works well with correlated characteristics. Although the ALE visualization does not focus on the correlated features, it is difficult to interpret the changes in prediction when the features are highly correlated and analyzed in isolation. In this case, only plots that show changes in both correlated features together help understand the changes in prediction.

So far, there are fewer methods to combine local and global XAI principles to obtain more informative explanations. For example, when explaining the heterogeneity of observations, PDPs should be accompanied by ICEs. However, combining methods requires specific model architectures. Finally, they require additional constraints on the training procedures or the availability of data, which makes *post hoc* application to arbitrarily pre-trained models practically impossible. Achtibat *et al.* (2022) present the concept relevance propagation (CRP) approach. The approach combines XAI's local and global perspectives, thus answering both the "where" and "what" questions for individual predictions.

4.4 Model agnostic vs. model specific

This criterion distinguishes XAI methods at the level of agnosticism. Model agnostic methods mean that their XAI algorithm can be applied to any ML model (Belle and Papantonis, 2021). The agnostic criterion could be a fuzzy boundary between different methods. Sometimes simplification techniques are used to generate proxies. They mimic their antecedents to obtain something comprehensible and less complex. One can aggregate the results of some local model-specific methods (such as integrated gradients or SHAPLY) to recover the entire prediction space using aggregation operations, such as averages and medians. Such methods are referred to as hybrid methods. In other cases, the goal is to extract knowledge directly from the models or visualize them to facilitate the interpretation of their behavior. Kursuncu *et al.* (2019) propose knowledge-infused learning. It measures information loss in latent features learned by ANNs through knowledge graphs. This incorporation of external knowledge is expected to help outperform feature learning for the model.

4.4.1 *Model agnostic*

Model agnostic methods separate the explanation from a machine learning model so that the method is compatible with various models. This separation has several advantages. For example, the XAI method can work with multiple ML models. In addition, these methods provide different forms of explainability (e.g., visualization of feature importance and linear formula) for a given model. Model-agnostic methods include LIME, SHAP, Individual Conditional Expectation (ICE) (cf. Section 4.3.1), Partial Dependence Plot (PDP), and Accumulation Local Effects (ALE) (cf. Section 4.3.2), as well as feature interaction, feature importance, and global surrogate (cf. Section 4.6). Model agnostic techniques may rely on model simplification, feature relevance estimation, and visualization techniques (Islam *et al.*, 2021; Arrieta *et al.*, 2020).

Explanation by simplification is the most comprehensive technique under model-agnostic *post hoc* methods. Local explanations are also found in this category since simplified models are sometimes representative only of certain parts of a model. Almost all techniques that follow this path of model simplification are based on rule extraction techniques. Among the best-known contributions to this approach is the LIME technique (cf. Section 4.3.1). Besides LIME and related variants, another approach to rule extraction is G-REX. Although it was not initially intended for extracting rules from opaque models, the generic set of G-REX has also been extended to consider the explainability of models.

Feature relevance explanation techniques such as Permutation Feature Importance (PFI) aim to assess or measure each feature's influence, relevance, or importance in predicting the model being explained. Various proposals can be found within this category, each relying on different algorithmic approaches with the same goal. One fruitful contribution to this path is SHAP (cf. Section 4.3.1). The method takes an additive feature weighting for each prediction with a number of desirable properties (local accuracy, missingness, and consistency) that its predecessors lacked.

Feature Interaction (FI) is used when features interact with each other. Then the individual feature effects do not sum to the total feature effects of all features. An H-statistic can help identify different types of interactions. The interaction strength between two characteristics is the difference between the partial dependence function for these two characteristics together and the sum of the partial dependence functions for each individual characteristic. Calculating the interaction between features is very computationally intensive. In addition, using samples instead of the entire dataset usually shows discrepancies. The method is often used in credit scoring.

Feature importance is the increase in the model's prediction error when the values of the feature are swapped. Then the genuine relationship between the feature and the accurate result should be broken. If the errors increase after swapping the values of the feature, then the feature is essential. Feature importance provides a compressed and global insight into the behavior of the ML model. Although feature importance considers both the feature's main effect and the interaction, this is a drawback because the feature interaction is included in the importance of the correlated features. It is worth mentioning that feature importance also falls under global methods (Section 4.3.2).

Visual explanation techniques are one means of achieving model-agnostic explanations. Visual explanations are less common in the field of model-agnostic methods for *post hoc* explainability. The design of these methods must ensure that they can be seamlessly applied to any ML model without regard to its internal structure. For this reason, creating visualizations of only the inputs and outputs of an opaque model is a complex task. All visualization methods that fall into this category work in conjunction with feature relevance techniques. They provide the information that is eventually displayed to the end user. Finally, visualization techniques provide exciting ways to visualize the results of feature relevance techniques to facilitate the interpretation of the model. In contrast, visualization techniques for other aspects of the trained model (e.g., its structure and operations) are closely related to the model explained.

4.4.2 *Model specific*

Model-specific methods, on the other hand, are designed for specific types of ML models. Examples are methods that depend on some intrinsic parts of the model learning methods, such as neural network methods. DeepVis, Keras-vis, and Lucid represent the XAI methods of an ANN. TreeInterpreter, for example, enables the explainability of a tree-based ML model.

Since their introduction, multi-layer neural networks (also known as multi-layer perceptrons, MLPs) have been widely hailed for their tremendous ability to infer complex relationships between variables (cf. Section 4.2.3). However, modelers tasked with applying these models in practice often need clarification about their questionable explanatory power. For this reason, NNs have always been considered black-box models. As a result, several explainability techniques have been developed for multi-layer neural networks. It includes model simplification approaches, feature relevance estimators, text explanations, local explanations, and model visualizations.

4.5 Explanation type-based methods

A variety of explicit explanatory methods also differ in explanatory power (Belle and Papantonis, 2021). For example, techniques such as feature summaries provide feature statistics that measure the proportional contribution of a feature to the prediction. Other returned data points also assist in better understanding the models. Some approaches help build simple models around complex models. These simple models, called surrogate models, can be used to derive explanations. Other explanation-based methods extract concepts, decision rules, correlation diagrams, and other visualizations.

A global surrogate model attempts to approximate the predictive function of a black-box model as correctly as possible using an explanatory model. It assumes that the prediction is explainable. It is also called a metamodel. Although a surrogate model offers explanatory power and flexibility (e.g., model agnosticism), different explanations for the same black box are a disadvantage. It could be true for multiple decision trees with different structures. Moreover, some would argue that this is just an illusion of explainability (Islam *et al.*, 2021).

LIME is a local surrogate model (cf. Section 4.3.1). Although the learned LIME model may have a good approximation to the local behavior, it does not have an excellent global approximation. This feature is also referred to as "local fidelity". LIME also shows which feature contributes to decision-making and to what extent. Non-ML experts can understand explanations of machine predictions.

In some cases, non-experts cannot see how the explanation is arrived at, making LIME a black-box explainer. Since LIME is a proximity model and the local model may not cover full attribution due to generalization, it may not be suitable for cases where full explanations are needed for a decision from a legal perspective. In addition, there is no consensus on neighborhood boundaries for the local model; sometimes, it provides very different explanations for two nearby data points (Islam *et al.*, 2021).

4.6 Example-based methods

Example-based explanatory methods use specific features from the dataset to explain the model's behavior and the data's distribution in a model-independent way. Example-based methods create an illusion of explainability as opposed to those that find the actual behavior or where the method alone is inherently interpretable. The following XAI methods fall under this type:

Various counterfactual methods (DICE) indicate what changes are required on the input side to achieve significant changes (e.g., a reversal of the prediction) in the prediction/output. Counterfactual explanations can be used to explain individual, local predictions. It involves examining how a particular prediction (e.g., borrower default) might have changed due to small changes in the values of the risk drivers. Counterfactual explanations can suffer from the so-called "Rashomon effect." Each counterfactual explanation tells a different story to achieve instance-level prediction. The challenge is to choose the best one. The counterfactual methods do not require access to data or models. They could work with a system that does not use ML at all. In addition, this method is unsuitable for categorical variables with many values (Islam *et al.*, 2021). For example, if a customer's credit score can be increased (similar to another customer's) and the other characteristic values remain unchanged, the customer will not default. In short, there are several ways to adjust the characteristic values so that a customer moves from nonpayment to payment default or vice versa.

An adversarial technique can reverse the decision through counterfactual examples. Small intentional perturbations of the input take place to make an incorrect prediction. However, negative examples can help discover hidden vulnerabilities and improve the model. For example, an attacker can intentionally create counterexamples to cause the ML system to make a mistake (Islam *et al.*, 2021). It could pose a more significant cybersecurity threat, for example. The adversarial technique can also be used to predict loan defaults. The customer is deceived by simply increasing the credit score, resulting in an inverse prediction. For example, RNNs are well suited for sequential data analysis. Adversarial training techniques can significantly reduce the attack surface (Gianfagna and Di Cecco, 2021).

The prototype method consists of a selected set of instances representing the data well. Conversely, the set of instances that do not represent the data well is called critical points. However, determining the optimal number of prototypes and critical points is challenging. The distance between the data points expresses the respective representativeness of the classes.

Influential instances are data points from the training set that are important for the prediction and parameter determination of the model. While they help debug the model and better understand the model's behavior, determining the correct cutoff point to separate influential and noninfluential instances is challenging (Islam *et al.*, 2021). For example, certain customers may be treated as influential instances based on the values of their credit score and delinquency characteristics because they are strong representatives of the corresponding target. On the other hand, other customers are not influential instances because they would be on the edge of the decision boundary for classification.

The prediction of the KNN model can be explained using the k-neighbor data points (neighbors averaged to produce the prediction). Visualizing each cluster containing similar instances interprets why an instance is a member of a particular group or cluster. A visualization provides insight into why a particular sample belongs to a particular class.

Case-based reasoning (CBR) as an XAI method has played a minor role in risk management (Li *et al.*, 2022). In this method, problems are to be solved with empirical knowledge. Experiential knowledge is formalized with the help of so-called cases. CBR establishes a particular form of knowledge representation and processing in which analogy is the primary reasoning principle.

4.7 Data type-based methods

In addition to all the above criteria, a distinction can be made according to the data type. Not all XAI methods can work with all data types. Examples of data types are numeric, graphic, image, text/language, and tables. In risk management, it is mainly the numeric, text, and tabular data types that are processed.

Existing XAI methods also have limitations based on the type of data used (Joshi, 2022). Often such data need to be more structured. In an environment where users and policymakers want an explanation, a powerful XAI method should be able to handle any type or combination of data. However, existing algorithms in XAI methods need to be prepared to handle all data types (Bertossi and Geerts, 2020).

Overall, each XAI method has different guarantees, limitations, and computational requirements in explaining the results. Nonetheless, these basic methods help create some model understanding and provide pieces of human-interpretable understanding. The methods are only a panacea for some XAI challenges. Table 1 summarizes the explanatory methods under the criteria presented in this section.

Table 1. Comparison of different explainability methods from a set of crucial perspectives.

Method	Approximate	Inherent	Intrinsic/ *Post hoc*	White/ Black/ Gray	Local/ Global	Agnostic/ Specific
Linear/logistic regression	No	Yes	Intrinsic	White/Gray	Both	Specific
Decision trees	No	Yes	Intrinsic	White/Gray	Both	Specific
Decision rules	No	Yes	Intrinsic	White/Gray	Both	Specific
k-nearest neighbors	No	Yes	Intrinsic	White/Gray	Both	Specific
Decision sets	Yes	No	*Post hoc*	Black	Local	Agnostic
Matrix factorization	Yes	No	*Post hoc*	Black	Local	Agnostic
Meaningful perturbation	Yes	No	*Poot hoc*	Black	Local	Agnostic
Partial dependence plot (PDP)	Yes	No	*Post hoc*	Black	Global	Agnostic
Individual conditional expectation (ICE)	Yes	No	*Poot hoc*	Black	Both	Agnostic
Accumulated local effects (ALE)	Yes	No	*Post hoc*	Black	Global	Agnostic
Permutation feature importance	No	Yes	Both	Black	Global	Agnostic
Feature interaction	No	Yes	Both	Black	Global	Agnostic
Globale surrogate	Yes	No	*Poot hoc*	Black/Gray	Global	Agnostic
Local explanation (LIME)	Yes	No	*Post hoc*	Black/Gray	Local	Agnostic
Shapley value (SHAP)	Yes	No	*Post hoc*	Black/Gray	Local	Agnostic
Break down	Yes	No	*Post hoc*	Black/Gray	Local	Agnostic
Diverse counterfactual explanations (DICE)	Yes	No	*Post hoc*	Black	Local	Agnostic
Adversarial examples	Yes	No	*Post hoc*	Black	Local	Agnostic
Prototypes	Yes	No	*Post hoc*	Black	Local	Agnostic
Influential instances	Yes	No	*Post hoc*	Black	Local	Agnostic

Source: In accordance with Islam *et al.* (2021, p. 11).

5 Lessons Learned

While ML can help in more precise estimation of risk parameters, the increase in predictive power comes with increased complexity, where the relationship between input and output variables is more difficult to evaluate and understand. Therefore, there is a trade-off between the interpretability of a model and its performance. The understandability of an ML model could degrade the quality of the decisions it makes. In this respect, there must be an optimal balance between the interpretability and performance of ML models. Until now, it seemed inevitable that more complex ML models would achieve higher performance. Equally, however, explainability declined with it. However, the emergence of more sophisticated methods for explainability may reduce this tendency. Figure 8 shows how new XAI techniques can improve the trade-off between model interpretability and performance.

Another aspect that should be mentioned here because of its close connection to model interpretability and performance is the approximation dilemma: explanations for an ML model must be drastic and approximate enough to meet the audience's requirements. At the

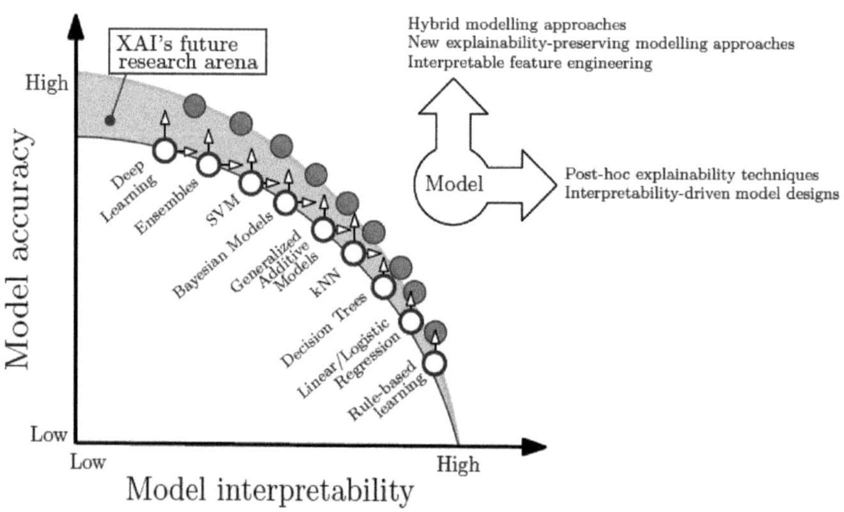

Figure 8. Trade-off between model interpretability and performance.
Source: Arrieta *et al.* (2020, p. 31).

same time, it must be ensured that the explanations represent the model under study and do not oversimplify its essential features.

In practice and the literature, there is a demand for a unified concept of explainability. For this to happen, it is essential to establish a common ground on which the community can contribute new techniques and methods. There needs to be a clear consensus on how to evaluate explainability methods. As a result, the standard of evaluation varies considerably across papers. It makes it difficult for even professional users to select appropriate methods. An explainability method must improve at least one of the features (predictive accuracy, descriptive accuracy, or relevance) to represent an improvement. The other features must be considered. While improvements in predictive accuracy are easy to measure, measuring improvements in descriptive accuracy and relevance remains challenging (Murdoch, 2019).

However, descriptive accuracy is generally complicated to measure or quantify, unlike predictive accuracy. One solution might be individual interpretations that appear to be "reasonable." These types of assessments are limited and not falsifiable. The results are often limited to a few examples and are only generally applicable to some datasets. The use of simulation studies could be a viable approach to solving this problem. Another starting point for developing improved explanatory methods is increasing interpretations' relevance to a particular audience or problem. It can take the form of feature heatmaps, rationales, or feature hierarchies. Care should be taken to focus on something other than the novel output and ignore what real-world problems it can actually solve (Murdoch, 2019).

There are two predominant approaches to demonstrating improved relevance. The first and most robust approach uses the introduced method to solve a domain-specific problem. Whether the audience is an expert, a decision maker, or a user with no knowledge of ML, comprehensibility can be at a different level to provide an understanding to the audience. Therefore, objective measures of what constitutes a good explanation are needed.

A second, less direct approach is to use human studies. Here, one draws inspiration from human psychology, sociology, or cognitive science experiments to create objectively convincing explanations (Khan *et al.*, 2022; Islam *et al.*, 2021). While difficult to structure and conduct, these studies are essential to demonstrate that new interpretive methods are relevant to potential practitioners. The process must be multi-disciplinary and integrative to make an AI-based model interpretable. In this process, it is paramount to examine and adequately address the interests, requirements, and needs of all stakeholders interacting with the system which are explained. It starts with the developers of the system, the decision-makers who use the results it produces, and the users who feel the consequences of the decisions made (Johs *et al.*, 2022).

Another essential feature required to relate a particular model to this specific concept is the presence of a metric. A metric or group of metrics should provide a meaningful comparison of how well a model meets the definition of explainable. These metrics should express how well the model performs on a particular aspect of explainability. In general, XAI measures should assess the goodness, usefulness, and satisfaction of explanations; the improvement of the audience's mental model by model explanations; and the impact of explanations on model performance. Measurement techniques such as goodness checklist, explanation satisfaction scale, mental model survey methods, computerized measures of explanation fidelity, explanation trustworthiness, and model reliability are a good push towards evaluating XAI techniques (Murdoch, 2019). Amparore *et al.* (2021) defined a general metric (prescriptiveness). It evaluates the extent to which a local linear explanation can be used to change the outcome of a black-box classifier. It is implemented in the Python library under LEAF (Local Explanation Evaluation Framework).

If model-based explainability can achieve reasonable predictive accuracy and relevance, its high descriptive accuracy makes it preferable to fitting a more complex model and relying on *post hoc* interpretability. Thus, the main focus of intrinsic explainability is to expand the possible use cases by increasing predictive accuracy through more accurate models and transparent feature engineering. A combination of intrinsic and *post hoc* interpretability is also ideal in risk management.

In many cases, intrinsic interpretation methods fail to achieve adequate predictive accuracy. Risk modelers are forced to abandon model-based explainability and seek more accurate models in these cases. Thus, an effective way to increase the applicability of model-based explainability is to develop new modeling methods that achieve higher predictive accuracy while maintaining their high descriptive accuracy and relevance. One way is through improved tools for exploratory data analysis. Examples include interactive environments, visualization tools, and data exploration tools. In unsupervised learning, clustering and matrix factorization techniques can lead to more valuable features.

In contrast to model-based explainability, much *post hoc* interpretability is still relatively new. Many fundamental concepts still need to be clarified. Given a black-box predictor and a real-world problem, it is generally unclear which format is best suited to capture a model's behavior fully. One approach could be feature hierarchies or identifying essential elements in the training set (Murdoch, 2019). There needs to be more clarity between the simple information these explanations provide and what the model has learned. Consideration must be given to whether any current interpretive formats can fully capture a model's behavior or whether an entirely new format is required.

In some cases, *post hoc* explanations reveal that a model has learned relationships that the risk modeler knows to be incorrect. However, it must be possible for the risk modeler to correct these relationships learned by the model, thus increasing predictive accuracy. DL models are now used in credit risk management. In automated credit decision environments (e.g., one-click loans), they can minimize default rates. Nevertheless, DL models still exhibit low explainability. Although many efforts are being made in the area of XAI, many challenges still need to be overcome before explainability can be achieved in DL models. It is the case that there is yet to be agreement on the vocabulary and various definitions around XAI. For example, feature importance and relevance are often used for the same concept. The goal must be to have standardized terminology for XAI as well.

There is an urgent need to reach a consensus on what explainability means in AI. In risk management, there is the additional requirement that the ML model must meet various regulatory requirements. Selected applications in the financial industry (primarily lending applications) are classified as a "high-risk system" (Fritz-Morgenthal *et al.*, 2022). Thus, the ML model must be subject to comprehensive risk management over the system's lifetime. In addition, there are data governance procedures to ensure, for example, the representativeness of the data used. Comprehensive technical documentation, permanent logging, and ongoing human oversight complete the requirements (EC, 2021). Supervisory authorities have far been distant from ML-based methods for capital adequacy of credit risks (internal ratings-based approach, IRB). The European Banking Authority (EBA, 2021) is now offering a positive view of ML — citing the technology's ability to improve risk differentiation in IRB models. Therefore, it is likely that standards that reduce implementation efforts could become established in the foreseeable future. An essential prerequisite is that the procedures be explicable to the various levels of management functions and bodies.

Finally, other critical challenges for these methods are internal and external validation. Internal validation requires that we rule out alternative explanations, determine the direction of causality, and account for simultaneity and selection bias. However, it has been shown that internal validation of a method is strongly challenged by changes in the input data (characteristics or other data parameters). In contrast to the precision and internal mechanics of the model, external validation would require the successful application of XAI methods from a small validation dataset to a larger population or set of data. Existing XAI methods suffer from external validity problems and cannot handle all data types. Some methods work with visual data, while others only handle text and speech. The issue of validity is even more problematic when methods applied to the same data produce different predictions.

Finally, we come back to the term "explain". It is derived from the Latin verb "explanare," which means "to make level." So the discussions and scientific efforts around XAI may involve the idea that we are "putting ourselves on the same level" with AI systems. It leads us to the old question about our relationship to and with AI systems. When considering what constitutes a "good explanation," at a minimum, contextual factors, potential implications, and domain-specific needs should be considered when developing a concept of interpretability. It includes a thorough understanding of the ML model's purpose, the complexity of the explanations needed by the audience, and the performance and interpretability levels of existing technologies, models, and methods.

When considering explainability in the development of an ML system, the decision of which XAI approach to choose should take into account domain-specific risks and needs, available data resources and domain knowledge, and the suitability of the ML model to meet the requirements of the computational task to be addressed (Dikmen and Burns, 2022). Davis *et al.* (2022) show the importance of domain-specific knowledge for consumer credit risk to explain black-box models. These domain-specific constraints must be obtained from experts in the field but can provide pragmatically valid suggestions and explanations.

In practice, the above issues (contextual factors, impacts, and domain-specific requirements) may lead to the preference of transparent models over complex modeling alternatives whose interpretability requires the application of *post hoc* XAI techniques. In contrast, black-box models (e.g., SVM, ensemble methods, and NN) should be selected only when their superior modeling capabilities best fit the characteristics of the problem at hand.

Overall, there need to be more valid and reliable assessments of the impact on user experience and behavior in response to explanations. New XAI methods are often based on an intuitive notion of what a practical explanation should be. An adequate explanation differs depending on the different explanation methods presented in Section 4. Evaluating the different explanation styles improves system understanding, persuasiveness, and task performance in risk management decision support.

Walambe *et al.* (2020) propose to leverage the immutable nature of the blockchain to store explanations of machine learning models for credit scoring. Local interpretations of the global model should be publicly available to customers securely. A report of model decisions can be accessed for each user. This approach helps users better understand the events that led to their credit decisions (Nassar, 2020).

With the widespread use of ML in risk management, new commercial approaches are resulting that split parts of the ML development process across multiple companies or organizations. This trend leads us to consider the ML value chain. It refers to the organizational process by which a single ML model is developed and implemented. This focus on the organizational process distinguishes the ML value chain from the technical steps involved in building an ML model. By splitting the ML model development process across multiple organizations, some implementations of the ML value chain create an increased risk of loss. In these approaches, the organization using the ML system to make decisions may need to understand or explain the ML model fully.

6 Conclusion

Machine learning is becoming increasingly important in financial services, for example, pre-approval, loan underwriting, investments, and various front-end and back-end activities. ML is also playing an increasingly important role in risk management. ML can automatically detect nonlinearities and interactions in training data, enabling faster and more accurate risk decisions. AI-based systems enable potent predictions.

However, due to their partial black-box nature, they are not readily explainable. It is where the issue of explainability comes in — a rapidly growing area of ML. Various XAI methods strive to break through the black box. So-called model explainer systems, which aim to make a model's prediction understandable to humans, build on the prediction results to clarify the crucial features, intermediate results, or solution paths, such as how a classifier arrived at its result. The paradox here is that a transparent design for humans can again happen in a black-box process. Kumar *et al.* (2020) show that the solutions to mitigate these problems necessarily introduce further complexity, such as the need for causal reasoning. Ultimately, the crucial data are revealed, to be sure. However, there is a risk of not ensuring that the explanation is correct, as it may again happen in a black-box system.

For this reason, there is an urgent need for an XAI framework. The framework proposed in this chapter highlights the advantages and disadvantages of different XAI procedures and methods. Thus, the framework intends to build confidence among the various stakeholders in risk management. Such a framework ideally provides complete, accurate, consistent, reliable, and meaningful explanations that can be understood in different cases across multiple domains, both in the laboratory and in the practical world of risk management in a financial institution.

It is also essential in a bank's risk management to properly understand the opportunities and caveats opened up by XAI techniques. The application of these techniques can also be challenging in its own right. It is related to the underlying mathematical hypotheses. However, it also relates to the computational capabilities required. In addition, it should be noted that each technique provides only a partial understanding of a model and that its usefulness may vary greatly depending on the case. The shortcomings of the purely functionalist approach to *post hoc* interpretability must be overcome. Model interpretability and explainability must be addressed along with requirements and constraints related to privacy, model confidentiality, fairness, and accountability. Responsible implementation and use of AI methods in financial institutions can only be ensured if all these AI principles are considered.

References

Achtibat, R. *et al.* (2022). From "where" to "what": Towards human-understandable explanations through concept relevance propagation. *arXiv*. Available from: doi: 10.48550/arXiv.2206.03208.

Amparore, E., Perotti, A., and Bajardi, P. (2021). To trust or not to trust an explanation: Using LEAF to evaluate local linear XAI methods. *PeerJ Computer Science*, 7: e479. Available from: doi: 10.7717/peerj-cs.479.

Ancona, M. *et al.* (2019). Gradient-based attribution methods. In Samek, W. *et al.* (Eds.), *Explainable AI: Interpreting, Explaining and Visualizing Deep Learning*. Springer, Cham, pp. 169–191. Available from: doi: 10.1007/978-3-030-28954-6.

Arrieta, A.B. *et al.* (2020). Explainable artificial intelligence (XAI): Concepts, taxonomies, opportunities and challenges toward responsible AI. *Information Fusion*, 58: 82–115. Available from: doi: 10.1016/j.inffus.2019.12.012.

Asimit, A.V. *et al.* (2022). Robust classification via support vector machines. *Risks*, 10: 154. Available from: doi: 10.3390/risks10080154.

Aziz, S., and Dowling, M. (2019). Machine learning and AI for risk management. In Lynn, T. *et al.* (Eds.), *Disrupting Finance*. Springer, Cham, pp. 33–50. Available from: doi: 10.1007/978-3-030-02330-0_3.

Aziz, S. *et al.* (2022). Machine learning in finance: A topic modeling approach. *European Financial Management*, 28: 744–770. Available from: doi: 10.1111/eufm.12326.

Baghdasaryan, V. *et al.* (2021). Comparison of econometric and deep learning approaches for credit default classification. *Strategic Change*, 30: 257–268. Available from: doi: 10.1002/jsc.2408.

Barboza, F., Kimura, H., and Altman, E. (2017). Machine learning models and bankruptcy prediction. *Expert Systems with Applications*, 83: 405–417. Available from: doi: 10.1016/j.eswa.2017.04.006.

Bastos, J.A. (2022). Predicting credit scores with boosted decision trees. *Forecasting*, 4: 925–935. Available from: doi: 10.3390/forecast4040050.

Belle, V., and Papantonis, I. (2021). Principles and practice of explainable machine learning. *Frontiers in Big Data*, 4: 688969. Available from: doi: 10.3389/fdata.2021.688969.

Bennetot, A. *et al.* (2022). Greybox XAI: A neural-symbolic learning framework to produce interpretable predictions for image classification. *Knowledge-Based Systems*, 258: 109947. Available from: doi: 10.1016/j.knosys.2022.109947.

Bertossi, L., and Geerts, F. (2020). Data quality and explainable AI. *ACM Journal of Data and Information Quality*, 12(2): 11. Available from: doi: 10.1145/3386687.

Biecek, P. *et al.* (2021). Enabling machine learning algorithms for credit scoring — Explainable artificial intelligence (XAI) methods for clear understanding complex predictive models. *arXiv*. Available from: doi: 10.48550/arXiv.2104.06735.

Blattner, L., Nelson, S., and Spiess, J. (2021). Unpacking the black box: Regulating algorithmic decisions. *arXiv*. Available from: doi: 10.48550/arXiv.2110.03443.

Breeden, J.L. (2021). A survey of machine learning in credit risk. *Journal of Credit Risk*, 17(3): 1–62. Available from: doi: 10.21314/JCR.2021.008.

Bücker, M. *et al.* (2022). Transparency, auditability, and explainability of machine learning models in credit scoring. *Journal of the Operational Research Society*, 73(1): 70–90. Available from: doi: 10.1080/01605682.2021.1922098.

Bussmann, N. *et al.* (2020). Explainable AI in fintech risk management. *Frontiers in Artificial Intelligence*, 3: 26. Available from: doi: 10.3389/frai.2020.00026.

Bussmann, N. *et al.* (2021). Explainable machine learning in credit risk management. *Computational Economics*, 57: 203–216. Available from: doi: 10.1007/s10614-020-10042-0.

Cao, J. *et al.* (2013). A loan default discrimination model using cost-sensitive support vector machine improved by PSO. *Information Technology and Management*, 14: 193–204. Available from: doi: 10.1007/s10799-013-0161-1.

Casabianca, E.J. *et al.* (2022). A machine learning approach to rank the determinants of banking crises over time and across countries. *Journal of International Money and Finance*, 129: 102739. Available from: doi: 10.1016/j.jimonfi n.2022.102739.

Chi, G. *et al.* (2019). Hybrid model for credit risk prediction: An application of neural network approaches. *International Journal on Artificial Intelligence Tools*, 28(5): 1950017. Available from: doi: 10.1142/S0218213019500179.

Chi, G. *et al.* (2021). A hybrid model for credit risk assessment: Empirical validation by real-world credit data. *Journal of Risk Model Validation*, 14(4): 1–39. Available from: 10.21314/JRMV.2020.228.

Cox, Jr., L.A. (2021). Information structures for causally explainable decisions. *Entropy*, 23: 601. Available from: doi: 10.3390/e23050601.

Davis, R. *et al.* (2022). Explainable machine learning models of consumer credit risk. Available from: https://ssrn.com/abstract=4006840.

Dikmen, M., and Burns, C. (2022). The effects of domain knowledge on trust in explainable AI and task performance: A case of peer-to-peer lending. *International Journal of Human — Computer Studies*, 162: 102792. Available from: doi: 10.1016/j.ijhcs.2022.102792.

Dumitrescu, E. *et al.* (2021). Machine learning or econometrics for credit scoring: Let's get the best of both worlds. Available from: hal-02507499v3f.

Enisa. (2021). Securing machine learning algorithm. Available from: https://www.enisa.europa.eu/news/enisa-news/artificial-intelligence-how-to-make-machine-learning-cyber-secure. Accessed: 18th January 2021.

European Banking Authority (EBA). (2021). Discussion Paper on Machine Learning for IRB Models (EBA/DP/2021/04). November 11, 2021. Available from: https://www.eba.europa.eu/eba-consults-machine-learning-internal-ratings-based-models. Accessed: 12th December 2021.

European Commission (EC). (2021). Proposal for a regulation of the European parliament and of the council laying down harmonised rules on artificial intelligence (artificial intelligence act) and amending certain union legislative acts. April 21, 2021.

Feng, Y., Min, M., and Fouque, J.P. (2022). Deep learning for systemic risk measures. *arXiv*. Available from: doi: 10.48550/arXiv.2207.00739.

Fritz-Morgenthal, S., Hein, B., and Papenbrock, J. (2022). Financial risk management and explainable, trustworthy, responsible AI. *Frontiers in Artificial Intelligence*, 5: 779799. Available from: doi: 10.3389/frai.2022.779799.

Fong, R., and Vedaldi, A. (2017). Interpretable explanations of black boxes by meaningful perturbation. *arXiv*. Available from: doi: 10.48550/arXiv.1704.03296.

Gianfagna, L., and Di Cecco, A. (2021). *Explainable AI with Python*. Springer, Cham.

Gilpin, L.H. *et al.* (2022). Explanation' is not a technical term: The problem of ambiguity in XAI. *arXiv.* Available from: doi: 10.48550/arXiv.2207.00007.

Giudici, P., and Raffinetti, E. (2022). Explainable AI methods in cyber risk management. *Quality and Reliability Engineering International*, 38(3): 1318–1326. Available from: doi: 10.1002/qre.2939.

Gramegna, A., and Giudici, P. (2021). SHAP and LIME: An evaluation of discriminative power in credit risk. *Frontiers in Artificial Intelligence*, 4: 752558. Available from: doi: 10.3389/frai.2021.752558.

Gramespacher, T., and Posth, J.-A. (2021). Employing explainable AI to optimize the return target function of a loan portfolio. *Frontiers in Artificial Intelligence*, 4: 693022. Available from: doi: 10.3389/frai.2021.693022.

Hamori, S. *et al.* (2018). Ensemble learning or deep learning? Application to default risk analysis. *Journal of Risk and Financial Management*, 11: 12. Available from: doi: 10.3390/jrfm11010012.

Heng, Y.S., and Subramanian, P. (2022). A systematic review of machine learning and explainable artificial intelligence (XAI) in credit risk modelling. In *Proceedings of the Future Technologies Conference (FTC) 2022*, Vol. 1, pp. 596–614. Available from: doi: 10.1007/978-3-031-18461-1_39.

Hoffman, R.R. *et al.* (2019). Metrics for explainable AI: Challenges and prospects. *arXiv.* Available from: doi: 10.48550/arXiv.1812.04608.

Hu, K. *et al.* (2022). Supply chain characteristics as predictors of cyber risk: A machine-learning assessment. *arXiv.* Available from: doi: 10.48550/arXiv.2210.15785.

Hurley, C.B., O'Connell, M., and Domijan, K. (2022). Interactive slice visualization for exploring machine learning models. *Journal of Computational and Graphical Statistics*, 31(1): 1–13. Available from: doi: 10.1080/10618600.2021.1983439.

Hussin, A.A., Khatir, A., and Bee, M. (2022). Machine learning models and data-balancing techniques for credit scoring: What is the best combination? *Risks*, 10: 169. Available from: doi: 10.3390/risks10090169.

Islam, R. *et al.* (2022). A systematic review of explainable artificial intelligence in terms of different application domains and tasks. *Applied Science*, 12: 1353. Available from: doi: 10.3390/app12031353.

Islam, S.R. *et al.* (2021). Explainable artificial intelligence approaches: A survey. *arXiv.* Available from: doi: 10.48550/arXiv.2101.09429.

Islam, T., Vasilopoulos, C., and Pruyt, E. (2013). Stress-testing banks under deep uncertainty. In *Paper Presented at the 31st International Conference of the System Dynamics Society*, Cambridge, MA, USA, July 21–25, 2013.

Johs, A.J., Agosto, D.E., and Weber, R.O. (2022). Explainable artificial intelligence and social science: Further insights for qualitative investigation. *Applied AI Letters*, 3(1): e64. Available from: doi: 10.1002/ail2.64.

Joshi, K. (2022). Deep dive into explainable AI: Current methods and challenges. Arya-xAI 2022. Available from: https://medium.com/arya-xai/deep-dive-into-explainable-ai-current-methods-and-challenges-2e9912d73136. Accessed: 14th March 2022.

Jullum, M. *et al.* (2020). Detecting money laundering transactions with machine learning. *Journal of Money Laundering Control*, 23(1): 173–186. Available from: doi: 10.1108/JMLC-07-2019-0055.

Khan, M.S. *et al.* (2022). Explainable AI: A neurally-inspired decision stack framework. *Biomimetics*, 7: 127. Available from: doi: 10.3390/biomimetics7030127.

Kim, J., and Seo, J. (2017). Human understandable explanation extraction for black-box classification models based on matrix factorization. *arXiv*. Available from: doi: 10.48550/arXiv.1709.06201.

Kou, G. *et al.* (2019). Machine learning methods for systemic risk analysis in financial sectors. *Technological and Economic Development of Economy*, 25(5): 716–742. Available from: doi: 10.3846/tede.2019.8740.

Kumar, E. *et al.* (2020). Problems with Shapley-value-based explanations as feature importance measures. *arXiv*. Available from: doi: 10.48550/arXiv.2002.11097.

Kursuncu, U., Gaur, M., and Sheth, A. (2019). Knowledge infused learning (k-il): Towards deep incorporation of knowledge in deep learning. *arXiv*. Available from: doi: 10.48550/arXiv.1912.00512.

Lakkaraju, H., Bach, S.H., and Leskovec, J. (2016). Interpretable decision sets: A joint framework for description and prediction. In *Proceedings of the 22nd ACM SIGKDD International Conference on Knowledge Discovery and Data Mining*, pp. 1675–1684. Available from: doi: 10.1145/2939672.2939874.

Leo, M., Sharma, S., and Maddulety, K. (2019). Machine learning in banking risk management: A literature review. *Risks*, 7: 29. Available from: doi: 10.3390/risks7010029.

Lessmann, S. *et al.* (2015). Benchmarking state-of-the-art classification algorithms for credit scoring: An update of research. *European Journal of Operational Research*, 247: 124–36. Available from: doi: 10.1016/j.ejor.2015.05.030.

Li, W., Paraschiv, F., and Sermpinis, G. (2022). A data-driven explainable case-based reasoning approach for financial risk detection. *Quantitative Finance*, 22(12): 2257–2274. Available from: doi: 10.1080/14697688.2022.2118071.

Linardatos, P., Papastefanopoulos, V., and Kotsiantis, S. (2021). Explainable AI: A review of machine learning interpretability methods. *Entropy*, 23: 18. Available from: doi: 10.3390/e23010018.

Lipton, Z.C. (2017). The mythos of model interpretability. *arXiv*. Available from: doi: https://doi.org/10.48550/arXiv.1606.03490.

Liu, R., and Pun, C.S. (2022). Machine-learning-enhanced systemic risk measure: A two-step supervised learning approach. *Journal of Banking & Finance*, 136: 106416. Available from: doi: 10.1016/j.jbankfin.2022.106416.

Lundberg, S.M., and Lee, S.-I. (2017). A unified approach to interpreting model predictions. In *Proceedings of the 31st International Conference on Neural Information Processing System*. Curran Associates Inc., Long Beach, CA.

Melsom, B. *et al.* (2022). Explainable artificial intelligence for credit scoring in banking. *Journal of Risk*, 25(2): 1–25. Available from: doi: 10.21314/JOR.2022.046.

Meske, C. *et al.* (2022). Explainable artificial intelligence: Objectives, stakeholders, and future research opportunities. *Information Systems Management*, 39(1): 53–63. Available from: doi: 10.1080/10580530.2020.1849465.

Minh, D. *et al.* (2022). Explainable artificial intelligence: A comprehensive review. *Artificial Intelligence Review*, 55: 3503–3568. Available from: doi: 10.1007/s10462-021-10088-y.

Misheva, B.H. *et al.* (2021a). Audience-dependent explanations for AI-based risk management tools: A survey. *Frontier of Artificial Intelligence*, 4: 794996. Available from: doi: 10.3389/frai.2021.794996.

Misheva, B.H. *et al.* (2021b). Explainable AI in credit risk management. *arXiv*. Available from: doi: 10.48550/arXiv.2103.00949.

Mueller, S.T. (2019). Explanation in human-AI systems: A literature meta-review, synopsis of key ideas and publications, and bibliography for explainable AI. *arXiv*. Available from: doi: 10.48550/arXiv.1902.01876.

Murdoch, W.J. (2019). Definitions, methods, and applications in interpretable machine learning. *PNAS*, 116(44): 22071–22080. Available from: doi: 10.1073/pnas.1900654116.

Nassar, M. *et al.* (2020). Blockchain for explainable and trustworthy artificial intelligence. *WIREs Data Mining Knowledge Discovery*, 10(1): e1340. Available from: doi: 10.1002/widm.1340.

Pintelas, E., Livieris, I.E., and Pintelas, P.A. (2020). A grey-box ensemble model exploiting black-box accuracy and white-box intrinsic interpretability. *Algorithms*, 13: 17. Available from: doi: 10.3390/a13010017.

Pun, J., and Lawryshyn, Y. (2012). Improving credit card fraud detection using a meta-classification strategy. *International Journal of Computer Applications*, 56(10): 41–46.

Raei, R. *et al.* (2016). A hybrid model for estimating the probability of default of corporate customers. *Iranian Journal of Management Studies*, 9: 651–673.

Renftle, M. *et al.* (2022). Explaining any ML model? – On goals and capabilities of XAI. *arXiv.* Available from: doi: 10.48550/arXiv.2206.13888.

Ribeiro, M.T., Singh, S., and Guestrin, C. (2016). 'Why should I trust you?': Explaining the predictions of any classifier. *arXiv.* Available from: doi: 10.48550/arXiv.1602.04938.

Stanton, B., and Jensen, T. (2021). *Trust and Artificial Intelligence.* National Institute of Standards and Technology NISTIR 8332. Available from: doi: 10.6028/NIST.IR.8332-draft.

Tantri, P. (2021). Fintech for the poor: Financial intermediation without discrimination. *Review of Finance*, 25(2): 561–593. Available from: doi: 10.1093/rof/rfaa039.

Tavana, M. *et al.* (2018). An artificial neural network and Bayesian network model for liquidity risk assessment in banking. *Neurocomputing*, 275: 2525–2554. Available from: doi: 10.1016/j.neucom.2017.11.034.

Tyagi, S. (2022). Analyzing machine learning models for credit scoring with explainable AI and optimizing investment decisions. *American International Journal of Business Management*, 5(1): 5–19.

Vilone, G., and Longo, L. (2021). Classification of explainable artificial intelligence methods through their output formats. *Machine Learning & Knowledge Extraction*, 3: 615–661. Available from: doi: 10.3390/make3030032.

Walambe, R. (2020). Integration of explainable AI and blockchain for secure storage of human readable justifications for credit risk assessment. *International Advanced Computing Conference 2020: Advanced Computing*, pp. 55–72. Available from: doi: 10.1007/978-981-16-0404-1_5.

Wang, H., Xu, Q., and Zhou, L. (2015). Large unbalanced credit scoring using Lasso-logistic regression ensemble. *PLoS One*, 10: e0117844. Available from: doi: 10.1371/journal.pone.0117844.

Yang, S.C.-H., Folke, T., and Shafto, P. (2021). Abstraction, validation, and generalization for explainable artificial intelligence. *Applied AI Letters*, 2(4): e37. Available from: doi: 10.1002/ail2.37.

Yeh, C.-K., and Ravikumar, P. (2021). Objective criteria for explanations of machine learning models. *Applied AI Letters*, 2(4): e57. Available from: doi: 10.1002/ail2.57.

Zhang, H.G. *et al.* (2017). Calculating value-at-risk for high-dimensional time series using a nonlinear random mapping model. *Economic Modelling*, 67: 355–367. Available from: doi: 10.1016/j.econmod.2017.02.014.

Zschech, P. *et al.* (2022). GAM(e) changer or not? An evaluation of interpretable machine learning models based on additive model. *arXiv.* Available from: doi: 10.48550/arXiv.2204.09123.

https://doi.org/10.1142/9781800615212_0005

Chapter 5

How Can Sentiment Analysis Contribute to Financial Markets and Services?

Abraham Itzhak Weinberg
AI-Weinberg, AI Experts, Tel Aviv, Israel
aviw2010@gmail.com

Abstract

In recent years, the use of Sentiment Analysis (SA) has proliferated across a wide variety of fields, including financial markets and services. SA can help predict market trends, detect changes in consumer behavior, and identify potential investment opportunities. In this chapter, we explore the impact and applications of SA in financial markets and services and review both traditional and state-of-the-art algorithms for sentiment analysis. We demonstrate how SA approaches can help make better decisions and predictions in financial markets, stock exchange, trading, and cryptocurrencies. We provide examples of popular algorithms used in financial SA and discuss their pros and cons. In addition, we mention the main metrics for evaluating SA performance. By the end of this chapter, readers will have a deeper understanding of how sentiment analysis can contribute to financial markets and services, and the tools and techniques used to achieve accurate and reliable results.

Keywords: Sentiment analysis, artificial intelligence (AI), machine learning, financial markets, financial services.

1 Introduction

The last decade has contributed to rapid growth in the field of SA and its use in financial applications (Hussein, 2018). This can be explained by the exponential growth of Machine and deep Learning (ML) algorithms, as well as their usage, vast growth of data storage such as the cloud, and an increase in computational resources. Simultaneously, the growth of social networks, online news, and financial services has contributed to the potential resources and usage of SA (Yue *et al.*, 2019; Mäntylä *et al.*, 2018).

SA is defined as an "analysis of data to estimate the emotions and attitudes of creators" (Sánchez-Rada and Iglesias, 2019). The SA also plays an important role in sentic computing field. Sentic computing uses many different soft fields such as sociology and psychology in combination with computational techniques (Valle-Cruz *et al.*, 2021). The analyzed data used for SA are usually text processed computationally using ML algorithms. The data can be extracted from the Internet, social networks such as Twitter, YouTube, Facebook, LinkedIn, Google News, Instagram, and Yahoo Finance, as well as other finance news data. The text can be written by every entity that has a relationship with the company, such as investors, journalists, experts, employees, partners, customers, suppliers, analysts, and consultants.

Typically, the output of the SA process has two values: positive and negative, also known as polarity, and in some cases, neutral. These values are considered the target classes for the ML SA tasks. Das and Chen (2007) used the SA values for predicting the market stocks: bullish for positive or optimistic, bearish for negative or pessimistic, and neutral. In the literature, we found more fine-grained sentiment values. The two main aspects of SA are polarity and intensity (Tian *et al.*, 2018). In Mishev *et al.* (2020), we developed a formula for polarity. It calculates the number of positive and negative words based on their sentiments in the lexicon. Polarity was calculated as the difference between positive and negative values divided by their sum. Intensity is defined as the intermediate value between the polarity values.

As the vast majority of SA are implemented on textual datasets, SA is considered a Natural Language Processing (NLP) task (Ma *et al.*, 2018). However, SA can be used for other sources such as audio and videos, and the interaction between them is known as multi-modal SA. The SA task is challenging because a machine must predict the emotions of a human being. Moreover, the only input for the machine is text, and usually, there is no additional information about human gestures, voice changes, and body and face language.

Despite these challenges, ML models show very high accuracy levels in solving SA tasks in general and for financial purposes in particular (Zhang *et al.*, 2018).

In scientific papers, we can find other related tasks for SA, such as opinion-mining/analysis, perception analysis, emotion detection, and stance detection. SA and opinion mining are typically synonymous and interchangeable (Bakshi *et al.*, 2016). Currently, the term SA is popular. Perception analysis is typically a product of sentiment analysis. It attempts to predict the support level of the author for a brand or statement (Arief and Pangestu, 2021; Soleymani *et al.*, 2017).

Emotion detection relates not only to the sentiment value of the data (positive or negative) but also to human emotion types, such as anger, disgust, fear, sadness, and joy (Nandwani and Verma, 2021). Stance detection or classification refers to the author's stance towards a statement and usually has values equivalent to SA: favor, against, or neither (Küçük and Can, 2020).

SA works on different levels of text from a corpus that includes several documents for a specific word. It can be implemented for the entire document, paragraph, sentence, word, or aspect. In the literature, we find four components of sentiment: entity, aspect, opinion holder, and aspect sentiment (Soleymani *et al.*, 2017). Entities usually "refer to names mentioned in the text, such as products, organizations, or services, where aspects refer to their attributes" (Schouten and Frasincar, 2015). There are several approaches and algorithms called Aspect-Based Sentiment Analysis (ABSA) that extract and analyze the sentiments of aspects (Laskari and Sanampudi, 2016). Hence, the ABSA target is to discover sentiments about entities and their related aspects (Mukherjee and Liu, 2012).

In the following paragraph, we review the relevant and popular metrics and indices for SA usage, in general, and in the context of finance, in particular.

2 SA Metrics

The SA task is a challenging process that comprises several stages. The evaluation of SA results is usually accompanied by metrics. Several metrics are commonly used to evaluate and compare the final results of SA pipeline processes and algorithms. These metrics are also used in SA finance tasks. In the financial context, SA is usually an intermediate stage that is considered an estimator for other financial indices or tasks. Usually, the better the performance of the SA process, the better the solution for the relevant financial task.

The most commonly used metrics for SA evaluation are accuracy, F measure (score) known also as F1, recall, and precision (Birjali *et al.*, 2021). Accuracy is the ratio of corrected SA prediction to the total number of input items. Recall divides the number of correctly positive SA predictions into all positive input items. Where precision divides this into the total number of predicted positive input items. The F1 measure multiplies recall by precision by 2 and divides it by the sum of recall and precision. Its value is between 0 and 1 and is known as the Harmonic mean or balance between recall and precision (Birjali *et al.*, 2021). An additional metric is called the specificity. Specificity is also considered the opposite of recall and is used for calculating the confidence of precision. SA robustness measures how much the model's performance changes when using data different from the model's trained data (Fei *et al.*, 2023; Hazarika *et al.*, 2022).

In the following subsections, we classify the different SA approaches. We provide a short description of SA approaches and algorithms, and in the last paragraphs, we explain what SA algorithms are commonly used for solving financial tasks.

3 SA Approaches and Algorithms

SA approaches can be divided into (Birjali *et al.*, 2021) lexicon-based, machine learning, and hybrid approaches. These approaches have evolved in the past few years. The first approaches were used at the inception of the SA field, where ML and, more specifically, the Deep Learning (DL) approaches are the most recent approaches for solving SA tasks.

Generally, lexicon-based approaches are based on calculating the polarity of words or phrases, as they appear in dictionaries or corpora of texts. The lexicon approach includes dictionary, corpus, and manual approaches. The difference between the dictionary and corpus approaches is that the dictionary approach uses dictionaries to tag words, whereas the corpus is based on statistical and syntactic analysis of the patterns and occurrences of words in the analyzed text (Darwich *et al.*, 2019). The manual approach used human sentiment-tagged lexicons and lists.

The SA–ML approach is the richest class in terms of algorithms and usage. Unlike dictionary-based approaches, ML deduces polarity or emotions from the trained data. ML implements the model deduced by the learning phase on the trained text and implements it on an unseen text called testing. In comparison to the dictionary-based approach, ML does not necessarily stick to a list of words but deduces conclusions learned automatically by the model. ML approaches can be subdivided into supervised, unsupervised, and semi-supervised.

The supervised SA approach uses sentiment-labeled data. This is the main reason that there are more algorithms for handling supervised tasks. Supervised approaches can be subdivided into traditional ML and DL approaches. Some traditional approaches are rule-based, decision tree, linear regression, probabilistic, Support Vector Machine (SVM), and ensemble approaches. DL is based on an architecture that is typically based on layers.

The SA DL approach includes Neural Networks (NN), Restricted Boltzmann Machines (RBM) (Karthik and Sethukarasi, 2022; Wang *et al.*, 2015), Deep Neural Networks (DNN) (Chen *et al.*, 2018), Deep Multi-Layer Perceptron (DMLP) (Akhtar *et al.*, 2017), Long Short-Term Memory (LSTM) networks (Miedema and Bhulai, 2018), Deep Belief Network (DBN) (Ruangkanokmas *et al.*, 2016), Convolutional Neural Networks (CNN) (Dos Santos and Gatti, 2014), Recurrent Neural Network (RNN) (Arras *et al.*, 2017), and Autoencoders (AE) (Ahmed *et al.*, 2022; Rekha and Sabu, 2022). In recent years, transformers have been increasingly used to solve SA tasks that demonstrate a high level of accuracy (Gong *et al.*, 2022; Mishev *et al.*, 2020). Transformers typically use a self-attention mechanism to predict DNN weights. This is usually performed using an encoder and a decoder.

As can be seen, there are many different approaches for solving SA tasks. The reason for the large number of algorithms is that each has its own benefits and can better fit specific data or tasks. Additional SA related approaches that use unsupervised approaches include Transfer Learning (TL) (Liu *et al.*, 2019) and Aspect-Based Sentiment Analysis (ABSA) approaches (Zhang *et al.*, 2022). For instance, TL can be used by applying and adopting an SA model trained on one domain to another (Liu *et al.*, 2019). ABSA includes many algorithms and can be subdivided into single and compound tasks. This depends on the desired output, whether it is a single or multiple sentiments (Zhang *et al.*, 2022). A single ABSA includes tasks, such as Aspect Term Extraction (ATE) (Manek *et al.*, 2017), Aspect Category Detection (ACD) (Schouten *et al.*, 2017), Opinion Term Extraction (OTE) (Fan *et al.*, 2019; Wang *et al.*, 2016a), and Aspect Sentiment Classification (ASC) (Zainuddin *et al.*, 2018). The compound ABSA tasks are mainly pair (Wang *et al.*, 2018b; Zhao *et al.*, 2020), triplet (Peng *et al.*, 2020; Wan *et al.*, 2020), and quad extraction (Cai *et al.*, 2021).

Additional approaches used in the context of SA include Reinforcement Learning (RL) (Chen *et al.*, 2017) and Deep Reinforcement Learning (DRL) (Kaur, 2017). RL agents dynamically learn sentiments using a trial-and-error method, whereas DRL learns sentiments from a pre-labeled text and applies it to a new text.

An additional category of SA approaches is called Semi-Supervised Learning (SSL). It is suitable for SA tasks because the portion of sentiment-labeled texts is usually much smaller than that of labeled examples (Silva *et al.*, 2016). The SSL category includes approaches and algorithms, such as the generative approach (Mesnil *et al.*, 2014) which generates input texts for each sentiment and a co-training approach that trains two (or more) classifiers based on different sentiments of the input text (Wan, 2009). In addition, SSL includes a self-training approach that assigns sentiments to unlabeled texts (Becker *et al.*, 2013; He *et al.*, 2022), a graph-based approach that extracts sentiments using graph nodes (Wang *et al.*, 2011), and multi-view learning approaches based on different sentiment classes (Birjali *et al.*, 2021; Niu *et al.*, 2016). AL is an additional learning approach complementary to SSL which is called Active Learning (AL). AL queries the user in cases where the machine confidence level of SA is low. An example of using AL for SA is solving imbalanced sentiment classification tasks (Smailović *et al.*, 2014).

In the following sections, we briefly explain how the abovementioned SA algorithms and approaches can be used to solve financial tasks.

4 SA Implementation in Finance Markets and Services

SA is commonly used in many financial applications. We find its roots at the beginning of the 2000s. The initial tasks predicted the financial and stock indices using SA. The research results showed significant improvements in metrics and index prediction. Hansen and Borch (2022) define the SA as a financial and stock exchange alternative data source. SA helps in prospecting market metrics and values hand-in-hand with the analytical tools. In addition, SA supports the trading process by transferring data to valuable assets.

One of the most famous SA financial tasks is the Morgan Stanley High Tech Index (MSH). Das and Chen (2007) predicted the index by using SA classes: bullish, bearish, and neutral. Additional SA prediction uses Twitter to predict several movements of stock market indices, such as the Dow Jones Industrial Average (DJIA) (Bollen *et al.*, 2011), S&P 500, and NASDAQ. To predict the Industrial Average (DJIA), Bollen *et al.* (2011) used tweets and extracted a six-dimensional daily time series of public mood: calm, alert, sure, vital, kind, and happy.

Other approaches use additional sources for predicting stock behavior, such as expert investor opinions (Bar-Haim *et al.*, 2011) and stock-related articles (Feldman *et al.*, 2011). Other studies use blogs and news sentiments to design trading strategies (Song *et al.*, 2017). An additional technique combines actual indexes with topic-based sentiment time-series techniques to predict the S&P 100 index (Si *et al.*, 2013).

The SA approach in finance has different characteristics from regular texts because it has unique content and format (Mishev *et al.*, 2020). Additionally, it involves the integration of numbers, trends, and time series.

The challenge of SA tasks in the context of stock and financial analysis intensifies in cases where there is a need to analyze Low-Resource Languages (LRL) (Kastrati *et al.*, 2021; Lo *et al.*, 2017). Because SA is based on textual resources, there is a need to use languages that are not commonly used in English. Popular approaches for solving LRL SA tasks include translation techniques and the correlation between LRL sources and markets.

As mentioned above, SA is only a stage in the financial solution framework. The SA includes several stages that can be considered as a pipeline. The SA pipeline usually includes several preprocessing stages, such as choosing and connecting to relevant sources, text cleaning and cleansing, detection of relevant features and sentiments, polarity analysis, and prediction. The following section describes

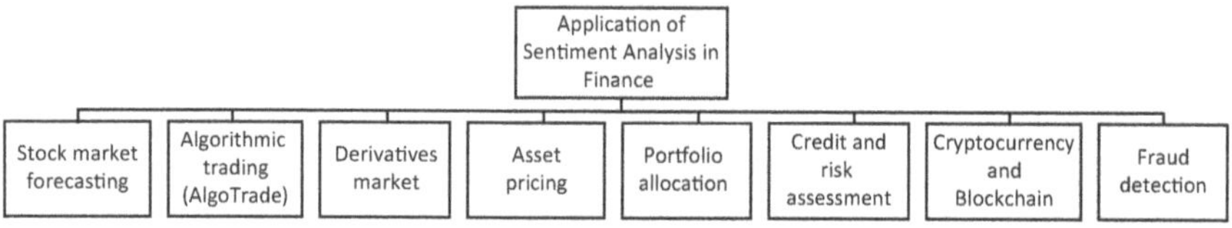

Figure 1. Taxonomy of application of sentiment analysis in finance.

financial tasks. As can be seen in Figure 1, in each task, we explain the challenges and how the SA approach solves them.

4.1 Stock market forecasting

Stock exchange market behavior is a challenging task (Kumar *et al.*, 2021). The stock price is difficult to predict because its chaotic characteristics are reflected in its complex, high noise, high volatility, and dynamic behavior. According to Mehta *et al.* (2021), there is a correlation between market price movement and public sentiment. This correlation can be explained by the fact that the inherent characteristics of both have the same challenges, such as chaotic behavior. According to Kalyani *et al.* (2016), sentiment analysis models can show an increase of approximately 20% in the accuracy of stock price predictions.

The stock market is an interesting challenge from two perspectives: the prediction of stock prices and market value. The stock markets are located worldwide. Hence, many languages are used in stock markets worldwide. As mentioned above, there is a need to use SA techniques for LRLs in markets that do not use popular languages for communication.

When forecasting stock market prices, we can distinguish between technical and fundamental analyses and computational methods (Sidogi *et al.*, 2021). The first looks at the price movement, whereas the second is the financial factors that influence the price. Computational methods use mathematical formulas and approaches for market factors (Diakoulakis *et al.*, 2002).

Many stock prediction models are based on three important indicators: trend, price actions, and momentum (Huang and Liu, 2019). The trend is the overall direction of the market, a specific indicator, or a specific asset (Huang and Liu, 2019). This is considered an important indicator of the Forex market. The price change can be used as an indication of entering or exiting an asset (Huang and Liu, 2019).

A momentum is an indication of strong changes in prices (Huang and Liu, 2019). SA can be used to predict each one of them and interact with each of them. For instance, SA and momentum can yield better estimations for trend. SA can also be analyzed in the context of different indicators and related to them.

To predict a specific indicator, the SA model must obtain its inputs prior to the required prediction time. When there is a combination of SA and an additional indicator, both the indicator and SA can be aligned and based on data at the same time. An example of an approach that combines technical indicators with SA is called Baker–Wurgler investor sentiment (Baker and Wurgler, 2006). This relates to both approaches, in the context of timelines (Baker and Wurgler, 2007).

Several popular SA indicators exist, also known as market sentiment or investor sentiment. These can be used in interactions with additional indicators to predict prices or other indicators.

Several approaches can be used to predict stock market prices. Some of these approaches use various strategies. It is based on indicators such as Moving Average (MA) and momentum. The indicator strategy uses the increase in an indicator as an indication of a positive trend of the price and vice versa. Other approaches used ML and DL to predict prices based on data from previous markets. Examples of such models include CNN, LSTM, RNN, and RBM (Birjali *et al.*, 2021; Kumar *et al.*, 2021). There are also approaches that use indicators in combination with SA, such as Directional Movement Index (DMI), High-Low Index (HLI), Bullish Percent Index (BPI), Chicago Board Options Exchange (CBOE), and Volatility Index (VIX). Examples of commonly used momentum-based indices are the Momentum Index (MI), Relative Strength Index (RSI), Commodity Channel Index (CCI), Stochastic Oscillator (SO), and pRice Of Change (ROC).

MA-type indicators such as Moving Average (MA), Moving Average Convergence and Divergence (MACD), Exponential Moving Average (EMA), and Triple Exponential Moving Average (TEMA) are dominant in the context of SA (Haritha and Rishad, 2020; Wang *et al.*, 2018a). DMI indicates trending by comparing highs and lows of price over time, and HLI indicates if the MA reached its record high percentage over a defined time window, such as ten-day period. BPI is calculated by dividing the total number of issues that signals "buy" by the total number of stocks in that group (Kumar *et al.*, 2021). The CBOE VIX represents the market"s volatility expectations over the coming 30 days (Kumar *et al.*, 2021). It is based on the option prices of the S&P 500 Index for the next month.

MI indicates the direction of price movement (upward or downward) and movement strength (Birjali *et al.*, 2021). The RSI is MI, which measures the speed and change in price movements (Birjali *et al.*, 2021). It calculates the closing prices of a recent trading period and tracks the speed of the price changes. CCI in comparison to RSI, CCI focuses on deviations from an asset's MA price (Huang and Liu, 2019). The SO is a momentum indicator that compares a particular closing price in the range of its prices over a certain period of time (Huang and Liu, 2019). The ROC is also a momentum indicator that measures the percentage change in price between the current price and the price for a certain number of periods (Huang and Liu, 2019). SO includes Stochastic K (SK) and stochastic D indexes (Huang and Liu, 2019). SK represents the current asset price in relation to the asset's recent price range, where SD is an SK MA and D represents the three-period average of K.

As mentioned above, the most popular strategy for stock market prediction involves MA and momentum, price, and trend-based indicators. These strategies can use SA as supportive input. The final decision involves the index values, SA polarity, and human decisions. Moreover, the decision-maker trader considers not only the SA polarity values but also the volume of data on which SA is based, such as the number of tweets that SA is based upon as well as its metrics. The SA indication output can align with the values of the other indicators or contradict them. In such conflicts, the trader must make the final decision.

In the following section, we explain an additional approach to market trading based on algorithms.

4.2 Algorithmic trading (algotrade)

Algorithmic trading differs from the conventional stock market forecasting techniques mentioned above. The main emphasis is on automated and rapid executable trading instructions (Kaur, 2017). The algotrade algorithms process an enormous number of transactions and orders per second and are called High-Frequency Trading (HFT)

(Kaur, 2017). They used novel big-data frameworks and strong computational resources (Kaur, 2017). Owing to rapid and unpredictable changes in the market, it is almost impossible to preprogram the algorithm. Most advanced algorithms react in real or near-real time to recent market changes (Bagate *et al.*, 2022).

Usually, there is a negative correlation between the model complexity and processed data with respect to the reaction time. One way to reduce the complexity of the model is to focus on reliable features. SA can be used to help trading algorithms either as a reliable input or can be combined with the algorithm's results. Usually, there is a time gap between sentiment and the actual behavior of the market. This time gap can be used by trading algorithms to analyze data. Many algorithms use predefined entry and exit strategies for trading in the stock market. This approach helps them work automatically. Adding SA to algorithms can improve their ability to observe human emotional perspectives. Usually, algorithms in the algotrade field use SA as an additional input to historical market data (Kaur, 2017).

The algotrade uses indicators such as MA, SO: SK and SD, RSI, and Larry–William's R% (LWR) index. The LWR is an oscillator momentum indicator that shows the current closing price in relation to the high and low of the past N days. R reflects how close the price is to the highest and lowest prices in the relevant period (Bagate *et al.*, 2022). Some traditional algorithms respond slowly to market changes, whereas others react instantaneously, even to minor changes. Combining the instant response algorithm with SA can improve accuracy. SA does not relate directly to market changes but to human opinions and texts that are usually analyzed before the market reaction.

Commonly used ML approaches in the context of algotrade and SA are RL, LSTM, CNN, AE, Wavelet Transforms (WT), Evolutionary Algorithm (EA), Piecewise Linear Representation (PLR), and traditional ML algorithms, such as DT, LR, KNN, RF, and SVM (Bagate *et al.*, 2022; Ozbayoglu *et al.*, 2020). In addition to indicators, the sources for SA algotrade are based on media such as Twitter and Facebook, market capitalization (value of companies' shares of stock), macroeconomic variables: Price Index (PPI), IPO first-day return (RIPO), Consumer Price Index (CPI), and Net Asset Value per Share and Price Earning (P/E) (Bagate *et al.*, 2022).

4.3 Derivatives market

Derivatives are considered important instruments in financial markets because of their large volumes and increasing usage. The notional value of outstanding Over The Counter (OTC) derivatives rose to 632 trillion at the end of June 2022 and from 598 trillion at the end of 2021 (McGuire *et al.*, 2022).

Derivatives in financial markets are general names for instruments that derive their values from an asset or stock exchange worth to which they relate. Derivatives include financial instruments, such as futures, contracts, and options. Future contracts (futures) value is based on a contract between two parties (or more) concerning selling or buying the asset. Derivatives are based only on futuristic asset values. These options are a category of derivatives. They allow the holder (give him an option) to buy or sell the underlying asset (McGuire *et al.*, 2022).

Swaps and forwards are additional tools that fall under the derivative category. Swap is a derivative contract between two or more entities that enables them to exchange cash flows or liabilities derived from two financial instruments (Coakley *et al.*, 2014). Forward is an additional contract that enables parties to buy or sell an asset or at a specified future time at a price agreed (Coakley *et al.*, 2014).

The use of SA in derivatives is based on predicting their derivative indices or combining them with them. Some popular approaches are VIX (previously explained in the above sections), Put Call Ratio (PCR), open interest, and models such as Black–Scholes (BSM). The abovementioned PCR metric is calculated by dividing the number of put contracts in the derivatives market by the total number of call contracts (Bandopadhyaya *et al.*, 2008; Jena *et al.*, 2019). The open interest index is based on the number of futures contracts or options held by the traders.

The BSM, on the other hand, is a theoretical model for estimating derivative values. It is based on input variables that include risk factors and investment instruments and takes into account the impact of time. SA is a complementary tool for BSM because all its inputs are based on financial values and not on audience sentiments. McGuire *et al.* (2022) developed a SA model based on BSM and deep networks: CNN and Recurrent CNN (RCNN) in order to predict VIX and derivatives values. The commonly used models using

SA for predicting derivative values are based on ML and DL models, such as LSTM, Bi-LSTM (Bidirectional LSTM), DNN, Multi-layer Perceptron (MLP) combined with the BSM model and CNN (Culkin and Das, 2017; Iwasaki, 2018; Ozbayoglu *et al.*, 2020).

4.4 Asset pricing

Asset Pricing (AP) explores the factors that determine prices and returns on financial and real assets (Houlihan and Creamer, 2017). Unlike liability, which its owner obligates to return value, the asset includes anything its holder owns that adds financial value. This includes stocks, bonds, currencies, and real estate (Pandey and Sehgal, 2019). From the SA perspective, the asset is similar to derivatives because the derivatives are usually based on it.

Fraiberger *et al.* (2021) find difference between the sources of SA on the AP results. The authors differentiated between local and global news sources. According to their research, SA based on global news have a larger impact on returns. In addition, local prices are affected mainly by foreign investors' SA. Additional research on India's AP used SA to predict AP factors (Pandey and Sehgal, 2019).

Several indices and models support the AP process. The commonly used models are Capital Asset Pricing Model (CAPM) and Fama models such as Fama and French three factor, Carhart four factor, Fama and French five factor, and Fama and French five factor with momentum (Xing *et al.*, 2018; Zeidan, 2022).

The CAPM is based on the expected returns on capital investments. Fama and French three factor is based on firms' size, excess return on the market (portfolio's return minus risk free rate of return), and book to market values (company's book value minus its market value) (Houlihan and Creamer, 2017). Fama and French five factor adds to the Fama and French three factor the following factors: quality and investment pattern.

The Carhart model is an extension of the Fama and French three factor model, with a momentum factor added. There are several approaches for predicting AP using Fama and French combined with DL approaches (Feng *et al.*, 2018). We have already explained in detail in the above sections how SA can help in predicting the momentum metric. A relatively new approach to AP is Zoo Factor (Feng *et al.*, 2017, 2020). This approach uses regression to predict AP by comparing relevant factors to control factors. Thus, it decreases redundant factors. It can be estimated that it has the potential to be combined with SA. In addition, SA can be used in combination with the Fama and French models as well as other indices to predict AP.

4.5 Portfolio allocation (PA)

PA (also known as portfolio optimization and portfolio selection) has two main aspects: assets and the proportion between them. Portfolio assets are typically stocks, bonds, and cash. Portfolio allocation and management is a more complex task than predicting one stock because it usually contains several stocks as well as additional assets (Micaletti, 2019).

PA encapsulates several tasks; hence, it is more challenging than trading each of its individual assets. One task is to choose the appropriate assets and match them to the portfolio holder's profile. The portfolio-holder profile can consist of parameters such as marital status, personal details, revenue expectations, and risk tolerance.

In addition, there is an interrelation between the different assets that affect the entire portfolio. Moreover, the mix of each asset in the portfolio has a strong impact on its value. In literature, we find several strategies for portfolio allocation such as strategic, constant weighting, tactical, insured policy, and integrated portfolio allocation (McIndoe, 2018; Micaletti, 2019; Muthivhi and van Zyl, 2022; Vaskikari *et al.*, 2020). Portfolio management is considered an optimization task; hence, the ML and DL approaches are commonly used. Some ML approaches are CNN, LSTM, RBM, RNN, AT, and RL (Ozbayoglu *et al.*, 2020).

Zeidan (2022) claim that using only metrics for investment in an Environmental, Social, and corporate Governance (ESG) companies portfolios is necessary but not a sufficient condition. Hence, there is a need to combine these metrics with additional approaches, such as SA. McIndoe (2018) distinguishes between SA strategies for PA: ranked sentiment strategy and extreme sentiment strategy. The first calculates a sentiment score for each commodity in comparison to other commodities in the PA, whereas the second considers each commodity independently. Muthivhi and van Zyl (2022) show that integration between LSTM and SA can improve portfolio selection strategy. SA can shed light on the portfolio management process, especially in cases in which financial metrics and ML-based systems are lagged to market responses.

Recent studies have used SA in different combinations of ML and DL. Koratamaddi *et al.* (2021) combine SA with DRL for predicting portfolios that consist of Dow Jones companies. Rane *et al.* (2022) offer an Hierarchical Risk Parity SA (HRP-S) approach that combines traditional Hierarchical Risk Parity (HRP) with SA and suggest an optimized portfolio weight distribution. In their work, Heiden and Parpinelli (2021) also combine LSTM with SA. On average, the combination shows a significant increase in portfolio revenue compared to models that do not use SA models.

The conclusion of this section is that SA can be helpful in solving PA tasks either by itself or in combination with other metrics and approaches.

4.6 Credit and risk assessment

Credit and risk assessments are common and widespread tasks. These tasks are relevant not only for businessmen or entrepreneurs who establish a new business but also for people who ask to open a new bank account.

Banks examine prospective customer profiles for applications, such as opening bank accounts, credit cards, loan requests, and mortgages. This is in addition to examining business and property risks. Risk has three aspects: the subject — the person or business who asks for the loan or credit, the object — the property or business the person asks to invest in, and the interaction between the two. Currently, the vast majority of banks use a predefined evaluation process for new customers. In addition, for mortgages, an appraisal is required to evaluate the asset's price.

Banks typically use ML systems to support this process (Wang *et al.*, 2016a). However, ML systems use data that is clear and based on specific details. In many cases, ML systems predict the Probability of Default (POD), Loss Given Default (LGD), and Exposure at Default (EAD) metrics (Wang *et al.*, 2016b).

POD is the probability that a borrower will return back the loan and is usually based on the credit score and debt-to-income metrics. LGD refers to the predicted loss of the borrower, and EAD predicts the amount of loss the lender is exposed to Wang *et al.* (2016a).

On the other hand, SA uses sentiment data based on relevant borrowers, businesses, markets, and assets. Each metric can be used in combination with SA, or alternatively, each ML input can be based on SA.

Wang *et al.* (2016a) found that SA is effective when traditional financial information is missing or as a complementary to traditional financial sources. In the literature, we find several credit and risk assessment tasks that use ML and DL approaches, such as bankruptcy prediction, credit scoring, credit evaluation, loan or insurance underwriting, bond ratings, loan applications, consumer credit determination, corporate credit ratings, mortgage choice decisions, and financial distress prediction (Ozbayoglu *et al.*, 2020).

Commonly used ML networks and algorithms that support the abovementioned tasks are DL, CNN, RBM, and SVM. The proposed ML and DL can work in combination with SA as an input or output (Ozbayoglu *et al.*, 2020).

Zhang *et al.* (2015) proposed a Generalized Multiple Kernel Learning (GMKL) ML model for credit risk evaluation that mimics the process of loan granting using SA. This shows an improvement in using SA in comparison to other models.

Nopp and Hanbury (2015) proposed a pipeline to assist European banks in predicting and handling risk management using SA. The researchers found a significant correlation between banks' aggregated SA and risk indicators.

As can be seen, the SA can be used an important tool for credit and risk assessment. It can be used as a complementary tool and has the potential to replace traditional approaches in some cases.

4.7 Cryptocurrencies

In recent years, the cryptocurrency market has grown exponentially. There are many different cryptocurrencies, such as Bitcoin, Ethereum, Litecoin, Cardano, Binance Coin, DogeCoin, Tether, XRP, Polkadot, and Solana. The main characteristic that differentiates cryptocurrencies from regular stock market behavior and digital currency is their decentrality (Balcerzak *et al.*, 2022; Sarode *et al.*, 2021; Vacca *et al.*, 2021).

Many cryptocurrencies are based on decentralized networks called blockchain. Blockchain is a distributed peer-to-peer database that enables a distributed ledger enforced by users' disparate computers (Sarode *et al.*, 2021). Owing to the decentrality characteristic, no one can control the cryptocurrency market. Hence, we can conclude that the overall picture of cryptocurrency is based on individual investors distributed worldwide.

One of the challenges in deducing cryptocurrency sentiment values is to cope with their diversity. The cryptocurrency SA task is based on analyzing different social media sources of investors from different geolocations, backgrounds, and knowledge. In addition, the cryptocurrency market tends to exhibit extreme fluctuations; therefore, it is usually riskier than the stock exchange market and more difficult to predict (Al-Yahyaee *et al.*, 2020).

In the literature, we find several factors that are correlated with cryptocurrency prices (Al-Yahyaee *et al.*, 2020): direct expenses of cryptocurrency mining such as electricity, macroeconomic factors, worldwide market trends, and indexes such as S&P 500, significant exchange rate for currencies such as USD and EUR, as well as worldwide political and regulation issues. There is also a specific influence of the government policy of exchanging cryptocurrencies into real money. Many of these factors can be predicted using the SA.

The most influential sources of cryptocurrencies are social media, such as Twitter, investors' opinions, and news (Aggarwal *et al.*, 2019). The need to integrate different language sources and LRL intensifies the SA analysis process of cryptocurrency.

An additional characteristic of the cryptocurrency market is the price change over short periods. This characteristic requires prompt response. Consequently, algotrading models have been developed in recent years. The most dominant model algorithms for cryptocurrency SA are DL-based (Ozbayoglu *et al.*, 2020).

Algotrade SA metrics are also used to integrate cryptocurrency and smart contracts. Smart contracts use blockchain as a platform for executing agreements or contracts between different parties both inside and outside the chain (Aggarwal *et al.*, 2019).

The most dominant cryptocurrency ML approaches for SA are based on CNN, LSTM, RNN, and RL. We can also observe the integration between DL approaches and RL (Ozbayoglu *et al.*, 2020). An additional approach used for predicting cryptocurrency prices is an ensemble. The ensemble approach integrates different models and uses decision criteria, such as majority voting. Prasad (2022) showed an accuracy of 94.2% predicting cryptocurrency price based on ensemble approach of YouTube comments. Guo and Li (2019) developed SA ensemble-based approach. This approach is based on the Twitter sentiment score (TSS) and is used for real-time prediction. The authors demonstrated that TSS achieved high levels of accuracy.

We were able to successfully predict cryptocurrency behavior using SA. This can be explained by the fact that cryptocurrency is highly influenced by investor psychology (Dwivedi and Vemareddy, 2023). This characteristic makes SA one of the most efficient approaches for predicting cryptocurrency markets.

Central Bank Digital Currency (CBDC) is a new approach for digital and cryptocurrency trading. This approach is planned to replace the decentrality characteristic of cryptocurrencies by issuing digital currencies to the central bank. Researchers have used SA to detect the public approach for this new initiative (Hoang *et al.*, 2023) and determine its vulnerability to cyberattacks (Tian *et al.*, 2022). As can be seen, the cryptocurrencies evolve over time. New tools and approaches have been developed rapidly. SA goes hand-in-hand with novel developments and finds solutions to new challenges that arise.

4.8 Fraud detection

Fraud detection is an important issue in the finance field. SA-based fraud detection uses a financial corpus or text to extract a sentiment indicator. According to the value of the sentiment indicator, a decision can be made whether the text is fraudulent. The input text can be structured or unstructured. There are several ways to detect fraud such as anomaly detection using DL, such as LSTM, CNN and AE (Studiawan *et al.*, 2020).

Goel and Uzuner (2016) examine several SA indicators for detecting fraud: polarity, subjectivity, and intensity in text. According to their research, SA indicators can successfully detect fraudulent texts. The authors found inherent characteristics of fraud texts. For example, texts that contain over-use of subjectivity clues or include more adjectives and adverbs than average can be indicated as fraud (Goel and Uzuner, 2016). The SA fraud-detection process is based on direct and indirect information sources. An example of direct information can be company reports, management discussions, and analysis of

(MD&As) section. Indirect sources can use data scraped from the internet, blogs, and other social media sources. SA output: intensity and polarity reflect the business reliability level and have the potential to detect fraud.

One of the reasons for the rise in popularity of SA for fraud detection in recent years is the growth and availability of social media and technical solutions, such as AI tools and transformers that process them. Nasrin *et al.* (2020) propose SA-based fraud detection for e-commerce sites based on Facebook. The authors propose a pipeline model and metrics that can be used for SA-based fraud detection tasks. As can be seen, SA can be used as a meaningful tool in the fraud detection field by itself or with additional AI solutions.

5 Conclusions

In this chapter, we discussed some important applications of SA in finance field. We mentioned the impact and the advantages of using SA in stock markets as well as financial services and cryptocurrency. SA contribution to the relevant tasks can be measured by using statistical metrics as well as financial and actuary indicators. This chapter demonstrated SA main approaches of commonly used financial tasks. In many cases, integrating between SA to other ML and traditional approaches leads to improvement in metrics and prediction accuracy. We estimate a growth of usage and implementation of SA in the coming years.

References

Aggarwal, G., Patel, V., Varshney, G., and Oostman, K. (2019). Understanding the social factors affecting the cryptocurrency market. arXiv:1901.06245 [online]. Available: http://arxiv.org/abs/1901.06245.

Ahmed, K., Nadeem, M.I., Li, D., Zheng, Z., Ghadi, Y.Y., Assam, M., and Mohamed, H.G. (2022). Exploiting stacked autoencoders for improved sentiment analysis. *Applied Sciences*, 12(23): 12380.

Akhtar, M.S., Kumar, A., Ghosal, D., Ekbal, A., and Bhattacharyya, P. (2017). A multilayer perceptron based ensemble technique for fine-grained financial sentiment analysis. In *Proceedings of the 2017 Conference on Empirical Methods in Natural Language Processing*, pp. 540–546.

Al-Yahyaee, K.H., Mensi, W., Ko, H.-U., Yoon, S.-M., and Kang, S.H. (2020). Why cryptocurrency markets are inefficient: The impact of liquidity and volatility. *The North American Journal of Economics and Finance*, 52: 101168.

Arief, N.N., and Pangestu, A.B. (2021). Perception and sentiment analysis on empathic brand initiative during the COVID-19 pandemic: Indonesia perspective. *Journal of Creative Communications*, 10, 1–17. https://doi.org/10.1177/09732586211031164.

Arras, L., Montavon, G., Müller, K.-R., and Samek, W. (2017). Explaining recurrent neural network predictions in sentiment analysis. *Proceedings of the 8th Workshop on Computational Approaches to Subjectivity, Sentiment and Social Media Analysis, WASSA@EMNLP 2017*, Copenhagen, Denmark, 8 September, 2017, pp. 159–168.

Bagate, R., Joshi, A., Trivedi, A., Pandey, A., and Tripathi, D. (2022). Survey on algorithmic trading using sentiment analysis. In *Proceedings of the 6th International Conference on Advance Computing and Intelligent Engineering: ICACIE 2021*. Springer, pp. 241–252.

Baker, M., and Wurgler, J. (2006). Investor sentiment and the cross-section of stock returns. *The Journal of Finance*, 61(4): 1645–1680.

Baker, M., and Wurgler, J. (2007). Investor sentiment in the stock market. *Journal of Economic Perspectives*, 21(2): 129–151.

Bakshi, R.K., Kaur, N., Kaur, R., and Kaur, G. (2016). Opinion mining and sentiment analysis. In *2016 3rd International Conference on Computing for Sustainable Global Development (INDIACom)*. IEEE, pp. 452–455.

Balcerzak, A.P., Nica, E., Rogalska, E., Poliak, M., Kliestik, T., and Sabie, O.-M. (2022). Blockchain technology and smart contracts in decentralized governance systems. *Administrative Sciences*, 12(3): 96.

Bandopadhyaya, A. *et al.* (2008). Measures of investor sentiment: A comparative analysis put-call ratio vs. volatility index. *Journal of Business & Economics Research (JBER)*, 6(8): 27–34.

Bar-Haim, R., Dinur, E., Feldman, R., Fresko, M., and Goldstein, G. (2011). Identifying and following expert investors in stock microblogs. In *Proceedings of the Conference on Empirical Methods in Natural Language Processing*, pp. 1310–1319.

Becker, L., Erhart, G., Skiba, D., and Matula, V. (2013). Avaya: Sentiment analysis on twitter with self-training and polarity lexicon expansion. In *Second Joint Conference on Lexical and Computational Semantics (* SEM), Volume 2: Proceedings of the Seventh International Workshop on Semantic Evaluation (SemEval 2013)*, pp. 333–340.

Birjali, M., Kasri, M., and Beni-Hssane, A. (2021). A comprehensive survey on sentiment analysis: Approaches, challenges and trends. *Knowledge-Based Systems*, 226: 107134.

Bollen, J., Mao, H., and Zeng, X. (2011). Twitter mood predicts the stock market. *Journal of Computational Science*, 2(1): 1–8.

Cai, H., Xia, R., and Yu, J. (2021). Aspect-category-opinion-sentiment quadruple extraction with implicit aspects and opinions. In *Proceedings of the 59th Annual Meeting of the Association for Computational Linguistics and the 11th International Joint Conference on Natural Language Processing (Volume 1: Long Papers)*, pp. 340–350.

Chen, M., Wang, S., Liang, P.P., Baltrušaitis, T., Zadeh, A., and Morency, L.-P. (2017). Multimodal sentiment analysis with word-level fusion and reinforcement learning. In *Proceedings of the 19th ACM International Conference on Multimodal Interaction*, pp. 163–171.

Chen, S., Peng, C., Cai, L., and Guo, L. (2018). A deep neural network model for target-based sentiment analysis. In *2018 International Joint Conference on Neural Networks (IJCNN)*. IEEE, pp. 1–7.

Coakley, J., Dotsis, G., Liu, X., and Zhai, J. (2014). Investor sentiment and value and growth stock index options. *The European Journal of Finance*, 20(12): 1211–1229.

Culkin, R., and Das, S.R. (2017). Machine learning in finance: The case of deep learning for option pricing. *Journal of Investment Management*, 15(4): 92–100.

Darwich, M., Mohd, S.A., Omar, N., and Osman, N.A. (2019). Corpus-based techniques for sentiment lexicon generation: A review. *Journal of Digital Information Management*, 17(5): 296.

Das, S.R., and Chen, M.Y. (2007). Yahoo! for amazon: Sentiment extraction from small talk on the web. *Management Science*, 53(9): 1375–1388.

Diakoulakis, I., Koulouriotis, D., and Emiris, D. (2002). A review of stock market prediction using computational methods. In *Computational Methods in Decision-Making, Economics and Finance*, pp. 379–403.

Dos Santos, C., and Gatti, M. (2014). Deep convolutional neural networks for sentiment analysis of short texts. In *Proceedings of COLING 2014, the 25th International Conference on Computational Linguistics: Technical Papers*, pp. 69–78.

Dwivedi, D., and Vemareddy, A. (2023). Sentiment analytics for crypto pre and post covid: Topic modeling. In *Distributed Computing and Intelligent Technology: 19th International Conference, ICDCIT 2023, Bhubaneswar, India, January 18–22, 2023, Proceedings*. Springer, pp. 303–315.

Fan, Z., Wu, Z., Dai, X., Huang, S., and Chen, J. (2019). Target-oriented opinion words extraction with target-fused neural sequence labeling.

In *Proceedings of the 2019 Conference of the North American Chapter of the Association for Computational Linguistics: Human Language Technologies, Volume 1 (Long and Short Papers)*, pp. 2509–2518.

Fei, H., Chua, T.-S., Li, C., Ji, D., Zhang, M., and Ren, Y. (2023). On the robustness of aspect-based sentiment analysis: Rethinking model, data and training. *ACM Transactions On Information Systems (TOIS)*, 41, 1–32.

Feldman, R., Rosenfeld, B., Bar-Haim, R., and Fresko, M. (2011). The stock sonar—sentiment analysis of stocks based on a hybrid approach. *Proceedings of the AAAI Conference on Artificial Intelligence*, 25(2): 1642–1647.

Feng, G., Giglio, S., and Xiu, D. (2017). *Taming the Factor Zoo*. Working Paper, Technical Report.

Feng, G., Giglio, S., and Xiu, D. (2020). Taming the factor zoo: A test of new factors. *The Journal of Finance*, 75(3): 1327–1370.

Feng, G., Polson, N., and Xu, J. (2018). Deep learning factor alpha. *SSRN Electron. J.*, 1–44.

Fraiberger, S.P., Lee, D., Puy, D., and Ranciere, R. (2021). Media sentiment and international asset prices. *Journal of International Economics*, 133: 103526.

Goel, S., and Uzuner, O. (2016). Do sentiments matter in fraud detection? Estimating semantic orientation of annual reports. *Intelligent Systems in Accounting, Finance and Management*, 23(3): 215–239.

Gong, X., Ying, W., Zhong, S., and Gong, S. (2022). Text sentiment analysis based on transformer and augmentation. *Frontiers in Psychology*, 13, 906061.

Guo, X., and Li, J. (2019). A novel twitter sentiment analysis model with baseline correlation for financial market prediction with improved efficiency. In *2019 Sixth International Conference on Social Networks Analysis, Management and Security (SNAMS)*. IEEE, pp. 472–477.

Hansen, K.B., and Borch, C. (2022). Alternative data and sentiment analysis: Prospecting non-standard data in machine learning-driven finance. *Big Data & Society*, 9(1): 20539517211070701.

Haritha, P.H., and Rishad, A. (2020). An empirical examination of investor sentiment and stock market volatility: Evidence from India. *Financial Innovation*, 6(1): 1–15.

Hazarika, D., Li, Y., Cheng, B., Zhao, S., Zimmermann, R., and Poria, S. (2022). Analyzing modality robustness in multimodal sentiment analysis. In *Proceedings of the North American Chapter of the Association for Computational Linguistics: Human Language Technologies*, pp. 685–696.

He, K., Mao, R., Gong, T., Li, C., and Cambria, E. (2022). Meta-based self-training and re-weighting for aspect-based sentiment analysis. *IEEE Transactions on Affective Computing*, 1, 1–13. http://dx.doi.org/10.1109/TAFFC.2022.3202831.

Heiden, A., and Parpinelli, R. (2021). Applying LSTM for stock price prediction with sentiment analysis. In *15th Brazilian Congress of Computational Intelligence*, pp. 1–8.

Hoang, Y.H., Ngo, V.M., and Vu, N.B. (2023). Central bank digital currency: A systematic literature review using text mining approach. *Research in International Business and Finance*: 101889.

Houlihan, P., and Creamer, G.G. (2017). Can sentiment analysis and options volume anticipate future returns? *Computational Economics*, 50(4): 669–685.

Huang, S., and Liu, S. (2019). Machine learning on stock price movement forecast: The sample of the taiwan stock exchange. *International Journal of Economics and Financial Issues*, 9(2): 189.

Hussein, D.M.E.-D.M. (2018). A survey on sentiment analysis challenges. *Journal of King Saud University-Engineering Sciences*, 30(4): 330–338.

Iwasaki, H. (2018). Topic sentiment asset pricing with dnn supervised learning. SSRN.

Jena, S.K., Tiwari, A.K., and Mitra, A. (2019). Put–call ratio volume vs. open interest in predicting market return: A frequency domain rolling causality analysis. *Economies*, 7(1): 24.

Kalyani, J., Bharathi, N., and Jyothi, R. (2016). Stock trend prediction using news sentiment analysis. *Int J Comput Sci Inf Technol*, 8: 67–76. https://doi.org/10.5121/ijcsit.2016.8306.

Karthik, E., and Sethukarasi, T. (2022). A centered convolutional restricted boltzmann machine optimized by hybrid atom search arithmetic optimization algorithm for sentimental analysis. *Neural Processing Letters*, 54(5): 4123–4151.

Kastrati, Z., Ahmedi, L., Kurti, A., Kadriu, F., Murtezaj, D., and Gashi, F. (2021). A deep learning sentiment analyser for social media comments in low-resource languages. *Electronics*, 10(10): 1133.

Kaur, S. (2017). Algorithmic trading using sentiment analysis and reinforcement learning. *Positions*. http://cs229.stanford.edu/proj2017/final-reports/5222284.pdf.

Koratamaddi, P., Wadhwani, K., Gupta, M., and Sanjeevi, S.G. (2021). Market sentiment-aware deep reinforcement learning approach for stock portfolio allocation. *Engineering Science and Technology, an International Journal*, 24(4): 848–859.

Küçük, D., and Can, F. (2020). Stance detection: A survey. *ACM Computing Surveys (CSUR)*, 53(1): 1–37.

Kumar, G., Jain, S., and Singh, U.P. (2021). Stock market forecasting using computational intelligence: A survey. *Archives of Computational Methods in Engineering*, 28: 1069–1101.

Laskari, N.K., and Sanampudi, S.K. (2016). Aspect based sentiment analysis survey. *IOSR Journal of Computer Engineering (IOSR-JCE)*, 18(2): 24–28.

Liu, R., Shi, Y., Ji, C., and Jia, M. (2019). A survey of sentiment analysis based on transfer learning. *IEEE Access*, 7: 85 401–85 412.

Lo, S.L., Cambria, E., Chiong, R., and Cornforth, D. (2017). Multilingual sentiment analysis: From formal to informal and scarce resource languages. *Artificial Intelligence Review*, 48: 499–527.

Ma, E., Cheng, M., and Hsiao, A. (2018). Sentiment analysis–a review and agenda for future research in hospitality contexts. *International Journal of Contemporary Hospitality Management*, 30(11): 3287–3308.

Manek, A.S., Shenoy, P.D., and Mohan, M.C. (2017). Aspect term extraction for sentiment analysis in large movie reviews using gini index feature selection method and svm classifier. *World Wide Web*, 20: 135–154.

Mäntylä, M.V., Graziotin, D., and Kuutila, M. (2018). The evolution of sentiment analysis — a review of research topics, venues, and top cited papers. *Computer Science Review*, 27: 16–32.

McGuire, P., Schrimpf, A., and Tarashev, N. (2022). OTC foreign exchange and interest rate derivatives markets through the prism of the triennial survey. *BIS Quarterly Review*, December. https://www.bis.org/publ/qtrpdf/r_qt2212.htm.

McIndoe, J. (2018). Power of the news: Tactical asset allocation strategies derived using sentiment analysis, Mathematics and Finance, Imperial College London.

Mehta, P., Pandya, S., and Kotecha, K. (2021). Harvesting social media sentiment analysis to enhance stock market prediction using deep learning. *PeerJ Computer Science*, 7: e476.

Mesnil, G., Mikolov, T., Ranzato, M., and Bengio, Y. (2014). Ensemble of generative and discriminative techniques for sentiment analysis of movie reviews. *arXiv preprint* arXiv:1412.5335.

Micaletti, R. (2019). Relative sentiment and machine learning for tactical asset allocation. *SSRN Electronic Journal, Available at SSRN 3475258.*

Miedema, F., and Bhulai, S. (2018). Sentiment analysis with long short-term memory networks. *Vrije Universiteit Amsterdam*, 1: 1–17.

Mishev, K., Gjorgjevikj, A., Vodenska, I., Chitkushev, L.T., and Trajanov, D. (2020). Evaluation of sentiment analysis in finance: From lexicons to transformers. *IEEE Access*, 8: 131 662–131 682.

Mukherjee, A., and Liu, B. (2012). Aspect extraction through semi-supervised modeling. In *Proceedings of the 50th Annual Meeting of the Association for Computational Linguistics (Volume 1: Long Papers)*, pp. 339–348.

Muthivhi, M., and van Zyl, T.L. (2022). Fusion of sentiment and asset price predictions for portfolio optimization. In *2022 25th International Conference on Information Fusion (FUSION)*. IEEE, pp. 1–8.

Nandwani, P., and Verma, R. (2021). A review on sentiment analysis and emotion detection from text. *Social Network Analysis and Mining*, 11(1): 1–19.

Nasrin, S., Ghosh, P., Chowdhury, S.M.H., Abujar, S., and Hossain, S.A. (2020). Fraud detection of facebook business page based on sentiment analysis. In *Proceedings of International Joint Conference on Computational Intelligence: IJCCI 2018*. Springer, pp. 279–287.

Niu, T., Zhu, S., Pang, L., and El Saddik, A. (2016). Sentiment analysis on multi-view social data. In *MultiMedia Modeling: 22nd International Conference, MMM 2016, Miami, FL, USA, January 4-6, 2016, Proceedings, Part II 22*. Springer, pp. 15–27.

Nopp, C., and Hanbury, A. (2015). Detecting risks in the banking system by sentiment analysis. In *Proceedings of the 2015 Conference on Empirical Methods in Natural Language Processing*, pp. 591–600.

Ozbayoglu, A.M., Gudelek, M.U., and Sezer, O.B. (2020). Deep learning for financial applications: A survey. *Applied Soft Computing*, 93: 106384.

Pandey, P., and Sehgal, S. (2019). Investor sentiment and its role in asset pricing: An empirical study for india. *IIMB Management Review*, 31(2): 127–144.

Peng, H., Xu, L., Bing, L., Huang, F., Lu, W., and Si, L. (2020). Knowing what, how and why: A near complete solution for aspect-based sentiment analysis. *Proceedings of the AAAI Conference on Artificial Intelligence*, 34(05): 8600–8607.

Prasad, G. *et al.* (2022). Sentiment analysis on cryptocurrency using youtube comments. In *2022 6th International Conference on Computing Methodologies and Communication (ICCMC)*. IEEE, pp. 730–733.

Rane, C., Pai, S., Dani, M., and Dhage, S. (2022). Financial portfolio management and optimization to maximize returns using a combination of hrp and sentiment analysis. In *Proceedings of the 2nd International Conference on Recent Trends in Machine Learning, IoT, Smart Cities and Applications: ICMISC 2021*. Springer, pp. 261–274.

Rekha, K., and Sabu, M. (2022). A cooperative deep learning model for stock market prediction using deep autoencoder and sentiment analysis. *PeerJ Computer Science*, 8: e1158.

Ruangkanokmas, P., Achalakul, T., and Akkarajitsakul, K. (2016). Deep belief networks with feature selection for sentiment classification. In *2016 7th International Conference on Intelligent Systems, Modelling and Simulation (ISMS)*. IEEE, pp. 9–14.

Sánchez-Rada, J.F., and Iglesias, C.A. (2019). Social context in sentiment analysis: Formal definition, overview of current trends and framework for comparison. *Information Fusion*, 52: 344–356.

Sarode, R.P., Poudel, M., Shrestha, S., and Bhalla, S. (2021). Blockchain for committing peer-to-peer transactions using distributed ledger technologies. *International Journal of Computational Science and Engineering*, 24(3): 215–227.

Schouten, K., and Frasincar, F. (2015). Survey on aspect-level sentiment analysis. *IEEE Transactions on Knowledge and Data Engineering*, 28(3): 813–830.

Schouten, K., Van Der Weijde, O., Frasincar, F., and Dekker, R. (2017). Supervised and unsupervised aspect category detection for sentiment analysis with co-occurrence data. *IEEE Transactions on Cybernetics*, 48(4): 1263–1275.

Si, J., Mukherjee, A., Liu, B., Li, Q., Li, H., and Deng, X. (2013). Exploiting topic based twitter sentiment for stock prediction. In *Proceedings of the 51st Annual Meeting of the Association for Computational Linguistics (Volume 2: Short Papers)*, pp. 24–29.

Sidogi, T., Mbuvha, R., and Marwala, T. (2021). Stock price prediction using sentiment analysis. In *2021 IEEE International Conference on Systems, Man, and Cybernetics (SMC)*. IEEE, pp. 46–51.

Silva, N.F.F.D., Coletta, L.F., and Hruschka, E.R. (2016). A survey and comparative study of tweet sentiment analysis via semi-supervised learning. *ACM Computing Surveys (CSUR)*, 49(1): 1–26.

Smailović, J., Grčar, M., Lavrač, N., and Žnidaršič, M. (2014). Stream-based active learning for sentiment analysis in the financial domain. *Information Sciences*, 285: 181–203.

Soleymani, M., Garcia, D., Jou, B., Schuller, B., Chang, S.-F., and Pantic, M. (2017). A survey of multimodal sentiment analysis. *Image and Vision Computing*, 65: 3–14.

Song, Q., Liu, A., and Yang, S.Y. (2017). Stock portfolio selection using learning-to-rank algorithms with news sentiment. *Neurocomputing*, 264: 20–28.

Studiawan, H., Sohel, F., and Payne, C. (2020). Anomaly detection in operating system logs with deep learning-based sentiment analysis. *IEEE Transactions on Dependable and Secure Computing*, 18(5): 2136–2148.

Tian, L., Lai, C., and Moore, J.D. (2018). Polarity and intensity: The two aspects of sentiment analysis. ACL 2018:40.

Tian, S., Zhao, B., and Olivares, R.O. (2022). Cybersecurity risks and central banks' sentiment on central bank digital currency: Evidence from global cyberattacks. *Finance Research Letters*: 103609.

Vacca, A., Di Sorbo, A., Visaggio, C.A., and Canfora, G. (2021). A systematic literature review of blockchain and smart contract development: Techniques, tools, and open challenges. *Journal of Systems and Software*, 174: 110891.

Valle-Cruz, D., Fernandez-Cortez, V., López-Chau, A., and Sandoval-Almazán, R. (2021). Does twitter affect stock market decisions? financial sentiment analysis during pandemics: A comparative study of the H1N1 and the covid-19 periods. *Cognitive Computation*, 13: 1–16.

Vaskikari, V. *et al.* (2020). Identifying tactical asset allocation signals for us and European equities, Department of Industrial Engineering and Management, Aalto University, Finland.

Wan, H., Yang, Y., Du, J., Liu, Y., Qi, K., and Pan, J.Z. (2020). Target-aspect-sentiment joint detection for aspect-based sentiment analysis. In *Proceedings of the AAAI Conference on Artificial Intelligence*, 34(05): 9122–9129.

Wan, X. (2009). Co-training for cross-lingual sentiment classification. In *Proceedings of the Joint Conference of the 47th Annual Meeting of the ACL and the 4th International Joint Conference on Natural Language Processing of the AFNLP*, pp. 235–243.

Wang, F., Lan, M., and Wang, W. (2018a). Towards a one-stop solution to both aspect extraction and sentiment analysis tasks with neural multi-task learning. In *2018 International Joint Conference on Neural Networks (IJCNN)*. IEEE, pp. 1–8.

Wang, L., Liu, K., Cao, Z., Zhao, J., and De Melo, G. (2015). Sentiment-aspect extraction based on restricted Boltzmann machines. In *Proceedings of the 53rd Annual Meeting of the Association for Computational Linguistics and the 7th International Joint Conference on Natural Language Processing (Volume 1: Long Papers)*, pp. 616–625.

Wang, Q., Xu, W., and Zheng, H. (2018b). Combining the wisdom of crowds and technical analysis for financial market prediction using deep random subspace ensembles. *Neurocomputing*, 299: 51–61.

Wang, S., Qi, Y., Fu, B., and Liu, H. (2016a). Credit risk evaluation based on text analysis. *International Journal of Cognitive Informatics and Natural Intelligence (IJCINI)*, 10(1): 1–11.

Wang, W., Pan, S.J., Dahlmeier, D., and Xiao, X. (2016b). Recursive neural conditional random fields for aspect-based sentiment analysis. In

Proceedings of the Conference on Empirical Methods in Natural Language Processing (EMNLP 2016).

Wang, X., Wei, F., Liu, X., Zhou, M., and Zhang, M. (2011). Topic sentiment analysis in twitter: A graph-based hashtag sentiment classification approach. In *Proceedings of the 20th ACM International Conference on Information and Knowledge Management*, pp. 1031–1040.

Xing, F.Z., Cambria, E., and Welsch, R.E. (2018). Intelligent asset allocation via market sentiment views. *IEEE Computational Intelligence Magazine*, 13(4): 25–34.

Yue, L., Chen, W., Li, X., Zuo, W., and Yin, M. (2019). A survey of sentiment analysis in social media. *Knowledge and Information Systems*, 60(2): 617–663.

Zainuddin, N., Selamat, A., and Ibrahim, R. (2018). Hybrid sentiment classification on twitter aspect-based sentiment analysis. *Applied Intelligence*, 48: 1218–1232.

Zeidan, R. (2022). Why don't asset managers accelerate esg investing? a sentiment analysis based on 13,000 messages from finance professionals. *Business Strategy and the Environment*, 31(7): 3028–3039.

Zhang, D., Xu, W., Zhu, Y., and Zhang, X. (2015). Can sentiment analysis help mimic decision-making process of loan granting? a novel credit risk evaluation approach using gmkl model. In *2015 48th Hawaii International Conference on System Sciences*. IEEE, pp. 949–958.

Zhang, L., Wang, S., and Liu, B. (2018). Deep learning for sentiment analysis: A survey. *Wiley Interdisciplinary Reviews: Data Mining and Knowledge Discovery*, 8(4): e1253.

Zhang, W., Li, X., Deng, Y., Bing, L., and Lam, W. (2022). A survey on aspect-based sentiment analysis: Tasks, methods, and challenges. *IEEE Trans. Knowl. Data Eng.*, 1–20.

Zhao, H., Huang, L., Zhang, R., Lu, Q., and Xue, H. (2020). Spanmlt: A span-based multi-task learning framework for pair-wise aspect and opinion terms extraction. In *Proceedings of the 58th Annual Meeting of the Association for Computational Linguistics*, pp. 3239–3248.

https://doi.org/10.1142/9781800615212_0006

Chapter 6

Quantum Fintech

Alessio Faccia
University of Birmingham Dubai, Dubai, UAE
a.faccia@bham.ac.uk

Abstract

This chapter explores Quantum Fintech, an innovative field at the intersection of quantum mechanics and finance, offering novel solutions for challenges in portfolio optimization, option pricing, risk management, algorithmic trading, and cryptography. Quantum Fintech promises to surpass traditional computing methods, address high-dimensional problems, and enable more accurate financial models by leveraging quantum computing's unique capabilities, such as parallelism and exponential speedup. Despite its potential, the field faces significant hurdles, including hardware limitations, noise and error correction, scalability, and ethical concerns. The chapter outlines a roadmap aligned with the IBM Quantum Roadmap, highlighting the progression from improved financial calculations to advanced quantum security measures. Through interdisciplinary research and advancements in quantum hardware, Quantum Fintech stands poised to revolutionize the financial industry, making financial models more efficient and transactions more secure.

Keywords: Quantum fintech, quantum computing, portfolio optimization, option pricing, risk management, algorithmic trading, cryptography, IBM quantum roadmap, quantum hardware, financial industry revolution.

1 Brief Overview of Quantum Fintech

Quantum fintech is an emerging field that applies the principles of quantum mechanics to finance. Integrating quantum computing and finance offers advantages over traditional computing techniques, especially in portfolio optimization, option pricing, risk management, and algorithmic trading. Quantum fintech is at the forefront of technological innovation and has the potential to revolutionize the financial industry (Pagano *et al.*, 2020; Zoufal *et al.*, 2019; Wong and Hayashi, 2018; Kumar and Bhat, 2020; Moşteanu and Faccia, 2021).

At its core, quantum mechanics is a theory that describes the behavior of matter and energy on a very small scale, such as atoms and subatomic particles. The principles of quantum mechanics, including wave–particle duality, superposition, and entanglement, are used in quantum computing to process information in new and unique ways (Nielsen and Chuang, 2010). Quantum computers use qubits, which can simultaneously be in a state of 0 and 1, enabling them to perform complex calculations in parallel and at an exponentially faster rate than classical computers. Even in the beginning of the digital age, finance has been one of the first sectors, after the military industry, to benefit from technological innovation. Indeed, big data processing, analysis, and execution speed are particularly relevant in finance (Kais, 2019; Peters and Crépeau, 2018; Woerner and Egger, 2019).

Given the existing knowledge, the key focus areas in quantum fintech are (a) portfolio optimization, (b) option pricing, (c) risk management, (d) algorithmic trading, and (e) cryptography.

Traditional portfolio optimization models have limitations in dealing with high-dimensional problems, such as optimizing large portfolios with many assets. However, quantum computing can be used to develop more efficient algorithms for solving these problems. For example, quantum annealing can optimize portfolios by finding the global minimum of a cost function, representing a given portfolio's expected return and risk (Rebentrost *et al.*, 2018).

The Black–Scholes model, widely used in finance, assumes that underlying asset prices follow a random walk, which may not reflect the actual behavior of financial markets. Quantum computing can be used to simulate more realistic market scenarios, leading to more accurate option pricing models. In addition, quantum Monte Carlo methods can be used to solve complex option pricing problems that are difficult to solve using classical methods (Woerner and Egger, 2019).

Financial institutions can use quantum neural networks and quantum Boltzmann machines to identify potential risks and take appropriate measures to mitigate them. These machine-learning techniques can also be used for fraud detection and credit scoring. Quantum computing can enable faster and more efficient market analysis and prediction and provide the ability to simulate various market scenarios. It can help traders make more informed decisions and respond to real-time market changes (Benedetti *et al.*, 2019a; Motta and Mott, 2019).

While quantum fintech offers many opportunities, significant challenges must be overcome. These include hardware limitations, noise and error correction, scalability, and complexity (Gomber *et al.*, 2018). In addition, legal and ethical considerations, such as data privacy and security, must be addressed (Lee, 2019). However, with advancements in quantum hardware and interdisciplinary research and collaboration, the potential for quantum fintech to transform the financial industry is vast (Taylor and Zohren, 2019).

2 Quantum Fintech Applications Roadmap

It is still difficult to determine the pace at which the applications analyzed in this chapter can be developed. However, it is possible to refer to a roadmap that has been traced and, so far, timely, perfectly executed for the development of quantum technology: the IBM Quantum Roadmap (IBM, 2020). IBM's Quantum Roadmap is a comprehensive plan to accelerate the development and adoption of quantum computing across various industries. Quantum fintech can fit into this roadmap in several ways, as the financial industry has the potential to benefit greatly from the advanced capabilities of quantum computing (IBM, 2021).

Initially, quantum computing can significantly improve the speed and efficiency of financial calculations, such as those used in option pricing and portfolio optimization. It aligns with the first phase of IBM's roadmap, which focuses on improving the performance of quantum hardware and software to solve specific problems (IBM, 2021). Consequently, quantum computing can enable more accurate risk assessment and management, which is critical in the financial industry. It aligns with the second phase of IBM's roadmap, which focuses on expanding quantum computing to address business problems and improve decision-making. In later development, quantum cryptography can provide new security for financial transactions, protecting sensitive data from potential breaches. It aligns with the third phase of IBM's roadmap, which focuses on advancing the development of quantum security and cryptography. Finally, quantum computing can lead to developing new financial products and services that are impossible using classical computing. It aligns with the fourth phase of IBM's roadmap, which focuses on fostering innovation and creating new markets for quantum computing.

Indeed, quantum fintech can fit into the IBM Quantum Roadmap by leveraging the advanced capabilities of quantum computing to improve financial calculations, risk assessment and management, security, and innovation. By working with IBM and other companies in the quantum computing ecosystem, the financial industry can accelerate the adoption of quantum computing and realize its full potential.

3 Portfolio Optimization

Portfolio optimization is selecting a portfolio of assets that maximizes returns while minimizing risk. It is an important area in finance, as investors aim to balance the risk–return trade-off in their portfolios. Traditional portfolio optimization techniques involve using mathematical models and algorithms to identify the optimal asset allocation. However, these techniques can be computationally expensive and may not be able to handle a large number of asset combinations in modern portfolios (Markowitz, 1952; Campbell *et al.*, 1997).

Quantum computing offers a new way to solve optimization problems, including portfolio optimization. By leveraging the unique properties of quantum mechanics, quantum computers can perform certain calculations exponentially faster than classical computers (Bruder, 2019; Zhang *et al.*, 2020).

In this section, we will discuss two types of quantum optimization techniques: quantum-inspired optimization and quantum annealing, and how they can be used to optimize portfolios.

3.1 Quantum-inspired optimization

Quantum-inspired optimization techniques are classical optimization techniques that quantum mechanics inspires. These techniques aim to mimic the behavior of quantum systems by introducing randomness and probabilistic search methods to traditional optimization algorithms. Quantum-inspired optimization algorithms have been shown to outperform classical optimization algorithms in certain optimization problems, including portfolio optimization (Lu *et al.*, 2019; Xu *et al.*, 2020; Wang *et al.*, 2020; Jindal *et al.*, 2021). Using randomness and probabilistic search methods allows for more efficient search space exploration, which can lead to better solutions (Niu *et al.*, 2020).

Several quantum-inspired optimization algorithms have been developed for portfolio optimization. Three of the most popular are quantum-inspired genetic algorithms, quantum-inspired particle swarm optimization, and quantum-inspired ant colony optimization.

(1) **Quantum-inspired genetic algorithms**: Genetic algorithms are a class of optimization algorithms inspired by natural selection. These algorithms use a population of candidate solutions and apply genetic operations, such as mutation and crossover, to evolve better solutions over generations. Quantum-inspired genetic algorithms incorporate the concepts of quantum mechanics, such as superposition and entanglement, to accelerate the evolution of the population. In the context of portfolio optimization, quantum-inspired genetic algorithms have been used to optimize the weightings of assets in a portfolio. The algorithm starts with a population of candidate portfolios and evolves the population over generations, selecting the best portfolios based on their fitness function (Zhang and Shen, 2019; Kim and Kim, 2020).
(2) **Quantum-inspired particle swarm optimization**: Particle swarm optimization is an optimization algorithm that simulates the movement of particles in a search space. Particles move towards the best solution found so far and adjust their velocity based on the best solution found by the swarm. In the context of portfolio optimization, quantum-inspired particle swarm optimization has also been used to optimize the weightings of assets in a portfolio. In this case, however, the algorithm starts with a swarm of particles moving towards the best solution. The particles adjust their velocity and position based on the best solution found by the swarm (Yang *et al.*, 2019; Sun *et al.*, 2021).
(3) **Quantum-inspired ant colony optimization**: Ant colony optimization is an optimization algorithm inspired by ants' foraging behavior. Ants deposit pheromone trails on the ground as they forage for food. Other ants follow these trails and reinforce them by depositing more pheromones. Over time, the shortest

trail to the food source becomes the most heavily reinforced, and the ants follow this trail. In the context of portfolio optimization, quantum-inspired ant colony optimization has again been used to optimize the weightings of assets in a portfolio. The algorithm starts with a colony of ants that explore the search space and deposit pheromone trails on the ground. The ants follow and reinforce these trails over time, eventually converging on the optimal portfolio (Zheng *et al.*, 2018; Ma *et al.*, 2019).

Quantum-inspired optimization techniques have been applied to several portfolio optimization problems, including enhancing Markowitz's mean–variance model, efficient frontier optimization, and hierarchical risk parity.

- **Enhanced Markowitz's mean–variance model**: Markowitz's mean–variance model is a popular portfolio optimization model that balances expected returns and variance. Quantum-inspired optimization techniques have been used to enhance this model by introducing additional constraints, such as transaction costs and liquidity constraints. The resulting portfolios are more efficient and better reflect real-world constraints (Zhang *et al.*, 2018).
- **Efficient frontier optimization**: Efficient frontier optimization is a portfolio optimization technique that seeks to maximize the expected return of a portfolio for a given level of risk. Quantum-inspired optimization techniques have been used to improve the efficiency of this technique by exploring the search space more efficiently and identifying better portfolios (Li *et al.*, 2021).
- **Hierarchical risk parity**: Hierarchical risk parity is a portfolio optimization technique that seeks to balance the risk of a portfolio across different levels of a hierarchy. Also, in this case, quantum-inspired optimization techniques have been used to improve this technique by introducing more efficient search methods and identifying better portfolios (Xu *et al.*, 2021).

3.2 Quantum annealing

Quantum annealing is a quantum optimization technique based on adiabatic quantum computing principles. Quantum annealing involves starting with a Hamiltonian that is easy to prepare and gradually transforming it into one that encodes the problem of interest. The system is then annealed or cooled to its ground state, which encodes the optimal solution to the problem (Kadowaki and Nishimori, 1998; Albash and Lidar, 2018).

Several quantum annealing algorithms have been developed for portfolio optimization, including adiabatic quantum computing, quantum Boltzmann machines, and quantum annealing.

(1) **Adiabatic quantum computing**: Adiabatic quantum computing is a quantum annealing technique that involves starting with a simple, known Hamiltonian and gradually transforming it into one that encodes the problem of interest. The system is then annealed to its ground state, which encodes the optimal solution to the problem. In the context of portfolio optimization, adiabatic quantum computing has been used to optimize the weightings of assets in a portfolio. The problem is encoded in the Hamiltonian, and the system is annealed to its ground state to find the optimal solution (Liu *et al.*, 2017; Gorman *et al.*, 2020).
(2) **Quantum Boltzmann machine**: A quantum Boltzmann machine is a quantum annealing technique that uses a network of interconnected quantum bits (qubits) to model a problem. Even in this case, a quantum Boltzmann machine can be used to optimize the weightings of assets in a portfolio. The problem is modeled as a network of interconnected qubits, and the system is annealed to its ground state to find the optimal solution. A quantum neural network uses quantum mechanics to learn and process data. It is based on the Boltzmann machine, an artificial neural network used in machine learning. QBM utilizes quantum entanglement to speed up the training and inference process, enabling it to analyze large and complex datasets more efficiently than classical machine learning methods. The potential applications of QBM include pattern recognition, optimization problems, and probabilistic modeling. However, QBM is still in the experimental phase, and developing quantum hardware that can support large-scale QBM calculations remains challenging (Huang *et al.*, 2020; Bian *et al.*, 2021).
(3) **Quantum annealing for portfolio optimization**: It is a quantum annealing technique specifically designed for portfolio optimization. This technique encodes the problem in the Hamiltonian, and the system is annealed to its ground state to

find the optimal solution. Quantum annealing is a quantum computing approach that solves optimization problems by finding the lowest energy state of a physical system. In the case of portfolio optimization, quantum annealing can be used to find the optimal mix of assets that maximizes the expected return for a given level of risk. The problem is mapped to a quadratic unconstrained binary optimization (QUBO) problem, which is a mathematical formulation of an optimization problem in which the objective function is quadratic, and the variables are binary (i.e., they can only take on values of 0 or 1). In this case, the variables represent the selection or nonselection of each asset in the portfolio. Once the problem is mapped to a QUBO form, it can be encoded in the quantum annealing hardware by programming the interactions between the qubits, which represent the binary variables, and the couplers, which represent the quadratic terms in the objective function. The quantum annealer then performs a series of annealing cycles to find the lowest energy state, corresponding to the optimal asset mix for the given risk level. One of the main advantages of using quantum annealing for portfolio optimization is that it can handle many assets and variables, leading to more accurate and comprehensive portfolio optimization. Additionally, quantum annealing can handle nonlinear relationships between assets and variables, improving the optimization process's accuracy (Carignan-Dugas *et al.*, 2018).

Quantum annealing techniques have been applied to several portfolio optimization problems:

- **D-Wave's quantum annealer**: It is a commercial quantum computer that is specifically designed for quantum annealing. It has been used to optimize portfolios by encoding the problem in the Hamiltonian and annealing the system to its ground state to find the optimal solution (Zhao *et al.*, 2018; Han and Wang, 2019).
- **Hybrid quantum-classical optimization**: It is a technique that combines the power of quantum computing with classical optimization methods. In the context of portfolio optimization, this technique can be used to find better solutions by leveraging the strengths of both classical and quantum computing (Benedetti *et al.*, 2019b; Rangoussi and Regan, 2020).

- **Portfolio rebalancing**: It is adjusting the weightings of assets in a portfolio to maintain a desired risk–return profile. Quantum annealing techniques can optimize this process by finding the optimal weightings of assets in a portfolio (Nastase and Zhu, 2020; Gutiérrez *et al.*, 2020).

3.3 Quantum-inspired vs. quantum annealing techniques

Quantum-inspired optimization techniques and quantum annealing techniques are promising portfolio optimization approaches. While quantum-inspired techniques are based on classical algorithms and are inspired by quantum systems' behavior, quantum annealing techniques are based on the principles of adiabatic quantum computing and use existing quantum systems to optimize (Delgado *et al.*, 2021).

They have both strengths and limitations. Quantum-inspired techniques are generally more accessible and easy to implement since they can run on classical computers, whereas quantum annealing techniques require up-to-date quantum hardware. This requirement explains why quantum annealing techniques have the potential to outperform classical algorithms in certain optimization problems, including portfolio optimization. Quantum-inspired optimization techniques also offer a range of search methods and can be adapted to various optimization problems. However, they may not be able to outperform classical optimization algorithms in all cases, and the size and complexity of the problem can limit their performance (Bernal and Munoz, 2020). Nevertheless, quantum annealing techniques have the potential to outperform classical optimization algorithms like problems that can be mapped to the Ising model or the QUBO problem. (Amin and Andriyash, 2012).

Choosing the appropriate technique for portfolio optimization depends on a range of factors, including the size and complexity of the problem, the availability of quantum hardware, and the performance requirements. Quantum-inspired optimization techniques are a good choice for smaller portfolios or problems that can be easily mapped to classical optimization algorithms. As already said, quantum annealing techniques are a good choice for larger portfolios or for problems that can be mapped to the Ising model or the QUBO problem, while hybrid quantum-classical optimization can also be a good choice for certain problems, as it combines the strengths of both classical and quantum computing (Abu-Jamous and Fa, 2019; Takahashi *et al.*, 2020; Albash and Lidar, 2018).

While quantum computing offers a promising new approach to portfolio optimization, several challenges and limitations must be addressed. Some of the key challenges and future directions for research include the following:

- **Technical challenges**: The optimization problem must be carefully formulated and mapped to the Hamiltonian of the quantum system (Farhi *et al.*, 2014; Lucas, 2014; Bian *et al.*, 2010).
- **Integration with existing portfolio optimization methods**: Quantum computing must be integrated with existing portfolio optimization methods to ensure it is compatible with current industry practices (Tang *et al.*, 2021; Capretta and Zdancewic, 2020). The use of quantum computing in portfolio optimization raises several regulatory and ethical considerations (Wilmer and Fehr, 2020). For example, quantum computing may require new regulations and standards for protecting sensitive information. Additionally, the development of quantum computing may raise questions about the impact of new technology on the workforce and the economy (Apte and Hill, 2020; Bucchi and Tognoli, 2021).

There are several directions for future research in quantum computing and portfolio optimization. For example, new quantum algorithms and techniques may be developed further to improve the efficiency and accuracy of portfolio optimization. Additionally, developing new quantum hardware may enable the optimization of larger portfolios or more complex optimization problems (Fösel and Troyer, 2019; Bian *et al.*, 2014).

Quantum computing offers a promising new approach to portfolio optimization, with both quantum-inspired optimization techniques and quantum annealing techniques showing great potential. While there are still challenges and limitations to be addressed, the development of quantum computing may significantly improve the efficiency and accuracy of portfolio optimization. We can harness the power of quantum computing to improve our understanding of finance and optimize our portfolios by carefully considering the strengths and limitations of different techniques and working to address technical, regulatory, and ethical challenges (Watanabe, 2019; Sun and Wang, 2021).

4 Option Pricing

Option pricing is a critical component of financial markets and plays a central role in determining the value of many financial instruments. Options give the holder the right, but not the obligation, to buy or sell an underlying asset at a predetermined price and date. The pricing of options has traditionally been done using classical models, such as the Black–Scholes model, which has successfully predicted the value of options in many cases. However, as financial markets become increasingly complex and the demand for more accurate pricing models grows, researchers have begun to explore the potential of quantum computing in option pricing (Rebentrost *et al.*, 2018; Biamonte *et al.*, 2017; Tognetti *et al.*, 2020).

Several approaches to option pricing use quantum computing, including quantum Monte Carlo simulation, quantum Fourier transform, and quantum artificial neural networks.

(1) **Quantum Monte Carlo simulation**: Monte Carlo simulation is a popular method for pricing options that involves generating many random simulations of the underlying asset price. Quantum Monte Carlo simulation is a quantum computing approach to this method that uses quantum bits to represent the different asset price paths. It allows for a much larger number of simulations than classical Monte Carlo simulation, leading to more accurate pricing (Bruschi and Zagoskin, 2020; McClean *et al.*, 2016; Aspuru-Guzik *et al.*, 2005).

(2) **Quantum Fourier transform**: The Fourier transform is a mathematical technique to transform a signal from the time domain to the frequency domain. Quantum Fourier transform is a quantum computing approach to this method that uses quantum bits to perform the transform. This approach can be used in option pricing to transform the payoff function of the option from the time domain to the frequency domain, making the pricing more efficient (Biamonte and Love, 2017; Biamonte and Wittek, 2017; Wang *et al.*, 2021).

(3) **Quantum artificial neural networks**: Artificial neural networks are a class of machine learning algorithms used to model complex relationships between variables. Quantum artificial neural networks are a quantum computing approach to this method that uses quantum bits to represent the variables. This approach can be used in option pricing to model the complex relationships between the variables that affect the options price (Dervovic *et al.*, 2020).

Quantum computing can also handle nonlinear relationships between variables, which can improve the accuracy of the pricing. Quantum computing has the potential to optimize the pricing process by reducing the time required to price options, providing traders with a potentially essential competitive advantage (in an industry where timely decisions and execution speed are crucial). Additionally, quantum computing can perform calculations in parallel, improving the pricing process's speed (Hu *et al.*, 2021).

While quantum computing offers a promising new approach to option pricing, several challenges and limitations must be addressed. Some of the key challenges and future directions for research include the following:

- **Technical challenges**: One of the main challenges is the development of more powerful and reliable quantum hardware, as current quantum devices are still prone to errors that can affect the accuracy of option pricing models. Another challenge is the need for better quantum algorithms that can handle the complex relationships between variables that affect option prices and the need for methods to verify the correctness of the results obtained from quantum algorithms. Additionally, integrating quantum computing into existing pricing workflows and protecting sensitive financial data in a quantum computing environment are technical challenges that must be addressed (Brandão *et al.*, 2020).
- **Integration with existing option pricing models**: Integration of quantum finance with existing option pricing models requires careful consideration of the strengths and limitations of both classical and quantum computing. Developing hybrid models that combine classical and quantum computing can optimize complex financial models and help ensure compatibility with current industry practices (Woerner and Egger, 2020).

New quantum algorithms and techniques may be developed further to improve the efficiency and accuracy of option pricing. Additionally, developing new quantum hardware may enable pricing larger and more complex options. As financial markets become increasingly complex and the demand for more accurate pricing models grows, researchers have begun to explore the potential of quantum computing in option pricing. By carefully considering the strengths and limitations of quantum computing and working to address technical, regulatory, and ethical challenges, we can harness the power of quantum computing to improve our understanding of finance and optimize our pricing models (Rattan and Singh, 2020).

4.1 Risk management

Risk management is a critical component of financial markets and plays a central role in managing the exposure to risks associated with financial instruments. The development of quantum computing has the potential to significantly enhance risk management practices by allowing for more complex and accurate risk assessment and analysis. Several potential quantum computing applications in risk management include portfolio optimization, asset allocation, and risk assessment:

(1) **Portfolio optimization**: It involves the selection of a portfolio of assets that maximizes the expected return for a given level of risk. Traditional portfolio optimization models are limited in handling the complexity of financial markets and often rely on simplifying assumptions. Quantum computing has the potential to handle the complexity of financial markets by allowing for the optimization of a much larger number of assets and variables (Woerner and Egger, 2020; Chen *et al.*, 2019).

(2) **Asset allocation**: It entails the selection of a mix of assets that is appropriate for a given investor or portfolio. Traditional asset allocation models are often based on statistical analysis and historical data. Quantum computing can enhance asset allocation by allowing for a more accurate and complex analysis of the risk–return characteristics of different assets (Rebentrost *et al.*, 2018; Woerner and Egger, 2020).

(3) **Risk assessment**: It regards the analysis of the risk associated with financial instruments. Traditional risk assessment models

are often based on statistical analysis and historical data. Quantum computing has the potential to enhance risk assessment by allowing for a more accurate and complex analysis of the risk associated with different financial instruments. Unlike traditional risk assessment models that rely on statistical analysis and historical data, quantum computing can handle much larger data and variables, enabling a more comprehensive and accurate financial risk analysis. It can lead to better risk management and more informed investment decisions (Gacitua-Mario *et al.*, 2020).

Indeed, quantum computing can provide a more accurate and efficient risk analysis than traditional models by handling more variables and scenarios, including nonlinear relationships. Quantum computing can optimize risk management by reducing the time required for risk assessment and analysis and performing calculations in parallel, leading to more efficient risk assessment and analysis. While quantum computing offers a promising new approach to risk management, several challenges and limitations must be addressed. Some of the key challenges and future directions for research include the following:

- **Technical challenges**: The technical challenges facing quantum finance include the development of scalable and reliable quantum hardware, efficient quantum software, and quantum-safe cryptography. Interdisciplinary collaboration and significant investment are necessary to overcome these challenges and mainstream quantum finance. While several companies are developing quantum hardware, it is still in its early stages and has limited capacity. Another technical challenge facing quantum finance is the need for large and diverse datasets. Quantum finance relies heavily on data, and the accuracy and efficiency of quantum algorithms depend on the availability of large and diverse datasets. However, obtaining and processing such datasets can be time-consuming and expensive. Furthermore, integrating quantum finance with existing financial systems and practices is another significant challenge. Quantum finance must be compatible with current industry practices to be useful, and this requires the development of new protocols and standards that can support the integration of quantum technologies into existing financial systems. Finally, there is a shortage of quantum computing and finance experts, making it difficult to find individuals with the interdisciplinary expertise needed for quantum finance. Addressing this challenge will require the development of educational programs that can train a new generation of experts with the necessary interdisciplinary skills (Biamonte and Bergholm, 2021; Hu *et al.*, 2021; Kearney *et al.*, 2019).

- **Integration with existing risk management models**: One of the significant challenges is the development of protocols and standards that can support the integration of quantum finance into existing risk management models. It requires a deep understanding of quantum computing and risk management, and finding individuals with the interdisciplinary expertise needed for this integration is challenging. Another challenge is the compatibility between existing risk management models and quantum finance. Integrating quantum finance into existing risk management models requires identifying areas where quantum computing can enhance risk management and the development of new models that can effectively incorporate quantum computing. Furthermore, developing quantum-safe cryptography is crucial to ensure financial transactions and data security and privacy in a post-quantum world. Integrating quantum finance with existing risk management models requires the development of new protocols and standards that can support the integration of quantum-safe cryptography (Shafiee and Javadi, 2020).

New quantum algorithms and techniques may be developed to improve risk assessment, analysis efficiency, and accuracy. Additionally, developing new quantum hardware may enable the analysis of larger and more complex portfolios and risk scenarios. Quantum computing offers a promising new approach to risk management in the financial industry, potentially enhancing risk assessment and analysis.

One example of a quantum machine learning algorithm is the quantum support vector machine, which can be used for binary classification and regression analysis in finance. This algorithm can be used for credit risk assessment and portfolio optimization, where it can identify the underlying structure of a dataset and separate it into different risk classes. Another example is the quantum principal component analysis, which can be used for dimensionality reduction in finance. This algorithm can extract the most relevant information from a large dataset and identify the factors contributing to different financial instruments' risk and return.

By carefully considering the strengths and limitations of quantum computing and working to address technical, regulatory, and ethical challenges, we can harness the power of quantum computing to improve our understanding of finance and optimize our risk management practices (Biamonte *et al.*, 2017).

4.2 Algorithmic trading

Algorithmic trading has become a critical component of financial markets and plays a central role in the execution of trades and optimizing investment strategies. The development of quantum computing has the potential to significantly enhance algorithmic trading practices by allowing for more complex and accurate analysis of financial markets (Brassard *et al.*, 2002).

There are several potential applications of quantum computing in algorithmic trading, including market prediction and optimization of trading strategies:

(1) **Market prediction**: It involves the analysis of market trends and the prediction of future market movements. Traditional market prediction models are often based on statistical analysis and historical data. Quantum computing has the potential to enhance market prediction by allowing for a more accurate and complex analysis of market trends and the underlying variables that affect market movements. Quantum machine learning algorithms can analyze large, complex datasets and uncover correlations and patterns not apparent to traditional models. Additionally, quantum algorithms such as quantum Fourier transform and quantum Monte Carlo simulation can provide more efficient and accurate predictions than their classical counterparts (Bausch *et al.*, 2021).

(2) **Optimization of trading strategies**: It involves selecting a strategy that maximizes the expected return for a given level of risk. Traditional optimization models are limited in handling the complexity of financial markets and often rely on

simplifying assumptions. Quantum computing has the potential to handle the complexity of financial markets by allowing for the optimization of a much larger number of variables and trading strategies. In trading strategy optimization, quantum-inspired optimization techniques can find the optimal mix of assets that maximizes investment returns while minimizing risks. These techniques can handle more variables and constraints than traditional optimization methods, providing a more accurate and comprehensive analysis of trading strategies (Chou *et al.*, 2019).

Future research on quantum algorithmic trading may focus on several areas, including developing new quantum algorithms: there is a need for developing more efficient quantum algorithms for analyzing financial data, forecasting market trends, and optimizing trading strategies. New algorithms can help enhance the accuracy and efficiency of quantum algorithmic trading. Furthermore, hardware and software improvements will play an essential role. As quantum computing technology advances, there will be a need for more advanced and efficient hardware and software for quantum algorithmic trading. Improvements in quantum processors, qubit coherence times, and error correction techniques will be critical for developing more efficient and reliable quantum trading systems (Neukart *et al.*, 2017).

4.3 Cryptography

Quantum cryptography, which uses quantum mechanics to ensure secure communication, is a promising technology for protecting sensitive information in the financial industry. However, it is still in the experimental stage and has not yet been widely adopted by banks.

Most banks use classical encryption techniques, such as the Advanced Encryption Standard (AES), to secure their communications and transactions. While these methods are robust, they are vulnerable to attacks by powerful quantum computers, which can easily break traditional encryption schemes.

Researchers are exploring the potential of quantum cryptography to address this vulnerability. The techniques are based on the fundamental principles of quantum mechanics to provide a new level of security for financial transactions. Unlike classical encryption techniques, which rely on complex mathematical algorithms, quantum cryptography is based on the laws of physics and provides an unbreakable level of security (Lo and Chau, 1999; Gisin *et al.*, 2002; Hsu *et al.*, 2021; Scarani *et al.*, 2009).

Quantum cryptography uses quantum key distribution (QKD) to distribute cryptographic keys between two parties. In QKD, information is encoded in individual photons sent from one party to another over a secure channel. Any attempt to intercept or measure the photons alters their state, allowing the two parties to detect eavesdropping attempts (Bennett and Brassard, 1984).

While QKD has the potential to provide unbreakable security, it is still in the experimental stage, and several technical and practical challenges need to be addressed before banks can widely adopt it. These challenges include the development of reliable and efficient quantum hardware, the standardization of protocols and implementation, and the integration of QKD with existing infrastructure.

Despite these challenges, quantum cryptography is a promising technology for securing financial transactions, and researchers and industry experts are working to overcome the technical and practical barriers to its adoption in the financial industry.

Several banks and financial institutions are exploring the potential of quantum cryptography to improve their security measures. For example, JPMorgan Chase has developed a quantum-resistant encryption algorithm designed to withstand attacks by quantum computers (JPMorgan Chase, 2021). The Bank of America has also filed a patent for a quantum encryption system using a quantum key distribution protocol to secure transactions (United States Patent and Trademark Office, 2019).

Moreover, several quantum computing companies, such as IBM and Microsoft, are developing quantum-safe encryption algorithms resistant to attacks by quantum computers (IBM, 2023; Microsoft, 2023). These algorithms are being developed in anticipation of the widespread adoption of quantum computing and the need for more secure encryption methods.

While quantum cryptography is not yet widely used by banks, it is an active research and development area. As the threat of attacks by quantum computers increases, banks and financial institutions are likely to adopt quantum-safe encryption methods to ensure the security of their transactions and communications. Cryptography is a critical component of financial markets, allowing for the secure transmission of financial information and protecting sensitive data.

The development of quantum computing can significantly enhance cryptography practices in the financial industry.

There are several potential applications of quantum cryptography in financial markets, including the secure transmission of financial information, digital signatures, and secure authentication:

(1) **Secure transmission of financial information**: It is critical in financial markets, as it allows for the secure transmission of financial transactions and the protection of sensitive data. Traditional encryption methods are based on mathematical algorithms and can be susceptible to attacks from quantum computers. Quantum cryptography provides a new approach to encryption, based on the principles of quantum mechanics, that can offer improved security for financial information (Dunjko and Briegel, 2018; Lo *et al.*, 2014).

(2) **Digital signatures**: Digital signatures are an essential aspect of financial transactions, as they provide a way to verify the parties' identity. Traditional digital signatures are based on mathematical algorithms that can be vulnerable to attacks from quantum computers. Quantum cryptography offers a new approach to digital signatures that leverages the principles of quantum mechanics, offering enhanced security for financial transactions. Specifically, quantum digital signatures use quantum key distribution to distribute a secret key between two parties, which is used to sign and verify digital documents. This approach provides an extra layer of security, as any attempt to intercept or measure the quantum signals used for key distribution would alter their state, alerting the parties to the attempted intrusion. The potential of quantum digital signatures to enhance the security of financial transactions has led to growing interest and research in this area. They are a critical component of financial transactions, as they provide a way to authenticate the identity of the parties involved in a transaction. Traditional digital signatures are based on mathematical algorithms and can be susceptible to attacks from quantum computers. Quantum cryptography provides a new approach to digital signatures, based on the principles of quantum mechanics, that can offer improved security for financial transactions (Shor, 1994; Bennett *et al.*, 1992; Gottesman *et al.*, 2004; Rivest *et al.*, 1978; Ekert, 1991; Liu *et al.*, 2016).

(3) **Secure authentication**: It is critical in financial markets, as it allows for secure access to financial information and the protection of sensitive data. Traditional authentication methods are based on mathematical algorithms and can be susceptible to attacks from quantum computers. Quantum cryptography provides a new approach to authentication, based on the principles of quantum mechanics, that can offer improved security for financial information. Using QKD for secure authentication offers improved security and confidentiality, reducing the risk of sensitive financial information being accessed by unauthorized parties. Using quantum cryptography for secure authentication, financial institutions can better protect their data and clients' data from potential attacks (Deng *et al.*, 2004; Dong *et al.*, 2017; Karimipour *et al.*, 2014).

Additionally, quantum cryptography can detect any attempts to intercept or tamper with data transmission, making it more difficult for hackers to compromise financial information.

Quantum cryptography provides a new approach to secure communication in financial markets, potentially enhancing security and data privacy for financial transactions. While traditional encryption methods rely on mathematical algorithms that can be vulnerable to attacks from powerful quantum computers, quantum cryptography utilizes the principles of quantum mechanics to create secure communication channels that can withstand such attacks. New quantum encryption and authentication algorithms that are resistant to attacks by quantum computers may be developed to improve the security and speed of encryption and authentication of financial information. Moreover, developing new quantum hardware could enable the encryption and authentication of larger and more complex financial datasets (Gottesman *et al.*, 2004; Werner and Holevo, 2002).

One promising approach for future research is the development of post-quantum cryptography, which involves exploring new cryptographic techniques resistant to attacks from classical and quantum computers. Post-quantum cryptography is an active area of research and development, with the potential to provide robust security for financial information in the face of future advances in computing technology.

Another promising direction for future research is the application of quantum machine learning to financial data analysis and decision-making. Quantum machine learning algorithms can improve the accuracy and speed of financial data analysis, leading to better investment decisions and risk management practices.

In general, quantum cryptography and quantum computing offer promising new approaches to enhance financial transactions' security, accuracy, speed, and data analysis. Continued research and development in these areas may significantly improve the financial industry's security practices and investment strategies.

5 Conclusions

Quantum fintech is an emerging field that explores the potential of quantum computing in the financial industry. While it is still in its early stages, quantum finance has shown promising results in improving financial modeling, risk management, and security.

One of the key potentials of quantum finance, and quantum fintech in particular, is its ability to handle many variables and scenarios, enabling more accurate financial modeling and risk assessment. Quantum computing can also handle nonlinear relationships between variables, improving the accuracy of pricing and risk management.

However, there are several constraints and challenges to adopting quantum fintech in the financial industry. One of the primary challenges is the current limitations of quantum hardware, which can be expensive and difficult to scale for larger financial datasets. Moreover, there is a shortage of trained personnel in quantum computing, particularly in the financial industry, and regulatory and ethical challenges must be addressed.

Despite these challenges, the potential of quantum finance in the financial industry is significant, and researchers and industry professionals are working to overcome these constraints and further explore the potential of quantum computing in financial technology. With the development of more advanced quantum hardware and software, quantum finance has the potential to revolutionize the financial industry, improve financial models, and enable more secure financial transactions.

References

Abu-Jamous, B., and Fa, R. (2019). Quantum-inspired algorithms for solving the multi-objective portfolio optimisation problem. *IEEE Access*, 7: 142500–142517. https://doi.org/10.1109/ACCESS.2019.2943129.

Albash, T., and Lidar, D.A. (2018). Adiabatic quantum computation. *Reviews of Modern Physics*, 90(1): 015002. https://doi.org/10.1103/RevModPhys.90.015002.

Amin, M.H., and Andriyash, E. (2012). Quantum annealing for problems with coulombic interactions. *Physical Review A*, 85(5): 052324. https://doi.org/10.1103/physreva.85.052324.

Apte, A., and Hill, C. (2020). Implications of quantum computing for financial services. *The Journal of Financial Data Science*, 2(1): 23–39. https://doi.org/10.3905/jfds.2020.1.112.

Aspuru-Guzik, A., Dutoi, A.D., Love, P.J., and Head-Gordon, M. (2005). Simulated quantum computation of molecular energies. *Science*, 309(5741): 1704–1707. https://doi.org/10.1126/science.1113479.

Bausch, J., Foulger, G., Goldberg, L.R., and Henry, C. (2021). Quantum computing: The next frontier in algorithmic trading. *Deloitte Insights.*

Benedetti, M., Garcia-Saez, A., Perdomo-Ortiz, A., and Wang, R. (2019a). A generative modeling approach for benchmarking and training shallow quantum circuits. *NPJ Quantum Information*, 5(1): 1–10.

Benedetti, M., Realpe-Gómez, J., and Biswas, R. (2019b). Quantum-inspired low-rank stochastic regression with logarithmic dependence on the dimension. *NPJ Quantum Information*, 5(1): 1–7.

Bennett, C. H., and Brassard, G. (1984). Quantum cryptography: Public key distribution and coin tossing. In *Proceedings of IEEE International Conference on Computers, Systems, and Signal Processing*, pp. 175–179. https://doi.org/10.1109/iccssp.1984.1172152.

Bennett, C.H., Brassard, G., and Mermin, N.D. (1992). Quantum cryptography without Bell's theorem. *Physical Review Letters*, 68(5): 557–559.

Bernal, C.A., and Munoz, L.E. (2020). Portfolio optimisation using quantum annealing and quantum-inspired algorithms. *Quantitative Finance*, 20(11): 1891–1912.

Biamonte, J.D., and Bergholm, V. (2021). Quantum finance: An introduction. *Contemporary Physics*, 62(2): 111–142. https://doi.org/10.1080/00107514.2020.1845643.

Biamonte, J.D., and Love, P.J. (2017). Realisable Hamiltonians for universal adiabatic quantum computers. *Physical Review A*, Riverdale, USA (APS – American Physical Society), 95(4): 042337. https://doi.org/10.1103/PhysRevA.95.042337.

Biamonte, J.D., and Wittek, P. (2017). Quantum machine learning for finance. In Hughston, L.P., Johnson, P.L., and Piterbarg, V.I. (Eds.), *The Oxford Handbook of Quantitative Asset Management*. Oxford University Press, pp. 235–263. https://doi.org/10.1093/oxfordhb/9780198754061.013.10.

Biamonte, J.D., Wittek, P., Pancotti, N., Rebentrost, P., Wiebe, N., and Lloyd, S. (2017). Quantum machine learning. *Nature*, 549(7671): 195–202. https://doi.org/10.1038/nature23474.

Dian, Z., Chang, S., Chen, J., and Chen, Q. (2021). A quantum Boltzmann machine approach to portfolio optimisation. *Neural Computing and Applications*, 33(19): 14005–14014.

Bian, Z., Chudak, F., Macready, W.G., and Clark, L. (2010). Hybrid quantum-classical approach to solving scheduling problems. *Physical Review A*, 81(3): 032323. https://doi.org/10.1103/physreva.81.032323.

Bian, Z., Chudak, F., Macready, W.G., and Clark, L. (2014). Portfolio optimisation for quantum computers. In Kim, T.H., Kim, H.S., and Kim, S. (Eds.), *Proceedings of the 14th International Conference on Quantum Communication, Measurement and Computing*. IEEE, pp. 54–58. https://doi.org/10.1109/QCMC.2014.6978963.

Brandão, F.G.S.L., Svore, K.M., and Temme, K. (2020). Quantum algorithms for optimisation and machine learning. *arXiv preprint* arXiv:2001.03622.

Brassard, G., Høyer, P., and Tapp, A. (2002). Quantum algorithms for the triangle problem. *SIAM Journal on Computing*, 31(6): 1687–1697. https://doi.org/10.1137/S0097539701397719.

Bruder, T. (2019). Quantum-enhanced finance. *Nature Reviews Physics*, 1(6): 330–341.

Bruschi, D.E., and Zagoskin, A.M. (2020). Quantum Monte Carlo simulation. In Bucchi, M., and Tognoli, C. (Eds.), *Quantum Computing in Finance*. Springer, Berlin, Germany, pp. 93–106. https://doi.org/10.1007/978-3-030-69288-5_6.

Bucchi, M., and Tognoli, C. (2021). Ethical implications of quantum computing in finance. In Bucchi, M., and Tognoli, C. (Eds.), *Quantum Computing in Finance*. Springer, Berlin, Germany, pp. 107–126. https://doi.org/10.1007/978-3-030-69288-5_7.

Campbell, J.Y., Lo, A.W., and MacKinlay, A.C. (1997). *The Econometrics of Financial Markets*. Princeton University Press, Princeton, US.

Capretta, V., and Zdancewic, S. (2020). Hybrid quantum-classical computing for portfolio optimisation. In de Angelis, F., Liò, P., Liotta, A., and Quattrociocchi, M. (Eds.), *Complex Networks and Their Applications VIII*. Springer, Berlin, Germany, pp. 312–324. https://doi.org/10.1007/978-3-030-65351-4_26.

Carignan-Dugas, A., Perdomo-Ortiz, A., and Benedetti, M. (2018). Variational quantum eigensolver for portfolio optimisation. *Physical Review A*, 97(1): 012303.

Chen, C.M., Tso, G.K.F., and He, K. (2023). Quantum optimized cost based feature selection and credit scoring for mobile microfinancing. In *Computational Economics*, pp. 1–32. Springer, Berlin, Germany.

Chen, Y., Chen, X., Liu, C., Lu, J., and Song, Z. (2019). A quantum-inspired particle swarm optimisation algorithm for portfolio optimisation. *Journal of Ambient Intelligence and Humanized Computing*, 10(4): 1561–1569. https://doi.org/10.1007/s12652-018-0774-8.

Chou, Y.H., Kuo, S.Y., Chen, C.Y., and Chao, H.C. (2014). A rule-based dynamic decision-making stock trading system based on quantum-inspired tabu search algorithm. *IEEE Access*, 2, pp. 883–896.

Delgado, M., Ortega, G., Martínez, A., and Martínez, J. (2021). A comparative study of quantum annealing and quantum-inspired optimisation for portfolio optimisation. *Expert Systems with Applications*, 166: 114107.

Deng, F.-G., Long, G.-L., and Liu, X.-S. (2004). Two-step quantum direct communication protocol using the Einstein-Podolsky-Rosen pair block. *Physical Review A*, 68(4): 042317.

Dervovic, E., Sotiropoulos, A., and Zuev, K. (2020). A survey on quantum machine learning: What is it and what could it be? *Journal of Quantum Computing*, 2(1): 1–50. https://doi.org/10.3390/jqc2010001.

Dong, L., Li, X., Huang, L., Wang, X., and Jiang, M. (2017). An efficient quantum remote authentication protocol based on EPR pairs. *Quantum Information Processing*, 16(5): 132.

Dunjko, V., and Briegel, H.J. (2018). Quantum-enhanced measurements without entanglement. *Scientific Reports*, 8: 3663. https://doi.org/10.1038/s41598-018-21928-6.

Ekert, A.K. (1991). Quantum cryptography based on Bell's theorem. *Physical Review Letters*, 67(6): 661–663.

Farhi, E., Goldstone, J., and Gutmann, S. (2014). *A Quantum Approximate Optimization Algorithm.* arXiv: Quantum Physics. Available at https://arxiv.org/abs/1411.4028.

Fösel, T., and Troyer, M. (2019). Optimising quantum annealers for hard optimisation problems. *NPJ Quantum Information*, 5(1): 1–8. https://doi.org/10.1038/s41534-019-0130-6.

Gacitua-Mario, E., Ortuño-Ortín, I., and Riera, J.V. (2020). A survey on quantum computing for finance: Applications, challenges, and opportunities. *International Journal of Financial Engineering*, 7(2): 2050006. https://doi.org/10.1142/S2424786320500063.

Gisin, N., Ribordy, G., Tittel, W., and Zbinden, H. (2002). Quantum cryptography. *Reviews of Modern Physics*, 74(1): 145–195. https://doi.org/10.1103/revmodphys.74.145.

Gomber, P., Haferkorn, M., Jentsch, P., and Zimmermann, K. (2018). High-frequency trading with and without quantum computing. *Journal of Banking & Finance*, 88: 115–131.

Gorman, J., Römisch, W., and Trück, S. (2020). Solving portfolio optimisation problems with an adiabatic quantum computer. *Journal of Computational Finance*, 24(3): 1–26.

Gottesman, D., Lo, H.-K., Lütkenhaus, N., and Preskill, J. (2004). Security of quantum key distribution with imperfect devices. *Quantum Information and Computation*, 4(5): 325–360.

Gutiérrez, E., Suárez, M.A., and del Pozo, M. (2020). Quantum annealing for portfolio rebalancing with multiple constraints. *Expert Systems with Applications*, 152: 113354.

Han, J., and Wang, Y. (2019). Portfolio optimisation via quantum annealing with an enhanced objective function. *Journal of Computational Science*, 31: 104–113.

Hsu, L.-Y., Wu, H.-C., and Liu, C.-Y. (2021). An overview of quantum cryptography: Threats, challenges, and solutions. *Symmetry*, 13(1): 92. https://doi.org/10.3390/sym13010092.

Hu, W., Gao, F., Li, Y., Li, C., and Li, X. (2021). Quantum computing in finance: Opportunities and challenges. *Journal of Parallel and Distributed Computing*, 151: 30–39. https://doi.org/10.1016/j.jpdc.2020.08.002.

Huang, Y., Zhou, D., Wang, H., Liu, D., and Xu, B. (2020). A quantum Boltzmann machine based method for portfolio optimisation. *Physica A: Statistical Mechanics and its Applications*, 557: 124836.

IBM (2020). IBM quantum roadmap. Retrieved from https://www.research.ibm.com/quantum-computing/roadmap/.

IBM (2021). Quantum for finance: Transforming industries with quantum computing. Retrieved from https://www.ibm.com/quantum-computing/industries/finance.

IBM (2023). Quantum-safe cryptography. https://www.ibm.com/quantum-computing/cryptography.

Jindal, A., Kaur, S., and Verma, A. (2021). Quantum-inspired optimisation techniques for portfolio optimisation: A review. *Mathematics*, 9(4): 353.

JPMorgan Chase (2021, June 24). JPMorgan Chase advances quantum computing efforts with quantum-resistant algorithm. https://www.jpmorganchase.com/news-stories/jpmorgan-chase-advances-quantum-computing-efforts-with-quantum-resistant-algorithm.

Kadowaki, T., and Nishimori, H. (1998). Quantum annealing in the transverse Ising model. *Physical Review E*, 58(5): 5355–5363.

Kais, S. (2019). Quantum computing for finance. *WIREs Computational Molecular Science*, 9(2): e1394.

Karimipour, V., Marvian, I., and Rabizadeh, S. (2014). Quantum strong authentication and key agreement protocols for elliptic curve cryptography. *Quantum Information and Computation*, 14(3–4): 323–341.

Kearney, M.J., Laflamme, R., and Kais, S. (2019). Quantum computing in finance: Overview and prospects. *NPJ Quantum Information*, 5(1): 1–17. https://doi.org/10.1038/s41534-019-0209-8.

Kim, Y.H., and Kim, H.J. (2020). Quantum-inspired genetic algorithms for multi-objective portfolio optimisation. *Quantitative Finance*, 20(6): 901–920.

Kumar, S.P., and Bhat, V. (2020). Quantum finance: A brief review. *Annals of Operations Research*, 291: 173–191.

Lee, K.H. (2019). Quantum machine learning for financial risk management. *Quantitative Finance*, 19(11): 1801–1810.

Li, X., Lu, S., and Huang, J.Z. (2021). A quantum-inspired multi-objective efficient frontier optimisation approach for portfolio selection. *Applied Soft Computing*, 98: 106803.

Liu, L., Lu, Z., Zhang, Y., and Sun, W. (2017). Adiabatic quantum computation for portfolio optimisation. *The European Physical Journal Plus*, 132(3): 115.

Liu, Y., Huang, Q., and Wong, K.K. (2016). A quantum digital signature scheme with verifiable signer and message recovery. *Quantum Information Processing*, 15(8): 3303–3313.

Lo, H.-K., and Chau, H.F. (1999). Unconditional security of quantum key distribution over arbitrarily long distances. *Science*, 283(5410): 2050–2056. https://doi.org/10.1126/science.283.5410.2050.

Lo, H.-K., Curty, M., and Tamaki, K. (2014). Secure quantum key distribution. *Nature Photonics*, 8: 595–604. https://doi.org/10.1038/nphoton.2014.149.

Lu, S., Li, X., Huang, J.Z., and Zhang, X. (2019). Quantum-inspired portfolio optimisation: A new computational finance paradigm. *Journal of Economic Dynamics and Control*, 103: 123–146.

Lucas, A. (2014). Ising formulations of many NP problems. *Frontiers in Physics*, 2: 5. https://doi.org/10.3389/fphy.2014.00005.

Ma, X., Li, Y., Li, Z., and Li, J. (2019). Quantum-inspired ant colony optimisation algorithm for portfolio optimisation. *Computational Economics*, 53(2): 801–824.

Markowitz, H. (1952). Portfolio selection. *The Journal of Finance*, 7(1): 77–91.

McClean, J.R., Kimchi-Schwartz, M.E., Carter, J., and de Jong, W.A. (2016). Hybrid quantum-classical hierarchy for mitigation of decoherence and determination of excited states. *Physical Review A*, 94(5): 052302. https://doi.org/10.1103/PhysRevA.94.052302.

Microsoft (2023). Microsoft quantum-safe cryptography. https://www.microsoft.com/en-us/security/quantum-safe-cryptography.

Moşteanu, N.R., and Faccia, A. (2021). Fintech frontiers in quantum computing, fractals, and blockchain distributed ledger: Paradigm shifts and open innovation. *Journal of Open Innovation: Technology, Market, and Complexity*, 7(1): 19.

Nastase, V., and Zhu, Q. (2020). Solving the portfolio rebalancing problem with quantum annealing. *Annals of Operations Research*, 293(1): 507–526.

Neukart, F., Ganzhorn, M., and Lengler, J. (2017). Quantum computing for finance: Overview and prospects. *Annals of Physics*, 529: 1700045.

Nielsen, M.A., and Chuang, I.L. (2010). *Quantum Computation and Quantum Information*. Cambridge University Press, Cambridge, UK.

Niu, B., Zhang, S., and Gao, X. (2020). A survey of quantum-inspired algorithms for combinatorial optimisation problems. *Annals of Operations Research*, 293(2): 463–498.

Pagano, G., Alioto, M., and Scala, M. (2020). Quantum computing for finance: State of the art and future prospects. *Quantitative Finance*, 20(12): 1927–1952.

Peters, E. E., and Crépeau, C. (2018). Quantum algorithms in computational finance. *Review of Financial Studies*, 31(5): 1725–1758.

Rangoussi, M., and Regan, K. W. (2020). A hybrid quantum-classical approach to solving large-scale quadratic assignment problems. *Journal of Global Optimization*, 77(2): 349–374.

Rattan, K.S., and Singh, G. (2020). Quantum computing in finance: A review and future research directions. *Journal of Accounting and Finance*, 20(8): 1–17. https://doi.org/10.33423/jaf.v20i8.2943.

Rebentrost, P., Gupt, B., and Bromley, T.R. (2018). Quantum computational finance: Monte Carlo pricing of financial derivatives. *Physical Review Research*, 1(3): 033063. https://doi.org/10.1103/PhysRevResearch.1.033063.

Rivest, R.L., Shamir, A., and Adleman, L. (1978). A method for obtaining digital signatures and public-key cryptosystems. *Communications of the ACM*, 21(2): 120–126.

Scarani, V., Bechmann-Pasquinucci, H., Cerf, N.J., Dušek, M., Lütkenhaus, N., and Peev, M. (2009). The security of practical quantum key distribution. *Reviews of Modern Physics*, 81(3): 1301–1350. https://doi.org/10.1103/revmodphys.81.1301.

Shafiee, M.A., and Javadi, B. (2020). Quantum computing in finance and risk management: A comprehensive review. *The Journal of Risk Finance*, 21(4): 390–416. https://doi.org/10.1108/JRF-08-2019-0155.

Shor, P.W. (1994). Algorithms for quantum computation: discrete logarithms and factoring. In *Proceedings 35th Annual Symposium on Foundations of Computer Science*. IEEE, pp. 124–134.

Sun, J., Feng, C., and Qian, Y. (2021). Quantum-inspired particle swarm optimisation algorithm for portfolio optimisation with transaction costs. *Symmetry*, 13(3): 503.

Sun, Q., and Wang, Y. (2021). A review of quantum computing in financial engineering. *Frontiers in Physics*, 9: 1–19. https://doi.org/10.3389/fphy.2021.622085.

Takahashi, D., Tanaka, R., and Ohzeki, M. (2020). Quantum-inspired optimisation for financial portfolio selection. *Journal of Physics: Conference Series*, 1529(1): 012014. https://doi.org/10.1088/1742-6596/1529/1/012014.

Tang, Q., Li, B., and Chen, Z. (2021). Quantum algorithm for multi-objective portfolio optimisation based on genetic algorithm. *International Journal of Theoretical Physics*, 60(1): 226–237. https://doi.org/10.1007/s10773-020-04587-w.

Taylor, M.A., and Zohren, S. (2019). Quantum machine learning in finance. In Gallopoulos, E., Herkersdorf, A., and Sauer, J.R. (Eds.), *Quantum Computing: An Applied Approach*. Springer, Berlin, Germany. pp. 287–315.

Tognetti, A., De Felice, G., and Giuseppe, A.D. (2020). A quantum model for pricing European options. *Quantum Reports*, 2(2): 253–259. https://doi.org/10.3390/quantum2020014.

United States Patent and Trademark Office. (2019). Quantum key distribution using polarisation states. https://patft.uspto.gov/netacgi/nph-Parser?Sect1=PTO2&Sect2=HITOFF&p=1&u=%2Fnetahtml%2FPTO%2Fsearch-bool.html&r=1&f=G&l=50&co1=AND&d=PTXT&s1=10,227,852&OS=10,227,852&RS=10,227,852.

Wang, J., Sun, Y., Li, C., and Li, X. (2021). A new quantum algorithm for option pricing based on Fourier transform. *Quantum Information Processing*, 20(4): 1–20. https://doi.org/10.1007/s11128-021-03043-x.

Wang, L., Wang, J., and Li, Y. (2020). Quantum-inspired algorithms for portfolio optimisation problems. *IEEE Transactions on Evolutionary Computation*, 24(4): 710–725.

Watanabe, Y. (2019). The promise and challenges of quantum computing in finance. *Journal of Investment Strategies*, 8(1): 1–22. https://doi.org/10.21314/jis.2019.180.

Werner, R.F., and Holevo, A.S. (2002). Counterexample to an additivity conjecture for output purity of quantum channels. *Journal of Mathematical Physics*, 43(9): 4353–4357.

Wilmer, E., and Fehr, S. (2020). Ethical considerations for quantum computing: The case of machine learning. *Journal of Business Research*, 109: 146–156. https://doi.org/10.1016/j.jbusres.2019.12.030.

Woerner, S., and Egger, D.J. (2019). Quantum computing for finance: Overview and prospects. *Reviews in Physics*, 4: 100028.

Woerner, S., and Egger, D.J. (2020). Quantum risk analysis. *Risk*, 33(8): 46–51. https://doi.org/10.21314/JOR.2020.406.

Wong, T., and Hayashi, A. (2018). Quantum finance: An introduction. *International Journal of Theoretical Physics*, 57(10): 2822–2838.

Xu, Q., Yu, H., Huang, T., and Xu, S. (2021). Quantum-inspired constrained hierarchical risk parity portfolio optimisation. *Neural Computing and Applications*, 33(10): 4845–4857.

Xu, S., Xu, Q., Huang, T., and Yu, H. (2020). A survey of quantum-inspired optimisation algorithms for portfolio optimisation problems. *Journal of Systems Science and Complexity*, 33(5): 1336–1360.

Yang, L., Peng, Y., and Chen, X. (2019). Quantum-inspired particle swarm optimisation for multi-objective portfolio optimisation. *Complexity*, 2019: 1–14.

Zhang, Y., and Shen, Y. (2019). Quantum-inspired genetic algorithm for portfolio optimisation. *Journal of Systems Science and Complexity*, 32(5): 1332–1352.

Zhang, Y., Luo, X., and Sun, W. (2018). A quantum inspired particle swarm optimisation algorithm for portfolio optimisation with transaction costs. *Neurocomputing*, 311: 262–273.

Zhang, Y., Luo, X., and Sun, W. (2020). A survey on portfolio optimisation. *Journal of Systems Science and Complexity*, 33(5): 1249–1281.

Zhao, X., Zhu, Y., Li, L., Li, C., Sun, N., and Guo, H. (2018). Portfolio optimisation with quantum annealing. *Annals of Operations Research*, 270(1–2): 395–409.

Zheng, X., Lu, S., Zhang, H., and Huang, J.Z. (2018). Quantum-inspired ant colony optimisation for portfolio optimisation with constraints. *Journal of Global Optimization*, 70(3): 487–507.

Zoufal, C., Fujii, K., and Woerner, S. (2019). Quantum computing and finance. In Zoufal, C., Fujii, K., and Woerner, S. (Eds.), *Quantum Computing for Finance*. Springer, Berlin, Germany, pp. 1–20.

https://doi.org/10.1142/9781800615212_0007

Chapter 7

Tail Dependence of Eurozone Bond Yields and Sovereign CDS Spreads*

Veni Arakelian[†,‡,§,**], **Roberto Savona**[¶,††] and **Marika Vezzoli**[‖,‡‡]

[‡]*Economic Research and Investment Strategy, Piraeus Bank, Vas. Sofias 94 & Kerasountos 1, Athens, Greece*

[§]*UCL Centre for Blockchain Technologies, London, UK*

[¶]*Department of Economics and Management, University of Brescia, Italy*

[‖]*Department of Molecular and Translational Medicine, University of Brescia, Italy*

[**]*veniarakelian@yahoo.com*

[††]*roberto.savona@unibs.it*

[‡‡]*marika.vezzoli@unibs.it*

Abstract

Using machine learning techniques, we detect clusters with high tail dependence obtained through a flexible threshold copula model applied pairwise to the Eurozone sovereign bond yields and credit default swap spreads. Our approach is also useful to inspect the evolution of the loss distribution, as we prove by computing a theoretical portfolio based on Clayton and Gumbel copulas for the highest values of the association parameters estimated by the model.

*This chapter has received funding from the European Union's Horizon 2020 research and innovation program "FIN-TECH: A financial supervision and technology compliance training programme" under grant agreement No 825215 (Topic: ICT-35-2018, Type of action: CSA).

†Disclaimer: The views expressed are those of the author and do not necessarily reflect those of the Piraeus Bank.

Keywords: Copula, regression trees, random forests, loss portfolio distribution.

1 Introduction

Machine learning is a sub-field of artificial intelligence (AI) and computer science that focuses on using data and algorithms to emulate how people learn while continuously improving its accuracy. Arthur Samuel of IBM is credited with coining the phrase "machine learning" with his study on the game of checkers in 1959. In 1962, Robert Nealey, the self-proclaimed checkers expert, played the game against an IBM 7094 computer and lost. This accomplishment looks modest compared to what is possible now, yet it is regarded as a key milestone in the science of artificial intelligence. Despite their close relationship, machine learning is distinct from artificial intelligence and was developed with the intention of generating AI. The easiest way to grasp this concept is to think of machine learning as the engine that drives artificial intelligence.

The objective of machine learning shifted from attaining artificial intelligence to tackling diverse practical issues as it developed into a distinct area. Models using machine learning analyze the supplied data to detect patterns and generate predictions. This is one method through which computers gain "intelligence." In contrast to machine learning algorithms, which can be seen on paper, artificial intelligence needs a performer. Via a virtual assistant, a bot, or any other AI-powered system, we are able to watch and use AI.

As a security precaution, finance and banking businesses use machine learning to monitor and analyze financial data. Machine learning models trained on historical data may identify underlying trends in financial activity, enabling the detection of fraudulent transactions, suspicious login attempts, etc. Although the purpose of this chapter is not to provide a systematic review of machine learning in finance, we have to provide some works that highlight the potential and the advantages of machine learning techniques over traditional econometric models next focusing on some sovereign risk. For example, Biau and D'Elia (2010) forecast GDP quarter-on-quarter growth in the euro area using random forests, showing that it's an effective tool for selecting the most relevant predictive variables. Manasse and

Roubini (2009) and later Savona and Vezzoli (2015) apply machine learning techniques to explore banking and sovereign crises and show that they are extremely robust and efficient in exploring complex and nonlinear relationships, offering an early warning system for the upcoming crisis. Döpke *et al.* (2017) use boosted regression trees to study the relative importance of leading indicators to forecast recessions in Germany. Arakelian *et al.* (2019) implement a machine learning approach to build a European sovereign risk stratification using macroeconomic fundamentals and contagion measures, detecting systemic risk zones. Bianchi *et al.* (2020) propose, compare, and evaluate several methodologies of machine learning: penalized linear regressions, partial least squares, regression trees, random forests, and neural networks, to show that they reliably detect movements in expected bond returns compared to the traditional dimensionality reduction techniques such as principal component analysis. Gu *et al.* (2020) identify trees and neural networks as the best-performing predictive methods in empirical asset pricing that allow nonlinear predictor interactions missed by traditional econometrics methods. Medeiros *et al.* (2021) explore advances of LASSO, random forests, and other machine learning techniques to produce more accurate forecasts of US inflation, noting the steadily smallest errors delivered by the random forests. Finally, Christensen *et al.* (2022) compare the heterogeneous autoregressive model with machine learning techniques for volatility forecasting, namely, regularization, tree-based algorithms, and neural networks, and show that the last performs better.

In theory, CDS spreads should be closely related to bond yield spreads, and despite the vast amount of papers examining the behavior of bond yields and sovereign CDS spreads, the literature on both the pairwise tail dependence and the behavior of the loan loss distribution for credit portfolios is scant. We will explain how regression trees work by examining the behavior of bond yields and the most popular credit derivatives, which are credit default swaps (hereafter CDS). A CDS contract provides protection against a default by a specific company or government entity. The company is known as the reference entity, and a credit event is a default by the company. The buyer of the insurance makes periodic payments to the seller in exchange for the right to sell a bond issued by the reference entity at face value in the event of a credit event. The behavior exhibited by each group is studied in a period that includes major unanticipated events, like the financial crisis of 2007, the largest global economic crisis due to the COVID-19 outbreak, and the war in Ukraine. In 2007, the world's economies were confronted with the biggest recession since the end of the Second World War. The financial crisis that started in the US sub-prime mortgage market in the summer of 2007 turned rapidly into a global financial system crisis and transferred to the real economy, driving a series of events that until some years ago seemed unlikely to happen. As the crisis unfolded, the intensity and extent of the increase forced governments, central banks, analysts, investors, entrepreneurs, and consumers to constantly review their perceptions and expectations. Past perceptions of a new era of low volatility of economic fundamentals, continuous prosperity, and self-regulation of markets collapsed in front of the rapidly deteriorating situation with major cross-border interconnections and interdependencies affecting financial markets. A year later, the continued deterioration in government finances led to a sudden loss of confidence in sovereign debt markets, which revealed itself in the form of widening credit spreads between several euro-area members and the Eurozone's largest economy, Germany. The response by Eurozone member states and international bodies such as the IMF and the EU has been a suite of interventions led by the ECB with the objective of mitigating sovereign spreads and related contagion dynamics. For example, Arghyrou and Kontonikas (2012) find evidence confirming changes in the regime for sovereign debt pricing, with a dominant role assumed by country-specific macro-fundamentals during the crisis. Later, Ait-Sahalia *et al.* (2014) capture the dependencies among Eurozone CDS spreads, proving the existence of clusters in time and space. On March 11, 2020, the World Health Organization characterized COVID-19 as a pandemic that caused the largest global economic crisis in more than a century. It has had direct effects on income due to premature deaths, workplace absenteeism, and a decline in productivity, and it has caused a negative supply shock, with manufacturing productive activity slowing due to disruptions in the global supply chain and factory closures. On February 24, 2022, Russia invaded Ukraine, which triggered turmoil in the financial markets and drastically increased uncertainty about the recovery of the global economy.

This chapter is organized as follows: in Section 2, we describe and explain the notion of tail dependence and how we obtain it.

In Section 3, we review the classification regression methods and particularly, the regression trees. In Section 4, we describe the data, and in Section 5, we provide the results, discussing the construction of the loss distributions based on copulas. In Section 6, we conclude with a brief summary.

2 Tail Dependence

A bivariate copula function C_t: $[0,1]^2 \to [0,1]$ is the joint distribution function of the random variables X and Y, $H(X,Y)$:

$$H(X,Y) = P(X_t \leq x, Y_t \leq y) = C_t(F(X_t), W(Y_t); \theta) \qquad (1)$$

where F and W are the marginal distributions of X and Y. In our analysis, we use the following copulas:

1. **Frank copula (Frank, 1979)**:

$$C_\theta^F(u,\nu) = -\frac{1}{\theta}\ln\left(1 + \frac{(e^{-\theta u}-1)(e^{-\theta\nu}-1)}{e^{-\theta}-1}\right)$$

$\theta \neq 0$. When $\theta = 0$, Frank copula is the independence copula.

2. **Clayton copula (Clayton, 1978)**:

$$C_\alpha^C(u,\nu) = [u^{-\alpha} + \nu^{-\alpha} - 1]^{-1/\alpha}$$

$\alpha \in [-1,\infty] - \{0\}$. Then $\alpha \to 0$, we obtain the independence copula. When $\alpha \to \infty$, the Clayton copula converges to the comonotonicity copula ($M(X_t,Y_t) = \min(F(X_t), W(Y_t))$), which is the Fréchet–Hoeffding upper bound. When $\alpha = -1$, we obtain the Fréchet–Hoeffding lower bound ($M(X_t,Y_t) = \max\{F(X_t) + W(Y_t) - 1, 0\}$), suggesting that the Clayton copula traces the countermonotonic, independence, and comonotonic copulas, as α moves from -1 through 0 to ∞.

3. **Gumbel–Hougaard copula (Gumbel, 1960; Hougaard, 1986)**:

$$C_\beta^G(u,\nu) = \exp\{-[(-\ln u)^\beta + (-\ln \nu)^\beta]^{1/\beta}\}$$

$\beta \geq 1$. Then $\beta = 1$, we obtain the independence copula. When $\beta \to \infty$, the Gumbel copula converges to the comonotonicity copula.

In our study, we perform transformations to the parameters of the Clayton and Gumbel copulas, i.e., $\theta = \log\alpha$ and $\theta = \log(\beta - 1)$, which allow them to lie in the $(-\infty, \infty)$ interval.

Tail dependence is a measure of dependence in the extremes of the distributions. It is specified for each tail and it describes the amount of dependence in the upper right quadrant tail or lower left quadrant tail of a bivariate distribution, describing the limiting proportion that one margin exceeds a certain threshold given that the other margin has already exceeded that threshold (Joe, 1997; Nelsen, 1999). Lower (upper) tail dependence measures the probability that two series are both below (above) a small (high) quantile:

$$\lambda_U^\theta = \lim_{u\to 1} P(X_2 > F_2^{-1}(u)|X_1 > F_1^{-1}(u)) = \lim_{u\to 1} \frac{1 - 2u + C_\theta(u,u)}{1-u}$$

$$\lambda_L^\theta = \lim_{u\to 0} P(X_2 \leq F_2^{-1}(u)|X_1 \leq F_1^{-1}(u)) = \lim_{u\to 0} \frac{C_\theta(u,u)}{u}$$

The upper tail dependence is the limiting value of the joint survival function $P(X_2 > F_2^{-1}(u), X_1 > F_1^{-1}(u))$ over $1 - u$, which is the conditional probability $P(X_2 > F_2^{-1}(u)|X_1 > F_1^{-1}(u))$. Similarly, the lower tail dependence is the limiting value of the conditional probability $P(X_2 \leq F_2^{-1}(u)|X_1 \leq F_1^{-1}(u))$. Put it simply, the tail dependence is the limiting proportion that one margin exceeds a certain threshold given that the other margin has already exceeded that threshold. We say that $X = (X_1, X_2)$ exhibits upper (lower) tail dependence if and only if $\lambda_U^\theta > 0$ ($\lambda_L^\theta > 0$). If $\lambda_U^\theta = 0$ ($\lambda_L^\theta = 0$), we say that X is upper (lower) tail-independent. Table 1 shows the tail behavior of the copulas used in this chapter. Frank copula is chosen for its nice symmetrical properties, whereas Clayton and Gumbel–Hougaard copulas are somehow complementary since they exhibit opposite upper and lower tail dependence properties. Comonotonicity copula mentioned before as a limiting case is the extreme case

Table 1. Upper- and lower-tail dependence coefficients.

Tail Dependence	**Frank**	**Clayton**	**Gumbel**
Upper tail dependence	0	0	$2 - 2^{-1/\beta}$
Lower tail dependence	0	$2^{-1/\alpha}$	0

where dependency is as strongly "positive" as possible. On the other hand, countermonotonicity copula is the extreme case where dependency is as strongly "negative" as possible. Modeling tail dependence using a bivariate model offers an important intuitive advantage (see, also, Meine *et al.*, 2015); the bivariate estimation setup ensures that our CDS tail dependence coefficients are directly comparable to alternative measures of downside and tail risk that are all estimated from bivariate rather than multivariate models (e.g., MES). Arakelian and Dellaportas (2012) generalize (1) by indexing the copula function C by a parameter θ that lies in $(-\infty, \infty)$ (if θ lies in another interval we just perform a simple transformation) and by introducing disjoint sets I_j, $j = 1, \ldots, J$, so that

$$C_t(u, v) = \sum_{j=1}^{J} I_j(t) C_{\theta_j}(u_j, v_j) \tag{2}$$

where $[0, T] = \bigcup_j I_j$, $I_j(t) = 1$ if $t \in I_j$, and in each interval I_j the parameter of the copula is θ_j and the corresponding samples x_j and y_j. The copula parameters are also indexed by the interval they belong, indicating that the parameters μ^X, μ^Y, σ^X, and σ^Y may be different in each interval I_j. A further generalization of (2) is achieved by employing a collection of copula functions $\{C_\theta^i, i = 1, \ldots, \ell\}$ so that

$$C_t(u, v) = \sum_{j=1}^{J} I_j(t) \sum_{i=1}^{\ell} w_{ij} C_{\theta_j}^i(u_j, v_j) \tag{3}$$

where $C_{\theta_j}^i$ denotes the copula function C_θ^i with $\theta = \theta_j$ and w_{ij} denotes the probability of having the copula i in the interval I_j, so $\sum_{i=1}^{\ell} w_{ij} = 1$ for all j. Their work is based on the assumption that different time periods, separated by thresholds, different volatilities, and copula formulations, can adequately explain the dependency between two financial assets which comove nonlinearly and possibly show changes in regime. By assuming that the number and location of thresholds are unknown and need to be estimated, the methodology considers models with different volatilities, copula functions, number of thresholds, and threshold locations. A reversible-jump MCMC algorithm is run thus obtaining samples from the posterior density of these models, and a Bayesian model-averaging estimation approach constructs a posterior density of the upper and the lower tail dependencies, λ_U and λ_L, respectively, marginalized over all models and parameters within each model. The use of copulas that allow for varying tail dependence is an important aspect of flexibility from a modeling viewpoint since there is an extension of the behavior of the random variables during extreme events.

3 Classification Regression Methods

Supervised machine learning is a type of machine learning where the algorithm is trained on labeled data, which means that the data are already categorized or classified. The algorithm learns from this labeled data and can then make predictions or decisions on new, unlabeled data. The process of supervised machine learning involves the following steps:

- **Gathering labeled data**: The first step is to gather a dataset with labeled data. The labeled data will typically include both input features and the corresponding output, such as a classification or prediction.
- **Splitting the data**: The labeled data are then split into a training set and a testing set. The training set is used to train the algorithm, and the testing set is used to evaluate the accuracy of the model.
- **Choosing a model**: Next, a suitable model is chosen for the data. This could be a decision tree, neural network, or other types of algorithms.
- **Training the model**: The chosen model is then trained on the labeled data. During this stage, the model adjusts its parameters to fit the data.
- **Testing the model**: Once the model has been trained, it is tested on the testing set. The accuracy of the model is evaluated, and any adjustments are made to improve its performance.
- **Using the model**: Finally, the trained model can be used to make predictions on new, unlabeled data.

Supervised machine learning is commonly used in various applications such as image recognition, speech recognition, natural language processing, and many more.

On the other hand, unsupervised machine learning is a type of machine learning where the algorithm is trained on unlabeled data, which means that the data are not categorized or classified. The algorithm learns from the patterns and structures that exist within the data and can then identify similarities and differences among the data points. The process of unsupervised machine learning involves the following steps:

- **Gathering unlabeled data**: The first step is to gather a dataset with unlabeled data. These data may include raw data from sensors, customer behavior data, or any other type of data where the categories are not known.
- **Choosing a model**: Next, a suitable model is chosen for the data. This could be a clustering algorithm, principal component analysis (PCA), or another type of algorithm.
- **Training the model**: The chosen model is then trained on the unlabeled data. During this stage, the model tries to identify patterns, similarities, and differences among the data points.
- **Evaluating the model**: Once the model has been trained, it is evaluated to see how well it has identified the patterns in the data. This may involve visualizing the data or using statistical methods to evaluate the performance of the model.
- **Using the model**: Finally, the trained model can be used to identify new patterns in new, unlabeled data.

Unsupervised machine learning is commonly used in various applications, such as anomaly detection, customer segmentation, image segmentation, and many more. It is advantageous when no labeled data are available or the categories are not well defined.

Coming back to supervised learning, regression trees are non-parametric models constructed by recursively partitioning a dataset through its predictor variables with the objective of optimally predicting a response variable that can be continuous or categorical. The beauty of the procedure, which is definitely what we need for our main objective, is in uncovering forms of nonlinearity and identifying multiple data regimes from a set of predictor variables. Moreover, regression trees are conceived with the aim of improving out-of-sample predictability, for modeling complex, nonlinear relationships between input features and continuous target variables. They are widely used in many fields, including finance, marketing, and engineering. However, they can be sensitive to outliers in the training data and may suffer from overfitting if the tree is too complex or the data are noisy.

The construction of a regression tree typically involves two main steps: tree construction and tree pruning. In the tree construction phase, the algorithm recursively partitions the input space using binary splits based on the input features until a stopping criterion is met, such as a minimum number of samples per leaf or a maximum depth of the tree. The procedure is performed for every branch (layer), where the data are divided into two categories. The objective is to identify a binary question that divides the data into two homogeneous groups at each branch of the tree, having a single root node, two branches from each parent node that each enter a child node, and numerous terminal nodes (or "leaves"). Several branches may connect to a node in nonbinary decision trees. The categorization is dependent on x_1 and x_2 as predictors or characteristics. To categorize an observation, beginning with the root node, one must determine if the value of feature x_1 for this observation is more than or less than a specified threshold x. Then, the value of characteristic x_2 becomes significant. The tree will ultimately identify the observation as either a circle or a triangle based on this information. In the instance of the tree in Figure 1, the probability associated with certain terminal nodes is 100%, but the probability associated with other terminal nodes is lower. This basic tree is incapable of appropriately classifying squares; a considerably deeper tree is required for it. In other words, more splits would be required to discover a space division where square-shaped data predominate.

To achieve this, they are estimated through a cross-validation estimation procedure whereby the sample is partitioned into subsets so that the analysis is initially performed on a single subset (the training sets), whereas the other subsets are retained for subsequent use in confirming and validating the initial analysis (the validation or testing sets).

Mathematically, having data consisting of R inputs and continuous response, Y, for each of N observations, the algorithm needs to decide on the splitting variables, the split points, and the topology (shape) of the tree. To do this, the algorithm partitions the input space $\mathcal{S}$, namely, the set of all possible values of $\mathbf{X}$ ($\mathbf{X} \in \mathcal{S}$),

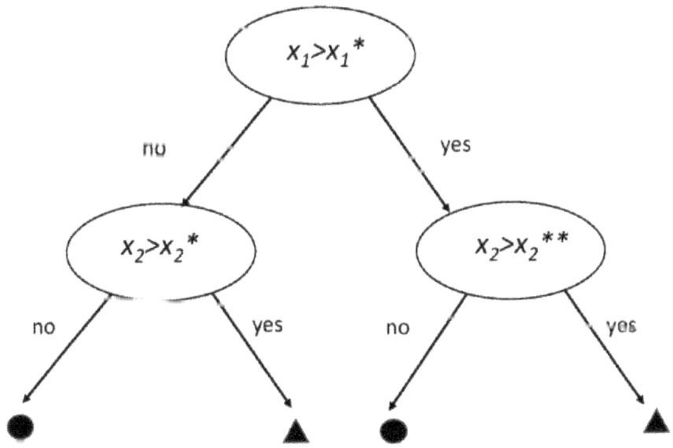


```
d = 0, endtree = 0
Note(0) = 1, Node(1) = 0, Node(2) = 0
while endtree < 1
    if Node(2^d−1) + Node(2^d) + .... +
     Node(2^{d+1}−2) = 2 − 2^{d+1}
        endtree = 1
    else
        do i = 2^d−1, 2^d, ... , 2^{d+1}−2
            if Node(i) > −1
                Split tree
            else
                Node(2i+1) = −1
                Node(2i+2) = −1
            end if
        end do
    end if
d = d + 1
end while
```

Figure 1. Basic regression tree.

into disjoint regions T_k with $k = 1, 2, \ldots, K$, so that $\mathcal{S} \subseteq \bigcup_{k=1}^{K} T_k$. The underlying response-predictor structure $f(\mathbf{X})$ is represented by the piecewise constant functions g_k fitted over the input sub-space:

$$f(\mathbf{X}) = \sum_{k=1}^{K} g_k I(\mathbf{X} \in T_k) \tag{4}$$

where g_k is the parameter that associates the kth value with the corresponding node and I denotes the indicator function taking the value of 1 if $\mathbf{X} \in T_k$. If the criterion minimization assumed is the sum of squares $\sum(Y - f(\mathbf{X}))^2$, then the predictions are computed by the average of the Y values within the terminal nodes, i.e.,

$$\widehat{Y}_i = \widehat{g}_k = \frac{\Sigma_{\mathbf{X} \in T_k} Y_i}{N_k}$$

thus obtaining a mapping of the response variable which is optimal for the number of final clusters, the best predictors and corresponding thresholds, and the predictions for the Y variable.

To find the best binary partition in terms of the minimum sum of squares is computationally infeasible, therefore a greedy algorithm is used. For each predictor, the procedure starts by considering all the possible binary splits obtained from the starting node (the first node is the sample as a whole) considering each realization as a possible splitting value (from min to max) and calculating the corresponding reduction in the MSE (node impurity) generated by the split from the starting node to the sub-nodes; the best split is the value for the predictor which attains the maximum reduction in node impurity. The procedure is run for each predictor at each split and the selected variables with the corresponding thresholds are those that most reduce the loss function in each partition. (See Hastie *et al.*, 2009 for more technical details.)

In the tree pruning phase, the algorithm prunes back the tree to avoid overfitting by removing branches that do not contribute to the overall accuracy of the tree.

4 Data

To measure the sovereign risk for Greece, Ireland, Italy, Portugal, Spain, France, Germany, the UK, and the US, we use the sovereign 5-year CDS spreads, Tables 2 and 3 contain the major events during the financial crisis of 2007 and the COVID-19 outbreak that could initiate dependency change. Figure 2 shows the evolution of the CDS spreads along with some key events of the financial crisis. We also collect the sovereign 10-year bond yields for the same period to compare the tail dependence behavior.

Table 2. Chronology of the financial and Euro debt crisis.

March 2008: The investment bank Bear Stearns is bought out by JP Morgan. ECB offers refinancing operations with longer maturities.
July 2008: ECB increases interest rates by 25 basis points September 2008: The US government bails out Fannie Mae and Freddie Mac — two huge firms that had guaranteed thousands of sub-prime mortgages. Lehman Brothers files for bankruptcy. ECB conducts a special term refinancing operation. Central banks announce measures to ease pressures in short-term US dollar funding markets. ECB and Fed step up efforts to alleviate tension in short-term funding markets. G7 vows to protect the financial system.
October 2008: ECB facilitates access to refinancing, decides on extraordinary liquidity measures, aims to improve protection for bank deposits, and calls other central banks in a joint move to cut rates.
November 2008: ECB cuts interest rates by 50 basis points. G20 seeks to boost growth and prevent crises.
December 2008: ECB's Governing Council decides to restore the standing facilities corridor to 200 basis points in January 2009. ECB cuts interest rates by 75 basis points.
January 2009: ECB cuts interest rate by 50 basis points. Fears for banking collapse.
February 2009: Key report on financial supervision published.
March 2009: ECB cuts interest rates by 50 basis points.
April 2009: ECB cuts interest rates by 25 basis points. G20 to set up Financial Stability Board.
May 2009: Launch of one-year maturity refinancing operations. ECB fears financial integration slowdown. The ECB cuts interest rates by 25 basis points.
June 2009: The ECB cuts interest rates by 25 basis points. ECB launches first covered bonds programme.
September 2009: G20 to step up economic cooperation.
October 2009: George Papandreou's socialist government is elected in Greece. Just over a week later, he reveals that the hole in Greece's finances is double what was previously feared.
November 2009: New Citigroup maven Buiter warns of sovereign debt delusion. Standard Bank says Greece and Ireland may leave Eurozone. Greece risks financial Armageddon while Ireland makes cuts — this marks the beginning of the Greek debt crisis. Before, Greece was the worst of many debtors but roughly equivalent to Ireland, for example. After this point, Greece became the singular focal point of all Eurozone debtors.
February 2010: Debt concealment in Greece. Greek death spiral hits bank credit ratings.

(*Continued*)

Table 2. (*Continued*)

March 2010: Anticipating Eurozone collapse. Europe puts the loaded gun on the table but no bailout.
April 2010: Fitch downgrades Greece to BBB- with a negative outlook. Merkel may force banks to take a haircut on Greek debt.
May 2010: The bailout for Greece is in. The first bailout package for Greece.
November 2010: European ministers agree on a bailout for Ireland worth 85bn euros.
March 2011: The Irish stress tests and Eurozone options: monetization, default, or break-up.
April 2011: S&P reckons 50–70% haircut for Greek debt restructuring, weakening euro — "the German finance minister and S&P both suggested that the risk of Greek debt restructuring has risen and may indeed be the most likely outcome. S&P, for example, envisions a 50–70% haircut with a 1-in-3 chance of default".
May 2011: The ECB bails out Portugal. Greece will eventually restructure.
June 2011: Can Greece CDS Trigger A European Lehman? — It took a while but Greek CDS made a return as a real issue. Stuffing bondholders in Greece and Ireland.
July 2011: The Eurozone debt crisis statement — This is the second bailout and third definitive Greek solution. Italian bonds are getting crushed and contagion is clearly spreading to the core.
August 2011: S&P downgrades US sovereign debt.
February 2012: Greece passes its most severe austerity package yet.
March 2012: The number of unemployed Europeans reaches its highest ever level.
June 2012: The level of Spanish borrowing reaches a record high.
July 2012: "Whatever it takes", ECB president Mario Draghi, gives his strongest defense yet of the Euro, prompting markets to rally.
July 2013: The European Commission and the IMF published their reports recommending that financial aid to Greece be continued. Further discussions on Greek debt sustainability.

5 Results

5.1 Tail dependence clusters

We apply our threshold copula model to the weekly differences in our data. From our threshold copula model, the pairwise upper and lower tail dependencies, λ_U and λ_L, of the sovereign bond yields and the CDS spreads are computed. To better explore results from our approach, we also used heatmaps, which are commonly used to

Table 3. Major timestamps of the COVID-19 pandemic.

December 31, 2019: Wuhan, China, confirmed dozens of cases of pneumonia of unknown cause. Days later, researchers in China identified a new virus that had infected dozens of people in Asia.
January 11, 2020: China reported its first death.
January 20, 2020: Other countries, including the United States, confirmed cases.
January 23, 2020: Wuhan, a city of more than 11 million, was cut off by the Chinese authorities.
January 30, 2020: The World Health Organization declared a global health emergency.
February 2, 2020: The first coronavirus death was reported outside China.
February 14, 2020: France announced the first coronavirus death in Europe.
February 23, 2020: Italy saw a major surge in cases.
February 29, 2020: The US reported a death.
March 11, 2020: The World Health Organization characterized COVID-19 as a pandemic.
March 17, 2020: The EU barred most travelers from outside the bloc.
March 26, 2020: The US led the world in confirmed cases.
April 6, 2020: Prime Minister Boris Johnson moved into intensive care.
April 26, 2020: The global death toll surpassed 200,000.
May 17, 2020: Japan and Germany, two of the world's largest economies, entered a recession phase.
May 27, 2020: Coronavirus deaths in the US passed 100,000.
June 30, 2020. The EU said it would reopen borders.
July 21, 2020: European leaders agreed on a $857 billion stimulus package.
August 22, 2020: Global virus deaths surpassed 800,000.
September 28, 2020: Global deaths reached 1 million.
December 18, 2020: Council and Parliament reach provisional agreement on the Recovery and Resilience Facility of €672.5 billion, to support public investments and reforms in member states, helping them to address the economic and social impact of the COVID-19 pandemic, as well as the challenges posed by the green and digital transitions.

emphasize data above or below specific thresholds as "hot" or "cold" colors, respectively. In our analysis, low values (cold colors) are in green, high values (hot colors) are in red, and values around the mean (warm colors) are in yellow. Heatmap also computes a hierarchical cluster analysis on the time-varying dependencies, thereby realizing dendrograms appended to the pairs of copulas, which help visualize homogeneous clusters among all possible pairs of copulas.

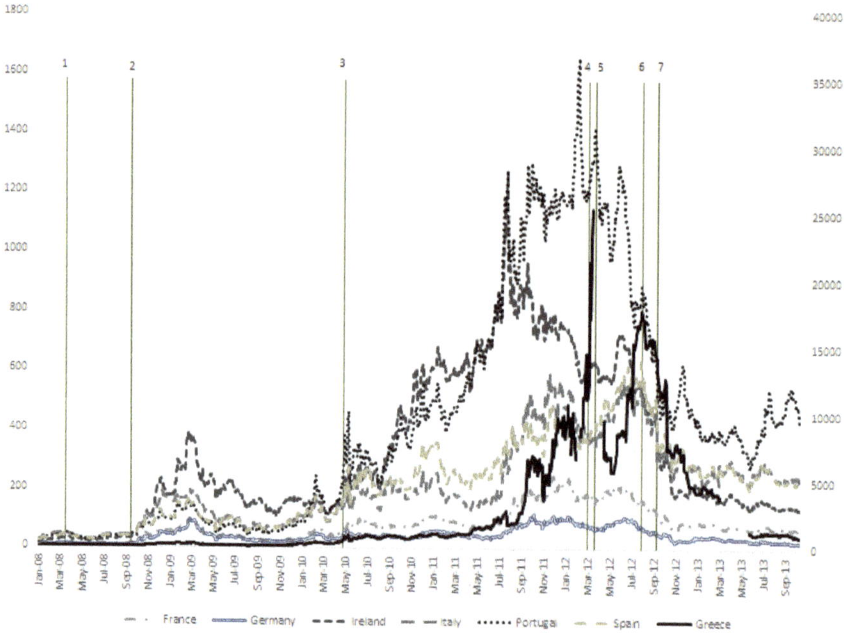

Figure 2. Left axis: Sovereign 5-year CDS spreads of France, Germany, Italy, Ireland, Portugal, and Spain from January 1, 2008, to October 10, 2013. Right axis: Greek 5-year CDS. Major events are highlighted: 1: Bear Stearns collapse, 2: Lehman Brothers collapse, 3: Greece asks for a bailout, 4: ECB suspends the use of Greek bonds as collateral, 5: Greek Default, 6: Draghi's "Whatever it takes", 7: Outright Monetary Transaction (OMT) programme starts.

Figure 3 shows the heatmaps of tail dependencies for all pairs with France. The missing pairs are referring to strong "positive" or "negative" tail dependencies. The lower tail dependence seems no significant changes throughout the years for each pair. Starting from the top and moving down, from the oldest observation to the latest, only the tail dependence between France and Germany changes from negative to positive, implying that only recently, the pair exhibits lower tail dependence. On the other hand, the pair France-Spain exhibits lower tail dependence before the crisis of 2008. Moving to the upper tail dependence of the bond yields, the behavior is mixed and changes more frequently in the majority of the pairs.

The tail dependence behavior of the CDS spreads differs significantly from that of the bond yields. France-Germany, France-Ireland, and France-Portugal show lower tail dependence in several

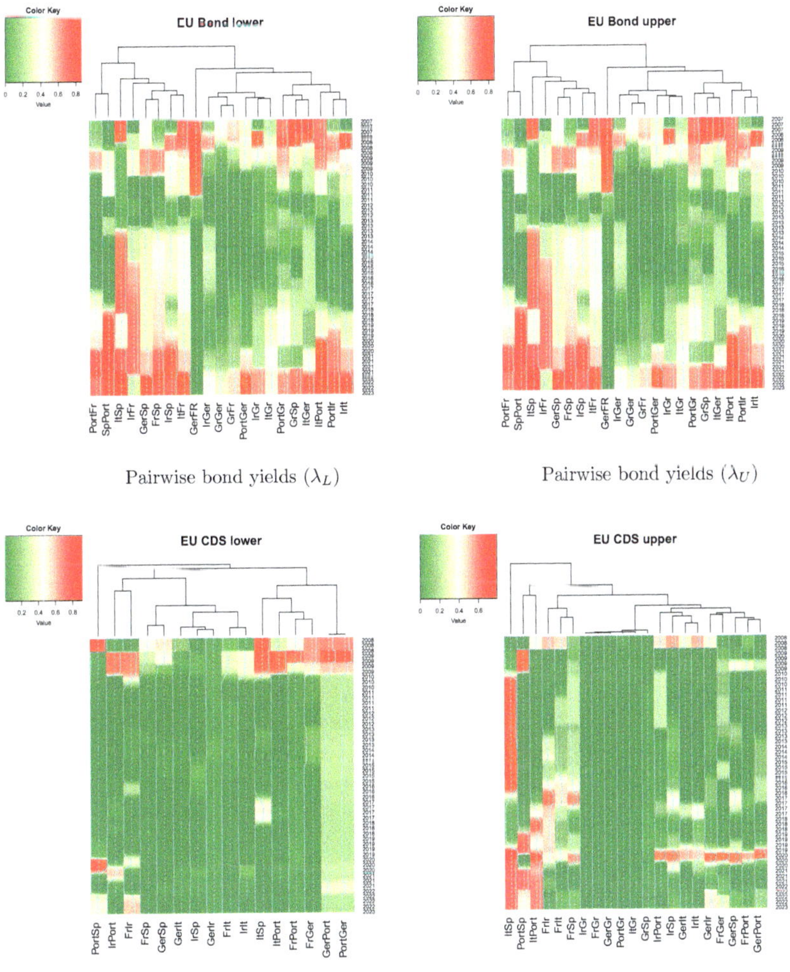

Pairwise bond yields (λ_L) — Pairwise bond yields (λ_U)

Pairwise CDS spreads (λ_L) — Pairwise CDS spreads (λ_U)

Figure 3. Posterior averaged upper and lower tail dependence for all the pairs of France bond yields and CDS spreads.

periods. The same holds for the upper tail dependence. Recall that the upper tail dependencies give the conditional probability of an extreme "upper" event, that is, the probability of one of the CDS spread moving towards very high and dangerous levels given that the other has already exceeded those values.

5.2 Application to loss distributions

A wide range of literature has been dedicated to the generation of loss distributions for credit portfolios, as they play a key role in pricing credit derivatives and in credit portfolio optimization. The loss distribution functions depend on each other[1] on the dependence structure, which in our case is assumed to change. The derivation of the loss distribution can be done either using Monte Carlo simulation techniques or other approaches. For a survey on the generation of loss distributions, see Jouravlev and Maurer (2009). [Vasicek (1987)] and [Vasicek (2002)] developed a large homogeneous portfolio approximation that played an important role in synthetic CDO pricing methods. In the first paper, he assumes an infinite number of entities in the portfolio with identical features (i.e., the same notional amount, default probability, and recovery rate) and a one-factor Gaussian copula modeling the correlation structure. Although these assumptions were very restrictive, the closed formula derived by Vasicek was easy to implement. Schönbucher (2002) used an algorithm from the theory of Archimedean copula functions to estimate limiting loss distributions that are driven by a random variable with different dependency structures.[2] This approach allowed for the presentation of simple and realistic formulas for the loan portfolio distribution. Following Schönbucher (2002), the distribution F and the density f of the limiting loss distribution are

$$F(q) = 1 - G\left(-\frac{\ln q}{\phi(p)}\right) \tag{5}$$

$$f(q) = \frac{1}{q\phi(p)} g\left(-\frac{\ln q}{\phi(p)}\right) \tag{6}$$

where p is the unconditional default probability of all obligators and q is the fraction of defaults in the portfolio. Details of the generator function can be found in Schönbucher (2002). Excluding Frank copula, as the mixing variable has an integer-value density,

---

[1]Other variables are the number of the portfolio entities, the individual credit rating and the recovery rate, the loss given default, and the probability of default.

[2]For an analytic discussion of portfolio loss distribution beyond Gaussian copula, see, for example, Andersen and Sidenius (2004).

we examine the loss distribution of the Clayton and Gumbel copulas based on the association parameters estimated by our flexible copula model described analytically in the following section. Our approach provided information about the changing upper and lower tail dependencies, which is very useful to compute loss distributions for portfolios of credit exposures based on the same copula functions. This is indeed what we prove by presenting an exercise to provide insight into the evolution of a theoretical portfolio of CDS, where all have the same profile in terms of notional amount, recovery rate, etc. We assume that the individual default probability of the obligator is 5% in all the cases (see Schönbucher, 2002), and we construct the loss distribution, Eq. (6), using either the Clayton or the Gumbel copula as generators, and the highest value of the association parameter, which corresponds to the strongest dependence detected between the CDS spreads. Figure 4 shows the portfolio loss with respect to the fraction q of the obligators that defaulted. For Clayton copula, the loss distribution reaches two different peaks for $q = 0$ and $q = 100\%$ defaults, contrary to Gumbel copula, which assigns the highest values to the loss distribution for small values of q and stays almost unchanged for the rest. Putting in other words, under Clayton copula, the probability of having more than a fraction q of defaults in the portfolio reaches its peak either with the scenario of a "few" defaults or "almost all" defaults, showing almost no change in the intermediate values of q, whereas with Gumbel copula, only a small fraction of defaults q is needed to reach the highest value of the probability of having more than q defaults.

6 Conclusions

In this study, we come up with a new way to find clusters in the pairwise tail dependence of sovereign bond yields and CDS spreads. We also look at the loss distribution function of a theoretical portfolio of CDS spreads, which is made up of the copula functions and the highest association parameters found by our method. Using a heatmap to visualize the tail dependencies across time, it is shown that the upper tail dependencies are high and that strong interconnections exist among the pair countries compared to each other. Based on the model's best estimate of the highest association parameters, we use

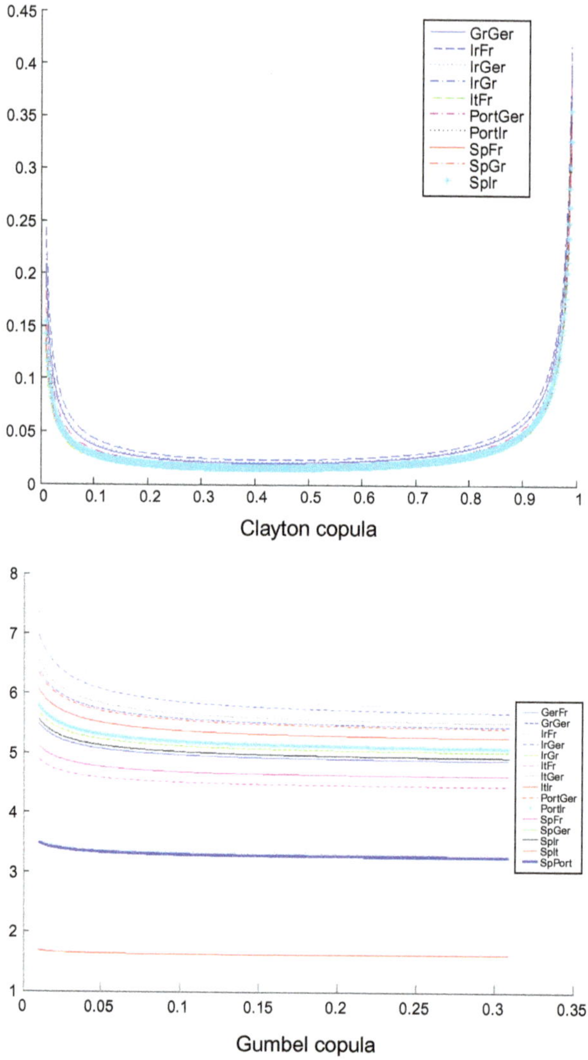

Figure 4. Loss distribution functions. In the x-axis, the fraction of defaulted obligators, q. In the y-axis, the density of the loss distribution function.

Clayton's and Gumbel's generator functions to build the loss distribution function, which tells us how likely it is that we will have more defaults than a given fraction. For Clayton copula, the loss distribution reaches two different peaks for close to 0% and 100% defaults. On the contrary, in the case of the Gumbel copula, only a small fraction of defaults lead to the probability of having more defaults reach their highest value. Both provide very interesting information about the probability of having more defaults when forming a portfolio of credit insurance contracts, like the CDS.

Acknowledgments

We also thank the members of the COST (European Cooperation in Science and Technology) Action 19130 for their comments. The first author thanks Elli Nobeli for providing editing assistance. This chapter is dedicated to Elli's father who passed away suddenly.

Declarations of Interest

The authors report no conflicts of interest. The authors alone are responsible for the content and writing of the chapter.

References

Ait-Sahalia, Y., Laeven, R.J.A., and Pelizzon, L. (2014). Mutual excitation in Eurozone sovereign CDS. *Journal of Econometrics*, 183: 151–167.

Andersen, L.B.G., and Sidenius, J. (2004). Extensions to the Gaussian copula: Random recovery and random factor loadings. *Journal of Credit Risk*, 1(1): 29–70.

Arakelian, V., and Dellaportas, P. (2012). Contagion determination via copula and volatility threshold models. *Quantitative Finance*, 12: 295–310.

Arakelian, V., Dellaportas, P., Savona, R., and Vezzoli, M. (2019). Sovereign risk zones in europe during and after the debt crisis. *Quantitative Finance*, 19(6): 961–980. Doi: 10.1080/14697688.2018.1562197. https://doi.org/10.1080/14697688.2018.1562197.

Arghyrou, M.G., and Kontonikas, A. (2012). The emu sovereign-debt crisis: Fundamentals, expectations and contagion. *Journal of International Financial Markets, Institutions and Money*, 22: 658–677.

Bianchi, D., Büchner, M., and Tamoni, A. (2020). Bond risk premiums with machine learning. *The Review of Financial Studies*, 34(2): 1046–1089. Doi: 10.1093/rfs/hhaa062. https://doi.org/10.1093/rfs/hhaa062.

Biau, O., and D'Elia, A. (2010). *Euro Area GDP Forecast Using Large Survey Dataset — A Random Forest Approach.* EcoMod2010 259600029, EcoMod, May 2010. https://ideas.repec.org/p/ekd/002596/259600029.html.

Christensen, K., Siggaard, M., and Veliyev, B. (2022). A machine learning approach to volatility forecasting. *Journal of Financial Econometrics*, 06 2022. Doi: 10.1093/jjfinec/nbac020. https://doi.org/10.1093/jjfinec/nbac020.

Clayton, D.G. (1978). A model for association in bivariate life tables and its application in epidemiological studies of familial tendency in chronic disease incidence. *Biometrika*, 65: 141–151.

Döpke, J., Fritsche, U., and Pierdzioch, C. (2017). Predicting recessions with boosted regression trees. *International Journal of Forecasting*, 33 (4): 745–759. Doi: https://doi.org/10.1016/j.ijforecast.2017.02.003. https://www.sciencedirect.com/science/article/pii/S0169207017300274.

Frank, M.J. (1979). On the simultaneous associativity of $f(x, y)$ and $x + y - f(x, y)$. *Aequationes Mathematicae*, 19: 194–226.

Gu, S., Kelly, B., and Xiu, D. (2020). Empirical asset pricing via machine learning. *The Review of Financial Studies*, 33(5): 2223–2273, 02 2020. Doi: 10.1093/rfs/hhaa009. https://doi.org/10.1093/rfs/hhaa009.

Gumbel, É.J. (1960). Distributions des valeurs extrêmes en plusieurs dimensions. *Publ. Inst. Stat. Univ. Paris*, 9: 171–173.

Hastie, T., Tibshirani, R., and Friedman, J. (2009). *The Elements of Statistical Learning: Data Mining, Inference and Prediction.* Springer, New York, NY.

Hougaard, P. (1986). A class of multivariate failure time distributions. *Biometrika*, 73: 671–678.

Joe, H. (1997). *Multivariate Models and Dependence Concepts.* Monographs on Statistics and Applied Probability, Vol. 73. Chapman & Hall, London.

Jouravlev, I., and Maurer, R.A. (2009). Loss distribution generation in credit portfolio modeling. *International Journal of Applied Management and Technology*, 8(1). https://scholarworks.waldenu.edu/ijamt/vol8/iss1/2/.

Manasse, P., and Roubini, N. (2009). "Rules of Thumb" for sovereign debt crises. *Journal of International Economics*, 78: 192–205.

Medeiros, M.C., Vasconcelos, G.F.R., Veiga, Á., and Zilberman, E. (2021). Forecasting inflation in a data-rich environment: The benefits of machine learning methods. *Journal of Business & Economic Statistics*, 39(1): 98–119. Doi: 10.1080/07350015.2019.1637745. https://doi.org/10.1080/07350015.2019.1637745.

Meine, C., Supper, H., and Weiß, G.N.F. (2015). Is tail risk priced in credit default swap premia?*. *Review of Finance*, 20(1): 287 336, 03. Doi: 10.1093/rof/rfv008. https://doi.org/10.1093/ rof/rfv008.

Nelsen, R.B. (1999). *An Introduction to Copulas.* Lecture Notes in Statistics, Vol. 139. Springer, New York.

Savona, R., and Vezzoli, M. (2015). Fitting and forecasting sovereign defaults using multiple risk signals. *Oxford Bulletin of Economics and Statistics*, 77: 66–92.

Schönbucher, P. (2002). Taken to the limit: Simple and not so-simple loan loss distributions. *Available at SSRN*: https://ssrn.com/abstract=378640.

Vasicek, O. (1987). Probability loss of a loan portfolio. Memo, KMV Corporation.

Vasicek, O. (2002). Loan portfolio value. *Risk*, 15(2): 160–162.

https://doi.org/10.1142/9781800615212_0008

Chapter 8

Stylized Facts of Decentralized Finance (DeFi)

Yuanyuan Zhang[*,¶], **Stephen Chan**[†,||], **Jeffrey Chu**[‡,**], **Xin Liao**[§,††] **and Helu Min**[§]

[*] *Center for Digital Trust and Society, Department of Criminology, University of Manchester, Oxford Road, Manchester, UK*
[†] *Department of Mathematics and Statistics, American University of Sharjah, PO Box 26666, Sharjah, UAE*
[‡] *School of Statistics, Renmin University of China, No. 59 Zhongguancun Street, Haidian District, Beijing, China*
[§] *Business School, University of Shanghai for Science and Technology, Shanghai, China*
[¶] *yuanyuan.zhang@manchester.ac.uk*
[||] *schan@aus.edu*
[**] *jeffrey.jchu@ruc.edu.cn*
[††] *liaoxin2010@163.com*

Abstract

Decentralized Finance (DeFi) represents an emerging sector within the cryptocurrency space. DeFi is currently one of the most groundbreaking and disruptive technologies impacting upon the centralized finance systems, bringing with it many distinctive features and huge potential. In this chapter, we present stylized facts on DeFi and shed light on the broader empirical features of market efficiency, volatility clustering, leverage effects, and the return volume relationship of this market.

Keywords: Decentralized finance, cryptocurrencies, efficient market hypothesis, market efficiency, tokens.

1 Introduction

Since the seminal work of Nakamoto (2009), the development of blockchain-based applications has taken us from pure cryptocurrencies such as Bitcoin, to decentralized applications such as the Ethereum network, and now to decentralized finance (DeFi). DeFi represents an emerging sector within the cryptocurrency space, where financial services "are made available on a public decentralized blockchain network in an attempt to remove intermediaries within financial transactions" (Corbet *et al.*, 2022). Since the introduction of DeFi in 2017, the total value locked (TVL) in DeFi products has grown to over $160 billion US Dollars. Although this may seem like a far cry from the $2 trillion US Dollars valuation of the cryptocurrency market, the two are very closely linked.

The foundations of DeFi are based on the movement towards a global financial system, which includes a wide range of concepts, such as decentralized applications (DApps), smart contracts, data oracles, stablecoins, and more. However, since DeFi is built upon blockchain technology, it also shares the same properties as traditional cryptocurrency systems, namely, decentralization, transparency, and permissionless. While traditional cryptocurrencies and DeFi share many similarities relating to digital monetary value, they also share a number of key differences. First, the DeFi ecosystem does not generally run on traditional cryptocurrencies such as Bitcoin but rather uses proprietary coins and tokens. Second, many traditional cryptocurrencies were developed with the intention of simply being used to transfer monetary value electronically. DeFi tokens, on the other hand, are primarily developed to be used with DApps and smart contracts. Third, DeFi tokens may be considerably more attractive to investors, as they not only can be bought and sold, but can also be used for staking and lending that can provide high interest rates.

Our motivations for studying the DeFi market are derived from the following three factors: (i) DeFi is currently one of the most groundbreaking and disruptive technologies impacting upon the centralized finance (CeFi) systems, bringing with it many distinctive features and huge potential. (ii) DeFi is currently in the early stages of its growth, however, within the past two years, the total value locked in the system has grown from nothing to over $160 billion US Dollars; the evolution of the TVL in the DeFi market is shown

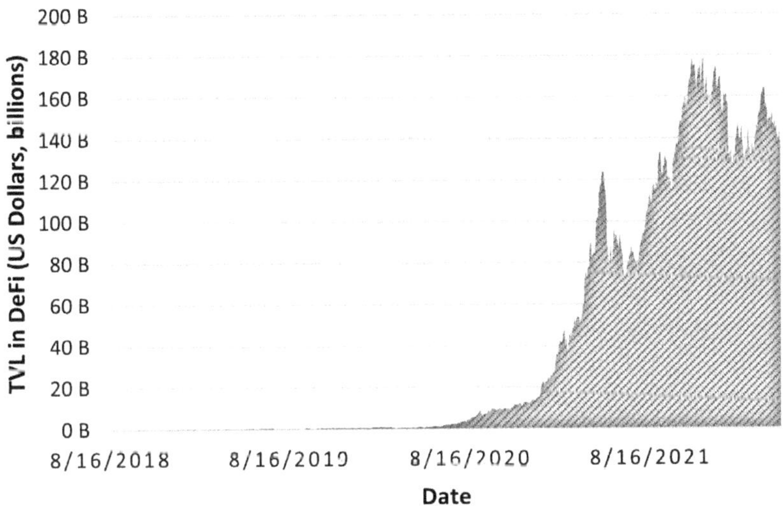

Figure 1. Total value locked (USD, billions) in DeFi markets over the period of 2018 to 2022.

in Figure 1. (iii) There is currently a mass adoption of DeFi from institutional investors — in Q2 2021, over 60% of DeFi transactions accounted for executions of over \$10 million US Dollars (Fixglobal, 2023). Hence, we believe that it is timely to undertake research on the DeFi ecosystem due to its disruptive and pivotal nature, which should be done in parallel to traditional financial markets.

At present, the literature exploring DeFi is scarce and there appears to be little research. The few studies that do exist only investigate the infrastructure and ecosystem of DeFi (Chen and Bellavitis, 2020; Gudgeon *et al.*, 2020; Popescu, 2020; Zetzsche *et al.*, 2020; Harvey *et al.*, 2021; Qin *et al.*, 2021; Schär, 2021; Katona, 2021; Werner *et al.*, 2021; Grassi *et al.*, 2022; Zhang *et al.*, 2022; Chu *et al.*, 2023). However, the closest comparison to this area are cryptocurrencies. The existing literature on cryptocurrencies is much more developed and is primarily from the perspective of classical financial economics, for example, the general price discovery and predictability (Godfrey, 2017; Brauneis and Mestel, 2018), the informational efficiency (Urquhart, 2016; Bariviera, 2017; Nadarajah and Chu, 2017), liquidity (Balcilar *et al.*, 2017; Loi, 2017; Zhang *et al.*, 2020), volatility (Brandvold *et al.*, 2015; Dyhrberg, 2016; Katsiampa, 2017;

Urquhart, 2017), Bitcoin system (Gandal *et al.*, 2018), the perspective of a currency or an asset (Yermack, 2015; Sapuric and Kokkinaki, 2014; Polasik *et al.*, 2015), and market regulations (Hendrickson and Luther, 2017; Pieters and Vivanco, 2017).

A notable omission in the early DeFi literature is the investigation into the statistical and financial properties of DeFi tokens or the stylized facts. These facts can refer to any consistent empirical finding across different assets, markets, and time periods. For example, for asset returns, this may include heavy tailed behavior, autocorrelation, volatility clustering, long-range dependence, leverage effects, the relationship between returns and trading volume, and so on. Such consistent empirical findings have been revealed in the traditional cryptocurrency markets (Cheah and Fry, 2015; Bariviera, 2017; Zhang *et al.*, 2018; Zhang *et al.*, 2019), so it is only natural that this should also be investigated in the DeFi markets. The importance of stylized facts stems from the fact that since they have been widely studied and acknowledged for traditional financial assets, this provides us with a set of common properties that can be used for comparison, not only to cryptocurrencies but also to other financial assets.

Our contributions to the literature and significance of our study are as follows. First, our work fills a gap in the existing literature exploring DeFi and provides the first investigation into the stylized facts of DeFi tokens comprehensively. Second, our work bridges the gap between the current literature investigating the stylized facts of traditional cryptocurrencies to the related sub-sector of DeFi, allowing us to provide a comparison to cryptocurrencies but also traditional financial assets.

The contents of this chapter are organized as follows. In Section 2, we outline the methods used to analyze the stylized facts. In Section 3, we provide a description of the data used in the analysis. Section 4 gives the empirical results. Section 5 discusses and summarizes this chapter and provides some concluding remarks.

2 Methodology

To test the stylized facts of the DeFi tokens, we implement a range of methodologies commonly used to describe the stylized statistical properties of financial assets. These properties include the heavy tails, autocorrelation, volatility clustering, leverage effect, long range dependence, and the return–volume relationship.

2.1 Basic statistics

Basic statistics of the skewness (second moment) and kurtosis (third moment) are implemented to describe the time series of the returns of DeFi tokens. The skewness provides a measure of symmetry in the data and the kurtosis measures whether the data exhibit a heavy- or light-tailed distribution. In addition, the presence of normality in the data was checked using the Jarque–Bera (JB) test (Jarque and Bera, 1987) and Kolmogorov–Smirnov (KS) test (Kolmogorov, 1933; Smirnov, 1948), testing the unit root (stationarity) using the Augmented Dickey–Fuller (ADF) test (Dickey and Fuller, 1979) and understanding the serial correlation using the Ljung–Box (LB) test (Ljung and Box, 1978).

2.2 Volatility clustering — GARCH model

The GARCH(1, 1) model is implemented to test the stylized fact for volatility clustering in a time series. Volatility clustering implies that large (small) changes in prices are clustered together resulting in continuous large (small) price movements. We implement the GARCH(1, 1) model to the returns of DeFi tokens specified as

$$X_t = \mu_t + \sigma_t \epsilon_t \tag{1}$$

where μ_t represents the conditional mean, σ_t represents a volatility process, and ϵ_t is the innovation process such that $\epsilon_t = \sigma_t \mu_t$.

The conditional variance σ_t^2 of the GARCH(1, 1) model is represented by

$$\sigma_t^2 = \kappa + \alpha\epsilon_{t-1}^2 + \beta\sigma_{t-1}^2 \tag{2}$$

for $\kappa > 0$, $\alpha > 0$, and $\beta > 0$. If $\alpha + \beta$ are significantly positive, this represents the existence of volatility clustering, and if $\alpha + \beta = 1$, this represents stationarity in the time series and that there is a strong persistence of volatility shocks. However, if $\alpha + \beta < 1$, this represents weak stationarity. When implementing the GARCH(1, 1) model to the time series, we have to test and confirm the existence of the ARCH(1) model effect beforehand. The ARCH(1) model effect will be tested with a GARCH(0, 1) model as it is identical to an ARCH(1) model.

2.3 Asymmetric volatility clustering — GJR model

The GJR (Glosten, Jagannathan, and Runkle) model (1993) is a dynamic model suitable in modeling the asymmetric volatility clustering and the leverage effect of a time series. The GJR model is a generalized GARCH model, and we implement the GJR-GARCH(1, 1) model. The key components of the GJR-GARCH(1, 1) model includes the lagged conditional variance (the GARCH polynomial), the lagged squared innovations (the ARCH polynomial), and the lagged squared negative innovations (the leverage polynomial). The conditional variance σ_t^2 of the GJR-GARCH(1, 1) model is represented by

$$\sigma_t^2 = \kappa + \alpha\epsilon_{t-1}^2 + \beta\sigma_{t-1}^2 + \xi_t I\left[_{\xi_{t-1}} < 0\right]\epsilon_{t-1}^2 \tag{3}$$

where ξ_t represents the leverage component coefficient and the $I\left[\cdot\right]$ is an indicator function.

The leverage effect describes the negative relationship between asset value and volatility. A general explanation is that negative shocks/news increases the volatility more than positive shocks/news of equal size (Black, 1976; Christie, 1982).

If $1 - \alpha - \beta - 0.5\xi > 0$, this represents stationarity in the time series and the volatility is mean reverting. The GJR-GARCH(1, 1) model is the particular case of the GARCH(1, 1) model for $\xi = 0$.

2.4 Long-range dependence — Detrended fluctuation analysis

The random walk hypothesis in DeFi tokens are examined by computing the Hurst exponent via the detrended fluctuation analysis (DFA) method. The method examines the dependence in these markets and indicates the random and nonrandom behavior in our time series. Compared to other well-known methods for testing the Hurst exponent such as the Rescaled Range (R/S), the DFA method has been shown to be more suitable in dealing with nonstationary time series data. In addition, as highlighted by Grau-Carles (2000), the DFA method avoids the spurious detection of long-range dependence; Zhang *et al.* (2019) showed the R/S method is not that stable. For instance, when a process under investigation has short memory, the R/S statistic may wrongly indicate the presence of long-term memory, leading to erroneous conclusions. Hence, the main reason for selecting to use the DFA method.

Zhang *et al.* (2019) provide detailed steps and explanation of the algorithm used to compute the Hurst exponent values. First, we generate an integrated time series (of total length M)

$$Z_i = \sum_{t=1}^{i} \left[X_{(t)} - \bar{X}\right] \quad (4)$$

where $X_{(t)}$ is the ith element of the stochastic time series X_t and $\bar{X}$ is the mean of the stochastic time series X_t. Furthermore, $Z_{(i)}$ is divided into M/m nonoverlapping sub-samples, and in order to determine the local trend of each subsample, a polynomial fit $Z_{\text{pol}(i,m)}$ is computed. Following this, we detrend the integrated time series $Z_{(i)}$, by subtracting the local trend, $Z_{\text{pol}(i,m)}$. The fluctuation function is defined as

$$F_{(m)} = \sqrt{\frac{1}{M} \sum_{t=1}^{M} \left[Z_{(i)} - Z_{\text{pol}(i,m)}\right]^2} \quad (5)$$

After many iterations using different values of m, it can be shown that the fluctuation function $F_{(m)}$ behaves as a power law of m, or $F_{(m)} \propto m^H$, where H is the value of the Hurst exponent. By regressing $\ln F_{(m)}$ on to $\ln(m)$, we obtain the Hurst exponent. The maximum block size to be used in partitioning the data follows `length(window)/2`, where `window` denotes the width of the data window or the time-series window vector. In our case, we use six points to estimate the Hurst exponent in the DFA method, and these points for the regression estimation are (as in Zhang *et al.*, 2019) $m = 4, 8, 16, 32, 64, 128$.

The computation of the Hurst exponent was conducted using the R statistical software package (R Development Core Team, 2022). We followed the method presented in Section 2.1 of Zhang *et al.* (2019) to compute Hurst exponent values, using the default parameters given in the procedure, and a rolling window of 30 (approximately one month) lagged data points.

The Hurst exponent (α) can take values of the range 0–1. A value of $\alpha = 0.5$ indicates a random walk process in the time series. On the contrary, a value of $\alpha \neq 0$ indicates that the considered time series exhibits evidence of long-term correlations, where $0.5 \leq \alpha \leq 1$, represents a series of trend-reinforcing behavior, and if $0 \leq \alpha \leq 0.5$, the series exhibits antipersistence behavior.

2.5 Return–volume relationship

The return–volume relationship is another widely studied stylized fact in many financial fields, for example, in stock markets (Ying, 1966), interest rates and currency futures (Puri and Philippatos, 2008), commodities (Chiarella *et al.*, 2016), and real estate (Tsai, 2014). The dynamic volume–return relationship can provide a crucial insight into the market microstructure and conveys valuable information about future price movements for market participants. From an economic and financial perspective, it can acknowledge how market information is conveyed and incorporated in financial instrument prices.

We apply the quantile-on-quantile (QQR) regression method proposed by Sim and Zhou (2015) to investigate the return–volume relationship. The QQR method allows the regression model to account for the quantiles of both the dependent variable and independent variable(s). This means that the relationship can vary at different points in their respective distributions. The QQR method Sim and Zhou (2015) is specified in the following way.

Let the quantile of a DeFi token's returns be denoted as the superscript θ. The regression model for the θ-quantile of the DeFi token's returns (DeFi_t) as a function of its lagged returns (DeFi_{t-1}) and returns of its trading volume (VOLM_t) is

$$\mathrm{DeFi}_t = \beta^{\theta}\left(\mathrm{VOLM}_t\right) + \alpha^{\theta}\mathrm{DeFi}_{t-1} + \epsilon_t^{\theta} \tag{6}$$

where $0 \leq \theta \leq 1$ and ϵ_t^{θ} is an error term that has a zero θ-quantile.

As in Sim and Zhou (2015), the link function $\beta^{\theta}(\cdot)$ is assumed to be unknown, since it would be reasonable that we do not know exactly how DeFi token returns and the returns of their trading volume are related prior to our analysis. To investigate the relationship between the θ-quantile of the DeFi token's returns and some κ-quantile of the returns of its trading volume (VOLM^κ), this function can be linearized by taking a first-order Taylor expansion of $\beta^\theta(\cdot)$ around VOLM^κ, resulting in

$$\beta^\theta\left(\text{VOLM}_t\right) \approx \beta^\theta\left(\text{VOLM}^\kappa\right) + \beta^\theta\left(\text{VOLM}^\kappa\right)\left(\text{VOLM}_t - \text{VOLM}^\kappa\right) \tag{7}$$

It can be seen that since VOLM^κ is a function of κ and $\beta^\theta(\cdot)$ is a function of θ, the link function of a particular quantile of volume returns, $\beta^\theta\left(\text{VOLM}^\kappa\right)$, is a function of both θ and κ. For convenience, Eq. (7) can be expressed as

$$\beta^\theta\left(\text{VOLM}_t\right) \approx \beta_0(\theta, \kappa) + \beta_1(\theta, \kappa)\left(\text{VOLM}_t - \text{VOLM}^\kappa\right) \tag{8}$$

where $\beta_0(\theta, \kappa) = \beta^\theta\left(\text{VOLM}^\kappa\right)$ and $\beta_1(\theta, \kappa) = \beta^{\theta'}\left(\text{VOLM}^\kappa\right)$, respectively (Sim and Zhou, 2015).

Substituting Eq. (8) back into (6), we get

$$\begin{aligned}\text{DeFi}_t = {} & \beta_0(\theta, \kappa) + \beta_1(\theta, \kappa)\left(\text{VOLM}_t - \text{VOLM}^\kappa\right) \\ & + \alpha(\theta)\text{TOKEN}_{t-1} + \epsilon_t^\theta\end{aligned} \tag{9}$$

which gives us an expression for the relationship between the θ-quantile of a DeFi token's returns and the κ-quantile of the returns of its trading volume. As mentioned above, this provides a more complete picture of the relationship between the returns of a DeFi token's prices and trading volume over their whole distributions.

The final step is to estimate Eq. (9). We note that in this analysis we work directly with the sample values of the returns of the prices and trading volume, so unlike Sim and Zhou (2015), it is not necessary to estimate any values. To estimate Eq. (9), the following minimization problem is solved

$$\begin{aligned}\min_{b_0, b_1} \sum_{t=1}^{n} \rho_\theta & \left[\text{DeFi}_t - b_0 - b_1\left(\text{VOLM}_t - \text{VOLM}^\kappa\right) - \alpha^\theta \text{DeFi}_{t-1}\right] \\ & \times K\left(\frac{F_n\left(\text{VOLM}_t\right) - \kappa}{h}\right)\end{aligned} \tag{10}$$

where ρ_θ denotes the tilted absolute value function giving the θ-conditional quantile of TOKEN_t as the solution, $F_n(\cdot)$ is the empirical distribution function, $K(\cdot)$ is the Gaussian kernel, h is the bandwidth, and the estimates $\hat{\beta}_0(\theta, \kappa)$ and $\hat{\beta}_1(\theta, \kappa)$ can be obtained as the solutions. For this analysis, a bandwidth value of $h = 0.10$ was selected.

The method is presented for DeFi tokens in general, thus, the process is identical for all DeFi tokens and can be seen by simply replacing the DeFi token with a selected token. For further details and discussion regarding this method, we refer the readers to Sim and Zhou (2015).

3 Data

The data we analyze consists of the historical daily closing prices of Chainlink (LINK), Aave (LEND), Maker (MKR), Kyber Network (KNC), and 0x (ZRX) in terms of the US Dollar (USD), for the period of 1st July 2018 to 11th June 2022. The data were obtained from CoinMarketCap (2022), which provides a unified daily closing price for each of the five DeFi tokens. These prices are computed as the volume weighted average of all market pair prices from all available exchanges, and therefore, we believe that it provides us with a suitable estimate of the global price. The tokens were selected based on their ranking in terms of the largest market capitalization in the DeFi market, trading volume, and ease and availability of purchase. The combined market capitalization of the five De-Fi tokens during the sample period was approximately 80% CoinMarketCap (2022), thus we believe that the data obtained give a satisfactory representation of the most prominent DeFi tokens. In order to obtain stationarity for the returns, we applied the data adjustment procedure as in Gallant *et al.* (1992), allowing us to use the log returns of each token in our main analysis. The log returns for each token are computed as

$$R_t = \ln\left(\frac{P_t}{P_{t-1}}\right)$$

where P_t and P_{t-1} denote the closing prices on days t and $t-1$, respectively.

A brief summary of the key properties of the five DeFi tokens are given in Table 1. These comprise the initial issue date of the token, the location of the issuer's headquarters, the blockchain that

Table 1. DeFi token properties.

Token	Issue Date	HQ Location	Blockchain	Mineable	dApp Platform
LINK	2017	Cayman Islands	Ethereum	No	Chainlink
XTZ	2017	Switzerland	Tezos	No	Tezos Network
MKR	2017	United States	Ethereum	No	Maker Protocol
KNC	2017	Singapore	Ethereum	No	Kyber
ZRX	2017	United States	Ethereum	No	0x Protocol

the token runs on, whether the token is mineable, and the corresponding dApp platform. It can be seen that all five tokens were issued first issued in 2017 but have headquarters that are located around the world. Note that parts of some token systems (e.g., ideas and networks) were developed slightly earlier or later than the issue date. The majority of the DeFi tokens utilize the standard Ethereum blockchain, with the exception of Tezos that runs on its own blockchain network. All five of the tokens are not mineable, however, each system has its own dApp platform that can run decentralized applications using the respective token.

4 Empirical Results

4.1 Descriptive statistics and heavy tails

Summary statistics of the daily log returns of the DeFi tokens versus the US Dollar are given in Table 2. The statistics computed include the number of observations (N), minimum, maximum, mean, median, skewness, kurtosis, standard deviation (SD), variance, range, and interquartile range. From Table 2, we find that the MKR/USD returns give the lowest minimum and LINK/USD the largest maximum. The median and mean of all DeFi tokens are close to zero.

For the returns of all five price series, the kurtosis values of all the returns are more peaked and heavier tailed than the normal distribution. The returns of all price series are negatively skewed, except the return of ZRX/USD which exhibit a positive skewness. With respect to the variability, all returns exhibit similar standard deviations (approximately 7% volatility), while the returns of the MKR/USD currency pair generate the smallest of all these values.

Table 2. Summary statistics of returns of the daily market price of the DeFi tokens LINK/USD, XTZ/USD, MKR/USD, KNC/USD, and ZRX/USD, over the full sample period.

Statistics	**LINK**	**XTZ**	**MKR**	**KNC**	**ZRX**
Observations	1441	1441	1441	1441	1441
Minimum	−0.618	−0.605	−0.818	−0.632	−0.460
Q1	−0.034	−0.032	−0.028	−0.038	−0.036
Median	0.001	0.000	0.000	0.000	0.000
Mean	0.002	−0.001	0.000	0.000	−0.001
Q3	0.037	0.030	0.027	0.038	0.035
Maximum	0.484	0.305	0.423	0.336	0.440
Skewness	−0.358	−0.776	−0.971	−0.353	0.027
Kurtosis	8.641	8.573	27.138	6.959	6.544
SD	0.068	0.066	0.062	0.071	0.066
Variance	0.005	0.004	0.004	0.005	0.004
Range	1.102	0.910	1.241	0.968	0.900
IQR	0.071	0.063	0.054	0.076	0.071
Jarque–Bera	4530.7*	4574.4*	44582*	2949.4*	2581.6*
Kolmogorov–Smirnov	0.428*	0.426*	0.437*	0.428*	0.430*
Augmented Dickey–Fuller	−11.489*	−11.006*	−10.994*	−11.307*	−10.460*
Ljung–Box	5.923*	2.552*	11.157*	8.835*	3.560*

Note: The tests for normality, stationarity, and serial correlation are represented by their test statistics shown in the last four rows respectively and * indicates statistical significance at the 1% level of significance.

The results of the JB test, KS test, the ADF test, and the LB test for the five DeFi token's returns are given in Table 1. We observe for all four tests on each of the five returns series that the test statistics and results are significant at the 1% level of significance. In all cases, the JB and KS tests reject the null hypothesis of normality of the returns data, supporting our previous results. The ADF test rejects the null hypothesis of the existence of a unit root in the returns, which implies the data exhibit stationarity. Finally, the LB test rejects the null hypothesis of no serial correlation.

The Hill tail index estimator (Hill, 1975) on the daily log returns of the five DeFi tokens over the period analyzed is plotted in Figure 2. The plots present a more robust indicator for analyzing the heavy tails for the DeFi tokens. The hill estimator for all plots decreases

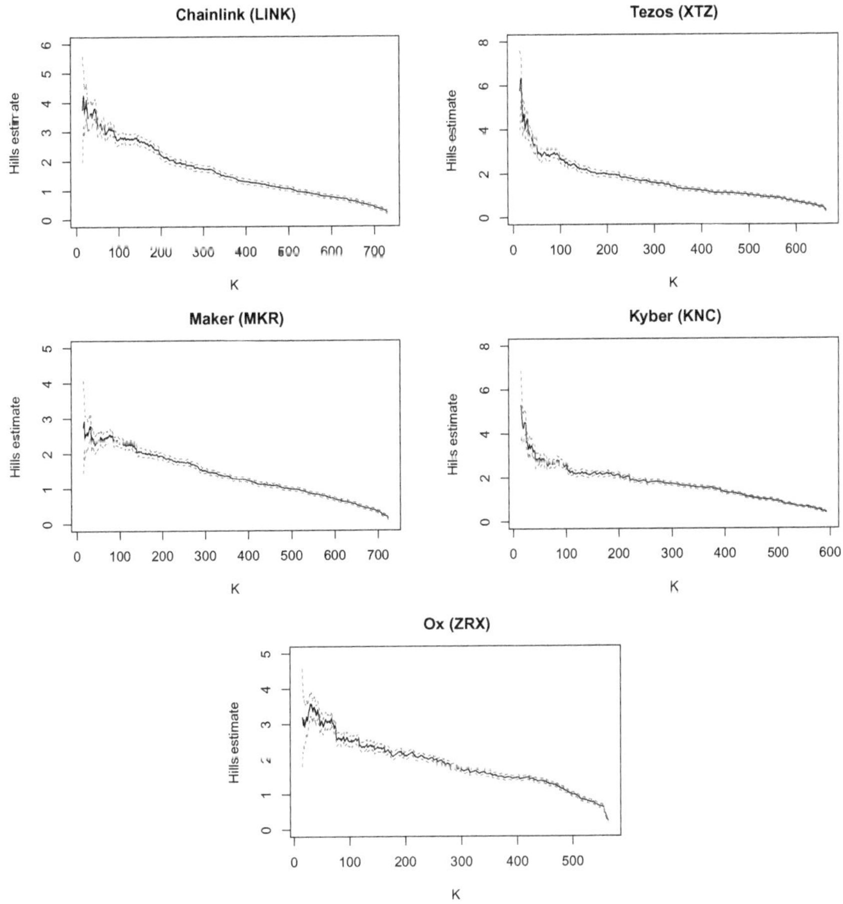

Figure 2. Hill tail index estimators of the log returns of the DeFi tokens. The 95% confidence intervals are indicated by the dashed lines.

for increasing k samples, and this illustrates that the returns of DeFi tokens exhibit heavy tail.

4.2 Autocorrelation

The autocorrelation on the daily log returns of the five DeFi tokens over the period analyzed is shown in Figure 3. The dashed lines represents the 95% confidence interval, and it can be seen that

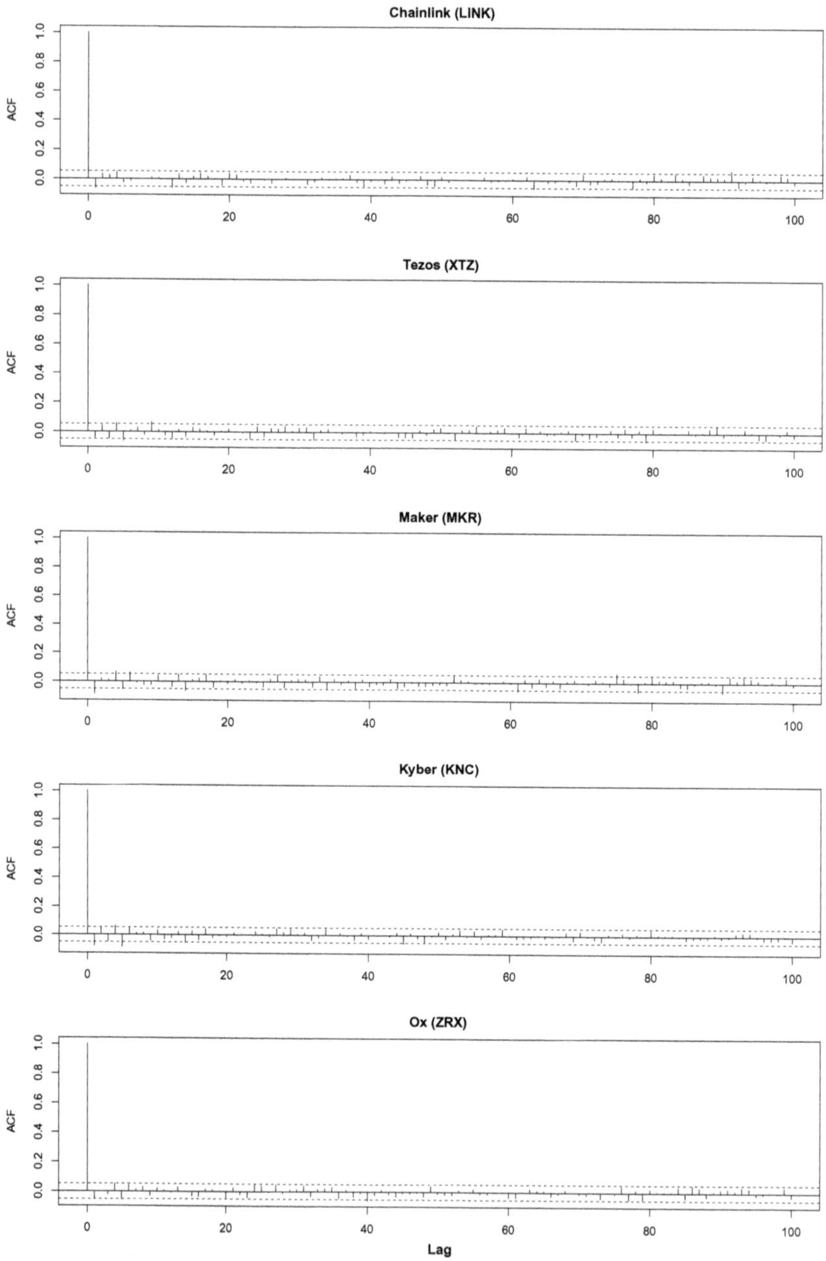

Figure 3. Autocorrelation function of the log returns of the DeFi tokens, for lags 1–100 over the full sample period. The 95% confidence intervals are indicated by the dashed lines.

autocorrelation decays within this confidence band after a few lags for all DeFi tokens. This represents the daily log returns of the five DeFi tokens that exhibit no significant autocorrelations between each lag.

4.3 Volatility clustering

The daily log returns of the five DeFi tokens over the period analyzed is shown in Figure 4. It can be seen that all five DeFi tokens exhibit extreme daily volatility, with the large price changes for all DeFi tokens clustered together. We apply the ARCH test and GARCH(1, 1) model to all of daily returns of DeFi token prices to analyze the volatility clustering. The ARCH test and GARCH(1, 1) model were performed in R (R Development Core Team, 2022) using the `fGarch` package and the results of the test and models are presented in Table 3. Before a GARCH model can be implemented, the existence of the ARCH(1) model effect must be present. We observe the estimator of the ARCH test to be statistical significance at the

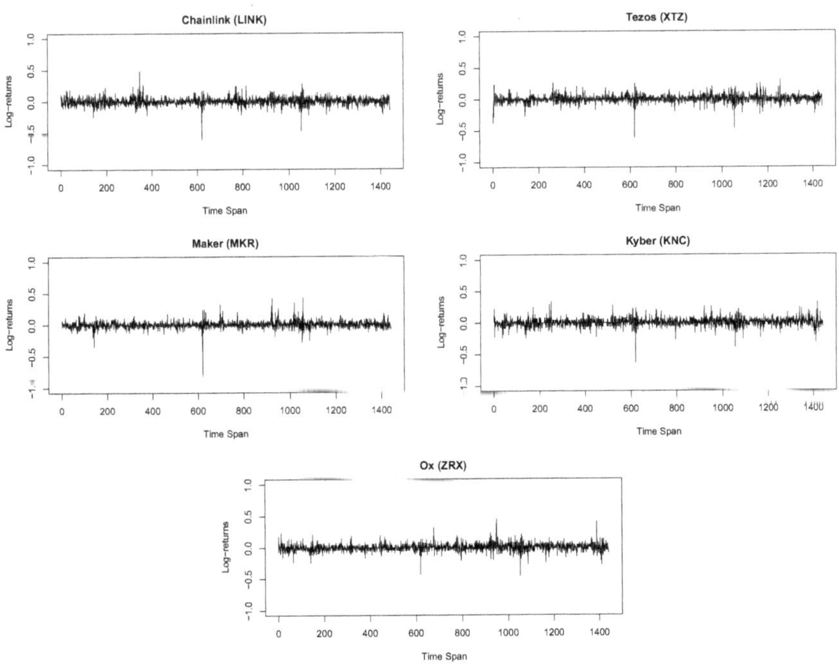

Figure 4. Log returns of the DeFi tokens.

Table 3. Estimate of the ARCH test and the estimation of GARCH(1, 1) model.

DeFi Tokens	ARCH Test	ARCH (α)	GARCH (β)	$\alpha + \beta$
LINK	4561.1*	0.090	0.873	0.963
XTZ	4586.4*	0.194	0.742	0.936
MKR	44620*	0.112	0.790	0.902
KNC	2963.2*	0.179	0.701	0.880
ZRX	2621.2*	0.126	0.780	0.906

Note: *Indicates statistical significance at the 1% level.

1% level for all five DeFi tokens, which helps us infer the existence of a time-varying phenomenon in the conditional volatility of the five DeFi tokens. Hence a GARCH(1, 1) model can be implemented to test the volatility clustering of these DeFi tokens. The parameters of $\alpha + \beta$ are significant positive for all DeFi tokens, this represents the existence of volatility clustering. Moreover, the $\alpha + \beta$ values are less than one for all DeFi tokens, which shows weak stationarity in the time series.

4.4 Leverage effects

We apply the GJR (Glosten, Jagannathan, and Runkle) model (1993) to analyze the leverage effect in the daily returns of DeFi token prices, presented in Table 4. The leverage effect is inferred through the parameter value ξ in the GJR model. The leverage (ξ) value is positive for the majority of DeFi tokens (LINK, MKR, KNC and ZRK) except XTZ which is negative. This indicates the presence of leverage effect in DeFi tokens. As well, for all DeFi tokens, the value of $1 - \alpha - \beta - 0.5\xi > 0$ represents stationarity in the time series and the volatility is mean reverting, which reiterates the results seen in the previous section.

4.5 Long-range dependence

The Hurst exponent DFA method not only gives us a numerical value indicating deviations from market inefficiency but could provide further information, such as trend-reinforcing or antipersistence behavior through out the period.

Table 4. Estimates of the GRJ(1, 1) model.

DeFi Tokens	Constant	ARCH (α)	GARCH (β)	Levearage (ξ)	$1-\alpha-\beta-0.5\xi$
LINK	0.000	0.086	0.878	0.002	0.035
XTZ	0.000	0.203	0.757	−0.031	0.056
MKR	0.000	0.084	0.803	0.047	0.090
KNC	0.000	0.162	0.718	0.008	0.116
ZRX	0.000	0.106	0.793	0.018	0.092

Figure 5 gives the plot of the Hurst exponent DFA (using a sliding window of 90 lagged data points) over the whole period for each DeFi token. Figure 5 shows the Hurst exponent plot for LINK. Throughout the whole period (2018–2022), we observe the Hurst exponent values exhibit significant variations within the bounds of 0.2 and 0.8. This indicates that the returns of LINK are relatively inefficient (a nonrandom walk behavior) and exhibit fluctuating trend-reinforcing or antipersistence behavior through out the whole period. In general, it can be seen that for the three other DeFi Tokens, XTZ, KNC, and ZRX, a similar conclusion is reached. Surprisingly, the DeFi token MKR exhibits a unique pattern when compared to the other DeFi tokens. We observe the Hurst exponent values exhibit a stable converging variation of Hurst values around 0.5 in the first half of 2019 and after the middle of 2021, which reflects a general random walk behavior in these periods. In contrast, during the year of 2020, MKR exhibits an extreme volatile variation in the Hurst exponent value [0.0–0.8], indicating a interchanging form of trend-reinforcing and antipersistence market efficiency behavior through out 2020.

4.6 Return–volume relationship

The quantile-on-quantile regression method provides a robust approach in analyzing the relationship between all pairs of daily returns of DeFi token prices and trading volumes at varying quantiles. The method described in Section 2.5 was implemented and performed in R (R Development Core Team, 2022) using the `quantreg` package. Figure 6 gives the plot of the results of the regression, for the returns of prices and trading volumes of the five DeFi tokens. For each

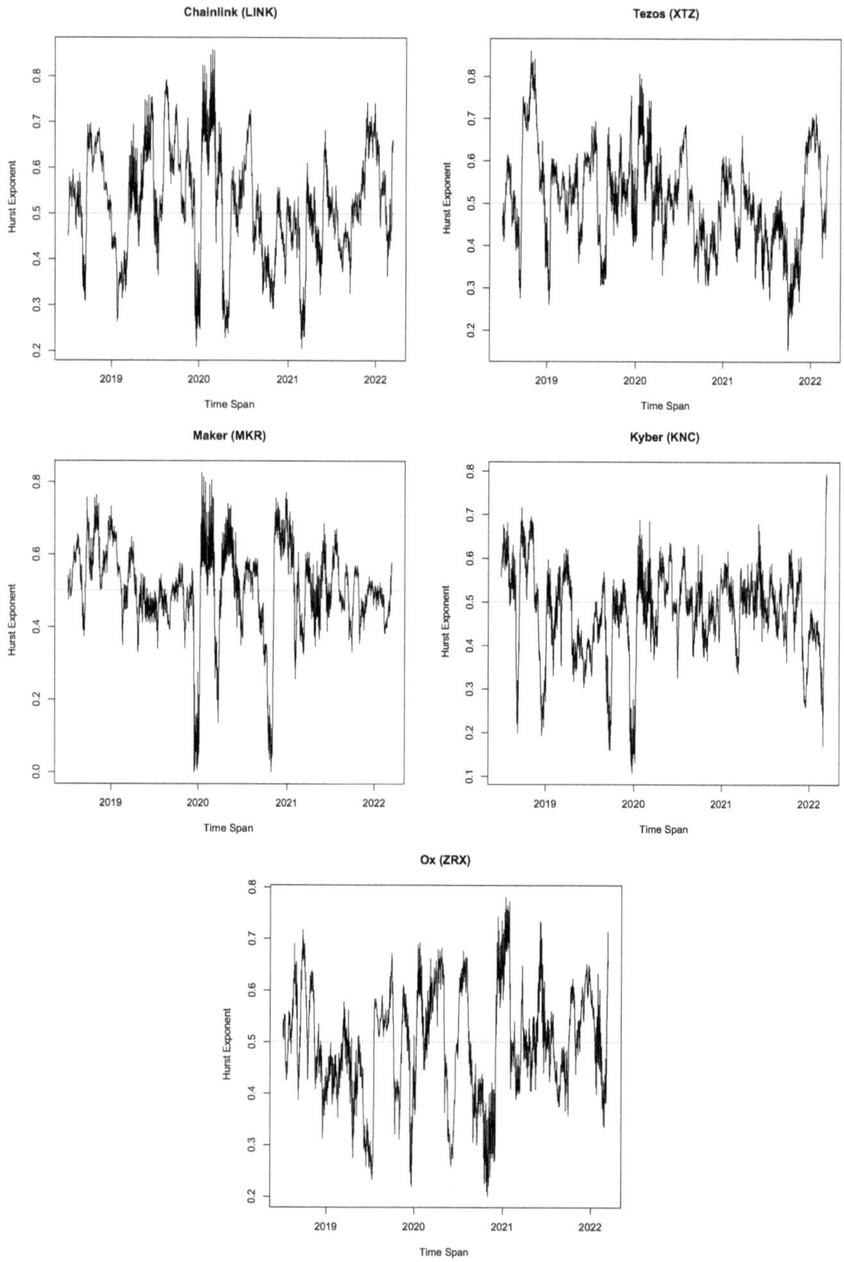

Figure 5. Plots of the Hurst exponent (DFA method) for the daily log returns of the DeFi tokens, using a sliding window of 90 lagged data points. The dotted horizontal line indicate the Hurst value at 0.5.

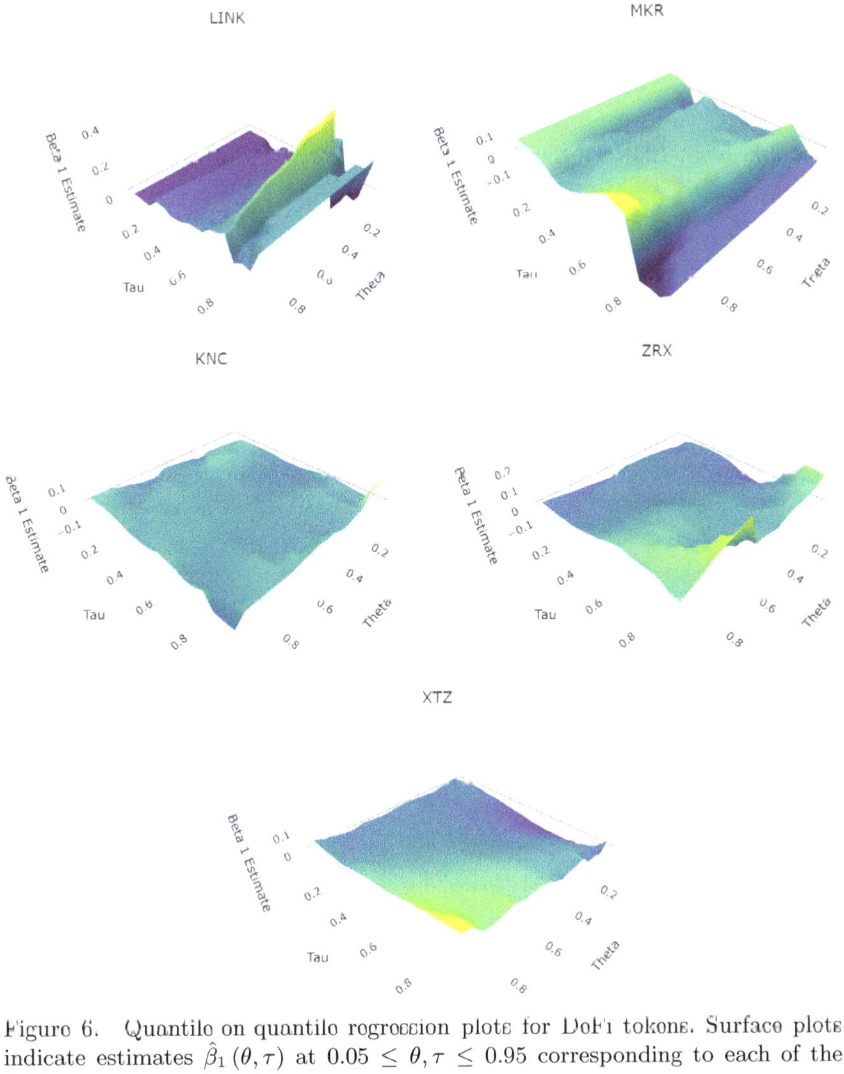

Figure 6. Quantile on quantile regression plots for DeFi tokens. Surface plots indicate estimates $\hat{\beta}_1(\theta,\tau)$ at $0.05 \leq \theta,\tau \leq 0.95$ corresponding to each of the DeFi tokens.

plots, it show the estimates of $\hat{\beta}_1$, at the corresponding quantiles of the returns of DeFi token prices (θ) and returns of trading volumes (τ), as in Eq. (9), for $0.05 \leq \theta,\tau \leq 0.95$. An assumption we make is that the extreme lower and upper quantiles of the returns of DeFi prices reflect bullish and bearish periods in the respective markets.

There are some similarities and differences in all five plots across the range of (θ and τ) quantile values. However, at the upper quantiles of trading volume returns (τ above 0.6), $\hat{\beta}_1$ is generally positive and larger than at any other quantile. This suggests that in times when trading volume is increasing, the returns of the DeFi tokens are positively related regardless of the state of the market. At the median (τ around 0.5) and at the lower quantiles (τ below 0.5) of the trading volume returns, $\hat{\beta}_1$ is generally close to zero. This resembles when trading volume is relatively stable and low, the returns of DeFi tokens do not appear to move together with volume.

The magnitudes of the $\hat{\beta}_1$ computed vary between the DeFi tokens, being largest for LINK and MKR and smallest for XTZ. Furthermore, at the extreme upper quantiles of trading volume returns (τ above 0.8), it can be seen that $\hat{\beta}_1$ is positive for all DeFi tokens except for MKR being negative. This resembles that in times when trading volume is increasing significantly for all DeFi tokens (except MKR), the returns of the DeFi tokens are positively related to trading volume. However, for MKR, when trading volume is increasing significantly, the returns of MKR token appear to be negatively related to trading volume.

Furthermore, to provide a more in depth analysis of the quantile-on-quantile regression plots, Table 5 depicts the average estimates of the coefficient value $\hat{\beta}_1$ obtained from each 10% quantile of τ

Table 5. Average estimates of the coefficient value $\hat{\beta}_1$ at each 10% quantile of τ corresponding to each of the DeFi tokens.

Quantile (τ)	LINK	MKR	KNC	ZRK	XTZ
0.1	−0.023	0.056	−0.002	−0.004	0.012
0.2	−0.021	−0.007	0.010	0.015	0.015
0.3	0.011	−0.008	0.007	0.014	0.016
0.4	0.016	0.002	−0.001	0.017	0.018
0.5	0.034	0.012	−0.003	0.027	0.023
0.6	0.059	0.026	−0.002	0.044	0.031
0.7	0.128	0.038	0.001	0.057	0.047
0.8	0.327	−0.029	0.004	0.069	0.063
0.9	0.156	−0.076	0.003	0.102	0.074

corresponding to each of the DeFi tokens. In most cases, we observe that as the τ quantile increases, the average $\hat{\beta}_1$ coefficient value increases too, except for the case of MKR where the average $\hat{\beta}_1$ coefficient decreases and becomes negative. In general, we see that at τ quantiles close to the median, the average estimates of the coefficient value $\hat{\beta}_1$ are positive. However, at τ quantiles below the median, results vary, and we find for LINK, MKR, KNC, and ZRK, the average $\hat{\beta}_1$ coefficient value is negative. For XTZ, we find the average $\hat{\beta}_1$ coefficient is positive for all τ quantiles.

5 Discussion and Conclusion

Since DeFi is currently one of the most groundbreaking and disruptive technologies in the blockchain, and with the current mass adoption from institution investors, the need for stylized facts on DeFi token is of significant interest. This study investigates the stylized facts (heavy tails, autocorrelation, volatility clustering, leverage effect, long-range dependence, and the return–volume relationship) of the five largest decentralized finance tokens: Chainlink, Tezos, Maker, Kyber Network, and 0x, using the daily returns on prices over the period from July 2018 to June 2022.

Results from the descriptive statistics indicate the existence of heavy tails, high intra-volatility, and the absence of autocorrelation in returns of DeFi tokens. In addition, the DeFi tokens exhibit volatility clustering, weak stationarity, and the existence of a leverage effect. The results of the long-range dependencies of DeFi tokens return are relatively inefficient and exhibit a fluctuating trend-reinforcing or antipersistence behavior throughout the whole period (2018–2022). Furthermore, the results of the volume–return relationship of DeFi suggest that larger changes in trading volume are positively related to the returns of DeFi prices. In comparison with markets of stable or low trading volume, there appears to be no significant relationship to the returns of DeFi prices.

As the decentralized finance market is still in the early stages of its development, we may expect that the market should exhibit similar properties to emerging markets. The stylized facts findings show some unique and common properties when compared to other similar assets (fungible assets and cryptocurrencies). The descriptive statistics are similar to those in cryptocurrencies (Chu *et al.*, 2015; Chan *et al.*, 2017; Zhang *et al.*, 2018) and other fungible assets (Nadarajah *et al.*, 2015; Battern *et al.*, 2017). Volatility clustering and leverage effects are also commonly seen in fungible assets (Tully and Lucey, 2007; Baur, 2012) and cryptocurrencies (Phillip *et al.*, 2018; Zhang *et al.*, 2018). With regard to the long-range dependencies, our findings are in line with the studies of Harvey (1995), Ratner and Leal (1999), and Lagoarde (2008) who found that returns in emerging financial markets are generally more predictable than returns in the developed financial markets. Our results also showed similarities with those of Khuntia (2018), Chu *et al.* (2019), and Zhang *et al.* (2019, 2020), who observed that cryptocurrency returns (high frequencies and daily) display mostly an inefficient market behavior. Surprisingly, our findings of the volume return relationship appear to be similar with literature on the developed markets. For example, Ying (1966) and Jain *et al.* (1988) find that the S&P500 has a strong positive relationship between the trading volume and returns. In addition, Llotente *et al.* (2002) find that stocks listed on the NYSE and AMEX exhibit variations in volume–return dynamics, which are similar to what we observed. However, studies of cryptocurrencies have found a contrast in results. Alaoui *et al.* (2019) find that the return–volume relationship of Bitcoin prices appear to exhibit a nonlinear relationship. Chan *et al.* (2022) find that high-frequency returns in cryptocurrencies exhibit weak positive correlation between return and volume at the extreme tails, which are partially in line with the lower tails of our results.

More importantly, our study of the stylized facts of DeFi markets provides an essential stepping stone to further understand the economic and financial perspective in acknowledging how market information is conveyed and incorporated in DeFi token prices. For industrial practitioners, these stylized facts will be useful in creating portfolios for hedging and developing utility pricing models for DeFi tokens. Future work would be to investigate if other blockchain products such as NFTs and the Metaverse exhibit similar stylized fact features.

Bibliography

0x (2020). Powering the decentralized exchange of tokens on Ethereum. Available at: https://0x.org/.

Aave (2020). Aave — Open source DeFi protocol. Available at: https://aave.com/.

El Alaoui, M., Bouri, E., and Roubaud, D. (2019). Bitcoin price–volume: A multifractal cross-correlation approach. *Finance Research Letters*, 31.

Bariviera, A.F. (2017). The inefficiency of bitcoin revisited: A dynamic approach. *Economics Letters*, 161: 1–4.

Bartels, R. (1982). The rank version of von Neumann's ratio test for randomness. *Journal of the American Statistical Association*, 77: 40–46.

Batten, J., Lucey, B., McGroarty, F., Peat, M., and Urquhart, A. (2017). Stylized facts of intraday precious metals. *PloS One*, 12(4): e0174232.

Baur, D.G. (2012). Asymmetric volatility in the gold market. *The Journal of Alternative Investments*, 14(4): 26–38.

Chainlink (2020). Chainlink. Available at: https://chain.link/.

Chan, S., Chu, J., Nadarajah, S., and Osterrieder, J. (2017). A statistical analysis of cryptocurrencies. *Journal of Risk and Financial Management*, 10(2): 12.

Chan, S., Chu, J., Zhang, Y., and Nadarajah, S. (2022). An extreme value analysis of the tail relationships between returns and volumes for high frequency cryptocurrencies. *Research in International Business and Finance*, 59: 101541.

Cheah, E.T., and Fry, J. (2015). Speculative bubbles in Bitcoin markets? An empirical investigation into the fundamental value of Bitcoin. *Economics Letters*, 130: 32–36.

Chiarella, C., Kang, B., Nikitopoulos, C.S., and To, T.D. (2016). The return-volatility relation in commodity futures markets. *Journal of Futures Markets*, 36: 127–152.

Chu, J., Chan, S., and Zhang, Y. (2023). An analysis of the return–volume relationship in decentralised finance (DeFi). *International Review of Economics & Finance*, 85: 236–254. https://doi.org/10.1016/j.iref.2023.01.006.

Chu, J., Nadarajah, S., and Chan, S. (2015). Statistical analysis of the exchange rate of bitcoin. *PloS One*, 10(7): e0133678.

Chu, J., Zhang, Y., and Chan, S. (2019). The adaptive market hypothesis in the high frequency cryptocurrency market. *International Review of Financial Analysis*, 64: 221–231.

Coinbase (2020). A beginner's guide to decentralized finance (DeFi). Available at: https://blog.coinbase.com/a-beginners-guide-to-decentralized-finance-defi-574c68ff43c4.

CoinMarketCap (2022). Cryptocurrency prices, charts and market capitalizations. Available at: https://coinmarketcap.com/.

Consensys (2020). Blockchain for decentralized finance (DeFi). Available at: https://consensys.net/blockchain-use-cases/decentralized- finance/.

Corbet, S., Goodell, J.W., and Günay, S. (2022). What drives DeFi prices? Investigating the effects of investor attention. *Finance Research Letters*, 48: 102883.

Dickey, D.A., and Fuller, W.A. (1979). Distribution of the estimators for autoregressive time series with a unit root. *Journal of the American Statistical Association*, 74: 427–443.

Durlauf, S.N. (1991). Spectral based testing of the martingale hypothesis. *Journal of Econometrics*, 50: 355–376.

Escanciano, J.C., and Lobato, I.N. (2009). An automatic portmanteau test for serial correlation. *Journal of Econometrics*, 151: 140–149.

Escanciano, J.C., and Velasco, C. (2006). Generalized spectral tests for the martingale difference hypothesis. *Journal of Econometrics*, 134: 151–185.

Fixglobal (2023). DeFi activity dominated by large transactions. Available at: https://www.fixglobal.com/defi-activity-dominated-by-large-transactions/.

Gallant, A., Rossi, P., and Tauchen, G. (1992). Stock prices and volume. *The Review of Financial Studies*, 5: 199–242.

Glosten, L.R., Jagannathan, R., and Runkle, D.E. (1993). On the relation between the expected value and the volatility of the nominal excess return on stocks. *The Journal of Finance*, 48(5): 1779–1801.

Grau-Carles, P. (2000). Empirical evidence of long-range correlations in stock returns. *Physica A: Statistical Mechanics and Its Applications*, 287: 396–404.

Harvey, C.R. (1995). Predictable risk and returns in emerging markets. *The Review of Financial Studies*, 8(3): 773–816.

Hill, B.M. (1975). A simple general approach to inference about the tail of a distribution. *The Annals of Statistics*, 1163–1174.

Jain, P.C., and Joh, G.H. (1988). The dependence between hourly prices and trading volume. *Journal of Financial and Quantitative Analysis*, 23(3): 269–283.

Jarque, C.M., and Bera, A.K. (1987). A test for normality of observations and regression residuals. *International Statistical Review*, 55: 163–172.

Jiang, Y.H., He, N., and Ruan, W.H. (2018). Time-varying long-term memory in the bitcoin market. *Finance Research Letters*, 25: 280–284.

Khuntia, S., and Pattanayak, J.K. (2018). Adaptive market hypothesis and evolving predictability of bitcoin. *Economics Letters*, 167: 26–28.

Kim, J.H. (2009). Automatic variance ratio test under conditional heteroskedasticity. *Finance Research Letters*, 3: 179–185.

Kolmogorov, A. (1933). Sulla determinazione empirica di una legge di distribuzione. *Giornale dell'Istituto Italiano degli Attuari*, 4: 83–91.

Kyber Network (2020). The on-chain liquidity protocol for the tokenized world. Available at: https://kyber.network/.

Lagoarde-Segot, T., and Lucey, B.M. (2008). Efficiency in emerging markets—Evidence from the MENA region. *Journal of International Financial Markets, Institutions and Money*, 18(1): 94–105.

Ljung, G.M., and Box, G.E.P. (1978). On a measure of the lack of fit in time series models. *Biometrika*, 65: 297–303.

Llorente, G., Michaely, R., Saar, G., and Wang, J. (2002). Dynamic volume-return relation of individual stocks. *The Review of Financial Studies*, 15(4): 1005–1047.

Maker. (2020). Maker. Available at: https://makerdao.com/en/.

Nadarajah, S., and Chu, J. (2017). On the inefficiency of Bitcoin. *Economics Letters*, 150: 6–9.

Nadarajah, S., Afuecheta, E., and Chan, S. (2015). GARCH modeling of five popular commodities. *Empirical Economics*, 48: 1691–1712.

Nakamoto, S. (2009). Bitcoin: A peer-to-peer electronic cash system. Available at: https://bitcoin.org/bitcoin.pdf.

Phillip, A., Chan, J.S., and Peiris, S. (2018). A new look at cryptocurrencies. *Economics Letters*, 163: 6–9.

Puri, T.N., and Philippatos, G.C. (2008). Asymmetric volume-return relation and concentrated trading in LIFFE futures. *European Financial Management*, 14: 528–563.

R Development Core Team (2011). *R: A Language and Environment for Statistical Computing*. R Foundation for Statistical Computing, Vienna, Austria.

Ratner, M., and Leal, R.P. (1999). Tests of technical trading strategies in the emerging equity markets of Latin America and Asia. *Journal of Banking & Finance*, 23(12): 1887–1905.

Sim, N., and Zhou, H. (2015). Oil prices, US stock return, and the dependence between their quantiles. *Journal of Banking and Finance*, 55: 1–8.

Smirnov, N. (1948). Table for estimating the goodness of fit of empirical distributions. *Annals of Mathematical Statistics*, 19: 279–281.

Tiwari, A.K., Jana, R.K., Das, D., and Rouband, D. (2018). Informational efficiency of bitcoin. *Economics Letters*, 163: 106–109.

Tsai, I.C. (2014). Ripple effect in house prices and trading volume in the UK housing market: New viewpoint and evidence. *Economic Modelling*, 40: 68–75.

Tully, E., and Lucey, B.M. (2007). A power GARCH examination of the gold market. *Research in International Business and Finance*, 21(2): 316–325.

Urquhart, A. (2016). The inefficiency of Bitcoin. *Economics Letters*, 148: 80–82.

Wald, A., and Wolfowtiz, J. (1940). On a test whether two samples are form the same population. *Annals of Mathematical Statistics*, 11: 147–162.

Ying, C.C. (1966). Stock market prices and volumes of sales. *Econometrica*, 34: 676–685.

Zhang, W., Wang, P., Li, X., and Shen, D. (2018). Some stylized facts of the cryptocurrency market. *Applied Economics*, 50(55): 5950–5965.

Zhang, Y., Chan, S., Chu, J., and Nadarajah, S. (2019). Stylised facts for high frequency cryptocurrency data. *Physica A: Statistical Mechanics and its Applications*, 513: 598–612.

Zhang, Y., Chan, S., Chu, J., and Shih, S.H. (2022). The adaptive market hypothesis of decentralized finance (DeFi). *Applied Economics*, 55(42): 4975–4989.

Zhang, Y., Chan, S., Chu, J., and Sulieman, H. (2020). On the market efficiency and liquidity of high-frequency cryptocurrencies in a bull and bear market. *Journal of Risk and Financial Management*, 13(1): 8.

https://doi.org/10.1142/9781800615212_0009

Chapter 9

Effective Systems for Bot Detection and Real-Time Stock Market Predictions

Reem Abdulla Alkhalifa[*,§], **Riadh Ksantini**[†,¶] **and Khaoula Tbarki**[‡,||]

[*] *College of Science, Department of Postgraduate Studies, University of Bahrain, Bahrain, Kingdom of Bahrain*
[†] *College of IT, Department of Computer Science, University of Bahrain, Bahrain, Kingdom of Bahrain*
[‡] *Private Higher School of Technology and Engineering (Tek-Up University), Ariana, Tunisia*
[§] *202012269@stu.uob.edu.bh*
[¶] *rksantini@uob.edu.bh*
[||] *khaoula.tbarki@gmail.com*

Abstract

Social media has reshaped the way in which individuals communicate with disruptive negative and positive externalities, alongside being breeding grounds for bot activities. Social media, limited to Twitter in this research, is rarely monitored and has accelerated the dissemination of disinformation, most of which is attributed to bot activities. To date, bot detection techniques are challenged by their inability to keep abreast with bot progression, while its importance is increasingly being bought to the forefront of political discussions. Therefore, the research will introduce a local-global SVM (LG-SVM) model to increase flexibility in detection methods to keep abreast with the ever-evolving world of Twitter. The end-to-end framework has increased accuracy in detection by treating the data as unsupervised and introducing an autoencoder to reduce dimensionality, which has solved for over-fitting. The multi-level framework starts with a convolutional layer that reduces dimensionality and learns key short-term characteristics, followed by a max pooling layer, two bi-LSTM models, a bottleneck layer, an upscaling layer, and a deconvolution layer. Dimension reduction oversaw the reduction of the dataset into 3 lengths: 70, 100, and 130, resulting in a 99% accuracy rate. Additionally, a multilayer perceptron model is built to predict the impact Bot Tweets have on stock market volatility with a 96.53% coefficient correlation.

Keywords: Bot detection, stock market prediction, dimension reduction, incremental models.

1 Introduction

Social media is a relatively new phenomenon that has reshaped society with disruptive negative and positive externalities. Although primarily intended for human use, social media has been known to be breeding grounds for bot activities. The coexistence of humans and bots in a single platform that is rarely monitored has accelerated the dissemination of disinformation (Australian Government, 2021) with real-life consequences, such as the January 6, 2021, attack on the US's democracy (Hendrix, 2021).

To date, bot detection techniques are challenged by their inability to keep abreast with bot progression as bots upgraded as bots now resemble human activity (McKenzie *et al.*, 2021). Therefore, this research will increase bot detection methods' flexibility to keep abreast with their evolving nature on Twitter and measure their influence on stock market volatility. The research will assume that investors are rational and undertake the best decision given the limited information presented with bots being one of many sources; thus, their presence influences decision-making processes.

2 Literature Review

Bot detection took off in 2010, using simple techniques as the dataset was labeled manually and suffered from bias that was accepted due to bot's simplistic activities, being merely "fake followers" or spammers. Researchers detected bots using a baseline of characteristics and multiple classifier models, including decision tree; however, it suffered from over-fitting and required trimming to be generalized (Cresci *et al.*, 2015). Features were later minimized to avoid over fitting while using contextual LSTM, which was used to incorporate the nonsequential metadata. The metadata incorporation increased accuracy when combined with tweet content (Kudugunta and Ferrara, 2018).

However, traditional machine learning methods fell short when compared to a more dynamic model known as the "Digital DNA model." The higher accuracy was accredited to the model's ability to take into consideration different behaviors at once, allowing for an overall comprehensive analysis that identifies similar behaviors shared by bots. Despite the higher accuracy, it fell short of detecting a new set of behaviors because it depends on a given baseline (Cresci *et al.*, 2017).

Other analysis includes social network analysis of what is coined "botnets:" a group of bots working in coordination. A social network and similar behavior were analyzed using a B-corr model that classifies output based on the network traffic flow. The research faced similar shortcomings in the digital DNA model (Hostiadi *et al.*, 2020).

As a response to bot evolution and AI advancement, researchers utilized generative adversarial networks (GANs), through which multiple models are trained jointly in a simulated environment. The generator was responsible for creating the data and the discriminator model with classifying. Researchers questioned whether the high accuracy holds in real life (Randhawa *et al.*, 2021).

Recent publications updated older models to bypass limitations. An example of this includes upgrading the generative adversarial network (GAN), a method that extracts behavioral patterns, to create GANBOT, by incorporating a layer of LSTM between the generator and the classifier. This improved accuracy which the authors attributed to the method's ability to learn behavioral patterns (Shaghayegh *et al.*, 2021).

2.1 Data extraction

The data utilized in this thesis are extracted from a private database shared by researcher Louis Daniel (Daniel *et al.*, 2021). The dataset then underwent cleaning with the goal of eliminating the traditional bot due to their diminishing activity on the platform, thus building a model that reflects current activities as much as possible. Data cleaning also included removing punctuations, hashtags, and user handles, alongside stemming the word to its bases. Stock market volatility data are extracted from the Chicago Board Options Exchange, which publishes data in several different intervals, such as daily.

Traditional bots have been decreasing in popularity as they have become relatively more recognizable, among human users, and Twitter has been growing in popularity as expected. Likewise, spambot has seen a rise in popularity due to technological advancement and its relatively lower probability of getting detected.

On a usage trend level, spambots have utilized Twitter the least with a slightly higher usage towards the end of the day, while human usage witnessed an uptake towards the end of the day. Spambots tend to use Twitter heavily with almost equal activation level throughout the day except for the morning hours.

Generally speaking, genuine users and spam bots both used real words. Traditional bots behaved as expected with their mandate of sharing URLs, with a majority sharing blog posts or advertising for followers' purchase.

Moreover, sentiment analysis has shown that human users tend to tweet in a neutral manner, which could be a result of the timeframe in which the tweets were collected as political polarity is yet to take over in the time period from 2009 and 2014. Likewise, traditional bots followed the same trend of neutrality, in line with their activity mandate of spamming users with links and advertisements. Spam bots, although created to follow genuine users' behavior patterns, tend to overly use positive vocabularies, as well as using a higher relatively negative sentiment.

3 Method

The LG-SVM classifier is motivated by the combination of the merits of the discriminant-based classifiers and the Support Vector Machine (SVM) classifier. These two are combined by incorporating the between-class and within-class scatter matrices, calculated in the input space, into the SVM optimization problem. Calculating the scatter matrices in the input space will overcome the limitations in terms of time and memory storage while considering the global information provided through discriminant-based classifiers.

Then, combining these characteristics with local ones provided by SVM will improve the performance. Thus, the proposed approach enhances output by considering class distributions' near-global variation, as well as the utilization of the Kernel Nonparametric Discriminant Analysis (KNDA) classifier in the calculation of observations that are both part of a class and fall between classes, during the input phase.

The model's input phase is denoted by formula 1, where N is the total number of samples that are split into two different classes denoted as $N1$ and $N2$, where $N1$ refers to the total number of samples in class one (x_1) and $N2$ in class two (x_2). The output of the model is outlined in formula 2, where the output is a number between 0 and 1 associated with the probability of falling a given class:

$$X = \{x_i\}_{i=1}^{N} \tag{1}$$

$$Y = \{y_i\}_{i=1}^{N} \tag{2}$$

Additionally, the observations that fall between classes are calculated with the nearest neighbor mean vectors as outlined in formula 3, where K refers to the number of neighbors considered, x_m refers to the observations that belong to x_1, and $(x_m)nn(i)$ refers to the i-th nearest neighbor of x_2:

$$M_q^k(x_m) = \frac{1}{k}\sum_{i=1}^{K}(x_m)NN(i) \tag{3}$$

Therefore, building on the above, the scatter matrix corresponding to the observations that fall between classes is calculated during the input phase utilizing formula 4 with $L1$ and $L2$ formulated in formulas 4 and 6, respectively:

$$S_b = \frac{1}{N_1 + N_2}\left(\sum_{i=1}^{N_1}\Psi_i L1(i)^T L1(i) + \sum_{i=1}^{N_2}\Psi_i L2(i)^T L2(i)\right) \tag{4}$$

$$L1(i) = x_i - M_2^k(x_i) \tag{5}$$

$$L2(i) = x_i - M_1^k(x_i) \tag{6}$$

The model has put control factors in space to ensure its continuity as data noise increases. The weighted function, denoted as $\mathbf{\Psi}$, counters and minimizes the influence observations further away from the decision boundary have on the output by deaccelerating the rate at which values recede to zero as they move further from the decision boundary through the introduction of parameter **Y**. This is presented in formula 7:

$$\Psi_i = \frac{\min(d(x_i, M_1^k(x_i))^{\Upsilon}, d(x_i, M_2^k(x_i))^{\Upsilon}}{(d(x_i, M_1^k(x_i))^{\Upsilon} + d(x_i, M_2^k(x_i))^{\Upsilon}} \tag{7}$$

On the other hand, the observations fall under a given category's scatter matrix as computed as outlined in formula 8 during the input phase. The formula considers I as the identity matrix, 1_{N1} and 1_{N2} as the umbrella matrix with all entries belonging to $\frac{1}{N_1}$ and $\frac{1}{N_2}$, respectively:

$$S_w = X_1(I - 1_{N_1})X_1^T + X_2(I - 1_{N2})X_2^T \tag{8}$$

The overall matrix, denoted as Θ, is outlined in formula 9, where η is a control parameter, calculated in formula 10, for the weight vector and M sets the upper limit boundary of the dataset as it equates to or is a lesser value than N:

$$\Theta = \eta S_w(S_{b+}\beta I)^{-1}S_w + I \tag{9}$$

$$n = 1 - \sum_{i=1}^{M} \frac{\Psi_i}{M} \tag{10}$$

The above symbol of M symbolizes the Mu, which reflects the 0.000001 preceded multiplier. The computation of the trade-off parameter M is computed by taking into account the effect of the near-global characteristics of the dataset, which, in return, reduces the calculation time, in which $M \leq N$, total samples available, and Ψ_i are the computational terms in accordance with Eq. (7), which penalizes observations based on their distance from the decision boundary as new observations are considered incrementally. Figure 1 outlines the above graphically (Soula *et al.*, 2020).

To further deliver on the SVM's objective, the formula undergoes minimization by incorporating Θ into the optimization phase as outlined in formula 11 and further reformulated into formula 12 through the insertion of a Karush–Kuhn–Tucker (KKT) condition. α_i in formula 12 is a number equal to or greater than zero and equal to or

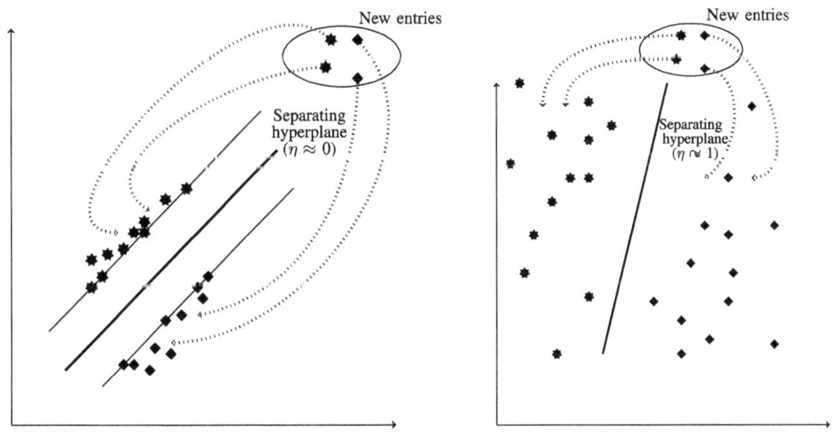

(a) (b)

Figure 1. Hyperplane separation of (a) low data spread and (b) wide data spread.

less than C. For all i from 1 to N, and $\sum_{i=1}^{N} y_i, \alpha_i = 0$. The new kernel matrix, K_{DSVM}, refers to $X_T\Theta$:

$$\min w \neq 0, \quad w_0 \left\{ \frac{1}{2} w^t \Theta w + c \sum_{i=1}^{N} \max(0, 1 - y_i(W^T x_i + w_0)) \right\} \tag{11}$$

$$\max \alpha \sum_{i=1}^{N} \alpha_i - \frac{1}{2} \sum_{i=1}^{N} \sum_{j=1}^{N} \alpha_i \alpha_j y_i y_j K_{\text{DSVM}}(x_i x_j) \tag{12}$$

The mathematical computation denoted to date is a linear function that needs to undergo further transformation to support dynamic learning, which is done by the introduction of a singular value decomposition on Θ, as denoted in formula 13, where $\mathbf{U}$ refers to the initial matrix and Σ the transverse matrix, under which $Q = \Sigma - \frac{1}{2}U$ is applied to the sample to calculate the new sample $xi' = Qx_i$ to obtain formula 14, which results in formula 15 if extended to the whole initial matrix:

$$\Theta = U^T \sum U \tag{13}$$

$$x_{i'T} x_{ji} = x_i^T Q^T Q x_j = x_i^T \Theta^{-1} x_j \tag{14}$$

$$X' = [x'_1, \ldots, x'_N] = [Qx_1, \ldots, Qx_N] = QX \tag{15}$$

Thus, solutions are attained using standard linear SVM with samples xi' and $x'TX'$ as a kernel matrix, which if extended to the transformed xi' samples would result in a nonlinear flexibility in $x'TX'$ and xj as outlined in function 16 with an RBF kernel in formula 17:

$$x'^T x' = X^T Q^T Q X = X^T \Theta^{-1} X \tag{16}$$

$$K_{\text{DSVM-RBF}}(x_i, x_j) = e^{-\frac{(x_i - x_j)^T \Theta^{-1} (x_i - x_j)}{2\sigma^2}} \tag{17}$$

Next, the model underwent further alteration to support incremental learning, in which each additional observation X_c is added to the optimal solution. This is achieved by identifying the scatter matrix of the discriminant-based classifier during the input phase to detect near-global features, which are added to the information retained on local and global characteristics. Computing the feature identification during the input space allows for the reduction of costs associated with time. The initial data are then moved to a higher-dimensional feature space with a singular value decomposition to allow the classifier to process big and complex datasets with a relatively high rate of accuracy. In this model, the Karush–Kuhn–Tucker condition is of utmost importance for achieving optimality. By preserving the KKT conditions for all trained data, an adiabatic increment is maintained, to which formula 6 is reformulated to formula 18, where K is equal to $X^T \Theta^{-1} X$. It is worth noting that the model only accepts new observations if all of the KKT requirements are met, and its weight is set to 0 as is nonsupport vectors. However, weights and bias values are updated if the newly added observation is proven to be a support vector using formula 19 and will keep undergoing updates until an optimal solution is reached:

$$g_i = -1 + \sum_{j=1}^{N} K_{i,j} a_j + y_i w_0 \geq 0,$$

$$\text{if } \alpha i = 0 = 0, \quad \text{if } 0 < \alpha i < C \quad \text{if } \alpha i = C \tag{18}$$

$$\frac{\partial W}{\partial W_0} = \sum_{j=1}^{N} y_i, a_j = 0 \tag{19}$$

To reach such a goal, the dataset **X** is divided into subsets while taking into consideration the following KKT conditions: the first set

S will hold an unbounded support vector with weight values between 0 and C, the second set, **E**, is constrained by weights equal to C, the last set, **N**, comprises of a nonsupport vector points with weight values of 0, and P = E U N. The conditions may be expressed in a matrix form denoted in formula 20:

$$[\Delta g_c \ \Delta g_s \ \Delta g_p \ 0] = \left[y_c \ K_{cs} \ y_s \ K_{ss} \ y_p \ K_{ps} \ 0 \ y_s^T\right] [\Delta w_0 \ \Delta \alpha_s] + \Delta \alpha_c \left[K_{cc}^T \ K_{cs}^T \ K_{cp}^T \ y_c\right] \tag{20}$$

As such in formula 20, any change to the value $\Delta\alpha_c$ is captivated by the required modifications in $\Delta\alpha_s$ and ΔW_0. Therefore, rows two and four are further modified in formulas 21 and 22, respectively, as $\Delta g_s = 0$:

$$[0\,0] = \left[0\, y_s^T \ y_s K_{ss}\right] [\Delta w_0 \, \Delta \alpha_s] + \left[y_c \, K_{cs}^T\right] \tag{21}$$

$$[\Delta w_0 \, \Delta \alpha_s] = \beta \, \Delta \alpha_c \tag{22}$$

$$\beta = [\beta_{w0} \, \beta_m] = -Q \left[y_c \, K_{cs}^T\right], \quad \forall m \in S \tag{23}$$

$$Q = \left[0\, y_s^T \ y_s \, K_{ss}\right] - 1 \tag{24}$$

$$\beta_{w0} = \frac{\Delta_{W0}}{\Delta a_c} \tag{25}$$

$$\beta_m = \left\{\frac{\Delta a_m}{\Delta a_c}, 0\right\} \ \forall m \in S, \ \forall m \notin S \tag{26}$$

In the above formulas, $\boldsymbol{\beta}$ refers to the gradient of all optimal solutions, denoted as $\boldsymbol{\alpha}\mathbf{c}$ that is tasked with regulating model revisions. β_{w0} refers to the sensitivity of changes in the weight as corresponds to $\Delta\alpha_c$, while β_m refers to the sensitivity of $\Delta\alpha_s$ as corresponds to $\Delta\alpha_c$; thus, we can replace formula 20 with rows one and three of formula 21 to obtain formula 27:

$$[\Delta y_c \ \Delta y_p] = \gamma_m \Delta \alpha_c, \quad \forall m \in P \cup c \tag{27}$$

$$\gamma_m = \left\{K_{mc} + \sum_{i \in s} K_{mi} \beta_i, 0\right\} \quad \forall m \in S, \ \forall m \notin S \tag{28}$$

A new update strategy is introduced to circumvent mathematical limits by referring to the largest possible change in α_s as a migrant point that will be moved to another subset. This strategy is made possible under four conditions, as follows:

- Weight α_i reaches the lower bound 0 or the upper bound C when ε is small and $\Delta\alpha_c^s$ represents the greatest incremental jump as follows in formula 29:

$$\Delta\alpha_c^s = \left\{\frac{C - \alpha_i}{\beta_i},\ \text{if}\ \beta_i > \varepsilon\ \frac{\alpha_i}{\beta_i},\ \text{if}\ \beta_i < \varepsilon\right\} \tag{29}$$

- A weight reaches the lower or upper boundary in formula 30:

$$\Delta\alpha_c^p = \frac{-g_i}{\Upsilon_i} \tag{30}$$

- A gradient denoted as x_c reaches zero in formula 31, or its weights equate to C as formula 32:

$$\Delta\alpha_c^g = \frac{-g_i}{\Upsilon_c} \tag{31}$$

$$\Delta\alpha_c^a = C - \alpha_c \tag{32}$$

Finally, we take the smallest of the four case values to compute the maximum feasible increment of α_c as outlined in formula 33, following which the inverse matrix Q is recalculated with every addition using the Woodbury formula, included in formula 34, while formula 35 is used to calculate datapoint exclusions from the matrix:

$$\Delta\alpha_c^{\max} = (\Delta\alpha_c^s,\ \Delta\alpha_c^p,\ \Delta\alpha_c^g,\ \Delta\alpha_c^a) \tag{33}$$

$$Q = [Q\,0\,0\,0] + \frac{1}{\Upsilon_c}\left[\beta^2\,\beta\,\beta\,1\right] \tag{34}$$

$$Q_{i,j} = Q_{i,j} - Q_{s,s}^{-1}Q_{i,s}Q_{i,j}, \quad \forall i,j \in s;\ \ i,j \neq s \tag{35}$$

The LG-SVM is presented in Algorithm 1 as a pseudo-code. As outlined in the following, the incorporation of the Woodbury formula has scaled the matrix θ with O(D2), which represents data points' total attributes and N the number of training points. Computational complexity equates to $O(N_s^2)$, with $N_s \leq N$.

3.1 Autoencoder

In a simple autoencoder, the bottom and top layers have the same number of neurons, while the middle layer usually has a fewer number of neurons with a number of weights connecting the bottom and middle layers, denoted as W_1, and connecting the middle and top layers, denoted as W_2. Thus, the input X is fed through the bottom layer to the middle with the following function, 36, and output function of 37:

$$h = \sigma(W_x + b) \tag{36}$$

$$\sim X = \sigma(W^T h + c) \tag{37}$$

The autoencoder works to minimize the deviation between $\sim X$ and X by compressing the data in the middle layer, denoted as h, creating formulas 38 and 39:

$$h = C(x) \tag{38}$$

$$\sim X = \int (C(x^{(i)})) \tag{39}$$

When combined, the encoder and decoder give formula 40, with an error in formula 41 (Choi, 2017):

$$X^{(i)} = \int (C(x^{(i)})) \tag{40}$$

$$E = \frac{1}{2} \sum_i \sum_k |\sim X^i - x^i|^2 \tag{41}$$

4 Results

The model is evaluated in terms of its prediction accuracy and the time it takes to build the model. The LG-SVM model is compared to similar classifiers: the batch kernel support vector machine (KSVM) (Mohammed *et al.*, 2022), the kernel nonparametric support vector machine (IKSVM) (Maji *et al.*, 2008), the batch kernel nonparametric support vector machine (KNSVM), the kernel support vector machine (IKSVM) (Salhi *et al.*, 2022), and the batch kernel nonparametric support vector machine (IKNSVM).

The model was tested using the 10-fold cross-validation process and the area under the curve (AUC). All data processed were limited to vectors of 130 words. Results related to model accuracy are shared in Table 1, while training times are shared in Table 2. The average score illustrated in Table 1 averaged at 79% with the LG-SVM recording the highest at 79.7% and the KSVM the lowest at 78.979%, relatively high when compared to the Bi-LSTM that stood at 52%.

4.1 Data transformation

To increase accuracy, an autoencoder was used. Three autoencoder models were created with dimensional reduction of 100, 130, and 70,

Table 1. Average AUC and average training time (in seconds) of each classifier for the original data.

Classifier	Average AUC	Average Training Time
LG-SVM	79.712	0.2533
KNSVM	79.431	338.6508
IKNSVM	79.455	0.5386
KSVM	78.979	4.7579
IKSVM	79.238	0.2444

Table 2. Required training times for the LG-SVM vs. different classifiers (in seconds).

LG-SVM	IKNSVM	IKNSVM	KNSVM	KSVM
0.03066	1.5475	0.47015	238.5659	0.47015
0.024035	0.82895	0.81168	368.7075	4.9631
0.02433	0.53863	0.02094	706.2941	8.0256
0.030496	0.49988	0.05545	1073.1679	12.6043
0.030352	0.9582	0.01929	1412.6015	18.0922
0.03026	0.2965	0.02248	1749.4815	23.0433
0.028874	0.6043	0.0512	2010.3415	25.2483
0.022455	0.66271	0.0161	2472.4615	28.1733
0.029001	0.66944	0.02094	2810.0515	31.7876

Table 3. Average AUC and average training time (in seconds) of each classifier.

	Classifier	Average AUC	Average Training Time
Dimensional reduction of 100	LG-SVM	99.75	2.4086
	KNSVM	99.68	639.966
	IKNSVM	99.73	6.692
	KSVM	99.31	50.0272
	IKSVM	99.39	1.644
Dimensional reduction of 70	LG-SVM	99.91	0.1797
	KNSVM	99.89	349.2133
	IKNSVM	99.904	6.151
	KSVM	99.859	0.49398
	IKSVM	99.89	0.029763
Dimensional reduction of 130	LG-SVM	99.86	0.2957
	KNSVM	99.8	387.8444
	IKNSVM	99.84	0.43334
	KSVM	99.76	2.6575
	IKSVM	99.83	0.2102

as outlined in Table 3. The results demonstrated in Table 3 follow a U-shaped curve in which a dimensional reduction of 130 had a relatively high accuracy score, which took a dip at 100, only to increase again at 70.

Table 4 demonstrates the time it took to build the models. As expected, batch processing took a longer time to train for the same reason.

5 Stock Market

The perceptron model has kept on par with the bot detection results. Data reduction to 70 yielded the best performance with a correlation of 96.58%, while mean absolute error stood at 8.9. The relative absolute error was also low at 18.4%. The errors, when normalized for the sample, also produced a low error rate, with a relative absolute error of 26.6%. The low error values recorded coupled with a high correlation coefficient are proof that the perceptron model can make predictions at a high accuracy level. Moreover, the stronger performance between the incorporation of an autoencoder and against the 130 dataset is reflected by the root relative squared error of 26.6%

Table 4. Required training times for the LG-SVM vs. different classifiers (in seconds).

LG-SVM	IKNSVM	IKSVM	KNSVM	KSVM
Dimensional reduction of 70				
0.20634	9.2123	0.059016	350.335	0.21143
0.24455	1.2679	0.021878	699.6986	0.47458
0.18545	5.4905	0.10818	1049.7615	0.63481
0.20002	2.4086	0.013309	1398.3695	0.91791
1.17704	8.5949	0.024096	1747.9796	1.3718
0.15755	3.3412	0.018002	2098.8932	1.7535
0.07111	9.1344	0.016572	2447.9545	2.0264
0.079729	4.4733	0.012405	2788.5784	2.4378
0.076965	6.0555	0.039655	3140.2585	3.0429
Dimensional reduction of 100				
0.03066	1.5475	0.47015	238.5659	0.47015
0.024035	0.82895	0.81168	368.7075	4.9631
0.02433	0.53863	0.02094	706.2941	8.0256
0.030496	0.49988	0.05545	1073.1679	12.6043
0.030352	0.9582	0.01929	1412.6015	18.0922
0.03026	0.2965	0.02248	1749.4815	23.0433
0.028874	0.6043	0.0512	2010.3415	25.2483
0.022455	0.66271	0.0161	2472.4615	28.1733
0.029001	0.66844	0.02094	2810.0515	31.7876
Dimensional reduction of 130				
0.3724	0.5256	0.1698	384.2309	1.3553
0.3275	0.6523	0.1303	745.1588	1.4737
0.0983	0.2364	0.0727	0.0014927	1.5802
0.3026	0.4521	0.2745	0.0018805	1.9422
0.3003	0.5852	0.1702	0.2000359	2.0633
0.1319	0.7854	0.4341	0.00281	2.2552
0.0977	0.3244	0.0708	0.0029933	2.3642
0.1689	0.2362	0.0926	0.0030728	2.4452
0.2144	0.5623	0.4770	0.0036806	2.7143

Table 5. Average performance metric and average training time (in seconds) of each classifier.

	Correlation Coefficient	Mean Absolute Error	Root Mean Squared Error	Relative Absolute Error	Root Relative Squared Error	Time Taken to Build the Model in Seconds
70	0.9658	6.0042	8.9126	18.4108%	26.6149%	189.87
100	0.9538	7.2202	9.9978	22.9191%	30.4901%	284.3
130	0.4662	25.6227	33.996	33.996%	81.3292%	462.68

versus 81%; this means that the model is capable of being closer to the actual value since it is normalized for the actual output. The findings in Table 5 demonstrate the statistical outcomes.

6 Discussion

Although recording almost similar accuracy scores, incremental learning methods are always preferred to batch processing in such dynamic environments. Batch learning models do not incorporate the latest information available as the model is shaped using N number of examples, only to drop old examples when its memory is depleted. As a result, the incremental model is preferred to the batch since it holds its accuracy by incorporating the latest example with no down time, which is an added value in dynamic environments (Read *et al.*, n.d.).

Despite the high accuracy rates, researchers have pointed out that there is no assurance of consistency in dynamic models, particularly when the models are continuously shaped by and measured against evolving data. Thus, observations that are either correctly or incorrectly classified by the current form of the model may be incorrectly or correctly classified by the newer format (Carbonara and Borrowman, 1998).

Moreover, the batch KSVM model has held the worst record when it comes to model accuracy, as expected. This is due to the fact that all other models, which it is compared to, are, arguably, subsequent models that have addressed the KSVM's shortcomings by computing the near-global variational in the input rather than the feature space.

The research has centered on analyzing the models' performance in terms of their accuracy; however, an in-depth comparison of the models' components would provide a stronger argument for the use of the LG-SVM. The in-depth comparison is not conducted at this time since it is challenging to investigate all the vast parameters involved; however, a recommendation is being made for future researchers to explore.

Future researchers are also encouraged to investigate the models' performance in terms of false positive and false negative to compute the business cost of implementing the model. A false positive would lead to barring human users from Twitter, which is costly to a business that depends on user-generated content to expand.

The models used to build and assess outcomes suffer from limited data. The data used in this research are outdated since they were collected between 2009 and 2014. This is a relatively old dataset since, as Chapters 1 and 2 demonstrated, Twitter is a highly dynamic environment with data evolving on a daily basis. Thus, a recommendation is also being made for data to be collected in real time to ensure that the performance is held at a high level in current terms.

In terms of model-building time, the incremental learning methods address batch processing's time inefficiencies. Incrementally incorporating new observations, rather than building a new model from scratch, allows for a smoother and more time-efficient learning method. Additionally, subsequent incremental models' modification of the core model outlines the relationship between the current and past models; thus, analyzing the changes gives researchers the opportunity to spot trends over time (Carbonara and Borrowman, 1998).

The dynamic models have recorded far better accuracy scores than the standard SVM model, as witnessed an estimated 20% increase in accuracy. This is in line with what was found in the literature review, which argued that standard models are unable to detect evolving bots due to their dependence on a set of baseline characteristics. The model used in this research is like the upgraded models that have addressed shortcomings in terms of its structure as well as its accuracy scores.

Turning to the stock market analysis, however, correlation does not indicate causation as the stock market may be influenced by a vast number of factors. The time factor was not incorporated in the perceptron model; therefore, time lag, which takes place between information dissemination over Twitter and human action, is not considered (Nisar and Yeung, 2018).

Additionally, not all accounts are found to be equal in terms of their impact on readers. It is found that *The New York Times*, Bloomberg, *CNN*, and Investing.com have a high level of impact on the stock market, offering a very high correlation between sentiments and market volatility (Valle-Cruz *et al.*, 2021). Thus, it is important to look into the metadata to distinguish not only bots from humans but also their level of influence.

It is worth noting that despite proving a possible relation, grounds for speculation expand far beyond Twitter. Users who depend on social media for information are more than likely to visit various platforms, such as Instagram; thus, any future model must include other platforms.

The relation between tweets and stock market volatility that is captured by the perceptron model might not reflect the reality of the situation since it did take into consideration other potential contributing factors. Therefore, future works should consider including other important economic factors such as the money supply and prices of other investment goods such as gold. Moreover, this study has not considered political factors that may impact the market. President Trump and Elon Musk are both widely known for their influential tweets that are known to influence the market; therefore, their tweets must be controlled for in future circumstances.

7 Conclusion

This research provided sufficient evidence supporting the notion that bot detection in a highly dynamic environment requires a model that is flexible and that Twitter has influence over public consensus. Contributions are as follows: incremental learning algorithms are more time efficient in detecting bots and create a trail that allows for analyzing trends. Third, the research provided proof of the autoencoder's advanced ability to learn nonlinear patterns and increase efficiency through dimension reduction (Sayantini, 2020).

Moreover, the perceptron model has proven to accurately predict short-term stock market volatility resulting from Twitter trends, alongside proving to be the best fit for stock market prediction as it works well with highly volatile datasets, which the stock market volatility is. However, the research can be extended by analyzing other financial indicators, global market trends, and deep diving into each account's reach to distinguish far-reaching accounts' influence from those with limited reach. Finally, data from other social media platforms should also be considered.

References

Australian Government (2021, June 23). Social media for business. Retrieved October 18, 2021, from Australian Government: Business: https://business.gov.au/online/social-media-for-business.

Bandyopadhyay, H. (2021, November 29). Computer vision: Everything you need to know. Retrieved January 15, 2022, from V7labs: https://www.v7labs.com/blog/what-is-computer-vision.

Basnat, A., Ahmed, A., El Ghazali, A., and Jain, V. (2014). Incremental learning approach for enhancing the performance of multi-layer perceptron for determining stock market trends. *IJSBAR*, 16(1): 15–23.

Boone, T. *et al.* (2015). Incorporating Google trends data into sales forecasting. *The International Journal of Applied Forecasting*, (38): 9–14.

Brownlee, J. (2019, July 05). A gentle introduction to computer vision. Retrieved Jan 15, 2022, from Machine Learning Mastery: https://machinelearningmastery.com/what-is-computer-vision/.

Brydon, A. (2019, October 30). Why AI needs human input (and always will). Retrieved January 15, 2022, from Forbes: https://www.forbes.com/sites/forbestechcouncil/2019/10/30/why-ai-needs-human-input-and-always-will.

Carbonara, L., and Borrowman, A. (1998). A comparison of batch and incremental supervised learning algorithms. Springer, Paris, France, pp. 264–272.

Cboe Volatility Index. (n.d.). External.

Choi, H.I. (2017). Lecture 16: Autoencoders. Retrieved from Seoul National University: http://www.math.snu.ac.kr/~hichoi/machinelearning/lecturenotes/Autoencoder.pdf.

Cresci, S., Pietro, R.D., Petrocchi, M., Spognardi, A., and Tesconi, M. (2015, September 14). Fame for sale: Efficient detection of fake Twitter followers. *Decision Support Systems*, 80: 56–71.

Cresci, S., Pietro, R.D., Petrocchi, M., Spognardi, A., and Tesconi, M. (2017). The paradigm-shift of social spambots. In *Proceedings of the 26th International Conference on World Wide Web Companion*, pp. 3–7.

Daniel, L., Loyola-González, O., Monroy, R., and Medina-Pérez, M.A. (2021). Bot datasets on Twitter: Analysis and challenges. *Applied Sciences*, 11(9): 4105.

Demush, R. (2019, February 26). A brief history of computer vision (and convolutional neural networks). Retrieved January 15, 2022, from Hackernoon: https://hackernoon.com/a-brief-history-of-computer-vision-and-convolutional-neural-networks-8fe8aacc79f3.

Dickson, B. (2020, January 06). What are convolutional neural networks (CNN)? Retrieved from TechTalks: https://bdtechtalks.com/2020/01/06/convolutional-neural-networks-cnn-convnets.

Gavali, P., and Banu, J.S. (2019). Chapter 6 — Deep convolutional neural network for image classification on CUDA platform. *Deep Learning and Parallel Computing Environment for Bioengineering Systems*. Academic Press, Cambridge, United States, pp. 99–122. doi:10.1016/B978-0-12-816718-2.00013-0.

Hajian-Tilaki, K. (2013). Receiver operating characteristic (ROC) curve analysis for medical diagnostic test evaluation. *PubMed Central*, 4(2): 627–635.

Hartley, R. (2004). *Multiple View Geometry in Computer Vision*. Cambridge University Press, Cambridge, United Kingdom.

Hendrix, J. (2021, October 6). How Facebook is misleading the public about its role in January 6. Retrieved October 18, 2021, from Just Security: https://www.justsecurity.org/78494/how-facebook-is-misleading-the-public-about-its-role-in-january-6/.

Hostiadi, D.P., Tohari, A., and Wibisono, W. (2020). B-corr model for bot group activity detection based on network flows traffic analysis. *KSII Transactions on Internet and Information Systems (TIIS)*, 14(10): 4176–4197.

Hutchinson, A. (2022, February 16). Twitter launches new bot labels to identify bot accounts in-stream. Retrieved from Social Media Today: https://www.socialmediatoday.com/news/twitter-launches-new-bot-labels-to-identify-bot-accounts-in-stream/618971/.

Jang, B., Kim, M., Harerimana, G., Kang, S.-U., and Kim, J.W. (2020, August 24). Bi-LSTM model to increase accuracy in text classification: Combining word2vec CNN and attention mechanism. *MDPI*, 10(17): 1–14.

Korteling, J.E., Boer-Visschedijk, G.C., Blankendaal, R.A., Boonekamp, R.C., and Eikelboom, A.R. (2021). Human- versus artificial intelligence. *Frontiers in Artificial Intelligence*, 4: 1–13. doi:10.3389/frai.2021.622364.

Kretinin, A., Samuel, J., and Kashyap, R. (2018). When the going gets tough, the tweets get going! An exploratory analysis of tweets sentiments in the stock market. *American Journal of Management*, 18(5): 23–36.

Kudugunta, S., and Ferrara, E. (2018, October). Deep neural network for bot detection. *Information Sciences*, 467: 312–322.

Kuepper, J. (2022, March 1). What caused the Russian financial crisis of 2014 and 2015. Retrieved from The Balance: https://www.thebalance.com/what-caused-the-russian-financial-crisis-of-2014-and-2015-1979012.

Lewis, T. (2014, December 04). A brief history of artificial intelligence. Retrieved December 01, 2021, from Live Science: https://www.livescience.com/49007-history-of-artificial-intelligence.html.

Lewis, C., and Monett, D. (2018). Getting clarity by defining artificial intelligence — A survey. In *Philosophy and Theory of Artificial Intelligence 2017*, pp. 212–214. doi:10.1007/978-3-319-96448-5_21.

Li, Q., Zhou, S., and Wei, F. (2017). Local kernel nonparametric discriminant analysis for adaptive extraction of complex structures. *Open Physics*, 15(1): 270–279.

Loureiro, A. *et al.* (2018). Exploring the use of deep neural networks for sales forecasting in fashion retail. *Decision Support Systems*, 114: 81–93.

Lowe, D.G. (1999). Object recognition from local scale-invariant features. In *Proceedings of the Seventh IEEE International Conference on Computer Vision*, Vol. 2. IEEE, pp. 1150–1157. doi:10.1109/ICCV.1999.790410.

Lutkevich, B., and Wigmore, I. (n.d.). Social media. Retrieved October 18, 2021, from Tech Target: https://whatis.techtarget.com/definition/social-media.

Macêdo, D.L. (2017). *Enhancing Deep Learning Performance using Displaced Rectifier Linear Unit.* Federal University of Pernambuco. doi: 10.13140/RG.2.2.23893.88807.

Madiraju, N.S., Sadat, S.M., Fisher, D., and Karimabadi, H. (2018). Deep temporal clustering: Fully unsupervised learning of time domaine features. Master Thesis Report, Arizona State University, 2018.

Mahanta, J. (2017, July 10). Introduction to neural networks, advantages and applications. Retrieved from Towards Data Science: https://towardsdatascience.com/introduction-to-neural-networks-advantages-and-applications-96851bd1a207.

Maji, S., Malik, J., and Berg, A. (2008). Classification using intersection kernel support vector machines is efficient. In *IEEE Conference on Computer Vision and Pattern Recognition*, pp. 1–8.

McKenzie, H.-W., Curtis, B., Leggio, L., Devoto, A., Giorgi, S., David, E.H., Ungar, L., Schwartz, H.A., and Rahman, M. (2021, May 20). Bots and misinformation spread on social media: Implications for COVID-19. *Journal of Medical Internet Research*, 23(5): e26933.

Mohammed, A., Noaman, M., and Azzai, H. (2022). A combining two KSVM classifiers based on true pixel values and discrete wavelet transform for MRI-based brain tumor detection and classification. *Engineering and Technology Journal*, 40(2): 322–333.

Nisar, T.M., and Yeung, M. (2018). Twitter as a tool for forecasting stock market movements: A short-window event study. *The Journal of Finance and Data Science*, 4(2): 101–119. doi: https://doi.org/10.1016/j.jfds.2017.11.002.

Prince, S.J. (2012). *Computer Vision: Models, Learning, and Inference.* Cambridge University Press, Cambridge, United Kingdom.

Randhawa, R.H., Aslam, N., AlAuthman, M., Rafiq, H., and Comeau, F. (2021, June 3). Security hardening of botnet detectors using generative adversarial networks. *IEEE Access*, 9: 78276–78292.

Read, J., Bifet, A., Pfahringer, B., and Holmes, G. (n.d.). *Batch-Incremental vs. Instance-Incremental Learning in Dynamic and Evolving Data.* The University of Waikato, New Zealand.

Rhodes, A.D., Quinn, M.H., and Mitchell, M. (2016). Fast on-line kernel density estimation for active object localization. *Computer Vision and Pattern Recognition*: 1611.05369. Retrieved from https://arxiv.org/abs/1611.05369.

Roberts, S. (2020, June 16). Who's a bot? Who's not? Retrieved from *New York Times*: https://www.nytimes.com/2020/06/16/science/social-media-bots-kazemi.html.

Salhi, M., Ksantini, R., and Zouari, B. (2022). A real-time image-centric transfer function design based on incremental classification. *Journal of Real-Time Image Processing*, 19: 185–203.

Savage, N. (2020, December 09). The race to the top among the world's leaders in artificial intelligence. Retrieved January 15, 2022, from *Nature*, 588(7837): S102–S104. https://www.nature.com/articles/d41586-020-03409-8.

Sayantini (2020, May 14). Autoencoders tutorial: A beginner's guide to autoencoders. Retrieved from Edureka: https://www.edureka.co/blog/autoencoders-tutorial/.

Soula, A., Tbarki, K., Ksantini, R., Said, S.B., and Lachiri, Z. (2020). A novel incremental kernel nonparametric SVM model (iKN-SVM) for data classification: An application to face detection. *Engineering Applications of Artificial Intelligence*, 89: 103468.

Stevens, K. (2012). The vision of David Marr. *Perception*, 41: 1061–1072. doi: 10.1068/p7297.

Szeliski, R. (2010). *Computer Vision: Algorithms and Applications.* Springer, Cham, Switzerland.

Temür, A. *et al.* (2019). Predicting housing sales in Turkey using ARIMA, LSTIM and hybrid models. *Journal of Business Economics and Management*, 20(5): 920–938.

Tian, Z., Shen, C., Chen, H., and He, T. (2019). FCOS: Fully convolutional one-stage object detection. In *2019 IEEE/CVF International Conference on Computer Vision (ICCV)*. IEEE, pp. 9626–9635. doi:10.1109/ICCV.2019.00972.

Udom, P. (2014). A comparison study between time series model and ARIMA model for sales forecasting of distributor in plastic industry. *IOSR Journal of Engineering*, 4(2): 32–38.

UW Bothell and Cascadia College: Campus Library. (2021, October 5). News: Fake news, misinformation & disinformation. Retrieved October 18, 2021, from UW Bothell and Cascadia College: https://guides.lib.uw.edu/c.php?g=345925&p=7772376.

Valle-Cruz, D., Sandoval-Almazán, R., López-Chau, A., and Fernandez-Cortez, V. (2021). Does Twitter affect stock market decisions? Financial sentiment analysis during pandemics: A comparative study of the H1N1 and the COVID-19 periods. Springer, Volume 14, pp. 372–387.

Victoriaruss (2013, Mar 13). Feature detectors/Hubel & Wiesel experiment/Prosopagnosia. Retrieved January 15, 2022, from goodpsychology: https://goodpsychology.wordpress.com/2013/03/13/235/.

Wang, P. (2019). On defining artificial intelligence. *Journal of Artificial General Intelligence*, 10(2): 1–37. doi:10.2478/jagi-2019-0002.

Zhou, H.P. (2020). Study on convolutional neural network and its application in data mining and sales forecasting for E-commerce. *Electronic Commerce Research*, 20(2): 297–320.

https://doi.org/10.1142/9781800615212_0010

Chapter 10

Reinforcement Machine Learning Optimization Algorithms for the Computation of Downside Risk and Investable Portfolios in Post 2007–2009 Financial Meltdown

Mazin A.M. Al Janabi

Full Professor of Finance & Banking and Financial Engineering, Mexico City, Mexico

mazinaljanabi@gmail.com

Abstract

The objective of this chapter is to examine reinforcement machine learning quadratic optimization techniques for the computation of downside-risk limits and investable portfolios in post 2007–2009 global financial meltdown. The modeling techniques are based on the notion of Liquidity-adjusted Value-at-Risk (LVaR) as well as the application of reinforcement machine learning optimization algorithms with meaningful financial and operational constraints. In this chapter, some simulation case studies are presented for the computation of downside-risk limits and investable portfolios. The applied risk valuation techniques and quadratic optimization algorithms can help in advancing reinforcement machine learning methods, risk computations, and portfolio management practices in the wake of the 2007–2009 global financial turmoil.

Keywords: Emerging markets, financial risk management, GCC financial markets, liquidity-adjusted value-at-risk, optimization, portfolio management, reinforcement machine learning, stress testing.

1 Introduction

The recent financial crisis has emphasized the necessity of accurate identification and assessment of embedded liquidity risk in financial investment portfolios. In essence, liquidity trading risk arises due to the incapability of financial entities to liquidate financial assets holdings, at rational prices, as time passes across the liquidation (closeout) period. Undeniably, certain collapses in some well-known financial entities and the consequential financial turmoil were caused, to some degree, by the impact of asset liquidity risk on structured portfolios (Al Janabi, 2015).

To evaluate the risks included in their daily trading operations, major financial institutions are progressively developing and using Value-at-Risk (VaR) models. Currently, VaR is by far the most widespread and most acknowledged risk measure among financial institutions. While VaR is a very popular measure of market risk of financial trading portfolios, it is not a panacea for all risk assessments and has several drawbacks, limitations, and undesirable properties (Sanders, 2002; Al Janabi, 2013, 2015).

One important critique that can be leveled against the variance–covariance estimate of VaR is that it does not explicitly consider asset liquidity risk. Typical VaR models assess the worst change in the mark-to-market portfolio value over a given time horizon but do not account for the actual trading risk of liquidation. Indeed, neglecting asset liquidity risk can lead to an underestimation of the overall market risk and misapplication of capital cushion for the safety and soundness of financial institutions (Al Janabi, 2011, 2015).

In effect, the conventional VaR approach to computing market (or trading) risk of a portfolio does not explicitly consider liquidity risk. Typical VaR models are based on modern portfolio management theory and assess the worst change in mark-to-market portfolio value over a given time horizon but do not account for the actual trading risk of liquidation. In general, customary fine tunings are made on an *ad hoc* basis. At most, the holding period (or liquidation horizon) over which the VaR number is calculated is adjusted to ensure the inclusion of liquidity risk. As a result, liquidity trading risk can be imprecisely factored into VaR assessments by assuring that the liquidation horizon is as a minimum larger than an orderly liquidation interval. Moreover, the same liquidation horizon is employed for all trading asset classes, albeit some assets may be more liquid than others (Al Janabi, 2011, 2015).

In fact, some relevant studies have addressed the issues of liquidity risk but not necessarily within the portfolio optimization context. Their main focus, in fact, was on modeling merely transaction costs (that is, the widening of the bid–ask spread), however the effects of adverse market price impact have not been studied rigorously, though Al Janabi (2013, 2014), Al Janabi *et al.* (2017), and Al Janabi *et al.* (2019) are an exception. For the sake of brevity, we discuss in the following a concise description of some of the suggested modeling techniques for liquidity risk, detailed as follows: Within the VaR technique, Jarrow and Subramanian (1997) present a market impact model of liquidity by taking into consideration the optimal liquidation of a portfolio over a fixed horizon. On the other hand, Bangia *et al.* (2002) approach the liquidity risk from another angle and provide a model of VaR adjusted for what they call exogenous liquidity. In a different vein, Almgren and Chriss (1999) present a concrete framework for deriving the optimal execution strategy using a mean–variance approach.

In a different but related strand of research studies, Madoroba and Kruger (2014) introduce a VaR model that incorporates intraday price movements on high–low spreads and adjusts for a trade impact measure, a novel sensitivity measure of price movements due to trading volumes. Furthermore, the authors compare and contrast 10 worldwide-recognized liquidity risk management models including the Al Janabi model, which is used in this chapter for the computation of liquidly risk modeling and optimization process. On another front, Al Janabi (2012, 2013, 2014) tackles the issue of adverse market price impact on liquidity trading risk and coherent portfolio optimization using a parametric liquidity-adjusted VaR (LVaR) methodology. The proposed adverse price unwinding approach comprises a liquidation multiplier that can adjust the impact of unfavorable price movement throughout the closeout period along with an optimization algorithm that allocates assets subject to imposing meaningful financial and operational constraints.[1]

Against this backdrop and despite some research into asset liquidity risk measurement, the financial services industry still finds it difficult to quantify and predict measurable attributes of market liquidity risk. In fact, most financial institutions have committed or are preparing to commit significant resources to managing liquidity risk. However, there are no clear standards regarding the definition of the problem these entities' efforts are meant to solve, let alone the risk measures themselves. In the absence of accepted industry standards, risk professionals are faced with the challenge of defining an organization-specific internal approach that addresses market liquidity risk not only for a single trading security but also on an aggregate portfolio level (Al Janabi, 2011, 2015).

This is where this research chapter comes in, as we strive to clarify the essence of asset liquidity risk, offer a clear-cut explanation of the topic, and recommend scenario optimization modeling techniques for the computation of downside-risk boundaries. Further, we empirically test for optimal and investable portfolios and provide some practical recommendations for financial institutions. Effectively, the developed methodology and risk assessment algorithms can aid in evolving risk management practices in emerging markets, predominantly in light of the outcomes of the 2007–2009 global financial crunch and the ensuing financial chaos.

In this backdrop, the main objectives of this chapter are threefold: (1) to examine scenario optimization algorithms for the computation of market and liquidity potential risk exposure for multiple-asset portfolios under unfavorable circumstances, (2) to propose modeling techniques for the computation of maximum downside-risk threshold

[1]For other relevant literature on liquidity, internal risk models, asset pricing and portfolio choice and diversification, one can refer as well to Al Janabi (2021a), Al Janabi (2021b), Al Janabi (2022), Asadi and Al Janabi (2020), Uddin *et al.* (2022), Arreola-Hernandez and Al Janabi (2020), Grillini *et al.* (2019), Al Janabi *et al.* (2017), Al Janabi *et al.* (2019), Arreola-Hernandez *et al.* (2017), Arreola-Hernandez *et al.* (2015), among others. Furthermore, within the copula technique, and particularly the vine copula approach, there were indeed very few studies in this respect and most of published research is still focused on the issue of transaction costs (i.e., bid–ask spreads). In particular, Weiß and Supper (2013) investigate the issue of forecasting liquidity-adjusted intraday VaR with vine copulas.

limits, and (3) to consider optimization algorithms and techniques for the evaluation of optimal portfolios and investable portfolios under crisis market scenarios. In this chapter, the concept of investable market portfolios refers to rational portfolios that are contingent on meaningful financial and operational constraints. In this sense, investable market portfolios are not located on the efficient frontiers as defined by Markowitz (1952) and instead have logical and well-structured long/short asset allocation proportions.

To that end, in this chapter, we implement robust modeling techniques and optimization algorithms based on the Al Janabi model (Al Janabi, 2008; Madoroba and Kruger, 2014) for optimizing the risk–return profiles of different multiple-asset portfolios using rational operational and financial scenarios. The proposed optimization algorithms, investment portfolio analytics, and the attained empirical outcomes can have important practical uses and applications for portfolio managers and risk managers, particularly in the wake of the 2007–2009 global financial crisis. In addition, the recommended risk management modeling techniques and optimization algorithms can have key applications in reinforcement machine learning, expert systems, smart financial functions, Internet of Things (IoT), and financial technology (FinTech) in big data ecosystems.

The remainder of this chapter is organized as follows. Section 2 defines the mathematical procedure of a closed-form LVaR algorithm and a robust modeling technique that integrates the effects of illiquidity of financial assets using the Al Janabi model. Section 3 examines reinforcement machine learning optimization algorithms for the modeling of downside-risk exposures and investible portfolios. The outcomes of the reinforcement machine learning computational process, empirical tests, and simulations of investable portfolios are drawn in Section 3 as well. Section 4 provides certain concluding remarks.

2 Modeling Techniques for the Computation of Liquidity Adjusted Value-at-Risk (LVaR) Using Al Janabi Model

In line with the Al Janabi model (Al Janabi, 2008, 2015; Madoroba and Kruger, 2014), for a single trading position, the absolute value of VaR in monetary terms can be defined as follows:

$$\text{VaR}_i = |(\mu_i - \alpha * \sigma_i)[\text{Asset}_i * Fx_i]| \approx |\alpha * \sigma_i[\text{Asset}_i * Fx_i]| \quad (1)$$

where μ_i is the expected return of the asset, α is the confidence level (or in other words, the standard normal variant at confidence level α), and σ_i is the forecasted standard deviation (or conditional volatility) of the return of the security that constitutes the single position. Asset_i is the mark-to-market value of the trading asset and indicates the monetary amount of equity position in asset i and Fx_i denotes the unit foreign exchange rate of asset i (Al Janabi, 2013, 2015).

For multiple assets or portfolios of assets, VaR is a function of each individual security's risk and the correlation factor $[\rho_{i,j}]$ between the returns on the individual securities, detailed as follows:

$$\text{VaR}_P = \sqrt{\sum_{i=1}^{n}\sum_{j=1}^{n} \text{VaR}_i\, \text{VaR}_j\, \rho_{i,j}} = \sqrt{|\text{VaR}|^T\, |\rho|\, |\text{VaR}|} \quad (2)$$

In order to estimate VaR (of a portfolio of any number of financial assets), one needs first to generate a vector |VaR| of individual VaR positions — evidently n rows and one column $(nx1)$ matrix — a transpose vector $|\text{VaR}|^T$ of the distinct VaR positions — an $(1xn)$ vector, and for this reason, the superscript "T" donates transpose of the vector — and finally a correlation matrix, $|\rho|$, of all correlation factors (ρ) — explicitly an (nxn) matrix.

In fact, if asset returns are independent and they can have any elliptical multivariate distribution, then it is possible to convert the VaR horizon parameter from daily to any t-day horizon. The variance of a t-day return should be t times the variance of a 1-day return or $\sigma^2 = f(t)$. Thus, in terms of standard deviation (or volatility), $\sigma = f(\sqrt{t})$ and the daily VaR number [VaR (1-day)] can be adjusted for any t horizon to yield an LVaR estimate, such as

$$\text{LVaR}(t\text{-day}) = \text{VaR}(1\text{-day})\sqrt{t} \quad (3)$$

The above formula was proposed and used by *J.P. Morgan* in their earlier *RiskMetrics*^{TM} method (1994). This methodology implicitly assumes that liquidation occurs in one block sale at the end of the holding period and that there is one holding period for all assets, regardless of their inherent trading liquidity structure. Unfortunately, the latter approach does not consider real-life trading situations, where traders can liquidate (or re-balance) small portions of their trading portfolios on a daily basis. Moreover, this could generate unreliable risk assessments and can lead to considerable overestimates of LVaR figures, especially for the purposes of economic capital allocation between trading and/or investment units (Al Janabi, 2011, 2013, 2015).

The assumption of a given holding period for orderly liquidation inevitably implies that assets' liquidation occurs during the holding period. Accordingly, scaling the holding period to account for orderly liquidation can be justified if one allows the assets to be liquidated throughout the holding (closeout) period. In order to perform the calculation of LVaR under more realistic illiquid market conditions, we can define the following throughout the closeout period:

$$\text{LVaR}_{\text{adj}} = \text{VaR}\sqrt{\frac{(2t+1)(t+1)}{6t}} \tag{4}$$

where t is the number of liquidation days (t-day to liquidate the entire asset fully), VaR = Value-at-Risk under liquid market conditions (as presented formerly in equation [1]), and LVaR_{adj} = Value-at-Risk under illiquid market conditions. The latter equation indicates that $\text{LVaR}_{\text{adj}} > \text{VaR}$, and for the special case when the number of days to liquidate the entire assets is one trading day, then $\text{LVaR}_{\text{adj}} = \text{VaR}$. Consequently, the difference between $\text{LVaR}_{\text{adj}} - \text{VaR}$ should be equal to the residual market risk due to the illiquidity of any asset under illiquid market conditions.

3 Reinforcement Machine Learning Optimization Algorithms for the Modeling of Downside-Risk Exposures and Investable Portfolios

In this research chapter, databases of daily price returns of the Gulf Cooperation Council (GCC) stock markets indexes are implemented as a case study to demonstrate the applications of reinforcement machine learning modeling techniques and optimization algorithms. The total number of indexes that are considered in this work is seven, including two indexes for the UAE markets, with various liquidity horizons and conditional volatilities, detailed as follows:

(a) DFMGI General Index (Dubai Financial Market General Index, Country: United Arab Emirates).
(b) ADX Index (Abu Dhabi Stock Market Index, Country: United Arab Emirates).
(c) BSEX All Share Index (All Share Stock Market Index, Country: Bahrain).
(d) KSEGI General Index (Stock Exchange General Index, Country: Kuwait).
(e) MSM30 Index (Muscat Stock Market Index, Country: Oman).
(f) DSM Index (Doha Stock Market General Index, Country: Qatar).
(g) TASI Tadawul All Share Index (All Share Stock Market Index, Country: Saudi Arabia).

For this particular study, we have chosen a confidence interval of 95% (or 97.5% with a "one-tailed" loss side) and several liquidation time horizons (closeout periods) to calculate LVaR under crisis market situations. Historical databases (of more than six years) of daily closing index levels, for the period 17/10/2004–22/05/2009, are collected for the purpose of implementing this research study and further for the construction of market risk management parameters, downside-risk limits (or thresholds), and in the computations of optimal and investable portfolios. In fact, the selected time-series datasets fall within the period of the most severe part of the 2007–2009 sub-prime financial crunch. Next, based on the Al Janabi model (Al Janabi, 2008; Madoroba and Kruger, 2014), robust financial and optimizing algorithms and a software package are designed for constructing structured multiple-asset portfolios and for the implementation of LVaR and under adverse market perspectives. The analysis of data and discussions of relevant findings and results of this research are organized and explained as follows.

3.1 Reinforcement machine learning for the computation of maximum LVaR thresholds

How should we establish downside-risk limits to protect against maximum loss amounts? These are certain fundamental questions risk managers and/or portfolio managers must consider. In order to ascertain coherent maximum LVaR trading limits, the mathematical formulation of an algorithm for the optimization process is set as follows:

From Eq. (4), we can express the liquidation horizon factor (LHF_i) for each trading asset as

$$\mathrm{LHF}_i = \sqrt{\frac{(2t_i+1)(t_i+1)}{6t_i}} \geq 1.0; \quad \forall_i\ i = 1, 2, \ldots, n \tag{5}$$

After substituting Eq. (5) into Eq. (2), we can calculate the maximum portfolio downside-risk $\mathrm{LVaR}_{P_{\mathrm{adj}}}$ limits by resolving the following quadratic programming formulation (objective risk function) under illiquid and adverse (crisis) market state of affairs:

$$\begin{aligned} \text{Maximize: } \mathrm{LVaR}_{P_{\mathrm{adj}}} &= \sqrt{\sum_{i=1}^{n}\sum_{j=1}^{n} \mathrm{LVaR}_{i_{\mathrm{adj}}}\, \mathrm{LVaR}_{j_{\mathrm{adj}}}\, \rho_{i,j}} \\ &= \sqrt{|\mathrm{LVaR}_{\mathrm{adj}}|^T\, |\rho|\, |\mathrm{LVaR}_{\mathrm{adj}}|} \end{aligned} \tag{6}$$

The above objective risk function can be maximized conditional on the following operational and financial budget constraints as specified by the portfolios' trading risk manager and/or portfolio manager:

$$\sum_{i=1}^{n} R_i x_i = R_P; \quad l_i \leq x_i \leq u_i \quad i = 1, 2, \ldots, n \tag{7}$$

$$\sum_{i=1}^{n} x_i = 1.0; \quad l_i \leq x_i \leq u_i \quad i = 1, 2, \ldots, n \tag{8}$$

$$\sum_{i=1}^{n} V_i = V_P \quad i = 1, 2, \ldots, n \tag{9}$$

$$|\mathrm{LHF}| \geq 1.0; \quad \forall_i \quad i = 1, 2, \ldots, n \tag{10}$$

where R_P and V_P denote the target portfolio mean expected return and total portfolio volume, respectively, and x_i the weight or percentage asset allocation for each asset. The values l_i and u_i, $i = 1, 2, \ldots, n$, denote the lower and upper constraints for the portfolio weights x_i. If we choose $l_i = 0$, $i = 1, 2, \ldots, n$, then we have the situation where no short sales are allowed (Al Janabi, 2013). Moreover, |LHF| indicates an $(nx1)$ liquidity risk factor vector for all $i = 1, 2, \ldots, n$.

For this purpose, Tables 1 and 2 present four structural simulation case studies for the setting of maximum downside LVaR boundary trading limits. In all four case studies, the effects of various asset allocations (with or without short sales) are investigated for the purpose of deciding on acceptable LVaR threshold limits. In all case studies, the optimization algorithm is based on the definition of LVaR as the maximum possible loss over a specified time horizon within a given confidence level. The optimization technique solves the problem by locating market positions that maximize downside loss, subject to that all imposed constraints are fulfilled within their boundary values. For the sake of restraining the optimization process and thereafter its analysis, a volume trading limit of AED 200,000,000 (UAE Dirham) is assumed as a constraint, that is the financial entity must keep a maximum overall market value of stocks of no more than AED 200,000,000 (between long-only and short-sales positions). Further, in all cases, a liquidation horizon (or a closeout period) of 10 trading days is assumed constant during the optimization procedure for all trading assets. This indeed is in line with Basel rules on capital adequacy which stipulates that market risk usually has to be measured using longer horizons for regulatory purposes.

While in Case Study (1) diverse asset allocation percentages are postulated, in Case Study (2), all equity assets position is centered in one market index that has, under adverse market conditions, the highest daily return volatility, that is, the Dubai Financial Market General Index (DFMGI). Finally, in Case Study (3) and Case Study (4), the influence of short sales of the sample stocks (or stock market indexes) is also contemplated by randomly short-selling certain stocks.

The principal effect of diversification on LVaR downside limits setting seems to be through the long-only Case Study (1), that is, with uneven asset allocation. On the other hand, using empirical correlations only, we can stress that the highest downside LVaR figures, which are obtained from the optimization engine, are for Case Study (3), i.e., when the trading budget is allocated between long- and short-sales equity positions. Nonetheless, for correlation factors other than empirical (that is, $\rho = +1$ and 0), the optimization results

Table 1. Downside-risk parameters (LVaR limits threshold) in AED and with different correlation factors (ρ) (simulation under the assumption of normal market conditions).

Downside LVaR Limits Threshold with Different Correlation Factors	ρ **= Empirical**	$\rho = +1$	$\rho = 0$
Long-only Case Study 1	6,401,699	10,777,025	4,908,240
Long-only Case Study 2	15,111,606	15,111,606	15,111,606
Long/short-sales Case Study 3	21,553,941	7,832,512	22,772,680
Long/short-sales Case Study 4	15,414,438	19,433,231	12,775,513

Note: In all the above optimization case studies for the assessment of downside risk-budgeting threshold, the liquidity horizons for all equity indexes are assumed 10 trading days and in line with Basel accord on capital adequacy regulations.

Table 2. Downside-risk parameters (LVaR limits threshold) in AED and with different correlation factors (ρ) (simulation under the assumption of crisis market conditions).

Downside LVaR Limits Threshold with Different Correlation Factors	ρ **= Empirical**	$\rho = +1$	$\rho = 0$
Long-only Case Study 1	37,457,121	63,967,200	28,728,113
Long-only Case Study 2	95,417,112	95,417,112	95,417,112
Long/short-sales Case Study 3	125,538,018	60,978,300	131,830,223
Long/short-sales Case Study 4	87,355,735	92,984,460	76,297,610

Note: In all the above optimization case studies for the assessment of downside risk-budgeting threshold, the liquidity horizons for all equity indexes are assumed 10 trading days and in line with Basel accord on capital adequacy regulations.

are quite mixed and spread between Case Studies 2, 3, and 4 respectively as presented in the gray-shaded areas of Tables 1 and 2.

As a conclusion of these empirical case studies, the asset management entity can set the maximum daily downside LVaR threshold limits for their structured equity portfolios as follows:

- Maximum daily downside LVaR threshold limit under normal market conditions = AED 21,553,941.

- Maximum daily downside LVaR threshold limit under crisis market conditions = AED 125,538,018.
- Maximum daily volume limit = AED 200,000,000 (between long-only and short-sales trading positions).
- The maximum liquidity horizons (unwinding periods) of all equity indexes are set for 10 trading days and in line with Basel accord on capital adequacy regulations.

It should be noted here that the above maximum downside LVaR trading threshold limits are in their equivalent UAE dirham (AED) values at the prevailing foreign exchange rates of the other GCC countries against the UAE dirham.

3.2 Reinforcement machine learning for the computation of investable portfolios under crisis market scenarios

For more than five decades, a wide body of knowledge has been accumulated about the performance, strengths, and weaknesses of Markowitz's (1952) classical mean–variance approach when applied to equity portfolios. However, much less is known about portfolio optimization techniques in emerging equity markets, particularly under austere and crisis-driven market conditions (Al Janabi, 2013, 2015). Likewise, and given the fact that mean–variance optimizers have serious financial deficiencies (which could often lead to financially meaningless *optimal* portfolios) and since asset-allocation decision is the most fundamental issue facing portfolio managers who invest across multiple asset classes, the aim of this research chapter is to look at the scenario optimization problem from a different realistic operational angle.[2]

As such, the focus in this work is on the forecast of risk-adjusted-returns measure, rather than on expected returns for two reasons: first, several studies have analyzed the forecasts of expected returns in the context of mean–variance optimization (see, for instance,

[2]It is well documented (Michaud, 1989) that mean–variance optimizers, if left to their own devices, can sometimes lead to unintuitive portfolios with extreme positions in asset classes. Consequently, these "optimized" portfolios are not necessarily well diversified and exposed to unnecessary *ex post* risk (Michaud, 1989).

Best and Grauer, 1991). The common opinion is that expected returns are not easy to forecast and that the optimization process is very sensitive to these variations. Second, there exists a general notion that risk-adjusted returns, in a wide sense, are simpler to assess than expected returns from historical data (Al Janabi, 2013). Set against this background, in this work, we develop a model for optimizing portfolio risk–return with LVaR constraints using realistic operational and financial scenarios and conduct a simulation study on optimizing equity portfolios of the six GCC stock markets. The simulation study shows that the optimization algorithm, which is based on quadratic programming (QP) techniques, is very stable and efficient in handling different liquidity horizons and correlation factors.

Essentially, our approach is a robust improvement to the classic Markowitz (1952) mean–variance approach, where the original risk measure, variance, is replaced by LVaR algorithms. The task is attained here by minimizing LVaR while requiring a minimum expected return subject to several financially meaningful operational constraints. Thus, by considering different expected returns, we can generate an optimal LVaR frontier. Alternatively, we can also maximize expected returns while not allowing for large risks. For the purpose of this study, the optimization problem is formulated as follows:

It is possible to compute from Eqs. (2), (4), and (5) the minimum LVaR necessary to support current asset management operation by solving for the following quadratic programming objective function:

$$\begin{aligned}\text{Minimize: } \mathrm{LVaR}_{P_{\mathrm{adj}}} &= \sqrt{\sum_{i=1}^{n}\sum_{j=1}^{n} \mathrm{LVaR}_{i_{\mathrm{adj}}}\,\mathrm{LVaR}_{j_{\mathrm{adj}}}\,\rho_{i,j}} \\ &= \sqrt{|\mathrm{LVaR}_{\mathrm{adj}}|^{T}\,|\rho|\,|\mathrm{LVaR}_{\mathrm{adj}}|} \qquad (11)\end{aligned}$$

The above objective function can be minimized subject to operational and financial budget constraints as specified by the portfolio manager and as indicated in Eqs. (7)–(10).

Against this backdrop, the empirical optimization process is based on the definition of LVaR as the minimum possible loss over a specified time horizon within a given confidence level. The iterative optimization modeling algorithm solves the problem by finding the market positions that minimize the loss, subject to the fact that all constraints are satisfied within their boundary values. Further, in all cases, the liquidation horizons (closeout periods) indicated earlier are assumed constant throughout the optimization process. For the sake of restraining the optimization algorithm and thereafter its analysis, a volume trading position limit of 10 million AED is assumed as a constraint, that is the equity trading entity must keep a maximum overall market value of diverse equities of no more than 10 million AED (between long- and short-sales positions). As such, Figure 1 provides evidence of the empirical LVaR optimal frontier (under 10-day liquidation horizons and for crisis market conditions) defined using a 97.5% confidence level. As mentioned above, the optimal portfolio selection is performed by relaxing the short-sales constraint, for the different equity assets. On the other hand, optimal portfolios cannot always be attained (e.g., short sales without realistic lower boundaries on x_i) in the day-to-day real-world portfolio management operations and, hence, the portfolio manager should establish proactive investable portfolios under realistic and restricted dynamic budget constraints, detailed as follows:

- The total trading volume (between long and short-sales equity trading positions) of any investable portfolio is 10 million AED.
- For any investable portfolio, the asset allocation for a long equity trading position varies from 10% to 100%.
- For any investable portfolio, the asset allocation for short-sales equity trading position varies from −10% to −60%.

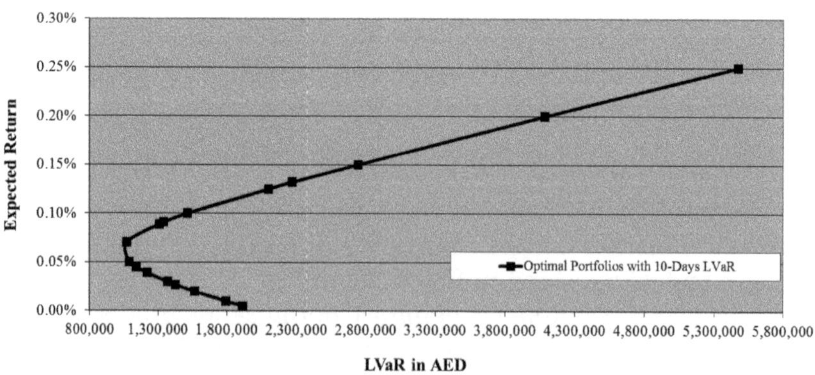

Figure 1. Optimal portfolios with 10-days LVaR technique (case of long and short-sales positions under crisis market conditions).

- All liquidity horizons (closeout periods) for all equities are kept constant and in accordance with the following values:
  (a) Liquidity Horizon (Closeout Period) of the DFMGI Index = 2 Days.
  (b) Liquidity Horizon (Closeout Period) of the ADX Index = 3 Days.
  (c) Liquidity Horizon (Closeout Period) of the BSEX Index = 4 Days.
  (d) Liquidity Horizon (Closeout Period) of the KSEGI Index = 3 Days.
  (e) Liquidity Horizon (Closeout Period) of the MSM30 Index = 4 Days.
  (f) Liquidity Horizon (Closeout Period) of the DSM Index = 3 Days.
  (g) Liquidity Horizon (Closeout Period) of the TASI Index = 2 Days.

- Overnight volatilities under crisis market notions are estimated as the maximum historical-simulation events with the highest downside risk. These conditional volatilities are kept constant throughout the optimization process and in accordance with the following values:
  (a) Conditional Volatility of the DFMGI Index = 12.16%.
  (b) Conditional Volatility of the ADX Index = 7.08%.
  (c) Conditional Volatility of the BSEX Index = 3.77%.
  (d) Conditional Volatility of the KSEGI Index = 3.74%.
  (e) Conditional Volatility of the MSM30 Index = 8.70%.
  (f) Conditional Volatility of the DSM Index = 8.07%.
  (g) Conditional Volatility of the TASI Index = 11.03%.

Now the asset allocation weights are allowed to take negative or positive values, however, since arbitrarily high or low percentages have no financial logic, we determined to introduce lower and upper boundaries for the weights and in accordance with reasonable trading practices. Furthermore, for comparison purposes and since the endeavour in this work is to minimize LVaR under crisis market prospects subject to specific expected returns, we decide to plot LVaR versus expected returns and not the reverse, as is commonly done in the various modern portfolio management literature. As a result,

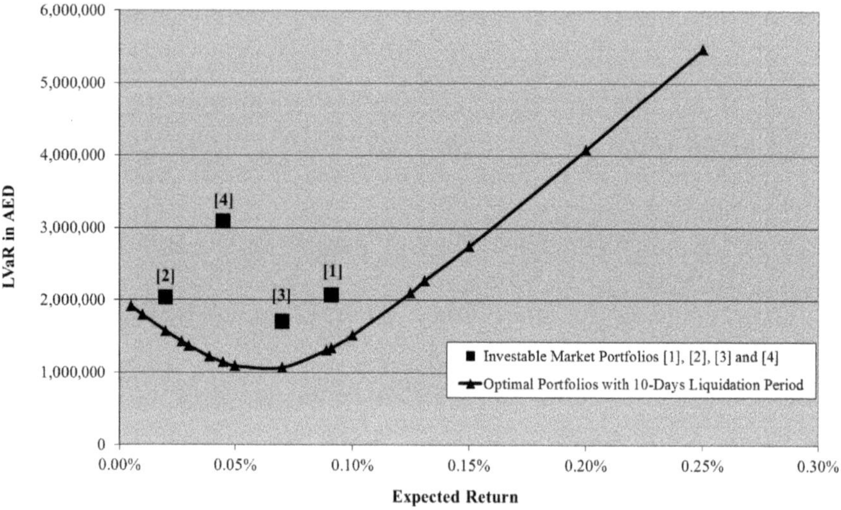

Figure 2. Optimal and investable portfolios with LVaR technique (case of long and short-sales positions under crisis market conditions).

it is worthy of note that the four benchmark investable portfolios (investable portfolios [1], [2], [3], and [4]) are not positioned near the optimal frontier as indicated in Figure 2. This is because financially and operationally real-world investment considerations make it unlikely that an investment portfolio will behave exactly as theory predicts under crisis-driven market's perspectives. Imperfections such as restriction on long- and short-sales trading positions, total trading volume, and liquidation horizons make it unlikely to create an optimal equity trading portfolio (Al Janabi, 2013). Thus, the portfolio manager should apply active strategies in order to earn excess returns, particularly under adverse market perceptions. These considerations are especially relevant for individual portfolio managers who may spread their trading positions across a few securities. In this way, portfolio managers should employ appropriate downside-risk measures which allow them to make prompt decisions which would produce a risk budget lower than a specific target. Thus, this analysis is substantially a generalized enhancement to the classical Markowitz's (1952) analysis that permits one to determine and verify the asymmetric aspects of risk and investable portfolios under crisis market notions.

4 Concluding Remarks

The outcomes of the results of this research study on the Gulf Cooperation Council (GCC) stock markets advocate that while there is a strong deviation from normality in the distribution of daily assets return, this matter can be addressed without the necessity of complex mathematical and analytical processes. In effect, it is feasible to handle these issues for equity cash assets with the clear-cut use of a closed-form parametric method within a matrix-algebra arrangement, along with the integration of a credible stress-testing tactic (under adverse crisis market conditions), as well as by complementing the risk analysis with a rational illiquidity risk factor that considers real-world trading situations all the way through the closeout period.

For this purpose, in this research chapter, a robust optimization technique for the assessment of illiquidity of both short-sales and long trading positions is incorporated. In contrast to other commonly used liquidity models, the liquidity technique that is applied in this work is more appropriate for real-world trading practices since it considers selling small fractions of the long/short trading securities on a daily basis. Further, this liquidity model can be implemented for the entire portfolio or for each individual security within the equity trading portfolio. Indeed, the developed methodology and risk assessment algorithms can aid in progressing risk management practices in emerging markets and above all in the wake of the 2007–2009 credit crunch and the ensuing financial upheavals.

In a nutshell, the attained empirical results can have many practical uses and applications and could aid in overcoming some of the shortcomings of traditional VaR methods and the classical mean–variance approach, above all in light of the aftermaths of the 2007–2009 global financial meltdown. In conclusion, the proposed optimization algorithms, investment portfolio analytics, and the attained empirical outcomes can have important practical uses and applications for portfolio managers and risk managers, particularly in the wake of the 2007–2009 global financial crisis. For instance, the proposed modeling techniques and reinforcement machine learning optimization algorithms can be of benefit to risk managers and portfolio managers for the computation of asset allocations for multiple-asset investable portfolios. Likewise, the modeling techniques and algorithms can be applied in optimization processes for determining rational asset management portfolios and in pacing maximum downside LVaR boundaries under different market circumstances. In addition, the recommended risk management modeling techniques and optimization algorithms can have key applications in reinforcement machine learning, expert systems, smart financial functions, Internet of Things (IoT), and financial technology (FinTech) in big data ecosystems.

Acknowledgment

Recognition of the original source of previous publications: This chapter is partially based on earlier research papers conducted by the same author (Mazin A. M. Al Janabi) and published by Springer, World Scientific Publishing (WSP), and Elsevier, under the following titles:

1. Al Janabi, M.A.M. (2013). Optimal and coherent economic-capital structures: Evidence from long and short-sales trading positions under illiquid market perspectives. *Annals of Operations Research*, 205(1): 109–139.
2. Al Janabi, M.A.M. (2015). Scenario optimization technique for the assessment of downside-risk and investable portfolios in post-financial crisis. *International Journal of Financial Engineering*, 2(3): 1550028-1–1550028-28.
3. Al Janabi, M.A.M. (2014). Optimal and investable portfolios: An empirical analysis with scenario optimization algorithms under crisis market prospects. *Economic Modelling*, 40: 369–381.

References

Al Janabi, M.A.M. (2008). Integrating liquidity risk factor into a parametric value at risk method. *Journal of Trading*, 3(3), 76–87.

Al Janabi, M.A.M. (2011). A generalized theoretical modeling approach for the assessment of economic capital under asset market liquidity risk constraints. *Service Industries Journal*, 31(13 & 14): 2193–2221.

Al Janabi, M.A.M. (2012). Optimal commodity asset allocation with a coherent market risk modeling. *Review of Financial Economics*, 21(3): 131–140.

Al Janabi, M.A.M. (2013). Optimal and coherent economic-capital structures: Evidence from long and short-sales trading positions under illiquid market perspectives. *Annals of Operations Research*, 205(1): 109–139.

Al Janabi, M.A.M. (2014). Optimal and investable portfolios: An empirical analysis with scenario optimization algorithms under crisis market prospects. *Economic Modelling*, 40: 369–381.

Al Janabi, M.A.M. (2015). Scenario optimization technique for the assessment of downside-risk and investable portfolios in post-financial crisis. *International Journal of Financial Engineering*, 2(3): 1550028-1–1550028-28.

Al Janabi, M.A.M. (2021a). Is optimum always optimal? A revisit of the mean-variance method under nonlinear measures of dependence and non-normal liquidity constraints. *Journal of Forecasting*, 40(3): 387–415.

Al Janabi, M.A.M. (2021b). Multivariate portfolio optimization under illiquid market prospects: A review of theoretical algorithms and practical techniques for liquidity risk management. *Journal of Modelling in Management*, 16(1): 288–309.

Al Janabi, M.A.M. (2022). Optimization algorithms and investment portfolio analytics with machine learning techniques under time-varying liquidity constraints. *Journal of Modelling in Management*, 17(3): 864–895.

Al Janabi, M.A.M., Arreola-Hernández, J., Berger, T., and Nguyen, D.K. (2017). Multivariate dependence and portfolio optimization algorithms under illiquid market conditions. *European Journal of Operational Research*, 259(3): 1121–1131.

Al Janabi, M.A.M., Ferrer, R., and Shahzad, S.J.H. (2019). Liquidity-adjusted value-at-risk optimization of a multi-asset portfolio using a vine copula approach. *Physica A: Statistical Mechanics and its Applications*, 536, Article 122579.

Almgren, R., and Chriss, N. (1999). *Optimal Execution of Portfolio Transaction.* Working Paper, Department of Mathematics, The University of Chicago.

Arreola-Hernandez, J., and Al Janabi, M.A.M. (2020). Forecasting of dependence, market and investment risks of a global index portfolio. *Journal of Forecasting*, 39(3): 512–532.

Arreola-Hernandez, J., Al Janabi, M.A.M., Hammoudeh, S., and Nguyen, D.K. (2015). Time lag dependence, cross-correlation and risk analysis of U.S. energy and non-energy stock portfolios. *Journal of Asset Management*, 16(7): 467–483.

Arreola-Hernandez, J., Hammoudeh, S., Khuong, N.D., Al Janabi, M.A.M., and Reboredo, J.C. (2017). Global financial crisis and dependence risk analysis of sector portfolios: A vine copula approach. *Applied Economics*, 49(25): 2409–2427.

Asadi, S., and Al Janabi, M.A.M. (2020). Measuring market and credit risk under solvency II: Evaluation of the standard technique versus internal models for stock and bond markets. *European Actuarial Journal*, 10(2): 425–456.

Bangia, A., Diebold, F., Schuermann, T., and Stroughair, J. (2002). Modeling liquidity risk with implications for traditional market risk measurement and management. In Figlewski, S., and Levich, R. M. (Eds.), *Risk Management: The State of the Art*. The New York University Salomon Center Series on Financial Markets and Institutions, Vol. 8. Springer, Boston, MA, USA, pp. 3–13.

Best, M.J., and Grauer, R.R. (1991). On the sensitivity of mean-variance-efficient portfolios to changes in asset means: some analytical and computational results. *Review of Financial Studies*, 4: 315–342.

Grillini, S., Sharma, A., Ozkan, A., and Al Janabi, M.A.M. (2019). Pricing of time-varying illiquidity within the Eurozone: Evidence using a Markov switching liquidity-adjusted capital asset pricing model. *International Review of Financial Analysis*, 64: 145–158.

Jarrow, R., and Subramanian, A. (1997). Mopping up liquidity. *Risk*, 10(12): 170–173.

Madoroba, S.B.W., and Kruger, J.W. (2014). Liquidity effects on value-at-risk limits: Construction of a new VaR model. *Journal of Risk Model Validation*, 8: 19–46.

Markowitz, H. (1952). Portfolio selection. *Journal of Finance*, 7(1): 77–91.

Michaud, R.O. (1989). The Markowitz optimization enigma: Is 'optimized' optimal? *Financial Analysts Journal*, 45(1): 31–42.

Morgan Guaranty Trust Company. (1994). *RiskMetrics-Technical Document*. Morgan Guaranty Trust Company, Global Research, New York.

Sanders, D.R. (2002). The role of value-at-risk in purchasing: An application to the foodservice industry. *The Journal of Supply Chain Management* (Spring Issue): 38–45.

Saunders, A., and Cornett, M. (2008). *Financial Institutions Management*, 6th edn. McGraw Hill International Edition, Singapore.

Uddin, M.S., Chi, G., Al Janabi, M.A.M., and Habib, T. (2022). Leveraging random forest in micro-enterprises credit risk modeling for accuracy and interpretability. *International Journal of Finance & Economics*, 27(3): 3713–3729.

Weiß, G.N.F., and Supper, H. (2013). Forecasting liquidity-adjusted intraday value-at-risk with vine copulas. *Journal of Banking & Finance*, 37(9): 3334–3350.

https://doi.org/10.1142/9781800615212_0011

Chapter 11

Deep Learning in Insurancc: An Incremental Deep Learning Approach for Pricing Prediction Strategy in the Insurance Industry

Alaa Tareq Mohamed[*,‡], **Riadh Ksantini**[†,§] **and Jihcnc Kaabi**[†,¶]

[*]*College of Science, Department of Postgraduate Studies, University of Bahrain, Bahrain, Kingdom of Bahrain*
[†]*College of IT, Department of Computer Science, University of Bahrain, Bahrain, Kingdom of Bahrain*
[‡]*202012448@stu.uob.edu.bh*
[§]*rksantini@uob.edu.bh*
[¶]*jkaapi@uob.edu.bh*

Abstract

Deep learning is a type of machine learning known for its competitive advantage in discovering complex relationships in all data types. However, the insurance applications of deep learning were used for damage detection and churn prediction applications, while the premium prediction received low attention from previous researchers. This study aims to build an incremental deep learning model to predict insurance premiums. The model contributes to the previously studied Usage-Based Insurance (UBI) concept. We propose a deep learning model consistent with the UBI concept that considers the available factors affecting the premium to predict the insurance premium. The proposed model consists of two parts. Part one is the Convolutional Neural Network (CNN) for deep features extraction. Part two is the Support Vector Regression (SVR) built on the extracted deep features to predict the premium. The proposed model is called CNN-SVR after combining the two parts of

CNN and SVR. The dataset was collected from an insurance company to train the proposed model and evaluate its performance compared to the other classical models adopted previously by other researchers, namely the Neural Network (NN), Random Forests (RF), Decision Trees (DT), Linear Regression and Support Vector Regression (SVR). The model performance evaluation was achieved using some metrics and the execution time needed to add a new data point to the model. The selected metrics are the Mean Squared Error (MSE), Root Mean Squared Error (RMSE), Mean Absolute Percentage of Error (MAPE), Explained Variance (EV), Correlation Coefficient (R), and t-test. The proposed CNN-SVR model reported the best averages among the other models of 1363.935 MSE, 36.838 RMSE, 18.774 MAE, 11.940 MAPE, 0.957 R, and $1 - p$ values close to 1 in the t-test. The proposed incremental model reported a faster execution time than the classical models, which need to be retrained fully to add a new data point. The study concluded that CNN-SVR model outperforms the other models in prediction performance and execution time, which supports the hypothesis. A possible future direction for this study is to use a larger dataset with more factors affecting the premium for a better contribution to the UBI and predictions.

Keywords: CNN, deep features, incremental SVR, prediction, insurance, UBI.

1 Introduction

Pricing insurance policy is an essential step that strengthens the insurance companies' positions and holds their competitive advantage within the operating market by offering policies at competitive and fair prices. From a customer's point of view, price is a factor and comparing it with others is a tool that affects the buying decision.

Currently, the prices of an insurance policy (premium) in most countries are calculated using classical ways of setting rates to different risk categories and adding charges to the additional services. This calculation differentiates the level of risk that an insurance company will be exposed to, which considers numerical factors like the vehicle value and claims history. The premium includes the additional services requested by the customer at a fixed price. The rates can vary according to the category of risks specified by the insurance company.

Researchers have discussed and introduced a new Generalized Linear Model (GLM) to price the insurance policies that overcome the issue of classical rate pricing. The classical rate pricing disregards differentiating between customers based on their behavior, creating unfair and inaccurate pricing, especially within motor insurance (Wamwea *et al.*, 2015). Other researchers have also proposed a behavior-based classification model using Convolution Neural Networks (CNN) to classify the customers based on their behavior to predict the grade to price the motor insurance accordingly (Yan *et al.*, 2020).

Although the pricing of an insurance policy lies within the actuarial framework using the actuaries' approaches in estimating the future costs to price the insurance product, the calculations need a model that works well with the dynamic and highly nonlinear real datasets.

Moreover, having reviewed the literature related to deep learning applications within the financial institutions, insurance companies have received relatively low attention from researchers than the banking and investment sectors in terms of the number of studies and DL applications.

Previous researchers have adopted many models using regression and classification learning to replace the traditional pricing techniques. To the best of our knowledge, none of them used incremental Deep Learning (DL) feature extraction to train the Support Vector Regression (SVR) model for price prediction, although, in recent years, the development of DL marked an enormous success in applications in almost all industries. Also, incremental learning has proven good results for highly nonlinear, real-time, and dynamic data prediction.

There are many types of insurance policies sold and services offered by an insurance company, such as property, marine, and motor insurance. However, researchers usually apply methods to motor insurance datasets that yield the highest income within the insurance sector. Motor insurance is also compulsory for all drivers or vehicles that operate in public in many jurisdictions, including the Kingdom of Bahrain.

The abovementioned motivations developed the need to propose an advanced model that caters for predicting the price of an insurance policy based on many factors in a dynamic dataset. The algorithm and results of the adopted method in this study (CNN-SVR) compared to classical batch learning methods of the previous studies are discussed in detail in this chapter.

An incremental DL approach that predicts the premium of motor insurance policies is proposed and compared with other classical batch Machine Learning (ML) models. All models used the available factors affecting the insurance premium, such as driver age, vehicle model, year of manufacture, vehicle type, and value of vehicle.

Finally, to the best of our knowledge, the adopted strategy in this study, the premium prediction, is the first to be used and applied on an insurance industry dataset and can outperform the classical batch DL methods used in previous studies to solve prediction problems. The adopted model extracts the deep features from a pre-trained Convolutional Neural Network (CNN) and trains a support vector regression to describe the real-time and highly nonlinear data.

1.1 Research setting

This study was conducted on the extracted 2019 transactions of the motor insurance underwriting. The datasets were extracted and provided by Solidarity Bahrain B.S.C, which is one of the Kingdom of Bahrain's leading insurance companies.

2 Literature Review

The conducted review is divided into two subsections: regression and classification applications. The review holds a specific interest in premium and price prediction applications within the sector as the basis of this study.

2.1 Classification in insurance

Within the insurance sector, insurance fraud detection, damage detection, customer retention, and claims prediction are the main issues that classification can resolve using historical data of various types, such as numerical, images, and video data.

The fraud detection models can minimize the losses an insurance company might incur from fraudulent transactions by avoiding the predicted fraud. The models can create an auto alert to the underwriters warning them about possible fraud to analyze the risk further and impose some warranties and exclusions on the customer at the underwriting assessment stage.

A study achieved by Itri *et al.* (2019) aimed to model the fraud and suspicious behavior of vehicle insurance policyholders through ML. The authors compared 10 algorithms: Random Forests (RF), AdaBoostM1, PART, J48, multilayer perceptron, decision table, logistic, SGD, naive Bayes, and SVM. The comparative results showed that the RF machine learning algorithm outperforms the other nine methods used to detect automobile insurance fraud. The comparison was made using four metrics, recall, precision, F-measure, and K-measure, which yielded 23.83%, 19.66%, 21.52%, and 99.46%, respectively, for the RF algorithm.

Researchers have adopted different methods to detect fraudulent transactions within the claims. A recent study done by Dhieb *et al.* (2020) reached a 7% higher accuracy than the previously adopted methods with the extreme gradient boosting (XGboost) machine learning algorithm applied to the motor insurance dataset. The study aimed to create an alert that informed the company about any possibility of a risky client and developed further to online learning emulating the blockchain using hyperledger fabric composer.

Subudhi and Panigrahi (2020) studied fraud detection on the motor dataset using the Genetic Algorithm-based Fuzzy C-Means (GAFCM). It is a supervised classifier applied to various algorithms. Researchers reported that the SVM applying the GAFCM outperforms the DT, Multi-Layer Perceptron (MLP), and Group Method of Data Handling (GMDH) algorithm. The performance comparison of the various models was made using three metrics: sensitivity, specificity, and accuracy. The SVM using the GAFCM reported 83.21%, 88.45%, and 87.02% for sensitivity, specificity, and accuracy.

On the other hand, the damage detection topic was popular in ML applications and essential at the stage of claims evaluation. Insurance companies can adopt damage detection models at many claims processing stages. Many insurance companies worldwide are moving towards implementing digitalization initiatives and reducing as many human interventions as possible in their daily work for an efficient process.

The models can be introduced as part of the claim registration process or during the vehicles' survey process to detect the damaged part and evaluate the level of damage.

Many studies conducted in this area mainly use the DL approaches as known by their ability to learn the features and analyze specific requirements from images, videos, and audio with high success rates.

Zhang *et al.* (2020) conducted a recent study to analyze the damaged area on a vehicle after the accident of 2,000 collected scratched vehicles images available online and from daily photographs under the conditions of normal light, weak light, close distance, multiple damage, strong exposure, and minor injury. The study concluded that the advanced detection algorithm (Mask RCNN) improved the previously adopted methods, with better average precision value and higher accuracy. The proposed method improved the mask accuracy by 1.89%, the detection accuracy by 2.15%, and the running speed by 0.52 fps compared to the normal Mask RCNN.

The third area to apply the classification within the insurance sector is customer retention and, in other words, churn prediction. Many companies are incorporating the level of the desired retention rates into their strategic plans and trying to reduce it as much as possible. Also, not only the insurance companies but all companies dealing with clients also plan to maintain a solid customer base, never lose any clients, and increase customer loyalty to their company. A helpful way to create and adopt a model that differentiates the characteristics of the clients the company might lose is to either focus on their needs or analyze the problem behind them, choosing not to continue with the company.

In insurance, a term when a policyholder decides not to renew his/her policy is called lapse. Many previous studies in the literature use the classification approach to determine the lapse risk by classifying a company's policyholders into risk levels.

In a previous study conducted by Spiteri and Azzopardi (2018), the accuracy rate reached 91.18% in forecasting the customer churn by using the RF model applied over the motor dataset collected from the Maltese insurance company. The study found that around 90% of the customers remain loyal for at least five years within the insurance company, and rarely a customer terminates a policy before the expiry date.

A study conducted by Xong and Kang (2019) developed a classification method that determines the lapse or surrender risk. The researchers compared four classification methods of NN, SVM, LR, and k-Nearest Neighbor (KNN) using the AUC criteria, which concluded that SVM outperforms the others at predicting the "bad" risks the lapsed policies on 800 observations from the Malaysian insurance company.

The fourth topic is claims prediction, which forms the basis for insurance pricing and is an essential part of the underwriting process within the insurance companies to assess the risk before accepting it. The claims prediction provides the necessary understanding for assessing the risk. All insurance industries aim to achieve a better understanding and closer prediction of the reality of whether a customer is going to file a claim or not.

So *et al.* (2020) studied the claims to capture the insured drivers' behavior to support the usage-based insurance idea whereby the policyholder should be charged a premium based on his/her history of driving. The premium is higher for the risky drivers with high claims frequency. The study focused on the imbalanced data because the claim's dataset contained zero claims, using the applied AdaBoost algorithm. The applied method outperforms the classical models to handle the dataset imbalances and classify the claims classes (0 claims, 1 claim, and 2+ claims). The results are presented in a confusion matrix, and the G-mean of the recall is 0.71 for the AdaBoost, which outperforms the other SMOTE RUSBoost and SMOTEboost models.

Abdelhadi *et al.* (2020) compared the performance of four models, ANN, DT, naïve Bayes, and XGBoost, to predict motor insurance claims in order to charge a proper and fair premium. The study concluded that the XGBoost obtained a higher accuracy of 92.53% using the publicly available insurance dataset on the Kaggle website.

Hanafy and Ming (2021) proposed that the AdaBoost model can accurately predict who is likely to file claims. The model outperforms the other seven methods used in the study: DT, bagging, and boosting methods, with an accuracy of 99.4%. Insurance companies can benefit from such models in charging a customer a higher premium after an alert from the prediction model that the customer might file a claim based on his characteristics. The underwriters can use the proposed model for a faster conclusion at the underwriting assessment stage.

The previously discussed studies use a variety of classification models ranging from the classical machine learning models to the DL models. A recent study by Yan *et al.* (2020) extracted the features from the DL approach of CNN and used those features to train the hull vector SVM to classify the customers based on their behavior. The study was conducted to replace the classical methods in pricing and come up with an appropriate pricing methodology. The study suggests that the underwriter considers at the pricing stage the grade obtained by the model representing the risk and behavior of the driver. The average accuracy rate obtained by the developed model is 86.1% using 10-fold cross-validation.

To sum up, most recent studies used the classification approaches in various areas of risk analyses, claims prediction, fraud detection, and damage detection. Only one study used DL with an objective to enhance the pricing strategy using classification approaches for customer grading (Yan *et al.*, 2020). Hence, a direction for future studies is to focus on the DL applications for pricing an insurance product.

A summary of the insurance-related works and the models applied previously by researchers using the machine learning classification approaches are presented in Table 1, along with the performance metrics used by the researchers.

2.2 Regression in insurance

The regression in insurance can solve many problems related to insurance, such as pricing an insurance policy, predicting costs, marketing, and fraud and severity detection.

Zhang and Walton (2019) developed the pricing model using the GLM, and Gaussian process and their study's initial findings on the pricing using a machine learning approach suggested that online machine learning algorithms are worth studying and future investigation and have the potential for insurance applications.

In addition to the studies on the motor insurance datasets, Rampal *et al.* (2020) applied an ensemble regression model to predict the price of health insurance policies. Their model was compared to four models: decision table, Gaussian process, linear regression, and zero R using different criteria of correlation coefficient Mean Absolute Error (MAE), Root Mean Squared Error (RMSE), relative absolute error, and Root Relative Squared Error (RRSE) which in all cases

Table 1. Overview of studies on classification applications within insurance.

Area	Related Work	Best Method	Performance Metric	Value
Fraud detection studies	Itri *et al.* (2019)	RF	Recall Precision F-measure K-measure	23.83% 19.66% 21.52% 99.46%
	Dhieb *et al.* (2020)	XGboost	Accuracy Precision Recall F1-score	99.25% 0.87 0.929 0.892
	Subudhi and Panigrahi (2020)	SVM using GAFCM	Sensitivity Specificity Accuracy	83.21% 88.45% 87.02%
Vehicle damage detection	Zhang *et al.* (2020)	Improved mask RCNN	Detection accuracy Mask accuracy Running time (fps)	96.68% 83.14% 4.78
Lapse and churn prediction	Spiteri and Azzopardi (2018)	RF	Accuracy	91.18%
	Xong and Kang (2019)	SVM	AUC	89.55%
Claims prediction	So *et al.* (2020)	AdaBoost	Recall	0.71
	Abdelhadi *et al.* (2020)	XGBoost	Accuracy ROC	92.53% 0.986
	Hanafy and Ming (2021)	AdaBoost	Sensitivity Specificity Accuracy	92.94% 99.82% 99.4%
Customer grading	Yan *et al.* (2020)	CNN-HVSVM	Accuracy	86.1%

the ensemble method outperforms the others with 0.97, 8.9, 36.35, 10.16, and 23.49, respectively.

Henckaerts *et al.* (2021) have published a study with an objective to develop a tariff plan using machine learning models which showed that after using several decision trees (simple regression trees, RF, and GBT), the GBT outperforms the typical GLMs, resulting in a more profitable tariff and less risk of adverse selection. The study compared the results using many aspects. The Gini index is one of the comparisons performed where the GBT achieved the minimal maximum Gini index of 3.93, and the GLM was in second place at 4.07 before the regression trees and RF.

A comparative study was conducted by Blier-Wong *et al.* (2021) to summarize the related work to the actuarial and insurance that uses machine learning and provide the status of development within this field. The study stated that several attempts were made towards implementing machine learning in insurance. However, few used Neural Networks (NN), and usually, the methods were applied to the motor insurance datasets.

At the beginning of 2022, a study was published by Lindholm *et al.* (2022) that uses the GLM and NN to develop a discrimination-free pricing model for the health insurance product. The study highlighted the importance of collecting the necessary policyholder's information, but it is a challenge in some companies due to concerns about policyholder's privacy.

Regression problems are not limited to pricing within insurance as in predicting the numerical values; the claims prediction is the second topic for regression application in insurance using several machine learning approaches.

In 2016, a study was conducted that used the Back Propagation Neural Network (BPNN) to model the claims frequency and severity of a Malaysian motor insurance dataset. After using several network structures, the study showed that the BPNN is successful in predicting due to the capability of the model in dealing with nonlinear data. The BPNN showed a Mean Absolute Percentage Error (MAPE) of the claims frequency of 0.2191 for the third party and 0.2169 for the own damage claims, and for the severity prediction, the MAPE is 0.6515 for the third-party claims and 0.3261 for the own damage claims (Yunos *et al.*, 2016).

The use of a GLM is widespread within insurance, but other methods can perform well. Duan *et al.* (2018) showed that the LR model on the Chinese insurance company motor data performs well when fitting the claim frequency and claim costs. The LR p-value of the residual deviance is 0.9419055, which could not deny the model hypothesis.

Within the context of claim prediction, Staudt and Wagner (2019) compared the ML models (RF and NN) with the traditional regression models (GLM and GAM) to predict the claims frequency and severity of the Swiss motor dataset. The results showed that the RF outperforms the other models under the RMSE with 0.893. Also, Dewi *et al.* (2019) studied the Allstate motor insurance dataset available on Kaggle. They applied the RF model to predict the claims frequency, showing a high success of 0.999 explained variance.

Zhou *et al.* (2020) studied the claims data, which contains many zero claims. Therefore, the study aimed to deal with significantly unbalanced data and, more specifically, zero-inflated data. The researchers developed a boosting-assisted Tweedie model to deal with the zero-inflated data that a standard and classical method would not work well on such data. The developed method called EMTboost outperformed all the classical models when comparing the results of Gini indices and Mean Absolute Deviation (MAD) under different circumstances and parameters.

Regression can also predict the conversion rates to understand the characteristics of the customers who most likely will buy a product, in other words, the rate of conversion from a quotation to a policy. Spedicato *et al.* (2018) studied the conversion and retention prediction on the motor liability cover quotations using traditional and machine learning models of the XGBoost, gradient boosting machine, RF, DL, and GLM. The models were used to predict the converted policies and then compared models using the log-loss and AUC metrics. The XGBoost performed well and is the best among the selected models, with 0.089 log-loss and 0.9064 AUC. Such a model can be applied in marketing and understanding any customer-based industry to focus on customers with high conversion rates.

From the above, most regression applications use the GLMs with a direction for fruitful machine learning applications in insurance. All listed references with the applied methodology on regression within the insurance industry are summarized in Table 2. Hence, the lack and gap of few studies applying the DL for pricing motivated us to develop an approach that predicts insurance premiums.

3 Methods and Procedures

The previously mentioned studies, models applied, and discussed applications within the insurance industry shaped the objectives, motivated the researchers to conduct this study, and helped design its theoretical framework.

As mentioned previously, many applications used the DL approach on the images' data type. For example, the images of the scratched vehicles within the insurance industry to locate the damages on the car and predict the damaged part using labeled images. This approach showed success with the high accuracy rates obtained

Table 2. Overview of studies on classification applications within insurance.

Area	Related Work	Best Model	Performance Metric	Value
Insurance pricing/ rating	Zhang and Walton (2019)	GLM and Gaussian process	—	—
	Rampal *et al.* (2020)	Ensemble regression	Correlation coefficient MAE RMSE RAE RRSE	0.97 8.9 36.35 10.16 23.49
	Henckaerts *et al.* (2021)	GBT	Gini indices	3.93
	Blier-Wong *et al.* (2021)	Overview & comparative study	—	—
	Lindholm *et al.* (2022)	GLM and NN	—	—
Claims prediction	Yunos *et al.* (2016)	BPNN	MAPE – severity MAPE – frequency	0.2191 0.6515
	Duan *et al.* (2018)	LR	p-value	0.9419
	Staudt and Wagner (2019)	RF	RMSE	0.389
	Dewi *et al.* (2019)	RF	Explained variance	0.999
	Zhou *et al.* (2020)	GBT	Gini indices Mean absolute Deviation	Best
Conversion	Spedicato *et al.* (2018)	XGBoost	Log-loss AUC	0.089 0.9064

in a previous study of 96.68% (Zhang *et al.*, 2020). On the other hand, the pricing of an insurance policy and premium predictions used various methods of regressions and NN but not through a DL approach.

In general, the objectives of modeling the pricing of an insurance product are presented in Figure 1. In contrast, factors such as the driver's age and model year affect and shape the policy premium. The relationship between factors and premiums can be explained and denoted by one of the ML models, which learns this relationship.

The aim and purpose of this study are to build an incremental DL model for predicting the premium of motor insurance policies that consider the factors affecting the premium within the collected numerical data. With such a model, an objective was set to fill a gap in the literature by applying a different model known for its high

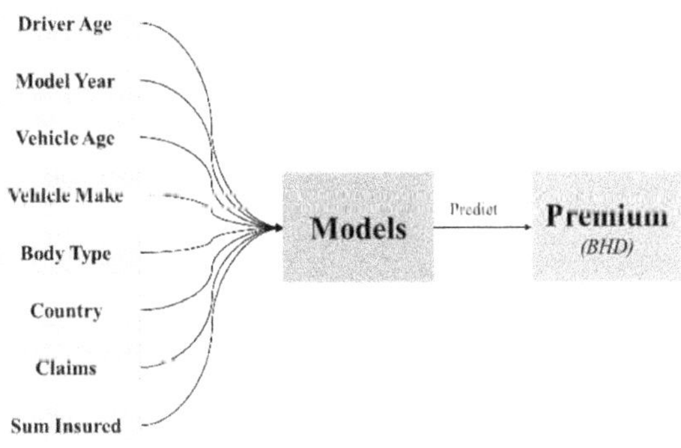

Figure 1. Process of premium prediction.

success in discovering nonlinear relationships and performing well on the actual numerical data, the CNN.

Having a pre-trained CNN on the part of the data to extract the deep features allows better understanding and fit to be carried forward to train an incremental SVR model used for premium prediction.

The theoretical framework of this study is outlined in Figure 2. After setting the objectives and direction of this study to build a prediction model, the framework starts with the collection of the motor underwriting insurance dataset.

The framework starts with the dataset collection obtained from Solidarity Bahrain B.S.C, a leading insurance company operating in the Kingdom of Bahrain. Second, explore the data and perform the data cleaning and preprocessing steps for a better prediction as they are real data.

Having cleaned data ready, the selected model and adopted strategy are then fitted to the preposessed dataset. The selected model consists of two stages: A and B. Stage A aims to build the one-dimensional CNN for deep features' extraction. In contrast, Stage B fits the incremental SVR on the extracted features for premium prediction. The adopted two-stage model of the convolutional neural network and support vector regression will be referred to as CNN-SVR for the rest of this study.

Besides the proposed CNN-SVR, other researchers selected different previously adopted models known for regression and prediction. Therefore, a selection of models was fitted on the same portion of

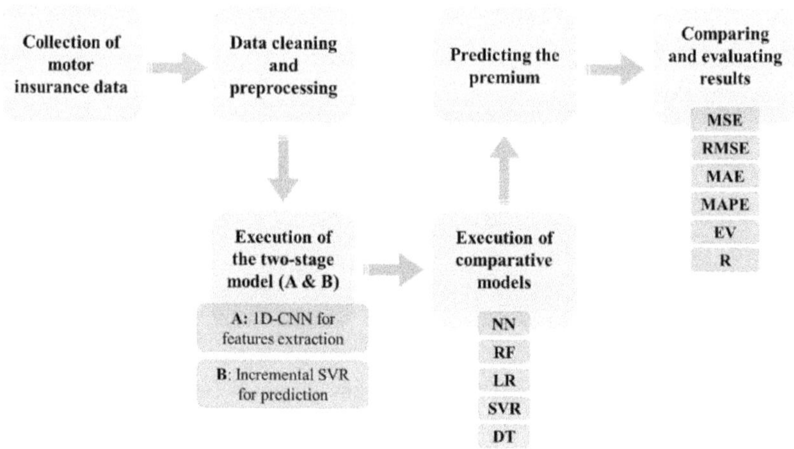

Figure 2. Process diagram detailing the adopted theoretical framework.

data to compare the performance of the CNN-SVR to the classical models, which are the NN, Ensemble Least Squares Tree Boosting (LSBoost), linear regression, SVR, and DT.

The final step in the framework is the evaluation of models in predicting the premium, which will take place after fitting all the models on the training dataset and predicting the premium of the testing dataset using all models. There are many evaluation techniques used for regression problems, but a selection of those techniques will be used to validate the performance of each method.

The selected evaluation techniques are the Mean Squared Error (MSE), Root Mean Squared Error (RMSE), MAE, MAPE, Explained Variance (EV), and regression correlation between the predicted values and the observed values (R) as evaluation techniques. The stated techniques were used to evaluate the performance of the CNN-SVR and the comparative models.

To ensure consistency in the model's outcome, the model training and evaluation process will take place twice on two different splits of the dataset. The details of the dataset splits, the evaluation metrics, and the results obtained are outlined in the preceding chapters of this book.

In addition to the above metrics, the CNN-SVR is an incremental model known to perform faster for a new prediction by updating the model with the information of the added point only rather than training a full dataset again. Therefore, the execution time of the models will also be recorded as a comparative tool for efficiency. An essential aspect of an online model is to have a fast outcome, especially for a customer-based company. It is not feasible for the insurance companies to wait too long for the training process to calculate the premium.

Following the above framework, the study's objective will be fulfilled: to build the CNN-SVR model and compare the performance with other classical methods. The built model will form a base for the premium prediction that could also be used on many types of data and factors.

The adopted strategy consisting of two parts was built to achieve the best predictions of the premium. The two parts are building the one-dimensional CNN and the incremental SVR compared to a selection of comparative models. The adopted models are explained separately as CNN and SVR.

3.1 Convolution neural network (CNN)

The CNN consists of two parts of the feature learning and fully connected layers. The first part of feature learning consists of a mathematical convolution technique that analyzes the input, e.g., images. In this part, two types of layers are available, namely, convolutions and pooling. The learning happens with convolution layers instead of matrix multiplications as in the classical NN.

There are many advantages of using the convolution layers in neural networks. Apart from the autodetection of the essential features of data, the advantages are the sparsity of connections and local connectivity or parameter sharing. Sparsity implies that the output of each layer depends on a few inputs rather than on the entire dataset. At the same time, the parameters sharing ensures efficient computations with all neurons sharing the weights at a feature map.

The second part of the CNN is the fully connected layer that takes the outcome from the convolution feature learning process and uses it for the prediction process. The fully connected layers extract the details from convolutions and have a complete connection between the nodes in the preceding and next layer. The last layer is responsible for the outcome.

The last part of the fully connected layers consists of weights, neurons, and biases representing the last linking point to the output layer where the classification or regression is happening.

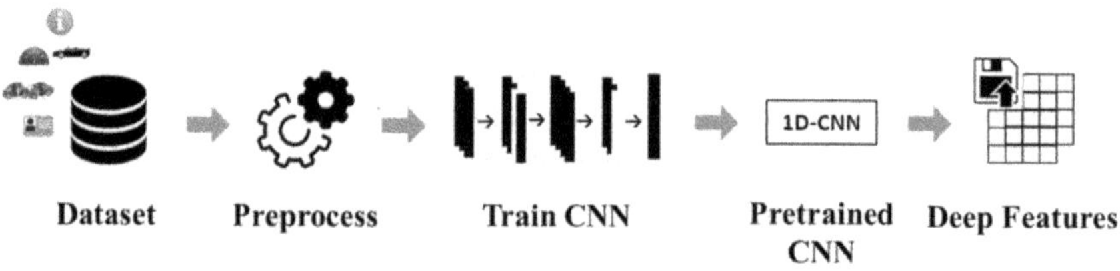

Figure 3. Steps of feature extraction (first stage).

In this study, the 1D-CNN was performed at the first stage, as presented in Figure 3. After cleaning and preprocessing the dataset that contains all the factors of interest which affect the premium of a motor insurance policy, the prepossessed data of the factors and premium will be the input to train the CNN.

The training process ensures choosing the best architecture of the 1D-CNN wherein many parameters can be changed in this step, such as the number and type of layers, optimizer function, number of epochs, and mini-batch size.

The best architecture can be achieved by having a minimal prediction error of the premium. The final chosen CNN having the lowest error is saved with all its weights and architecture for the deep feature extraction.

For better results and some improvement, there are some techniques followed by previous researchers, such as early training stopping and normalization of the input data to avoid the problem of overfitting. Normalization reduces the redundancy in the dataset, enhances the performance of models, provides consistency and flexibility in the design, and reduces the size of data for faster execution. It is discussed further in the data preprocessing stage.

The output of the first stage is a set of deep features representing the factors affecting the premium output from the pre-trained CNN. The deep features will be considered an input to the second stage of building the incremental SVR.

3.2 Incremental SVR

The difference between the SVM and SVR can be drawn from their objectives, as shown in Figure 4. The SVM is trying to reach a good fit and separation between classes with a low cost of instances laying on the specified margin. The SVR tries to fit the hyperplane with a

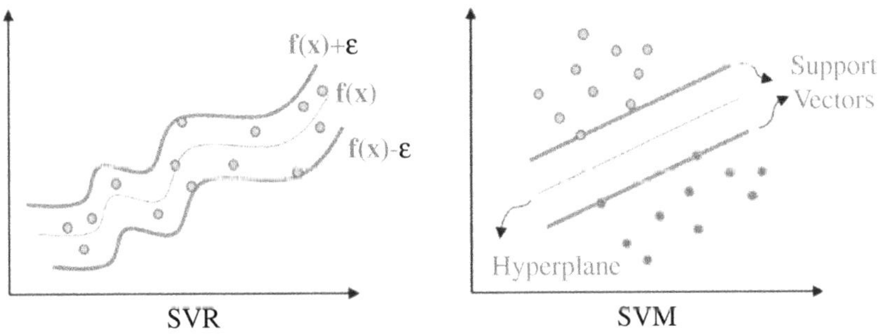

Figure 4. Comparison between SVR and SVM.

margin of minimum deviation on the observations where the epsilon defines the cost of instances laying outside the margin.

The epsilon (ε) value defines the accepted tolerance margin that any observations that fall within the margin will have a null cost, and no penalty is counted. Therefore, larger epsilon values represent a more comprehensive range of accepting errors in the model.

Within the daily work of an insurance company, many customers are requesting quotes on the spot, which requires immediate pricing. The training of a model will cause a delay in providing the customers and might affect the company's reputation. Therefore, incremental learning is proposed over the typical batch learning to have a prediction on the premium without training the whole model on the entire historical data. The main objective of incremental learning is to add knowledge to the trained model without forgetting the previous and existing knowledge.

The incremental learning would be faster for large datasets as there is no need to store extensive data to retrain the model again at the customer's request for a new prediction.

By applying the incremental model, the client information will be updated on the pre-trained model for prediction rather than retraining the whole model on the historical data, as Figure 5 explains the incremental part for a new prediction.

In incremental SVR, introducing a new data point represents the information about the customer. The information is the factor affecting the premium which is the predicted output. The incremental SVR prediction process adds those new factors to the historical knowledge that will best predict the premium based on the learned features from the data.

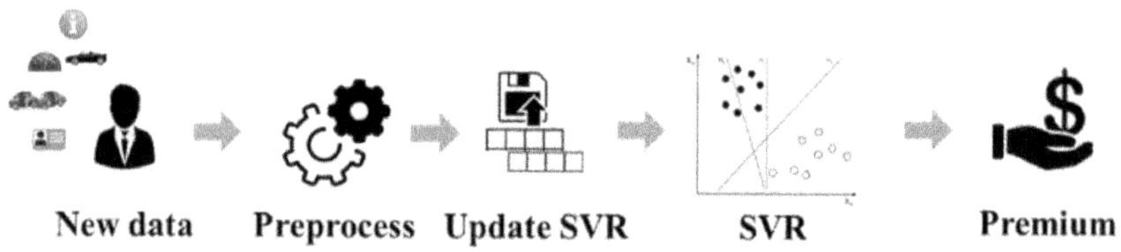

Figure 5. Incremental SVR process for premium prediction.

By performing the first and second stages on the dataset, the objective of this study to build an incremental model for premium prediction will be fulfilled. A selection of models gathered from the literature review will also be performed for premium prediction to compare the performance of the proposed model and the classical models.

4 Experiment Setting, Results, and Discussion

4.1 Data collection and preprocessing

The experimental study started with collecting an insurance dataset that contains factors affecting the insurance premium along with the actual premium charged. Solidarity Bahrain B.S.C provided us with the motor underwriting and claims data for the year 2019.

The company has provided the insurance data as comma-separated values (CSV) files, containing one year of quarterly reported claims and underwriting transactions. The underwriting dataset contains all the transactions recorded in a year, such as issuances, renewals, endorsements, and cancellations. Therefore, the transactions were filtered to keep only data related to the issuance of policies.

Additionally, the company has provided us with the claims data that contain the claim cost, which is one factor affecting the premium. Therefore, the claims data were also merged with the transactions data. The added columns contain an indicator of a claim and its associated cost. After performing data cleaning, the remaining data contain 32,879 rows and 9 columns.

Due to data confidentiality, only a sample of the filtered dataset is presented. Table 3 shows the first eight columns representing the

Table 3. A sample of the filtered insurance dataset.

Factors					Response			
Driver Age	**Model Year**	**Vehicle Age**	**Make of Vehicle**	**Vehicle Type**	**Country**	**Claims**	**Vehicle Value**	**Premium**
46	2018	2	Dodge charger	Saloon	US	0	11,730	268
...	...	...	...	...	...	...	...	...
37	2016	3	Toyota - Rav 4	Jeep	Japan	0	6,141	140
49	2016	3	GAC – GS5	Jeep	China	333	4,118	140

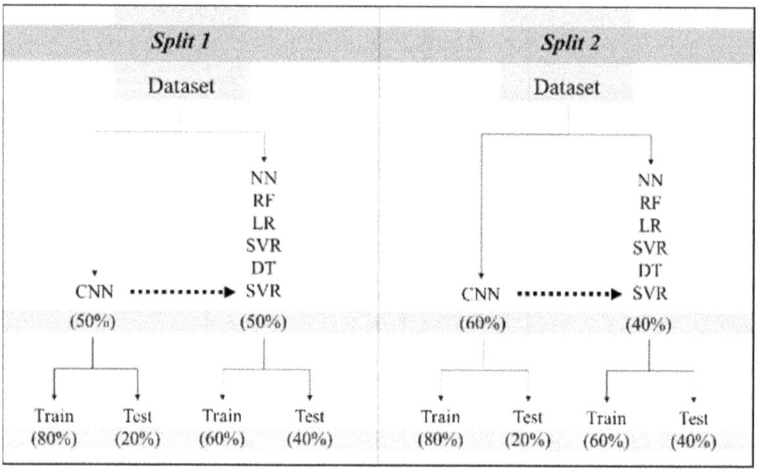

Figure 6. Dataset model training and testing splits.

values for eight factors. The last column represents the premium values.

The dataset was transformed and ready to build the models. Moving forward with it, the next step was to arrange the splits as the model needs to be trained and tested. Therefore, the training and testing processes were built on two different splits, as shown in Figure 6.

The first split (split 1) is 50:50, where 50% of the data was used to build the CNN and extract the deep features and the other 50% to train the incremental SVR on the deep features, as the figure shows a doted link between the CNN and SVR. The second 50% of the data was also used to build and compare the results of the CNN-SVR model with the other models of the NN, RF, linear regression, SVR, and DT.

Moreover, the first 50% of the CNN dataset was also divided into training and testing of 80:20. In other words, the training was on 80% and testing the model on 20% of the CNN data. Likewise, the second half of the dataset was divided into 60:40 for training and testing the SVR and comparative models.

Split 2 followed the same technique but with a 60:40 initial division of the CNN and SVR. The second split was introduced to validate further the results and strengthen the conclusion on the adopted model.

The dataset splits were done in MATLAB using the random split function. To ensure the consistency of the results at different random splits, five random splits were performed using different random seeds on both splits (a total of 10 runs). The random seeds were used to strengthen the conclusion of the best model after comparing the results with the other models.

4.2 Experiment setting

As mentioned previously, the CNN-SVR model consists of two parts. The first part is the CNN and the second is the incremental SVR. So, to reach an optimal structure of the CNN, several attempts in MATLAB were performed with different parameters on the training dataset of the two splits (1 and 2) to minimize the Mean Squared Error (MSE) of the testing dataset using Eq. (1):

$$\mathrm{MSE} = \frac{1}{n}\sum_{i=1}^{n}\left(Y_i - \hat{Y}_i\right)^2 \tag{1}$$

where n is the number of observations, Y_i is the actual value, and $\hat{Y}_i$ is the predicted value of observation i.

The MSE is the average of the sum of squares of the differences between the actual and predicted values. After several runs to the CNN, the final structure of the CNN, including the number of hidden layers, was fixed with the lowest MSE on the testing dataset.

The adopted CNN architecture after testing the lowest MSE is presented in Figure 7, which consists of nine layers. The first layer is the sequence input layer, followed by the first one-dimensional convolution layer, ReLU activation, and max-pooling layers. Similarly, the second one-dimensional convolution layer is followed by ReLU activation and Max pooling layers. The last layers are the fully connected and regression of the output.

The above CNN was performed on 50% of the dataset in split 1 and 60% of the dataset in split 2, out of which 80% for the training and 20% for testing the CNN. As the dataset contains eight factors, the input layer size was eight. Data normalization was performed using the Z-score, which subtracts the mean from the observation and divides the result by the standard deviation of the data, as illustrated in Eq. (2). It scales the values by their corresponding column mean

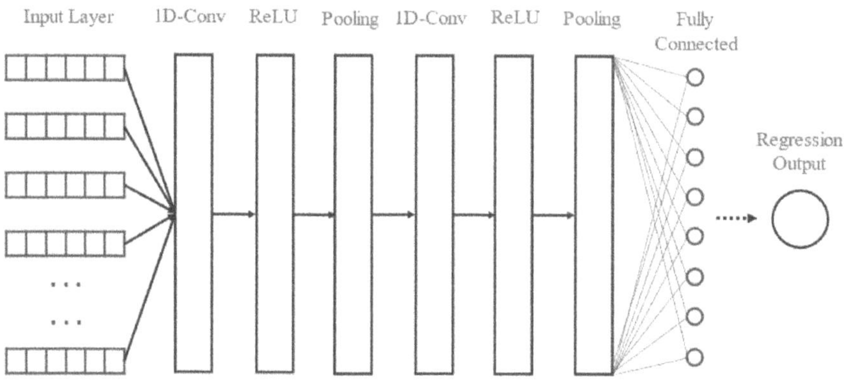

Figure 7. Layers of the adopted CNN.

and standard deviation:

$$z = \frac{x - \mu}{\sigma} \tag{2}$$

$$\text{where mean:} \quad \mu = \frac{1}{N}\sum_{i=1}^{N} x_i$$

$$\text{and standard deviation:} \quad \sigma = \sqrt{\frac{1}{N}\sum_{i=1}^{N}(x_i - \mu)^2}$$

where z is the normalized value, N is the number of observations, and x_i is the value of observation i.

The first one-dimensional convolution layer has a filter of size eight, while the second convolution layer filter size is two for each convolution layer, followed by a ReLU activation layer and Max pooling layer. This structure was achieved after several runs using different layers and parameters, which resulted in lower MSE on the 20% of the testing dataset.

There are several options to train CNN. The following are the best training options reached:

Optimizer: stochastic gradient descent with momentum (SGDM).
Execution Environment: NVIDIA GeForce MX330 GPU.
Epochs: 120.
Minibatch.
Shuffle.

The final structure of the CNN was saved for extracting the deep features from the last pooling layer. Only 50% of the dataset was used to build the CNN in split 1 and 60% in split 2. The remaining 50% and 40% of the data (split 1 and split 2) were spared for building the incremental SVR. The split is 60% for training the SVR and 40% for testing the SVR.

To train the incremental SVR, the first step focuses on extracting the deep features of the incremental SVR datasets from the pre-trained and saved CNN. The extracted features being the input to the incremental SVR were extracted from the last pooling layer, and therefore, the input data to train the incremental SVR were ready.

After having readied SVR datasets denoted by the deep features, the incremental SVR was trained using those extracted deep features from the CNN to predict the output of insurance premium. MATLAB optimizes the parameters of the SVR to reach the best-fit model.

The incremental model advantages allow storing the gained knowledge from the trained model on the historical data. Adding a new data point to the pre-trained model would not require retraining the whole model on the historical data. It requires updating the matrix of the incremental model with the new data point only.

On 40% of the testing dataset, the premiums were predicted and compared to the actual premiums using various metrics detailed in the upcoming sections of this chapter.

To further validate the efficiency of this study's results, the comparative models detailed in the following section were selected to predict the premium and compare the performance using the same metrics.

4.3 Comparative models

As a regression application, there are many classical models used previously by researchers for different prediction applications. However, for comparison purposes, the most famous models were selected. The selected models are NN, LSBoost, linear regression, SVR, and DT.

4.3.1 *Neural network (NN)*

The NN model was selected with a feedforward and fully connected layer for regression. The adopted NN used the loss function minimization of the limited-memory Broyden–Fletcher–Goldfarb–Shanno quasi-Newton algorithm (LBFGS) to minimize the MSE (Nocedal and Wright, 2006).

The structure of the NN starts with an input layer followed by a fully connected layer (FC), ReLU activation function, another FC layer, and finally, the output layer.

The standardization of input is also a method for faster and scaled execution which was performed before fitting the model on the data.

4.3.2 *Decision tree (DT)*

The second selected model is a decision tree (DT) on the input predictors to predict the response value and cross-validate the model using the 10-fold cross-validation method. The basic idea behind DT is splitting the dataset into subsets and, most likely, in the form of a tree. Building the DT on numerical values would split the data into ranges and conditions to reach the output.

4.3.3 *Linear regression*

The linear regression model was also selected for comparison. The linear regression is a simple model which performs exceptionally well on linearly separable datasets. The best-fit line of the linear model was chosen using the least MSE method.

4.3.4 *Support vector regression (SVR)*

The proposed model consists of the CNN and SVR models, so it is also worth discovering the performance of the SVR separately on the original dataset without using the deep features. Therefore, a support vector regression model was selected as one of the comparative models.

4.3.5 *Least squares boosting (LSBoost)*

One of the most popular models used previously by other researchers in insurance problems is the random forests, and therefore, the LSBoost model was selected to boost 100 regression trees.

The LSBoost returns a regression ensemble model to predict the response from the input table.

Finally, the prediction performance of the proposed CNN-SVR model compared to the models mentioned above is evaluated using various metrics outlined in the following section.

4.4 Evaluation metrics

After training the proposed and comparative models on the different splits, the resulting premium prediction compared to the actual premium of the testing datasets was reported and evaluated using several metrics. Each metric is defined and formulated as follows:

4.4.1 *Mean squared error (MSE)*

The MSE takes the square of the difference between the actual and the predicted values for each observation. After repeating for all observations, sum all the squared values and divide by the number of observations in the dataset, as explained in Eq. (3).

The MSE is a valuable tool to ensure a closer estimate of the actual values at the lower values of MSE:

$$\text{MSE} = \frac{1}{n}\sum_{i=1}^{n}(Y_i - \hat{Y}_i)^2 \tag{3}$$

4.4.2 *Root mean squared error (RMSE)*

One advantage to the root of the MSE is that it can be interpreted directly by the data unit for a better understanding of the resulting error. Moreover, RMSE is sensitive to significant and minor errors, and therefore, RMSE was selected to compare the error of the models using the formula in Eq. (4):

$$\text{RMSE} = \sqrt{\frac{\sum_{i=1}^{n}(Y_i - \hat{Y}_i)^2}{n}} \tag{4}$$

4.4.3 *Mean absolute error (MAE)*

The MAE measures the magnitude of the error regardless of its direction. The MAE was calculated for all the proposed and comparative models using Eq. (5) by taking the average of all the absolute errors to evaluate the proposed model. The error value is the difference between the actual and predicted values:

$$\text{MAE} = \frac{1}{n}\sum_{i=1}^{n} |Y_i - \hat{Y}_i| \tag{5}$$

4.4.4 *Mean absolute percentage error (MAPE)*

MAPE measures the percentage of error in the dataset to compare the performance of the models, which measures how far the predictions are from the actual dataset using Eq. (6):

$$\text{MAPE} = \frac{1}{n}\sum_{i=1}^{n} \left|\frac{Y_i - \hat{Y}_i}{Y_i}\right| \tag{6}$$

4.4.5 *Explained variance (EV)*

EV measures the proportion of variance of the dataset that the model accounts for using Eq. (7). The higher explained proportion indicates a better model:

$$\text{EV} = 1 - \frac{\sum_{i=1}^{n}(Y_i - \hat{Y}_i)^2}{\sum_{i=1}^{n}(Y_i\bar{Y}_i)^2} \tag{7}$$

4.4.6 *Correlation coefficient (R)*

The Correlation Coefficient (R) reports the correlation between the actual and predicted values by the model. R can be directly obtained from MATLAB after plotting the actual and predicted values.

At all the above-mentioned metric formulas (Eqs. (3)–(7)), n is the number of observations, Y_i is the actual value, and $\hat{Y}_i$ is the predicted value of observation i.

4.4.7 *Paired t-test*

The t-test calculates a number from a particular set of observations that quantifies whether the paired models are close or not based on initial hypotheses. The hypotheses are H_0, which presents the null hypothesis, and H_1, the alternative hypothesis.

The calculated number is the p-value which represents the probability that the null hypothesis H_0 is true. On the other hand, the 1 minus the p-value is the probability that the alternative hypothesis is true, where H_0 suggests no statistical or significant difference exists between the pair and H_1 signifies that the pairs are different.

For example, a p-value of 0.01 (1%) suggests that the alternative hypothesis is true, and there is a chance of 1% only that the difference happened by chance. In most cases, 5% is the accepted threshold to decide on the hypothesis, which is called the "significance level". The following steps present the process of the p-value calculation:

(a) Calculate the t-test of the pair using Eq. (8):

$$\text{Paired } t\text{-test } Z = \frac{\mu_1 - \mu_2}{\sigma/\sqrt{n}} \tag{8}$$

(b) Where, μ_1 and μ_2 are the mean of observations of the first and second lists, σ is the standard deviation, and n is the number of observations.
(c) Find the p-value from the t-test table.
(d) Compare the obtained value with the t-test table.

For a 5% significance level, if $Z < 0.05$, reject the null hypothesis and if $Z > 0.05$, accept the null hypothesis.

In this study, the 1 minus p-value was used to compare the difference between each pair of models. The pairs are between the adopted CNN-SVR and each comparative model. The test was conducted in MATLAB to conclude if there exists any statistical difference between each pair and that the results are not occurred by change to further strengthen the conclusion on the choice of the best model.

The following evaluation technique will be separately presented as it measures execution time.

4.4.8 *Execution time*

The last performed comparison is the execution time needed to add a new data point to each model. It measures the time needed to predict the premium of a new dataset in seconds. The time is helpful as the application of the premium prediction is an on-spot application where the premium output is needed immediately without any delay to offer the clients a policy quotation and update the model with new information.

5 Results and Discussion

Table 4 presents the average results of five runs in split 1 using different train and test data random partitioning. Similarly, Table 5 contains the averages of five runs at the second data split (split 2). Both tables present the evaluation of this study's proposed model and comparative models.

From Tables 4 and 5, the range of MSE obtained from all models was between 1363.935 and 2258.747, where the proposed CNN-SVR model holds the lowest MSE at 1454.628 in split 1 and 1363.935 in split 2. On the other hand, the DT model scored the highest MSE in both splits. These results were also extended to the RMSE by taking the root of the MSE for straightforward interpretation.

The RMSE, as interpreted by the data unit (BD), was relatively low, with values between 36.838 and 47.387 which indicates closer

Table 4. Split 1 comparative results of all models (average of 5 runs).

	Split 1						
Model	**MSE**	**RMSE**	**MAE**	**MAPE**	**EV**	**R**	**1-P**
CNN-SVR	**1454.628**	**37.939**	**18.488**	**11.940**	**0.915**	**0.957**	
NN	1820.959	42.354	21.351	13.475	0.883	0.948	0.9999
RF	2115.306	45.884	21.278	12.671	0.874	0.936	0.9999
LR	2065.948	45.205	25.856	15.900	0.878	0.940	0.9999
SVR	2095.306	45.566	24.829	14.941	0.878	0.941	0.9999
DT	2258.747	47.387	23.301	13.853	0.866	0.932	0.9999

Table 5. Split 2 comparative results of all models (average of 5 runs).

	Split 2						
Model	**MSE**	**RMSE**	**MAE**	**MAPE**	**EV**	**R**	**1-P**
CNN-SVR	**1363.935**	**36.838**	**18.774**	**12.717**	**0.912**	**0.955**	
NN	1613.269	40.085	21.079	13.969	0.895	0.948	0.9999
RF	1731.434	41.469	21.535	13.492	0.888	0.944	0.9999
LR	1898.410	43.527	26.243	16.626	0.877	0.938	0.9999
SVR	1939.835	43.977	24.987	15.530	0.876	0.939	0.9999
DT	2045.751	45.186	23.814	14.758	0.868	0.932	0.9999

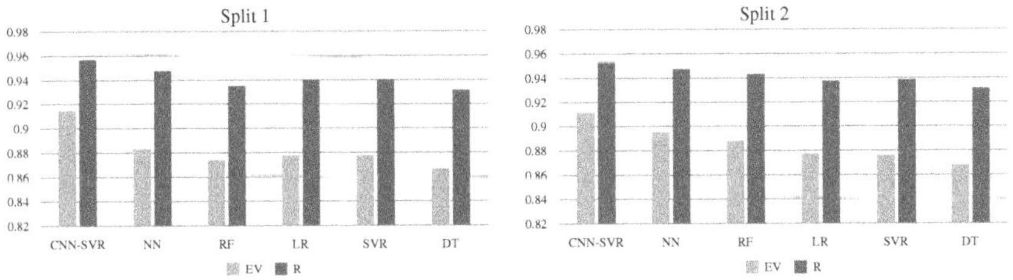

Figure 8 Comparison of EV and R of all models.

predictions to the actual values of the real data insurance premium using different models.

The results also show the lowest MAE and MAPE obtained by the CNN-SVR of 18.488 and 11.940, respectively, in split 1. Thus, it is noticeable from the tables that the adopted CNN-SVR model of this study outperforms the other comparative classical models in all the metrics outlined in bold text.

As mentioned previously, split 1 has 50% of the dataset for training the CNN, while split 2 has 60%, so split 2 has more data to train the model, and therefore, the CNN gained more information from the dataset.

The reported results show 1363.935 MSE in split 2 and lower than 1454.628 in split 1. The lower value of MSE at the split of more training data indicates that the error is reducing with increasing the size of CNN training data. In other words, the more input data and information gained by the CNN, the lower the error in predicting the premium.

Figure 8 summarizes the results of the EV and R obtained from all models. The figures show that CNN-SVR outperforms the other models with the highest R and EV. The NN model has an advantage over the other models in learning the complex relationships between the input and output; therefore, NN is the second-best model after the CNN-SVR.

Although the performance on several runs and splits was introduced to conclude that the best model is the CNN-SVR, the reported values of the evaluation metrics presented in Tables 4 and 5 have a narrow range between the highest and lowest scores. Therefore, to ensure that the evaluation values are not random, the t-test was performed, and $1 - P$ values were presented in the results tables.

Table 6. Comparison of the execution time.

Model	Type	Split 1 (Sec)	Split 2 (Sec)
CNN-SVR	**Incremental**	**0.0298**	**0.0265**
CNN-SVR	Batch	3.0320	2.4232
NN	Batch	1.2466	1.1751
RF	Batch	1.3274	1.0404
LR	Batch	0.5499	0.5234
SVR	Batch	1.5294	1.0142
DT	Batch	0.6977	0.4708

The t-test was done to compare the CNN-SVR to each other model as pairs. The 1-P scored values close to 1, indicating a solid rejection of the hypothesis that each pair is close. Alternatively, it can be concluded that there exists a statistical difference between the models in each pair, and the difference was not random.

The last evaluation technique to compare the overall performance of the adopted model is the execution time. Table 6 shows the execution time in seconds needed to add a new data point to each model. Adding a new data point represents including a new customer's information in the historical data.

The dataset was extracted for one year, containing relatively a small dataset compared to an insurance company's total historical data. Hence, the reported time needed to add a new point is low, as presented in Table 6, ranging between 0.0265 and 3.0230 seconds.

As presented in Table 6, the CNN-SVR is incremental, while other models are batch. The reported time shows a difference between the batch and incremental models whereby the latter performed faster in adding a new data point with 0.0298 seconds in split 1 and 0.0265 seconds in split 2. The other comparative models recorded higher execution times which makes the incremental CNN-SVR the best in terms of the execution time.

The faster performance of the incremental model was due to its learning way. The incremental learning will predict the output of the new data point and add it to the matrix of the pre-trained model without the need to re-train the model on the full dataset. In batch learning, adding a new data point requires re-training the model entirely with the new observation.

It can be concluded from the reported results that the incremental CNN-SVR model outperforms the batch CNN-SVR, NN, linear regression, SVR, RF, and DT in terms of the error rates metrics and execution time.

Deep learning also can scan large datasets and identify the correlations and the relationships between the input data and the required output. It is a complex model in terms of interpretability. However, the results show a high success where the proposed model outperforms the other classical models by reporting better evaluation metrics and execution time results.

6 Summary and Recommendations

This study touches on another area that received low attention from the researchers: premium prediction. The techniques to price an insurance policy were studied before by introducing a concept of pricing the insurance policy based on the customer behavior and were referred to as Usage-Based Insurance (UBI). This study provides the pathway to use deep learning, which examines an efficient deep learning model that can be further improved using many steps to contribute to the UBI idea.

The improvements can be made to the amount of data, as this study used one year data only. At the same time, it is recommended to consider insurance companies' historical data for many years. The model also can be further improved by considering other factors that affect the premium, such as mileage and driving behavior indicators considering speed and location.

To reach an optimal model that represents the UBI well, the company must set initial objectives first to plan the proper structure of needed data to start collecting it from their clients to base the pricing model on it. For example, in other jurisdictions, a tracker is placed in the customer's car to collect information related to the kilometre, speed, and location, which affects the premium.

After having a solid database with all the factors, the company can adopt a deep learning model to price its policies. As examined in this study, an acceptable choice of the model can be the proposed CNN-SVR as the model outperformed the other classical models of predicting the insurance premium.

In conclusion, the adopted model outperforms the other classical models with a recommendation to use a larger dataset and includes more data factors. Building a solid insurance database before implementing DL models for better and more efficient performance was also recommended.

The challenges to this study were the availability of the datasets and the quality of the currently available gathered data by the companies, which is based on the current way of pricing that does not support the UBI concept.

References

Abdelhadi, S., Elbahnasy, K., and Abdelsalam, M. (2020). A proposed model to predict auto insurance claims using machine learning techniques. *Journal of Theoretical and Applied Information Technology*, 98(22), 3428–3437.

Blier-Wong, C., Cossette, H., Lamontagne, L., and Marceau, E. (2021). Machine learning in P&C insurance: A review for pricing and reserving. *Risks*, 9(1): 4.

Dewi, K.C., Murfi, H., and Abdullah, S. (2019, October). Analysis accuracy of random forest model for big data–a case study of claim severity prediction in car insurance. In *2019 5th International Conference on Science in Information Technology (ICSITech)*. IEEE, pp. 60–65.

Dhieb, N., Ghazzai, H., Besbes, H., and Massoud, Y. (2020). A secure ai-driven architecture for automated insurance systems: Fraud detection and risk measurement. *IEEE Access*, 8: 58546–58558.

Duan, Z., Chang, Y., Wang, Q., Chen, T., and Zhao, Q. (2018). A logistic regression-based auto insurance rate-making model designed for the insurance rate reform. *International Journal of Financial Studies*, 6(1): 18.

Hanafy, M., and Ming, R. (2021). Improving imbalanced data classification in auto insurance by the data level approaches. *International Journal of Advanced Computer Science and Applications (IJACSA)*, 12(6): 493–499.

Henckaerts, R., Côté, M.P., Antonio, K., and Verbelen, R. (2021). Boosting insights in insurance tariff plans with tree-based machine learning methods. *North American Actuarial Journal*, 25(2): 255–285.

Itri, B., Mohamed, Y., Mohammed, Q., and Omar, B. (2019, October). Performance comparative study of machine learning algorithms for automobile insurance fraud detection. In *2019 3rd International*

Conference on Intelligent Computing in Data Sciences (ICDS). IEEE, pp. 1–4.

Lindholm, M., Richman, R., Tsanakas, A., and Wüthrich, M.V. (2022). Discrimination-free insurance pricing. *ASTIN Bulletin: The Journal of the IAA*, 52(1): 55–89.

Nocedal, J., and Wright, S.J. (2006). *Numerical Optimization*, 2nd edn. Springer, New York.

Rampal, J., Singh, P., Kaur, R., and Singh, K. (2020). An ensemble model to predict health insurance premium using machine learning. *Dogo Rangsang Research Journal*, 10(8): 191–199.

Spedicato, G.A., Dutang, C., and Petrini, L. (2018). Machine learning methods to perform pricing optimization. A comparison with standard GLMs. *Variance*, 12(1): 69–89.

Spiteri, M., and Azzopardi, G. (2018, September). Customer churn prediction for a motor insurance company. In *2018 13th International Conference on Digital Information Management (ICDIM)*. IEEE, pp. 173–178.

Staudt, Y., and Wagner, J. (2019). *Comparison of Machine Learning and Traditional Severity-Frequency Regression Models for Car Insurance Pricing*. Working Paper, University of Lausanne, Lausanne.

Subudhi, S., and Panigrahi, S. (2020). Use of optimized fuzzy C-means clustering and supervised classifiers for automobile insurance fraud detection. *Journal of King Saud University-Computer and Information Sciences*, 32(5): 568–575.

Wamwea, C.M., Muema, B.K., and Mung'atu, J.K. (2015). Modelling a pay-as-you-drive insurance pricing structure using a generalized linear model: Case study of a company in Kiambu. *American Journal of Theoretical and Applied Statistics*, 4(6): 527–533.

Xong, L.J., and Kang, H.M. (2019). A comparison of classification models for life insurance lapse risk. *International Journal of Recent Technology and Engineering*, 7(5S): 245–250.

Yunos, Z.M., Ali, A., Shamsyuddin, S.M, and Ismail, N. (2016). Predictive modelling for motor insurance claims using artificial neural networks. *International Journal of Advances in Soft Computing and Its Applications*, 8: 160–172.

Zhang, Y., and Walton, N. (2019). Adaptive pricing in insurance: Generalized linear models and gaussian process regression approaches. *arXiv preprint* arXiv:1907.05381.

Zhang, Q., Chang, X., and Bian, S.B. (2020). Vehicle-damage-detection segmentation algorithm based on improved mask RCNN. *IEEE Access*, 8: 6997–7004.

https://doi.org/10.1142/9781800615212_bmatter

Index

N

O

P

Q

R

S

T